High Leverage Practices for Inclusive Classrooms

High Leverage Practices for Inclusive Classrooms offers a set of practices that are integral to the support of student learning, and that can be systematically taught, learned, and implemented by those entering the teaching profession. The book focuses primarily on Tiers 1 and 2, or work that mostly occurs with students with mild disabilities in general education classrooms; and provides rich, practical information highly suitable for teachers, but that can also be useful for teacher educators and teacher preparation programs. This powerful, research-based resource offers twenty-two brief, focused chapters that will be fundamental to effective teaching in inclusive classrooms.

James McLeskey is Professor in the School of Special Education, School Psychology, and Early Childhood Studies at the University of Florida.

Lawrence Maheady is Professor and Horace Mann Endowed Chair in the Exceptional Education Department at SUNY Buffalo State.

Bonnie Billingsley is Professor of Teaching and Learning at Virginia Tech. She teaches in both the teacher preparation and doctoral programs at Virginia Tech.

Mary T. Brownell is Professor of Special Education at the University of Florida and Director of the Collaboration for Effective Educator Development, Accountability and Reform (CEEDAR) Center.

Timothy J. Lewis is Professor of Special Education at the University of Missouri. Dr. Lewis is the Associate Editor of the Journal of Positive Behavior Interventions and is a member of thirteen other editorial boards.

High Leverage Practices for Inclusive Classrooms

Edited by James McLeskey,
Lawrence Maheady,
Bonnie Billingsley,
Mary T. Brownell, and
Timothy J. Lewis

Routledge
Taylor & Francis Group

NEW YORK AND LONDON

First published 2019
by Routledge
711 Third Avenue, New York, NY 10017

and by Routledge
2 Park Square, Milton Park, Abingdon, Oxon, OX14 4RN

Routledge is an imprint of the Taylor & Francis Group, an informa business

© 2019 Taylor & Francis

The right of James McLeskey, Lawrence Maheady, Bonnie Billingsley, Mary T. Brownell, and Timothy J. Lewis to be identified as the authors of the editorial material, and of the authors for their individual chapters, has been asserted in accordance with sections 77 and 78 of the Copyright, Designs and Patents Act 1988.

Library of Congress Cataloging-in-Publication Data
A catalog record for this title has been requested

ISBN: 978-1-138-03919-3 (hbk)
ISBN: 978-1-138-03918-6 (pbk)
ISBN: 978-1-315-17609-3 (ebk)

Typeset in Minion Pro
by Apex CoVantage, LLC

Council for Exceptional Children

Contents

Introduction

For at least the last decade, teachers in every state in the U.S. have been faced with unprecedented accountability demands to increase achievement levels and ensure that *all* students are college or career ready when they complete high school. These demands require that teachers use the most effective available practices to improve student learning and behavior. This is especially important for students with disabilities, who continue to lag substantially behind their general education peers in academic achievement and post-school success.[1] While a range of effective practices have been identified to address the learning and behavioral needs of students with disabilities, these practices are not widely used in classrooms.[2]

The need to improve teacher practice and related student outcomes has led to a national effort to improve the preparation of teachers by "specifying teaching practices"[3] and preparing teachers to use these practices in their classrooms.[4] To address this need, several disciplines in education, including elementary education, mathematics, science, foreign language, and special education,[5] have begun to identify a limited number of teaching practices that have the highest leverage for improving student outcomes. These *high leverage practices* have been defined as "practices that are essential to effective teaching and fundamental to supporting student learning."[6] Furthermore, these practices 1) are supported by research as fostering improved student learning or behavior; 2) are broadly applicable across content areas; and 3) are frequently used in the classroom.[7]

This background information leads to several major reasons for developing high leverage practices that include the following:

- HLPs have been supported by research evidence to have significant potential for improving academic or behavioral outcomes for students with disabilities and others who struggle to learn.
- Identifying HLPs serves to specify the most effective practices that teachers must learn to use as a routine part of their practice.
- These practices provide a clear and limited focus for teacher preparation and professional development, increasing the likelihood that teachers will be well prepared to use these practices in their classrooms.
- Finally, the development of a set of effective core practices that are widely used in classrooms has the potential to significantly enhance the status of teaching as a profession that produces highly skilled professionals.[8]

Recently the Council for Exceptional Children approved a set of 22 high leverage practices (HLPs) for K–12 special education teachers that are intended to be a foundation for effective practice for teaching students with disabilities.[9] These practices may be used as a core curriculum for teacher preparation, as well as for continuing professional development for practicing teachers. For example, some teacher education programs have begun to use these HLPs as the core curriculum for teacher education, and teacher preparation is then designed to ensure that all program completers can use these practices at a beginning level of proficiency.[10] This ensures a level of proficient practice for all special education teachers and provides a foundation of skills for developing other aspects of practice as beginning teachers continue to learn and become highly accomplished professionals as their teaching careers progress.

Narrowing the Focus

As we developed this book, our primary goal was to provide a practical resource for in-service and preservice teachers who want to learn to use high leverage practices in their classrooms. To achieve this goal, we quickly recognized that we could not address the extraordinarily broad and varied roles and responsibilities that are assumed by special education teachers in a single book. We thus had to narrow the topic to ensure that rich, useful information about these practices could be provided. To do this, we decided to focus on how these practices may be used in general education classrooms (or Tiers 1 and 2) by teachers in grades K–12. With this focus, the practices we describe will often be useful to both special and general education teachers and are applicable to the large number of students with disabilities who spend most of the school day in general education classrooms. While we delimited the content in this way to make the book more usable for teachers, we also feel that a book is needed to provide descriptions of the application of the HLPs for students with more intensive needs, and also for early childhood special education, but unfortunately these books will have to wait for another day.

Chapter Overview

1. How were the HLPs identified?
2. What are the 22 HLPs for special education teachers?
3. Wrap up and tips for using the information in this book.

How Were the HLPs Identified?

The Council for Exceptional Children appointed a High Leverage Practices Writing Team in 2014 to develop a set of HLPs for special education teachers. This team consisted of 12 members, most of whom were teacher educators with extensive experience preparing special education teachers and working in schools. The HLP Writing Team initially determined that the major functions of special education teachers related to four areas of practice: collaboration, assessment, social/emotional/behavioral practices, and instruction. They further concluded that the HLPs would be developed for special education teachers in grades K–12.

Criteria were then developed for identifying the HLPs and are included in Table 0.1. These criteria were intended to support the development of HLPs that represent the essence of effective practice in special education. This included practices that are frequently used in the classroom and that have been shown to improve student learning or behavior. Criteria were also included to ensure that these practices were practical and useful for teacher education and professional development, and that a limited number of complex practices were identified that could be taught to novices at a reasonable

Table 0.1 Criteria for Identifying High Leverage Practices[11]

Applicable and Important to the Everyday Work of Teachers

- Focus directly on instructional practice
- Occur with high frequency in teaching
- Research-based and known to foster important kinds of student engagement and learning
- Broadly applicable and usable in any content area or approach to teaching
- So important that skillfully executing them is fundamental to effective teaching

Applicable and Important to Teacher Education

- Limited in number (about 20) for a teacher education program
- Can be articulated and taught
- Novices can begin to master
- Can be practiced across university and field-based settings
- Grain size (i.e., how detailed should the practice be) is small enough to be clearly visible in practice, but large enough to preserve the integrity and complexity of teaching
- System (or group of HLP) considerations
  - Embody a broader theory regarding the relationship between teaching and learning than would individual practices
  - Support more comprehensive student learning goals (the whole is more than the sum of its parts)

---

level of proficiency in a preparation program. It should be noted that while a primary criterion is that the HLPs should focus on instructional practice (including behavioral practices), collaboration and assessment practices were also included that addressed major functions of the role of special education teachers. While there is strong research support for at least one of these practices (i.e., HLP 6—Using assessment information to make instructional decisions or formative assessment), most of the practices in these areas were viewed as essential to the role of special education teachers and in most cases had policy support for their inclusion.

By April 2015, the group had developed a draft set of HLPs. These draft practices were then critically examined in focus group interviews that occurred over several months with teacher educators, teachers, and administrators. Based on this feedback, substantial revisions were made and the number of HLPs was reduced from 26 to 22 in a draft completed in October 2015. Further feedback was then sought for the revised version of the HLPs using an online survey and a presentation at a professional conference for teacher educators in November 2015. This feedback was then used by the HLP Writing Team to develop a near final set of 22 high leverage practices in January 2016. A final round of feedback was provided at the CEC Convention in April 2016, by the Representative Assembly (RA) of CEC. This feedback resulted in further changes, and a final version that included 22 HLPs was approved by the CEC Board in July 2016.

In the following section, a brief introduction and list of HLPs is provided across essential functions carried out by special education teachers: collaboration, assessment, social/emotional/behavioral practices, and instruction. These include 22 HLPs that are intended to address the most critical practices that every K–12 special education teacher should be able to use proficiently in the classroom. These practices are intended to provide a foundation for preparing effective special education teachers from initial preparation through induction and beyond. CEC has published a *Report of the HLP Writing Team*[12] that includes a more extensive description of each of the HLPs and research and/or policy support for each practice.

What Are the 22 HLPs for Special Education Teachers?

As previously noted, the HLP Writing Team determined that the major functions of special education teachers related to four areas of practice: collaboration, assessment, social/emotional/behavioral practices, and instruction. Here we provide a brief introduction to each area of practice, followed by a list of the HLPs for that section. It should be noted that the wording for HLPs 8 and 22 are the same, but HLP 8 applies to student behavior and feedback, while HLP 22 applies to feedback related to academic performance.

Collaboration High Leverage Practices

Effective special education teachers collaborate with a wide range of professionals, families, and caregivers to assure that educational programs and related services are effectively designed and implemented to meet the needs of each student with a disability. Collaboration allows for varied expertise and perspectives about a student to be shared among those responsible for each student's learning and well-being. This collective expertise provides collaborators with a more comprehensive understanding of each student's needs, and this knowledge is used to more effectively plan and implement instruction and services that benefit the student.

Teachers use respectful and effective communication skills as they collaborate with others, considering the background, socioeconomic status, culture, and language of the families and the professionals with whom they work. They focus collaborative activities on designing each student's instructional program to meet clearly specified outcomes and collecting data and monitoring progress toward these outcomes. Effective and purposeful collaboration should enlist support from district and school leaders, who foster a collective commitment to collaboration, provide professional learning experiences to increase team members' collaborative skills, and create schedules that support different forms (e.g., IEP teams, co-teachers, teachers and families, teachers and paraprofessionals) of ongoing collaboration. The three high leverage practices related to collaboration are as follows:

1. *Collaborate with professionals to increase student success.*
2. *Organize and facilitate effective meetings with professionals and families.*
3. *Collaborate with families to support student learning and secure needed services.*

Assessment High Leverage Practices

Assessment plays a foundational role in special education. Students with disabilities are complex learners who have unique needs that exist alongside their strengths. Effective special education teachers have to fully understand those strengths and needs. Thus, these teachers are knowledgeable regarding assessment and are skilled in using and interpreting data. This includes formal, standardized assessments that are used in the identification of students for special education services, in the development of their Individualized Education Programs, and to inform their ongoing services. Formal assessments such as statewide exams also provide data regarding whether students with disabilities are achieving state content standards and how their academic progress compares to students without disabilities. Teachers are also knowledgeable regarding and skillful in using informal assessments, such as those used to evaluate students' academic, behavioral, and functional strengths and needs. These assessments are used to develop students' Individualized Education Programs, design and evaluate instruction, and monitor student progress. As reflective practitioners, teachers are also continuously analyzing the impact and effectiveness of their own instruction. Finally, teachers are knowledgeable regarding how context, culture, language, and poverty might influence student performance, navigating conversations with families and other stakeholders, and choosing appropriate assessments given each student's profile. This is an especially important consideration given the over-representation of culturally and linguistically diverse students and those from high poverty backgrounds in special education. The three high leverage practices related to assessment are listed below.

4. *Use multiple sources of information to develop a comprehensive understanding of a student's strengths and needs.*
5. *Interpret and communicate assessment information with stakeholders to collaboratively design and implement educational programs.*
6. *Use student assessment data, analyze instructional practices, and make necessary adjustments that improve student outcomes.*

Social/Emotional/Behavioral High Leverage Practices

Effective special education teachers establish a consistent, organized, and respectful learning environment to support student success. To do this, they employ several practices that are critical in promoting student social and emotional well-being. First, effective teachers focus on increasing appropriate behavior by adopting an instructional approach and explicitly teaching social skills and offering multiple opportunities to practice appropriate social behaviors across the school day followed by positive specific feedback. Second, they implement evidence-based practices to prevent social/emotional behavioral challenges and provide early intervention at the first sign of risk. Third, effective teachers provide increasingly comprehensive supports through a team-based problem-solving strategy to match the intensity of student challenges guided by behavioral assessment. Finally, they implement all behavioral supports, even those in response to significant problem behavior, in a caring, respectful, and culturally relevant manner. Effective teachers recognize that academic and behavioral support strategies are more effective when delivered within the context of positive and caring teacher and student relationships. The four high leverage practices related to social/emotional/behavioral practices are listed below.

7. *Establish a consistent, organized, and respectful learning environment.*
8. *Provide positive and constructive feedback to guide students' learning and behavior.*
9. *Teach social behaviors.*
10. *Conduct functional behavioral assessments to develop individual student behavior support plans.*

Instruction High Leverage Practices

Teaching students with disabilities is a strategic, flexible, and recursive process, as effective special education teachers use content knowledge, pedagogical knowledge (including evidence-based practice), and data on student learning to design, deliver, and evaluate the effectiveness of instruction. This process begins with well-designed instruction. Effective special education teachers are well-versed in general education curricula and other contextually relevant curricula. They use appropriate standards, learning progressions, and evidence-based practices in conjunction with specific IEP goals and benchmarks to prioritize long- and short-term learning goals and plan instruction. This instruction, when delivered with fidelity, is designed to maximize academic learning time, actively engage learners in meaningful activities, and emphasize proactive and positive approaches across tiers of instructional intensity.

Teachers use the best available evidence, professional judgment, and knowledge of individual student needs. They value diverse perspectives and incorporate students' background, culture, and language to make instructional decisions. Their decisions result in improved student outcomes across varied curriculum areas and in multiple educational settings. They use teacher-led, peer-assisted, student-regulated, and technology-assisted practices fluently, and know when and where to apply them. They continually analyze instruction and monitor student progress in ways that allow them to improve student learning and refine their professional practice. The 12 high leverage practices related to instruction are listed below.

11. *Identify and prioritize long- and short-term learning goals.*
12. *Systematically design instruction toward a specific learning goal.*
13. *Adapt curriculum tasks and materials for specific learning goals.*
14. *Teach cognitive and metacognitive strategies to support learning and independence.*
15. *Provide scaffolded supports.*
16. *Use explicit instruction.*
17. *Use flexible grouping.*
18. *Use strategies to promote active student engagement.*
19. *Use assistive and instructional technologies.*
20. *Provide intensive instruction.*
21. *Teach students to maintain and generalize new learning across time and settings.*
22. *Provide positive and constructive feedback to guide students' learning and behavior. (Note that this HLP focuses on instruction, while HLP 8 focuses on behavior.)*

Wrap Up

In this introduction, we've provided an overview of what HLPs are and why they are important. We've also explained how the HLPs were developed and organized around the major functions of practice of special education teachers—collaboration, assessment, social/emotional/behavioral practices, and instruction. Finally, we provided a brief introduction to the 22 HLPs that were developed by the Council for Exceptional Children for K–12 special education teachers.

In the next 22 chapters, we provide more extensive information regarding each HLP. We begin each chapter with an introduction that provides a brief description and rationale for the practice, as well as its instructional purposes and intended targets. The HLPs are complex practices, so we could not describe every component and application of the practice in one chapter. Chapter authors thus carefully selected critical applications of each of the HLPs that we feel will be most useful for teachers. A "narrowing the focus" section is included following the introduction in each chapter to describe how and why we did this, as well as applications of practice that are the focus of the chapter. We then describe the essential functions or components of the HLP and general information regarding how to use the practice. This is followed by rich examples of the practice in real-life contexts. Finally, we conclude each chapter with a brief wrap up and tips for using the HLP.

Tips

1. Obviously, you can't learn to use all of the HLPs at once. We would encourage you to consider your teaching role and the students' needs, and then carefully review the HLPs to see which will be most useful to improve your practice and better meet your students' needs. Regardless of where you start, we would encourage you to pick a couple of HLPs that will be most useful for you and dive into the practices!

2. We would also encourage you to be opportunistic as you learn to use the HLPs. If you know a teacher who is well-skilled on one or more of the HLPs, seek them out, pick their brains for resources related to the practice, observe their teaching, and, if possible, have them observe you, provide feedback and respond to application-related questions. Information provided in the Wrap Up section at the end of each chapter should also be helpful in improving your understanding and application of these practices.

3. We would also encourage you to share information regarding these HLPs with your general education colleagues. As we've shared this information, many general educators have told us that these practices are also very useful for teaching students who struggle with academic content or behavior (which obviously includes most every classroom teacher). This is one reason we've focused HLP applications in each chapter on their use in general education classrooms. Many students struggle with learning or behavior in these classes, and most students with disabilities spend a large portion of the school day in these settings. We hope you'll find that these practices are useful in addressing the needs of these students.

All proceeds from this book are being donated to the Council for Exceptional Children to support their many initiatives directed toward improving services and outcomes for students with disabilities and their families. We want to acknowledge the many professionals who gave freely of their time to make this book possible. In particular we would like to acknowledge those who reviewed the chapters and provided valuable feedback, who are listed below.

Kristie Asaro-Saddler
Cynthia Baughan
B. Keith Ben
Dee Berlinghoff
Bryan Cook
Vivian Correa

Dane DiCesare
Scott Dueker
Grace Francis
Corrine Gist
Steve Goodman
Jessica Gugino
Dawn Hamilton

Andrew Hashey
Heather Hatton
Maria R. Helton
Michelle Hosp
Carl Liaupson
Andrew M. Markelz
Lisa Monda-Amaya
Tracy Gershwin Mueller
Rob O'Neill
Anna Osipova
Kathleen Pfannenstiel

Daniel Pyle
Nicole Pyle
Paul Riccomini
Benjamin Riden
Chris Riley-Tillman
Kristin L. Sayeski
Christian Shabey
Pamela Stecker
Jennifer Urbach
Annmarie Urso
Kimberly Vannest
Jocelyn Washburn
Peggy Weiss
Natalie Williams
Pamela Williamson

Notes

1 Albus, D., Lazarus, S. S., & Thurlow, M. L. (2015). *2012–13 publicly reported assessment results for students with disabilities and ELLs with disabilities* (Technical Report 70). Minneapolis, MN: University of Minnesota, National Center on Educational Outcomes. Rojewski, J. W., Lee, I. H., & Gregg, N. (2015). Causal effects of inclusion on postsecondary education outcomes of individuals with high-incidence disabilities. *Journal of Disability Policy Studies, 25*, 210–219.

2 Cook, B., Cook, L., & Landrum, T. (2013). Moving research into practice: Can we make dissemination stick? *Exceptional Children, 79*, 163–180.

3 McDonald, M., Kazemi, E., & Kavanaugh, S. (2013). Core practices of teacher education: A call for a common language and collective activity. *Journal of Teacher Education, 64*(5), 378–386. (quote from page 378).

4 McLeskey, J., & Brownell, M. (2015). *High leverage practices and teacher preparation in special education.* Gainesville, FL: CEEDAR Center. Retrieved from http://ceedar.education.ufl.edu/reports/

5 Davis, E., & Boerst, T. (2014). *Designing elementary teacher education to prepare well-started beginners.* Ann Arbor, MI: Teaching Works, University of Michigan School of Education.
Grossman, P., Hammerness, K., & McDonald, M. (2009). Redefining teaching: Re-imagining teacher education. *Teachers and teaching: Theory and Practice, 15*(2), 273–290.
Hlas, A., & Hlas, C. (2012). A review of high-leverage teaching practices: Making connections between mathematics and foreign languages. *Foreign Language Annals, 45*(51), S76–S97.
McLeskey, J., Berringer, M., Billingsley, B., Brownell, M., Jackson, D., Kennedy, M., . . . Ziegler, D. (2017). *High-leverage practices in special education.* Arlington, VA: CEC and CEEDAR Center.
Windschitl, M., Thompson, J., Braaten, M., & Stroupe, D. (2012). Proposing a core set of instructional practices and tools for teachers of science. *Science Education, 96*(5), 878–903.

6 McLeskey, J., Billingsley, B., Brownell, B., Maheady, L., & Lewis, T. (2017). *What are high leverage practices for special education teachers and why are they important?* Unpublished manuscript. Gainesville, FL: University of Florida. (p. 9).

7 McLeskey, J., & Brownell, M. (2015). *High leverage practices and teacher preparation in special education.* Gainesville, FL: CEEDAR Center. Retrieved from http://ceedar.education.ufl.edu/reports/

8 Ingersoll, R. M., & Merrill, E. (2011). The status of teaching as a profession. In J. Ballantine & J. Spade (Eds.), *Schools and society: A sociological approach to education* (pp. 185–189, 4th ed.). Los Angeles: Pine Forge Press/Sage Publications.

9 McLeskey, J., Berringer, M., Billingsley, B., Brownell, M., Jackson, D., Kennedy, M., . . . Ziegler, D. (2017). *High-leverage practices in special education.* Arlington, VA: CEC and CEEDAR Center.

10 Brownell, M., McLeskey, J., Barber, B., Spear-Swerling, L., & Benedict, A. (2016). *Practice-based approaches to improving teacher education.* OSEP U.S. Department of Education Project Directors Conference, Washington, DC.

11 Ball, D. L., Sleep, L., Boerst, T., & Bass, H. (2009). Combining the development of practice and the practice of development in teacher education. *Elementary School Journal, 109,* 458–476.

Grossman, P., Hammerness, K., & McDonald, M. (2009). Redefining teaching: Re-imagining teacher education. *Teachers and Teaching: Theory and Practice, 15*(2), 273–290.

McDonald, M., Kazemi, E., & Kavanaugh, S. (2013). Core practices of teacher education: A call for a common language and collective activity. *Journal of Teacher Education, 64*(5), 378–386. (quote from page 378).

Windschitl, M., Thompson, J., Braaten, M., & Stroupe, D. (2012). Proposing a core set of instructional practices and tools for teachers of science. *Science Education, 96*(5), 878–903.

12 McLeskey, J., Berringer, M., Billingsley, B., Brownell, M., Jackson, D., Kennedy, M., . . . Ziegler, D. (2017). *High-leverage practices in special education.* Arlington, VA: CEC and CEEDAR Center.

Section 1
Collaboration High Leverage Practices

Edited by Bonnie Billingsley

Co-edited by Dia Jackson

Introduction to Collaboration High Leverage Practices

Interacting positively and productively with professionals, families, and community members is a critical dimension of teacher effectiveness. Teachers interact with principals, other teachers, related-service providers, families, and paraprofessionals, and these interactions are important to assuring that educational programs and related services are designed and implemented to meet the needs of each student with a disability. Effective collaboration allows for varied expertise and perspectives about a student to be shared among all those responsible for each student's learning and well-being, increasing the possibility that learning experiences are coordinated and enhanced in ways that lead to successful student outcomes.

Becoming an effective collaborator is an ongoing process requiring self-awareness and an understanding of what collaboration means, what happens during effective collaboration, and how to assess whether collaboration is functioning in ways that support student learning. The collaboration high leverage practice chapters in this section address the why, what, and how of three interrelated areas: collaborating with colleagues to increase student success as teachers coordinate their efforts to plan, co-teach, and assess student learning; leading effective meetings with professionals and families, with a focus on instructional decision-making meetings; and collaborating with families to support students' learning and secure needed services across home and school environments. The chapters in this section focus on what effective collaboration means within each of these three contexts and provide detailed examples of effective collaboration in teachers' day-to-day work.

Specific collaborative skills are relevant across the three chapters. First, collaborative interactions are enhanced when professionals use respectful and effective communication skills to promote positive relationships and build trust among professionals and families. Effective collaborators are aware of and continue to hone their collaboration skills, attending to both their verbal and non-verbal interactions with others. They also encourage others to share their knowledge and perspectives, listen carefully to understand what others are saying, and use problem-solving strategies as they work with others to plan, teach, and assess using practices that lead to successful student outcomes. These collaborative practices are especially critical when there are interpersonal challenges or differences of opinion, which will inevitably occur during collaborative relationships.

Teachers who are effective collaborators are ready to interact positively and productively with diverse individuals in the school and community. Effective collaborators recognize that professionals and families with whom they work are unique and may differ from them in a variety of ways, such as primary language, race/ethnicity, socioeconomic background, family structure, beliefs, and communication preferences. Effective teachers take time to learn about the professionals and families with whom they work, and they use this knowledge to respond thoughtfully to others, considering others' unique perspectives and strengths. In particular, teachers in the U.S. are overwhelmingly White and female, while students of color are now the majority. Given the diversity of schools, teachers will at times need to seek guidance, training, and support in using culturally responsive practices that can lead to improved communication and involvement between schools and diverse families.

1

Collaborating With Colleagues
to Increase Student Success

Marilyn Friend and Tammy Barron

Introduction

Collaboration is integral to being a special education teacher. During the course of a school day, special educators may share teaching responsibilities with a general education teacher, participate in team meetings, interact with parents, contribute to a school committee or a department or grade-level professional learning community, ask for consultative assistance for responding to a student with challenging behaviors, touch base with other professionals instructing students on their case-loads, and share information with one or more paraprofessionals. However, interacting with others does not guarantee collaboration. Rather, collaboration is *how* professionals work together.[1] If one person dominates the conversation, one committee member dictates what he thinks others should do, or a teaching partner states that she does not plan to share instructional responsibilities, collaboration is not possible. On the other hand, when teachers plan together to create a learning environment that meets all their students' needs, when committee members carefully monitor to be sure each person has a voice in making key decisions, or when professionals and parents discuss students with a sense of respect and trust, collaboration is occurring. That is, collaboration relies on parity or a clear sense of value for each member's contribution, a mutual goal, shared responsibility for key decisions, joint accountability for outcomes, and pooled resources.[2]

Several factors explain the importance of collaboration for special education in today's schools. First, many provisions in the Individuals with Disabilities Education Act (IDEA) can be carried out only through collaboration. These include the teamwork involved in assessment and decision-making; the requirement for the provision of services in the least restrictive environment, often general education; and the joint efforts that occur during transition from school to post-school options or when hospitals, the courts, or other agencies play a role in a student's education. In addition, research supports collaboration: For example, positive achievement outcomes for students with disabilities often are associated with unwavering administrative leadership in a highly collaborative school culture.[3] Similarly, studies of collaborative endeavors such as co-teaching and consultation often demonstrate a positive impact on attaining student academic and behavioral goals.[4]

Narrowing the Focus

Collaboration is a broad topic, and this chapter emphasizes specific aspects of it. It overviews several of the most widely applicable collaboration skills special educators should develop and refine so that they effectively collaborate across situations. In addition, two applications of collaboration are explored: (a) co-teaching, the service delivery model in which a general and special educator share classroom responsibilities for all or part of the school day, and (b) interactions with paraprofessionals, a common special educator job responsibility that typically requires a blend of directive and collaborative approaches.

Chapter Overview

1. Describe collaboration skills special educators are likely to need as they work across settings, grade levels, and programs or services.
2. Explain the key structures that support professional collaboration for co-teaching teams.
3. Clarify the blend of collaborative and directive interactions that occur between special educators and paraprofessionals.

Universal Collaboration Elements

Collaboration is multi-dimensional. It begins with steadfast personal commitment, that is, a deeply held belief that the shared efforts of professionals generally are exponentially more powerful than those carried out in isolation. However, a commitment to collaboration is not sufficient. It must be accompanied by (a) skills for communicating with others and (b) the ability to efficiently and constructively complete the beginning-to-end steps of collaborative processes. These two skill sets are valuable regardless of the type of collaboration, and each is briefly described in the following sections.

Communication skills

The words professionals use (or avoid using) and the way they are said can have a profound impact on collaboration.[5] They can facilitate clear understanding and communicate respect and openness, or they can lead to confusion and defensiveness. These are examples of essential communication skills.

Listening

Skillful listening is an active process integral to constructive communication. First, the listener takes in the information being shared, perhaps mentally repeating it to maintain attention and remember what is said. In addition, the listener should convey to the speaker, without interrupting, that listening is occurring. This often is best accomplished by nodding or using vocalizations such as "Uh-hmmm." Listening, though, also involves demonstrating understanding, typically through a skill such as paraphrasing. Ms. Taylor says, "Joshua's behavior has really been deteriorating. At the beginning of the year he interacted appropriately with peers and adults, but at least four times in the past two weeks he ran from the classroom. He has also hit peers and refused to follow my directions." Mr. Randolph paraphrases by responding, "Joshua's behavior with peers and you recently has changed from acceptable to problematic." Notice how understanding is communicated by Mr. Randolph without adding meaning to the message as might have occurred if he had said, ". . . and you're frustrated with him." In addition, if any part of what Mr. Randolph said was not accurate, Ms. Taylor would be able to correct his understanding, thus ensuring communication accuracy.

Nonverbal communication

In face-to-face interactions, communication is strongly influenced by nonverbal factors that often suggest attitude and emotion. For example, leaning forward conveys interest in the conversation occurring while leaning back with crossed arms conveys the opposite. Facial expressions may suggest interest, boredom, surprise, disbelief, or many other emotions. Sitting at a right angle to another during a difficult interaction allows both participants to easily make or avert eye contact, while sitting across from one another can be awkward, as eye contact is more expected and difficult to avoid. In collaborative interactions, professionals should both note the nonverbal communication of others and its possible meaning while at the same time monitoring their own nonverbal communication so that it suggests openness, respect, and understanding.

Questions

Encouraging others to share information is largely accomplished through skillful question-asking. Think of how a colleague would respond to this question: "Of all the strategies you have tried to address this student's academic problems, which ones seem to have had the greatest positive effect?" Then consider this question: "Have any of the strategies you have tried been effective?" Notice that the first question is open and invites an elaborated response while the second is closed and can be answered with a simple "yes" or "no." Effective collaborators are skillful at asking more of the former type of question and fewer of the latter to increase engagement and contributions of their collaborative partners or team members.

Statements

Communication generally is clearest when statements made are accurate and descriptive. For example, Ms. Martinez communicates about Sophie's situation by saying, "Sophie has missed four days of school in the past two weeks, and she has been late for class an additional two times. She has not turned in the first part of her project, due last week." This is far more appropriate than if she had said, "Sophie is missing too much school and rarely completing assignments." The former type of statement leads to a productive conversation about reasons for the problems and potential solutions; the latter is too vague and evaluative to be useful.

Communication Skills in Action

Of course, the communication skills just described are not used in isolation; a careful blend of them fosters partnership. For example, Ms. Moore might begin an interaction intended to gather information about a student with a learning disability in a general education English class by saying, "You've mentioned that the students in your class are expected to complete and submit all their daily homework as well as two essays during the grading period and that their grades are significantly affected if they do not complete these assignments. They also have three or four unit tests during the same time. How is George doing in meeting these requirements?" She is leaning forward slightly as she speaks, and she makes direct eye contact. She also clearly pauses, a nonverbal strategy, so that her colleague can think and respond before Ms. Moore makes additional comments. Statements, questions, nonverbal communication, and listening have occurred in just this brief exchange.

In addition, cultural differences must be taken into account as part of constructive communication.[6] For example, some professionals may clearly state expectations based on their cultures related to student behavior as well as teachers' roles and responsibilities. Others may prefer an indirect approach to communication instead of the typical direct approach of American culture. Other differences, including nonverbal signals such as physical distance and eye contact, likewise may vary. Special educators who always consider culture as part of the context of their communication are most likely to be successful collaborators.

Interaction Processes

Communication skills alone seldom are sufficient for collaboration. Have you ever participated in a meeting or other interaction in which communication was clear and seemed exemplary, but the conversation seemed to be circular or to have no clear purpose? That occurs when the interaction process, that is, the steps necessary to get from the beginning to the end of an interaction, are neglected. By far the most common interaction process is problem solving.

Group Problem Solving

Reflect on the interactions that special educators have with others at school. They plan upcoming lessons with a co-teacher, respond to questions from a general education colleague regarding the reading intervention for a shared student, meet with a specialist to determine how instructional technology could assist a student, and interact with a paraprofessional who reports that a student seems to be increasingly dependent on adult attention. Each of these situation calls for problem solving facilitated through effective communication.

The steps of shared problem solving have been widely studied and repeatedly articulated.[7] They include these:

1. *Analyze the need for and appropriateness of a problem-solving process.* Professionals should first assess whether the problem at hand is one that shared problem solving can address and participants can positively influence. For example, addressing a teacher's concern about a student who is struggling academically probably is appropriate, but responding to a parent's decision against the use of medication likely is not.

2. *Identify the problem.* This step seems obvious, but often it is too rushed. For example, during co-planning a general educator says that students are not reading when given time during class. Is this the problem? Perhaps . . . but perhaps not. It may be that getting students to read is only a symptom; the underlying problem is matching student reading level and interest to the selected materials or providing specific purpose and accountability for completing the reading task.

3. *Generate potential solutions.* This well-known problem-solving step should be based directly on a careful articulation of the problem, and its success usually involves generating many options, often resulting in creative alternatives. In the reading example above, the teachers decide the problem is the need for a clearer purpose and accountability for reading. They generate solutions such as giving bonus points for completing comprehension questions, having students create skits about the passages, giving a quiz after each reading assignment, providing the material for some students through an audio recording, and eliminating all such reading tasks.

4. *Evaluate potential solutions.* Next, professionals determine which solutions are more likely to have the desired impact. Eliminating reading tasks is a whimsical idea unlikely to be selected, but thoughtful consideration might be given to a quiz and skits about the material. In weighing pros and cons, quizzes comprise specific accountability but have to be created, delivered, scored, and recorded. Skits might prove entertaining and illustrative of student understanding, but they would take considerable time to complete and evaluation would require a rubric.

5. *Select a solution and plan for its implementation.* If the teachers in the reading example decide to give brief quizzes after each reading assignment, they should determine who will create the quizzes, the format for delivery (e.g., paper/pencil, electronic), and the grading procedure. They also should identify students with accommodations for any type of testing and necessary arrangements.

6. *Implement the solution.* With careful planning, this is the most straightforward problem-solving step. The selected solution is implemented, and data are gathered related to its impact on the identified problem.

7. *Evaluate the solution's effectiveness and continue, discontinue, or revise it as needed.* The co-teachers giving brief quizzes may be pleased that students now are far more likely to read their assigned material, and so they continue this solution. Alternatively, they may find the quizzes are too time-consuming and decide to switch to unannounced periodic quizzes. Or they may decide the quizzes interfere too much with the pacing and priorities in the class, abandoning that solution to try another.

Shared problem solving should be proactive (e.g., "How can we prepare for our new student who is not reading grade-level materials with proficiency?") as well as reactive (e.g., "What strategies could we use to increase Simon's attention during large-group instruction?"). The more serious the problem, the more important it is that these steps be carefully followed, accomplished by well-phrased questions and statements (e.g., "How likely is it that we can change Susan's behavior?" "That is one idea. What else could we try?" "What are the potential negative outcomes of trying this with Mason?" "Our data show a 70 percent success rate. How could we increase that?"). Collaboration heavily relies on the power of shared problem solving.

Collaborating With School Colleagues

Collaboration is a means to an end, that is, a way professionals work together to design and deliver, directly and indirectly, a wide range of services for students with disabilities. Two examples of services that rely heavily on collaboration are outlined in the following sections: (a) co-teaching and (b) working with paraprofessionals.

Co-Teaching

Co-teaching occurs when a general educator and a special educator collaborate in the typical classroom to simultaneously (a) deliver the grade-level curriculum and (b) meet the specialized needs of students with disabilities.[8,9] Although co-teaching outcomes are not reported as universally positive,[10] co-teachers often report benefits to children, including increased academic performance as well as improved self-confidence, social skills, and peer relations, especially when they have resources such as shared planning time.[9,11]

Collaboration skills are essential to co-teaching practice. In the following sections, we illustrate collaboration in the co-teaching context during interactions to determine partners' roles and responsibilities and select co-teaching approaches to be used for a specific lesson.

Example 1: Co-Teacher Roles and Responsibilities

Ms. Deptha and Ms. Cassie are meeting just prior to the beginning of the school year. Ms. Deptha, the general educator, has had several years of experience with co-teaching, not all positive. Special educator Ms. Cassie is new to the school but successfully co-taught at her previous school. The purpose of the meeting is to discuss their co-teaching roles and responsibilities.

Ms. Deptha has taught fifth grade for nine years and has a routine beginning to her school year. She plans to spend the first day reviewing the expectations for the class and will send a welcome letter home to parents that must be signed and returned. The meeting begins with

Ms. Deptha stating, "I am looking forward to co-teaching with you this year, and I have put your name on the letter to parents and provided you a desk of equal size at the front of the room on the opposite side from mine, so we should be good to go." Ms. Cassie replies, "Thank you for providing a desk for me and placing my name on the letter to the parents. Those are very important ways to communicate to students and parents that I am a full teacher in this classroom. I would like to discuss a couple other items with you as we begin our work together." Ms. Cassie asks these questions:

- What are all the ways you communicate with parents? How do you see me involved in this communication?
- What is your tolerance for noise in the classroom?
- What have been your experiences in providing specialized instruction to students with disabilities as part of co-teaching?
- What is your approach to behavior management?
- What are the procedures for having students turn in their work? Paper and pencil? Electronic? What role might I play in grading student work?

Ms. Cassie's questions are open because she is seeking information to enable the teachers to develop a shared plan for behavior and academic procedures. Ms. Deptha is eager to discuss the topics Ms. Cassie raises, and she is grateful she understands what co-teaching should be. The teachers continue discussing their shared classroom and agree that Ms. Deptha will do most grading but that Ms. Cassie will lead on a class behavior management plan. They agree that their partnership is starting off with a strong, honest foundation that will enable them to best meet their students' needs.

Example 2: Co-Teaching Approaches

Ms. Deptha and Ms. Cassie share the goal of enabling their students to succeed in learning the grade-level curriculum. But the teachers approach the shared goals with somewhat different points of view. Ms. Deptha knows she must keep up the expected teaching pace, a requirement her principal has explicitly set. Ms. Cassie prioritizes a teach-to-mastery mindset over pacing, an integral dimension of being a special educator. During another planning meeting the alternative perspectives become a topic of discussion as the co-teachers determine the best approach to be used to deliver the content. Six basic co-teaching approaches can guide co-teachers on the delivery of instruction (see Table 1.1) as they think about the balance of curriculum pace and individual student learning needs. Determining which approach to implement requires teachers to consider the academic goals of individual students, curricular demands, the specific content that will be covered, and the unique expertise of each teacher illustrated as the teaching partners share these crucial decisions.

Ms. Deptha shows Ms. Cassie her already-made plans: Week 1 – Introduction and Inferences From Text. She adds that she expects to immediately begin work on close reading and using text evidence to support statements and conclusions. Ms. Cassie is concerned based on data for the seven students with disabilities in this class, though she realizes this instruction is a essential fifth-grade curriculum standard.

Ms. Deptha begins the meeting by saying, "We need to plan our lessons for this standard—this is critical content in fifth grade. Let me start by saying that I am fine taking the lead for the first several weeks while you get acclimated to the school, learn the content, and get to know the students.

So we should probably begin with me teaching and you assisting individual students." Ms. Cassie shares that "most of the students are reading on a third-grade level, and the activities in the lesson plans require reading the text independently and making inferences based on what has been read. The plans as written can help us be efficient, but based on student data I fear many will not be able to complete the work, and we'll lose them. I wonder about trying some of the other co-teaching approaches, so we can provide support for their learning." Ms. Deptha replies, "I agree we should try some new ideas, as long as we maintain our rigor; to get through this curriculum, we have to work at a fast pace." Ms. Cassie replies, "I believe strongly in high expectations and full access to the general curriculum, and I'm confident we can reach the objectives for this week's lessons while adding the additional scaffolding, especially for the students with disabilities." Ms. Cassie shares her co-teaching models chart (see Table 1.1), and the co-teachers collaborate to make the following list of how the six models would work with the current lesson.

Co-teachers share goals about student outcomes, but they should not try to be identical. General educators' first areas of expertise usually relate to academic content, while special educators' core expertise is the process of learning. By blending their knowledge and skills, Ms. Deptha and Ms. Cassie identified the co-teaching structure that would best fit the lesson. The initial tendency for Ms. Deptha was to help Ms. Cassie get oriented to the grade level and academic content by asking her to implement "one teach, one observe" or "one teach, one assist." When Ms. Cassie shared her expertise in scaffolding instruction using a research-based practice, Ms. Deptha recognized that the other models would more likely lead to the desired academic outcomes. The teachers eventually agreed that station teaching would enable them to effectively complete the instruction, and alternative teaching would facilitate unit review and re-teaching. Notice how they made decisions and completed detailed planning by employing communication and problem-solving strategies.

As these two examples clarify, co-teaching achieves its purpose when partners understand and practice collaboration. They have a strong commitment to their shared work; they communicate carefully; and they share resources, decision-making, and accountability. They interact using clear communication, problem solve, and ultimately create a true partnership that results in positive outcomes for students with disabilities.

Working With Paraprofessionals

Paraprofessionals, sometimes also called paraeducators, serve a vital function in special education.[12] Some work with individual students who need physical assistance or whose behavior must be closely monitored; others are assigned to work in general or special education settings to provide support as needed. Many special education teachers work with paraprofessionals, and the topic of collaboration often arises. These examples illustrate the interactions between special educators and paraprofessionals.

Example 1: A Collaborative Special Educator-Paraprofessional Interaction

In many locales, paraprofessionals work in general education classes to provide support. Although this is not co-teaching, this assistance is appreciated and vital to student success. However, the general educator, special educator, and paraprofessional should collaborate, especially when challenges occur. For example, high school English teacher Mr. Bushelli asks for a meeting with special educator Ms. Crane and paraprofessional Ms. Hawthorne, who is assigned to this class to provide support for two students with ADHD and a student with autism. Mr. Bushelli begins by noting Ms. Hawthorne's value to the class and then states, "We are beginning our most important writing assignment of the

Table 1.1 Co-Teaching Approaches Applied to Instructional Content

Co-Teaching Approach	Characteristics	Co-Teaching Meeting Notes of Ms. Deptha and Ms. Cassie
Teaming	Teachers function as partners with the entire class group and teach the content together; whole group instruction.	This approach is often used when one teacher introduces a concept and the other provides an example of it to clarify, with both teachers delivering content. The teachers agree that this requires a more advanced level of collaboration than they have currently and more content knowledge for Ms. Cassie.
One Teach, One Observe	While one teacher works with the class, the other observes specific student or the whole class for specific behaviors.	Both teachers believe this model is not appropriate as they set out to introduce new concepts; it might be utilized toward the end of the unit, depending on student need.
One Teach, One Assist	One teacher leads instruction while the other quietly assists student who need assistance.	Ms. Deptha is interested in the model because it seems to be the easiest to implement. However, Ms. Cassie explains that this co-teaching approach is the least effective and should rarely be used.
Station Teaching	Students work in three groups. Two stations are led by the teachers to address different dimensions of the day's lesson, while in the third group students complete an independent, paired, or small group activity or assignment. Students rotate to each station.	To facilitate student reading with comprehension, Ms. Cassie notes that one group of students can use the 3-2-1 strategy to record three things they discovered in the text, two interesting facts, and one question they still have.[1] Ms. Deptha likes this idea: Students can use this strategy with Ms. Cassie; they can independently write answers to inference questions in their journals; and with her they can work on skills related to inferences and finding evidence. The students would have three types of exposure to the same text using this approach.
Parallel Teaching	Each teacher leads half of the class—sometimes covering the same material so that all students can participate more and sometimes addressing the material in different ways to accommodate students' diverse learning needs.	Ms. Deptha thought this would be an effective approach if Ms. Cassie was familiar with the instructional material and expected outcomes because it would enable her to more carefully scaffold for students with IEPs. However, the teachers decided the groups would be too large and that they risked stigmatizing students by having a "high" group and a "low" group.
Alternative Teaching	While one teacher works with most of the class, the other selects a small group for remediation, additional practice, enrichment, pre-teaching, assessment, or any other instructional purpose.	Ms. Deptha and Ms. Cassie agreed that this model would work well if the 3-2-1 was only helpful to students that struggled in reading or if the number of students that did not need the strategy was small enough to support doing an enrichment activity in a small group as the rest of the students learned the 3-2-1 strategy. However, the students would not get the multiple exposures to text that the station teaching allows. They decided this may be an approach to use toward the end of the unit for remediation or enrichment, depending on formative assessment data.

[1]Zygouris-Coe, V., Wiggins, M. B., & Smith, L. H. (2004). Engaging students with text: The 3–2–1 strategy. *e Reading Teacher, 58*, 381–384.

semester in about a week, and I wanted to touch base about the needs of the identified students, the types of supports you might provide, Ms. Hawthorne, and ways to avoid inadvertently making those students—and others—too dependent on adult assistance. After all, a critical goal is for students to be able to tackle longer assignments independently."

Ms. Crane turns to Ms. Hawthorne and says, "According to the data I have, the students we're discussing all are capable of completing this type of assignment as long as we provide supports. Ms. Hawthorne, what is your view?" Ms. Hawthorne replies, "If I make sure to use the self-monitoring technique with Jason and Shawn, I think they will be ok. But Nicholas is overwhelmed with even short writing assignments; he usually produces just a paragraph in the time other students complete pages. We have work samples we can review to show what I mean."

They continue discussing the assignment and jointly decide that the self-regulation strategy already introduced is adequate for two students. Ms. Crane then explains that she will develop a specific teaching protocol for Ms. Hawthorne to use when introducing the visual supports and a specific writing strategy for Nicholas.[13] As is typical for these educators, Ms. Crane will teach the protocol to Ms. Hawthorne and share it with Mr. Bushelli so that communication is clear and instruction is effective. Gathering data about Nicholas' use of the writing strategy will be part of the process and will guide future discussion and instructional decisions.

This interaction is highly collaborative and represents proactive problem solving. The three educators contribute, and because Ms. Hawthorne rather than Ms. Crane is in the class daily, it is appropriate in this instance that she fully participates in deciding how to address student needs.

Example 2: A Directive Special Educator-Paraprofessional Interaction

Although collaboration with a paraprofessional sometimes is preferred, in other situations the special education teacher appropriately directs the activities of the paraprofessional. For example, Mr. Evans is the paraprofessional for Mr. Tillerson in 6th grade math. Special educator Ms. Murkowski meets with Mr. Evans and after touching base on several of his assignments, says, "I need to raise one item with you. Mr. Tillerson has mentioned that he thinks you are providing too much assistance for the students with IEPs and that they are capable of independently understanding most of the concepts. He said that he wants students to try to work on their own so that he can determine what they do and do not understand." Mr. Evans replies, "The math is really hard. I feel bad for the kids when they struggle. I thought I was in there to help them!"

Ms. Murkowski answers, "No doubt you have the students' best interests at heart, and I appreciate your caring approach with them. For the next two weeks, when students ask you to help them, please tell them that you know they probably can do the problems independently and encourage them to try. If a student doesn't respond, quietly alert Mr. Tillerson. Let's meet again to see how students are doing. I'll ask Mr. Tillerson for their weekly quiz grades so that we have some data to use in deciding how to proceed."

This example is quite different from the first one as it illustrates one of the complexities of being a special educator who works with paraprofessionals, namely, making decisions about which interactions should be collaborative and which should be directive. In the first example, the situation clearly called for input by each participant, and Ms. Hawthorne's input was equally valued to that of the teachers. However, in the second example, Ms. Murkowski had received a specific concern from a general educator, and her judgment was that the paraprofessional should change his interactions with students. His value and intentions were not in question, but it was appropriate for Ms. Murkowski to clearly communicate to him her expectations. Establishing a timeline, a data source, and a specific plan for follow-up contributed to a constructive but flexible solution.

Early career special educators sometimes report that they are uncomfortable providing direction to paraprofessionals, particularly when those individuals may have worked in the school for many years. However, special education teachers generally are charged with directing the work of these school personnel, and clarity regarding expectations, whether it pertains to individual students, classroom responsibilities, or other assigned tasks, enables paraprofessionals to do their jobs effectively.[14] In most instances, a blend of collaboration and direction is successful. If paraprofessionals disagree with the guidance they are given, the special educator should first try to resolve the matter using recommended communication skills. However, if difficulties persist it may be necessary to seek input from the administrator who is the paraprofessionals' formal supervisor.

Wrap Up

This chapter has illustrated how collaboration is integral to the practice of today's special educators. We first reviewed the applicable collaboration skills special educators should develop and refine so that they effectively work with other professionals across situations. Next, we focused on two specific applications of collaboration: co-teaching and working with paraprofessionals. The fundamental skills for collaboration apply across grade levels and subject areas, and they are relevant in many of a professional's daily activities.

Tips

1. Become a student of collaboration, seeking input from others, practicing your communication skills, learning how to use those skills to complete each step of a collaborative process, and remembering that collaboration should be practiced within the context of culture. Observe others who demonstrate sophisticated collaboration skills to further polish your skills, noting how they use verbal and nonverbal communication skills and a problem-solving process to accomplish goals for effectively educating students with disabilities.

2. Practice exemplary collaboration skills in routine situations. If you do this, when a situation is stressful or awkward you will be more likely to be able to respond in a way that is constructive. In challenging situations, take a moment to think before speaking, to ask questions before stating opinions, and to paraphrase to check that you heard another's perspective accurately.

3. If you encounter a situation in which you and a colleague (regardless of role) disagree on how to address a student's needs, you should not assume that, as a novice special educator, others' experience takes priority over your perspective. Try at least three times to influence the situation: Rely on data that supports your view, and note that you are accountable for implementing strategies and practices to educate the student. Suggest implementing the strategy you prefer, but with a specific time limit at which point you and the other individual can review its impact. If your efforts are not successful, ask a non-supervisory school leader (e.g., instructional coach, counselor) to facilitate a meeting to discuss the matter. If that is not successful, your options are to decide to defer temporarily or to ask for administrative input.

4. If you co-teach, clearly explain to your colleague your roles and responsibilities rather than asking what that person would like you to do. Remember that some general educators may only learn about co-teaching through your contributions, as it is not required in all teacher preparation programs and some districts may not provide related professional development.

These professionals may not realize exactly why you are there unless you expressly discuss this topic.

5. Review paraprofessional job descriptions and meet with paraprofessionals at the very beginning of the school year. Outline your understanding of the specific roles and responsibilities they have, and seek their perspective about their assignments. Make sure that they have a clear schedule and arrange to periodically meet with them to discuss their work. Being proactive in building your relationships with paraprofessionals is essential.

Notes

1 Friend, M., & Cook, L. (2017). *Interactions: Collaboration skills for school professionals* (8th ed.). Upper Saddle River, NJ: Pearson.
2 Cook, L., & Friend, M. (2010). The state of the art of collaboration in special education. *Journal of Educational and Psychological Consultation, 20,* 1–8.
3 Huberman, M., Navo, M., & Parrish, T. (2012). Effective practices in high performing districts serving students in special education. *Journal of Special Education Leadership, 25*(2), 59–71.
4 Walsh, J. M. (2012). Co-teaching as a school system strategy for continuous improvement. *Preventing School Failure, 56*(1), 29–36.
5 O'Hair, D., Friedrich, G. W., & Dixon, L. D. (2016). *Strategic communication in business and the professions* (8th ed.). Boston, MA: Pearson.
6 Cooper, J. E., & He, Y. (2011). *Developing critical cultural competence: A guide for 21st-century educators*. Thousand Oaks, CA: Corwin Press.
7 Laughlin, P. R. (2011). *Group problem solving*. Princeton, NJ: Princeton University Press.
8 Murawski, W. W., & Swanson, H. L. (2001). A meta-analysis of co-teaching research: Where are the data? *Remedial and Special Education, 22,* 258–267.
9 Scruggs, T. E., Mastropieri, M. A., & McDuffie, K. A. (2007). Co-teaching in inclusive classrooms: A metasynthesis of qualitative research. *Exceptional Children, 73,* 392–416.
10 Solis, M., Vaughn, S., Swanson, E., & McCulley, L. (2012). Collaborative models of instruction: The empirical foundations of inclusion and co-teaching. *Psychology in the Schools, 49,* 498–510.
11 Tremblay, P. (2013). Comparative outcomes of two instructional models for students with learning disabilities: Inclusion with co-teaching and solo-taught special education. *Journal of Research in Special Educational Needs, 13,* 251–258.
12 Causton-Theoharis, J. (2009). *The paraprofessional's handbook for effective support in inclusive classrooms*. Baltimore, MD: Paul H. Brookes.
13 Carnahan, C. R., Williamson, P., Clarke, L., & Sorensen, R. (2009). A systematic approach for supporting paraeducators in educational settings: A guide for educators. *Teaching Exceptional Children, 41*(5), 34–43.
14 Fisher, M., & Pleasants, S. L. (2012). Roles, responsibilities, and concerns of paraeducators: Findings from a statewide survey. *Remedial and Special Education, 33,* 287–297.

Key Resources

Friend, M. (2019). *Co-teach: Building and sustaining effective classroom partnerships in inclusive schools* (3rd ed.). Washington, DC: Marilyn Friend, Inc.
Griffin, C., Kilgore, K., Winn, J., & Otis-Wilborn, A. (2008). First-year special educators' relationships with their general education colleagues. *Teacher Education Quarterly, 35,* 141–157.
Martin, C. C., & Hauth, C. (2015). *The survival guide for new special education teachers* (2nd ed.). Arlington, VA: Council for Exceptional Children.

Nichols, S. C., & Sheffield, A. N. (2014). Is there an elephant in the room? Considerations that administrators tend to forget when facilitating inclusive practices among general and special education teachers. *National Forum of Applied Educational Research Journal, 27*(1), 31–44.

Rivers, D. (2012). *The seven challenges workbook: Communication skills for success at home and work.* Retrieved from http://www. newconversations.net/

Stockall, N. S. (2014). When an aide really becomes an aid: Providing professional development for special education paraprofessionals. *Teaching Exceptional Children, 46*(6), 197–205.

2

Leading Effective Meetings With Professionals and Families

Jocelyn Washburn and Bonnie Billingsley

Introduction

Becoming an effective teacher for students with disabilities requires collaborating with others to make instructional decisions that will help students achieve important educational outcomes. Leading and participating in effective meetings require the ability to work effectively with a range of individuals, including those from varied cultural and linguistic backgrounds; leadership and organizational skills needed to facilitate positive team functioning; and specific knowledge and practices related to teaching students with disabilities. The primary benefit of well-organized meetings is that they have the potential to have a positive impact teams working on behalf of students with disabilities and their families and consequently student learning.

Depending on specific school and district expectations, teachers may participate in or lead varied types of meetings for different purposes, such as (1) continuous school improvement meetings; (2) screening meetings to identify students who are not responding to instruction in the general education curriculum and to plan programs of assistance; (3) eligibility meetings to assess whether students meet criteria to receive special education services; (4) Individualized Education Program [IEP] meetings to develop plans about the instruction and services that students with disabilities will receive; and (5) ongoing instructional decision-making meetings for the purpose of monitoring student progress and adjusting instruction so that students continue to make progress toward their goals. Other meetings may be held in response to specific needs, and these meetings may be initiated by parents or professionals.

Unfortunately, many professionals have experienced meetings that were unproductive, which may decrease motivation to attend and participate. This is the case when participants are not clear about what is to be achieved in the meeting or how they should contribute. Another barrier to effective meetings is the absence of key people who are in the position to implement instructional decisions. Sometimes participants do not listen to each other, or tensions may interfere with effective teamwork. It may also be challenging to accomplish meeting goals even when they are well planned, given time limitations and the many competing priorities in schools. Fortunately, there are practices that can be used to improve the effectiveness of meetings.

Narrowing the Focus

This chapter provides specific recommendations about leading meetings that make it possible for school staff and parents to coordinate their efforts in ways that lead to improved student learning and behavior outcomes. We first provide general guidelines that are relevant for leading and participating in varied types of meetings. These guidelines are designed to ensure that each meeting has clear goals, that the meeting is planned and organized so teams are likely to meet stated goals, and that all involved know how to prepare for and participate in the meeting. These guidelines are applicable to most meetings.

Next, we focus on instructional decision-making meetings, emphasizing specific actions that help teams establish instructional goals and progress monitoring systems toward these goals. These team meetings often occur within a Multi-Tiered System of Supports (MTSS) framework, which includes Response-to-Intervention (RTI) and Positive Behavioral Interventions and Supports (PBIS).[1] Key activities include data synthesis, recognizing students' strengths, identifying and resolving instructional and behavioral problems, and setting goals and monitoring student progress.[2] Ideally, instructional decision-making meetings, including IEP team meetings, are those that teachers engage in most frequently, as they provide opportunities for school staff to monitor and make adjustments in ways that can impact student learning.

Chapter Overview

1. Describe the rationale and purposes served by meetings, with an emphasis on instructional decision-making meetings.
2. Describe how to organize and lead effective, goal-oriented meetings that involve all participants.
3. Describe the rationale, prerequisites, and processes needed to facilitate instructional decision-making meetings, including the use of guiding questions and checklists.
4. Describe specific requirements of IEP meetings and the interconnections of IEP components.

Leading Effective Meetings

In this section, we provide suggestions for organizing and leading effective, efficient, student-centered meetings that involve all participants, including parents. Teachers place a premium on using their time for instruction, leaving very little time for out-of-class meetings and other activities. Creating the structures for effective meetings requires that facilitators take steps before, during, and after meetings to ensure meetings are efficient and productive.

Preparing for Effective Meetings

1. Determine Meeting Goal(s)

All meetings should have a clear goal so that all participants can direct their attention toward what needs to be accomplished by the end of the meeting. Meetings are held for a range of reasons, and facilitators need to specify what is to be achieved prior to the meeting. The purposes of meetings vary, and examples include designing the IEP, creating a home-school communication plan, addressing parents' concern about their child, reviewing a student's progress in reading, and making instructional changes. Facilitators need to share specific goals with all participants prior to the meeting and outline specific information and materials that they need to be prepared to discuss at the meeting (e.g., compile reading benchmark assessments, bring student work samples).

2. Determine Who Should Attend the Meeting

The participants included in meetings will vary depending on the purpose of the meeting and may include teachers, administrators, parents, and others such as school psychologists, guidance counselors, and related services personnel. In some cases, who will attend is straightforward, and in other contexts, it may be less clear. In the case of eligibility and IEP meetings, there are specific requirements (see section on IEPs later in this chapter).

It may be helpful for the teacher to consult with the principal if there are questions about who should attend. For instructional team planning meetings, facilitators will usually invite and encourage participation from those who have responsibility for and expertise about the student. Co-teaching and grade-level meetings typically include partnering teachers and occasionally support personnel. Although principals will not typically attend all meetings, their presence helps in communication across teachers and administration, and they are often included when difficult decisions need to be made (e.g., manifest determination) and in addressing specific concerns. For example, in an instructional decision-making meeting, the team may be interested in securing an assistive technology device to assist a student with communication. The principal or administrative designee could then agree to work with the district in securing funds to purchase the device and arranging professional development regarding its use.

3. Schedule the Meeting and Share the Agenda

Prior to scheduling the meeting, it is important to find a time that works for all who need to attend. In the event that scheduling is difficult, an online program for scheduling might be considered. Once this is finalized, the date, time, place, and length of the meeting should be shared with all participants, giving an appropriate amount of notice. The leader also needs to schedule adequate time for the meeting, allowing sufficient time for agenda items and discussion. If an individual would like to contribute, yet cannot attend, facilitators should collect input to be shared at the meeting.

Meeting facilitators may need to confer with the principal to ensure attendance of needed individuals. Principals can establish expectations with the faculty about meeting participation and coordinate class coverage to ensure attendance. How meetings are scheduled should be considered carefully, as it is important to protect instructional time. Some questions to consider when scheduling team meetings:

- Can the meeting take place during a planning block to avoid missing instructional time?
- If participants must be away from their class, will teachers need substitute coverage for their class in order to attend?
- Are meetings taking place frequently enough so as to not lose track of instructional goals?

Finally, at least a week prior to the meeting, the facilitator should share the following with each participant: the agenda, which includes meeting purposes; materials that should be brought to the meeting; and any specific expectations for each member's preparation and participation.

Facilitating Meetings

Once participants have arrived at the meeting, they need to operate as a team. Effective meetings are facilitated by building trust,[3] communicating clearly,[4] listening carefully to others' concerns and opinions,[5] and holding a belief in equality as shown through genuine respect for others.[6] Good facilitators involve meeting participants, model active listening, and encourage consensus-building while maintaining efficiency.

Effective meeting facilitators use a range of strategies to encourage participation and effective communication. Teams that meet together frequently should agree on a set of behaviors or ground rules for their meetings, clarifying what each one means and how they will help each other use them.[7] Another strategy is for leaders to share ground rules that they would like participants to follow, such as beginning and ending the meeting on time, focusing on the agenda and meeting goals, allowing all participants opportunities to share, and focusing on "what's possible" instead of "what's wrong" (see resources for a website with many additional ground rules). Below are key activities for meeting facilitators.

1. Begin With a Clear Goal and a Positive Tone

The facilitator should begin the meeting on time and welcome participants. It is important to begin meetings with a positive tone and share or remind the team of the ground rules. If appropriate, a brief one- or two-minute sharing about student success in the classroom or at home may help set a positive tone for the meeting. If the facilitator is leading a new team or there are new team members, take time to introduce each member and share informally for a few minutes to develop rapport. If some members have not attended a specific type of meeting before (e.g., IEP, instructional decision-making meeting), an overview of the process should help team members understand how to participate. Facilitators may also encourage engagement in the meeting by asking specific participants to take on various roles, such as note-taker, timekeeper, or encourager.

2. Facilitate Discussion

The role of the facilitator is to promote discussion, equal voice, and contribution by all individuals within a group.[8] Techniques such as writing notes on chart paper or submitting ideas with technology, such as Padlet (https://padlet.com/), may be used to encourage participation. Special consideration may be given to facilitating parent input, such as suggesting topics for them to think about prior to the meeting (see Chapter 3 for more information about parent involvement). Specific processes, such as using guiding questions and checklists described later in this chapter, can be used to increase discussion among participants in instructional decision-making meetings.

3. Keep the Meeting on Track

Sometimes a discussion strays from the stated purpose of the meeting, and it requires care and sensitivity to encourage discussion and yet refocus the group when conversation is off topic. For example, the facilitator might state, "Let's take ten minutes to finalize our discussion about this data, and then we will move to determining the student's reading goal." However, it is important to use judgment to assure that decisions are not made in haste. If the meeting becomes unproductive, gently remind the group of the meeting purpose. If a participant complains or blames others, refocus on the goal and problem solve. For example, the facilitator may pose a question, such as, "In moving forward, what might we do together to address this need?"

4. Identify Next Steps

The facilitator should discuss any follow-up activities that need to occur after the meeting, as decisions may need to be communicated to others who also work with the student. For example, if related services are determined to be necessary at an IEP meeting, a member of the committee may need to follow up to assure that these are scheduled. Table 2.1 provides a format to record the specific actions, the date for completion, and the individuals who are responsible.

5. Summarize Key Points

In the last few minutes of the meeting, it is helpful if the facilitator summarizes what was accomplished (e.g., review student goals and plans); reviews the follow-up items; and, if needed, determines

Table 2.1 Post Meeting Follow-up Plan

Topic	Action	Date	By Whom	Completed √
Student schedule	Change Althea's schedule at the end of the first six weeks, adding the study skills class.	December 15	Guidance counselor	
Reading strategy generalization	Provide description of reading intervention DeMario is learning to his English and social studies teachers	October 12	Intervention Teacher	
	Gather English, science, and social studies passages for DeMario's intervention teacher	October 14	Case manager	

the date and the time of the next meeting. If there is extra time, the facilitator may ask for feedback about the meeting processes and make suggestions for improvement.

Instructional Decision-Making Meetings

Irrespective of the content emphasis (e.g., math, literacy, behavior), instructional decision-makers use data to develop students' learning goals and to monitor their performance. The use of student data in instructional decision-making accomplishes several critical needs, including:

- providing information about each student's present levels of performance, which is needed to determine individual goals and instructional entry points;
- providing the basis for determining students or groups of students who are not meeting performance expectations in specific content or behavior areas, signaling the need for more intensive supports;
- allowing teams to determine the extent to which students are benefiting from specific instructional interventions over time and to modify interventions as needed.

This section provides prerequisites for leading instructional decision-making meetings and demonstrates how guiding questions and checklists can be used to support the goals of these meetings.

Prerequisites for Instructional Decision-Making Meetings

A beginning point for facilitating instructional decision-making meetings is developing data-literacy skills. There are four basic prerequisites to instructional decision-making meetings: (1) understand varied types of student data; (2) analyze and chart student data to assess progress over time; (3) understand decision-making processes; and (4) identify and use effective instructional practices. We discuss each briefly here and also refer you to other HLP chapters in this book for additional resources.

1. Understand Varied Types of Student Data

Teachers need to be familiar with the varied student data sources in the school and the schedule that is used to collect this data. Additionally, teachers may need to select appropriate, validated skills-based assessments to determine student needs and to monitor progress (e.g., curriculum-based measures for oral reading fluency or math fluency). Figure 2.2 provides an overview of a comprehensive assessment system, illustrating the varied types of data teachers may use, including screening, formative assessments, benchmark tests, and skill-based assessments.

2. Analyze and Chart Student Data

Data literacy also requires that teachers are able to analyze and chart various sources of student performance data in combination with their knowledge about curricular demands and effective interventions in order to make sound instructional decisions.[9] A common way to compare results from differing assessments is through the use of percentiles. A percentile is not the same as a percent; rather it represents a comparison to norm age peers. For example, a student who scores at the 20th percentile performs better than 20 percent of other students taking the same assessment. Forthcoming examples use percentiles. Also, see Chapter 6 that provides additional information about using assessment data to make instructional decisions.

3. Understand Decision-Making Processes

Instructional decision-making meetings need to incorporate several important considerations, including:

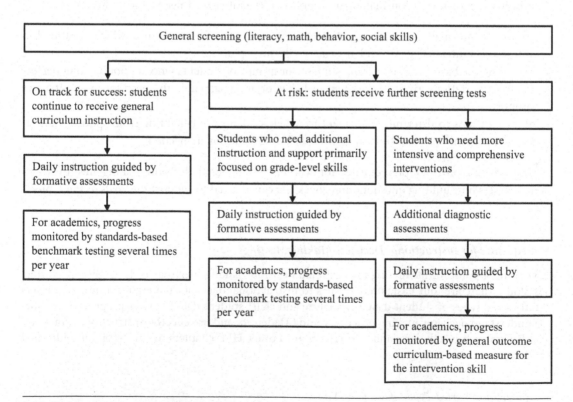

Figure 2.2 A Comprehensive Assessment System for Instructional Decision-Making

Source: Adapted from Torgesen, J. K., & Miller, D. H. (2009). *Assessments to guide adolescent literacy instruction*. Portsmouth, NH: RMC Research Corporation, Center on Instruction.

- What are key goals for the student (e.g., academic, behavioral, social)?
- What is the student's current level of performance? How are current instructional approaches working? Is the gap between the initial goal and student progress narrowing, or is progress stagnant?
- How will the student meet instructional goal(s)? What effective practices will be used? Prior to altering current instruction, how will fidelity and dosage of implementation be confirmed? Fidelity is the delivery of instructional strategies or interventions as designed with accurately and consistency, and dosage is the amount of instructional strategies or interventions delivered (usually refers to a recommended number of minutes per day and per week).
- How will student progress be monitored and assessed (e.g., measurement, frequency)?

These questions may be used flexibly, and teams may return to earlier questions as they consider new instructional strategies. The order of the questions may vary, depending on the type of meeting. For example, for a new student who has just entered the school, the team may want to begin with question "b" (what is the student's current level of performance?) and then return to question "a." If the goals are clear and progress monitoring plans are established, they may spend most of their time reviewing monitoring data to determine how well the current instructional plan is working as they assess effectiveness of interventions. If progress shows minimal growth, they will need to revisit their instructional plan and take steps to assure that it is being carried out as planned by confirming implementation with fidelity and correct dosage.

4. Identify and Use Effective Instructional Practices

Once instructional needs are determined, teams need to incorporate the use of effective instructional practices in the development of plans. Teachers need to be familiar with high-quality resources (e.g., HLPs, reviews and meta-analyses on effective instructional practices) in order to select practices that yield positive results for students with similar characteristics to the student with whom the team is working. The following websites also provide information about specific practices and the student populations for which practices are intended.

- Best Practices Encyclopedia: www.bestevidence.org
- Institute for Educational Sciences: https://ies.ed.gov/ncee/WWC/
- IRIS Center: http://iris.peabody.vanderbilt.edu/ebp_summaries

Preparing for Instructional Decision-Making Meetings

Using a decision-making process helps teachers develop their data-literacy skills, which in turn helps school staff distinguish between tiers of support required for students' needs to be met. For example, some students may need additional instruction and support to meet grade-level expectations, whereas other students (typically fewer) may need more intensive interventions in basic skills.

Prior to instructional decision-making meetings, facilitators will want to request that team members bring specific data relevant to the purpose of the meeting, such as:

- results of pre-test or baseline assessments;
- benchmark assessment results;
- behavior/performance checklists;
- progress charts for classwork and interventions;
- cumulative file to consider past performance, such as standardized assessments, course work, discipline record, attendance; and
- other information such as student work, observations about the student or student interviews.

The process of instructional decision-making meetings is sufficiently complex to warrant advance preparation in the form of guiding questions or checklists to ensure that all needed details are addressed during the meeting, just as surgeons use checklists to perform their job with consistency, accuracy, and safety.[10] There are a number of guiding questions and checklists that may be used, and several options are illustrated in the next sections.

Example 1. Using Guiding Questions to Review an Individual Student's Progress

In this example, a team gathers reading fluency data to assess how well DeMario is progressing in reading. At the beginning of the meeting, the facilitator posts the team's guiding questions (see Figure 2.3) on the wall and states, "The purpose of our meeting today is to determine how DeMario is progressing in reading and to determine any modifications needed in his instructional plan. We will use this visual to remind us of our decision-making process and to keep our focus on the goal we are working toward." The facilitator then begins with the first question:

1. What Are Key Goals for the Student (e.g., Academic, Behavioral, Social)?

His classroom teacher shares, "We would like DeMario to read 97 words correct per minute by December, as this would place him just above the 50th percentile in fluency (on par with typical third-grade readers), allowing him to practice reading comprehension skills with grade-level materials."

2. What Is the Student's Current Level?

At the start of this school year, DeMario read 55 words correct per minute in context, which was approximately 33rd percentile for a third grader in the fall.[11] At the time of this meeting, it appears that after seven weeks into the school year, his oral reading fluency is progressing, but not at the rate needed to meet his goal (see Figure 2.4). DeMario's mother expresses a concern: "When DeMario reads as fast as he can, he does not understand what he has read." His special education teacher

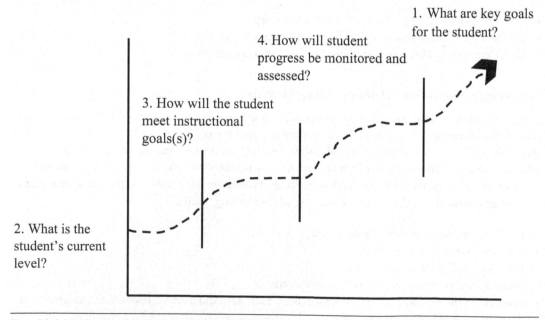

Figure 2.3 Guiding Questions for Instructional Decision-Making Meetings

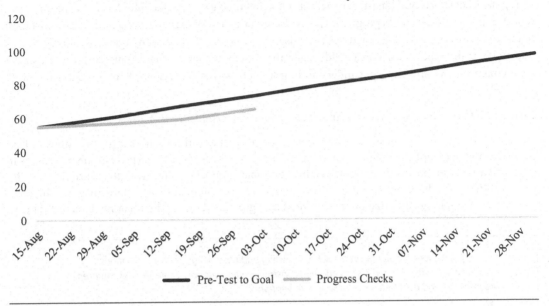

Figure 2.4 Results of an Oral Reading Fluency Curriculum-Based Measure

validates the mother's point by asking the team, "How are we helping him increase his reading speed without sacrificing his ability to comprehend?"

3. How Will the Student Meet Instructional Goal(s)?

The team confirms that fluency instruction is delivered with fidelity and for the recommended amount of time each day. Next, the team acknowledges his mother's concern and begins to brainstorm ways that DeMario can work on both fluency and comprehension. His classroom teacher asks, "While he is practicing, would it help if we emphasized different purposes for reading with each repeated reading? For example, we can use this evidence-based practice: the first read will be for accuracy; the second read will be for fluency (speed); and the third read will be for understanding."[12] Initially, DeMario's goal was focused on fluency as a means to increase access to grade-level materials; however, through conversation, the goal evolves to include a focus on accuracy, fluency, and comprehension. When DeMario reads for accuracy and meaning, his rate will likely be slower than when he reads for fluency (speed). The team concurs and believes DeMario will gain a lot by increased cognitive awareness about the reading process.

4. How Will Student Progress Be Monitored and Assessed (e.g., Measurement, Frequency)?

DeMario's special education teacher suggests, "When we assess his words correct per minute, let's add a quick comprehension check. This way we will know if his comprehension rises as his reading speed increases. Also, during typical classroom reading assignments, one of his teachers could do a spot-check by asking him to read a paragraph aloud as well as check his percentage of correct answers on the accompanying comprehension questions." The team agrees to meet in another month to see how this new instructional plan will increase DeMario's fluency and reading comprehension of grade-level materials.

To conclude, using guiding questions creates an opportunity for teams to review progress monitoring data, set short- and long-term goals, discuss potential issues, make intervention decisions, and monitor an individual child's progress. Teams also identify assessment tools (e.g., a curriculum-based fluency measure) and testing schedules (e.g., used bi-weekly). Using guiding questions allows everyone on the team to be focused on a child's goals, the plan for achieving these goals, clear criteria about achieving the goals, and a specific understanding about how they will know when the goal is achieved.

Example 2. Using Guiding Questions for Whole School Universal Screening

In this next example, we illustrate how a team uses guiding questions with supporting steps to lead them through a complex whole school universal screening process. The purpose of the meeting is to identify those students needing additional instructional support or intensive interventions. In order to ensure the consideration of multiple data points in a consistent and systematic manner, the team uses decision-making rules that are represented in Figure 2.5. During the meeting, a recorder keeps

---

Meeting Purpose: Identify students in the school needing additional support or interventions.
Guiding Question: Which students need additional instruction and support in grade-level comprehension skills or more intensive and comprehensive reading interventions?

Steps:
1. Organize the following data available, ideally using online databases:
   - student records and class schedules;
   - whole school reading universal screening results;
   - other reading assessment results, such as oral or silent reading fluency or Language Arts benchmarks;
   - standardized reading test scores; and
   - class rosters for groups of students receiving additional instruction in grade-level comprehension skills or intensive reading interventions.

2. For each grade level, print student reading levels sorted from highest to lowest.
3. Discuss one grade level and one student at a time. Start with the student with the lowest reading level and work up toward students reading with proficiency.
4. To determine if a student needs a more intensive reading intervention, consider assessing underlying reading skills, such as oral reading fluency or silent reading fluency. Based on the results, follow these guidelines:

   ⇑ 35 percentiles and higher: no additional instruction or intervention needed
   15–35 percentiles: recommend for additional instruction in grade-level comprehension skills; contact parents
   ⇓ 15 percentiles: administer program-specific placement tests (e.g., pre-test or baseline assessment); recommend for intensive reading intervention; contact parents

5. Complete the "Record of Data Analysis" table as the team discovers students who need additional instruction or intensive reading interventions.
6. If the student is identified with a disability or is an English Language Learner (ELL) and is found to need additional instruction or an intervention, check with case managers. IEPs may need to be amended. Consider functional and academic language development of ELL students prior to intervention placement.

*Developed by Jocelyn Washburn & Linda Freeman based on the comprehensive assessment system in Figure 2.2 above.

Figure 2.5 Review Process for Universal Screening*

Student	Identified as student with a disability or ELL	Reading comprehension level	Oral or silent reading fluency Score	Standardized test score(s)	Course grades/ GPA	Attendance issues	Discipline issues	Recommendation for additional instruction or intensive intervention	Next steps (Examples: Give skill-based assessment, confer with parents, retake prior assessment, make schedule change)
Cora		19th percentile		365	3.3	No	No		Give silent reading fluency assessment
Pranaya	ELL	10th percentile			3.8	No	No	Yes	Confer with ELL teacher

Figure 2.6 Record of Data Analysis

track of student data and action items using the organizing tool in Figure 2.6. This record of student performance data helps the team in subsequent meetings to monitor progress and provides team members with specific tasks, making follow-through easier to coordinate.

Example 3: Using Checklists to Monitor Progress of Small Groups

Another option to facilitate instructional decision-making meetings is to use a Do-Confirm style checklist,[13] which means team members naturally discuss students while one person, acting as facilitator, checks off items as they arise. The team revisits any items that remain for discussion based on the facilitator's guidance.

The example provided in Figure 2.7 is a checklist designed for progress monitoring with a Learning Strategy from the Strategic Instruction Model (SIM™) developed by the University of Kansas Center for Research on Learning. The SIM Learning Strategies Curriculum teaches adolescents *how* to learn with interventions relevant to the rigorous demands of the secondary level curriculum. Each SIM Learning Strategy prompts students to analyze and solve problems that they encounter with cognitive and meta-cognitive strategies, and thus a prerequisite for student participation in instruction with a Learning Strategy is to read at the fourth-grade level or higher.[14]

In the upcoming example of using checklists for instructional decision-making, two high school English teachers and one special educator meet monthly after school to share their students' progress, discuss areas of concern, and refine their instructional programs. Each of the three teachers are responsible for a one-semester elective course titled SIM Learning Strategies.

Purpose: Analyze student Learning Strategy data with the goal of accelerating student learning.

Note: This is a *Do-Confirm* checklist, so discussion should proceed naturally, and at ten-minute intervals a member of the team checks that these items have been addressed. Identify one person to be responsible for the checklist.

- Each member of the team has introduced themselves (as needed), and a few success stories with Learning Strategy instruction have been shared.
- A spreadsheet of students' scores (e.g., Classroom Management Chart in Google Docs) is up-to-date and referenced.
- Each teacher has reviewed at least one student folder to check progress charts, cue cards, and organization.
- The team discussed all students whose progress is stagnant, defined as showing no progress on three practice attempts at a similar level of difficulty.
- Students have goals with dates on their progress chart.
- Each student whose progress is stagnant has a plan for addressing potential barriers, such as consulting with a colleague, classroom support from an instructional coach, student support from a speech-language pathologist, special education teacher, or other specialist.
- The Learning Strategy manual has been consulted, specifically the troubleshooting section for each stage of instruction.
- Scoring procedures have been reviewed and/or samples of student products with score sheets have been shared and reviewed.

Developed by Jocelyn Washburn, SIM™ Professional Development Leader, based on the process of a Do-Confirm style checklist in Gawande, A., & Lloyd, J. B. (2010). *The checklist manifesto: How to get things right* (Vol. 200). New York: Metropolitan Books.

Figure 2.7 Do-Confirm Checklist for Progress Monitoring

Each teacher arrives at the meeting with their students' folders, which contain progress charts, cue cards that students created to guide themselves through strategy use, and evidence of their students' attempts at applying particular reading strategies to passages. For example, students have recorded main ideas and essential details about their reading passage or have annotated their reading passage with symbols. They also reference their students' records of past performance, such as standardized test scores and reading levels, as well as their current IEP goals (as applicable), intervention performance, such as assignment scores, and periodic silent reading fluency assessment results.

Ms. Odle shares, "Last week, some of my students reported using the strategy currently being taught in our Learning Strategies class in their social studies class." Next, Mr. Gonzales celebrates, "The students who are in my Learning Strategies class and in my English 9 class are outperforming other students in the class on their research papers, despite their history of struggling." Finally, Ms. Utz proudly reports, "All of my students are using their cue cards while practicing the strategy!"

- Each member of the team has introduced themselves (as needed), and a few success stories with Learning Strategy instruction have been shared.

The three teachers begin reviewing their spreadsheets with their students' strategy performance. During instruction, they use this same spreadsheet to stay organized and to discuss progress directly with students through individual conferencing. After studying the mastery level of all students, they identify individual students who are doing really well and those who are struggling. Reflecting on students who succeed helps the teachers notice behaviors needed to master the strategy and how to encourage or teach these behaviors to all students. Ms. Utz points out, "Kiki has advanced by three grade levels in reading while using this strategy." Ms. Odle shares with the team that she is concerned about Leland. Mr. Gonzales asks Ms. Odle to describe the situation and share current intervention performance data from her spreadsheet. At this point, the team suggests that they start completing the action plan sheet for Leland (see Figure 2.4). Reading from her class spreadsheet, Ms. Odle reports, "Leland has attempted a level 5 reading passage three times, and his scores for both strategy use (52%, 68%, 45%) and comprehension (40%, 25%, 38%) have not met mastery or shown improvement."

- A spreadsheet of students' scores (e.g., Classroom Management Chart in Google Docs) is up-to-date and referenced.

Ms. Utz asks to look through Leland's strategy folder as Ms. Odle wonders, "What behaviors do you notice about Kiki (who is doing well) when she is practicing the strategy? What might her strategy folder show us?" Ms. Utz pages through Kiki's folder and describes, "Her folder is really organized, and she has highlighted and written notes on her cue cards. When she uses the strategy, she looks like she is talking to herself." All three teachers start looking through their students' strategy folders to check for overall organization, up-to-date progress charts, and legible cue cards. While inside the folders, they ask each other to check a few of their scored assignments as a cross-check for accuracy.

- Each teacher has reviewed at least one student folder to check progress charts, cue cards, and organization.
- Students have goals with dates on their progress charts.
- Scoring procedures have been reviewed and/or samples of student products with score sheets have been shared and reviewed.

When Ms. Odle comments, "Leland complains a lot about not wanting to read. He says the passages are boring, and he takes longer than expected to complete the actual reading," Mr. Gonzalez suggests they look in the troubleshooting section of the Learning Strategy manual, which gives them some pointers. The team discusses how motivation for reading is a typical and understandable challenge for older readers who continue to struggle with reading. Mr. Gonzalez recommends seeking high-interest passages to help Leland find success with the strategy and then move to more complex or content-specific passages later on. Ms. Utz also reminds the team that Kiki talks to herself while using the strategy and actively uses her cue cards. Ms. Odle decides, "I'll ask the entire class to have their cue cards out, and I'll specifically ask Leland to think aloud for me, so I can hear how he is using or not using the strategy." The team records these ideas on the action plan sheet.

- The Learning Strategy manual has been consulted, specifically the troubleshooting section for each stage of instruction.

As a result of the team's problem-solving and discussion, they develop the following plan for Leland (see Figure 2.8).

Team members continue to problem-solve and develop action plans for other students whose progress is stagnant.

- The team has discussed all students whose progress is stagnant, defined as showing no progress on three practice attempts at a similar level of difficulty.
- Each student who is stagnant has a plan for addressing potential barriers, such as consulting with a colleague, classroom support from a SIM Professional Developer, student support from a speech-language pathologist, special education teacher, or other specialist.

Student Name: *Leland King*   **Date:**   **October 9, 2018**

Data that shows need for additional support:

Leland has attempted a level 5 reading passage three times, and his scores for both strategy use (52%, 68%, 45%) and comprehension (40%, 25%, 38%) have not met mastery or shown improvement.

Hypothesized barrier to success:

Leland complains a lot about not wanting to read. He says the passages are boring, and he takes longer than expected to complete the actual reading.

Actions to Take	Date to Accomplish
Check that Leland has his cue cards out while he is reading the passages and that he is using them.	October 10
Sit with Leland during his next practice assignment with the strategy and have him "think aloud."	October 10
Talk to driver's ed teacher to pull passages from their manual for Leland's practice with the strategy.	October 12
Survey Leland about his interests and find several options of passages at level 5 in order to offer him choice for his reading.	October 16

Figure 2.8 SIM™ Learning Strategy Action Plan

In summary, this team of three teachers, while each teaching separate classes, come together as a genuine partnership, engaging in meaningful discussion to assess student progress over time and modify instruction so that the progress of their students improves.

Steps for Facilitating Instructional Decision-Making Meetings

The examples above used the following processes in instructional decision-making, even though the purposes and tools were somewhat different:

1. Identify the purpose of the meeting.
2. Create a step-by-step process, using a checklist or set of guiding questions, to match the purpose of the meeting. Consider if the right tool already exists using available resources, such as online or within a school or district.
3. Create tables or charts to record trends in the data, identify roles for participants, outline key tasks, and determine the need for other graphic organizational tools.
4. Share the checklist or guiding questions before or at the beginning of the meeting along with participant assignments.
5. Give each participant data to present during the meeting or suggest an assignment for the meeting.
6. Teach participants how to use the checklist or guiding questions so that they are invested and can take on facilitation roles in future meetings.
7. Use the checklist or guiding questions to debrief about the outcome of the meeting.

Leading IEP Team Meetings

Individual Educational Program team meetings (IEPs) are critical to instructional decision-making as educators and parents design a plan to meet the educational needs of a student with disability. Consistent with the collaboration principles described throughout this chapter, IEP team meetings are designed to set learning goals and to describe the services a school will provide. The IEP team must develop an initial IEP, and review and revise an existing IEP at least annually. For the first several IEP team meetings, beginning special educators need to work closely with their mentors to prepare for, facilitate, and complete post-meeting responsibilities.

Preparing for IEP Team Meetings

Special educators must become familiar with the federal requirements of IEPs and learn district procedures, processes, and tools (e.g., online IEP development tools, IEP team meeting agendas) and methods for facilitating team discussion around IEP components. Solely meeting the requirements specified in the law may not produce an IEP that provides a student with optimal instructional programming. The following considerations will help special educators prepare for leading effective IEP team meetings:

- Read manuals, online materials, and attend orientations that describe IEP processes in the district.
- Resources developed for parents are especially helpful to understand the IEP process quickly in user-friendly language as well as prepare to communicate purposes and expectations of IEP meetings to parents.

- Review previously completed IEPs from your school or district.
- Observe a mentor or experienced teacher during an IEP team meeting.

IEP Components

Special education teachers who understand how IEP components are interrelated will be better able to participate in or lead IEP team meetings. Figure 2.9 shows how team member discussions about a student's strengths and needs, concerns, and evaluation results (i.e., information included in the IEP Present Level of Performance) can drive goal setting, which in turn can influence decisions regarding special education and related services. The four-step process in Figure 2.3 can be used to help all team members begin with the end in mind as they align student goals with the general education curriculum as well as each student's unique needs. Students are often involved in the development of their IEPs and participate in the IEP team meeting, especially during transition planning.

After discussing the team's vision for the student's future, the meeting facilitator should share and gather data to craft the IEP Present Level of Performance (PLOP). Discussion related to a student's current level of performance or functioning will include strengths, needs (e.g., academic, development, functional), parents' and others' concerns, and initial or most recent evaluation results (e.g., achievement tests, teacher observation, or completion of behavior checklists). The IEP *goals* will be directly related to the information provided in the PLOP. Next, the team will determine the IEP *services* needed for the student to reach his or her goals. Services include accommodations, assistive technology, testing participation, and placement (e.g., general education with varied degrees of special education support, such as co-teaching or consultative support). Once the IEP is developed, the team should monitor student progress throughout the year using the procedures described earlier in this chapter. The team needs to determine when and how progress will be measured for each IEP goal.

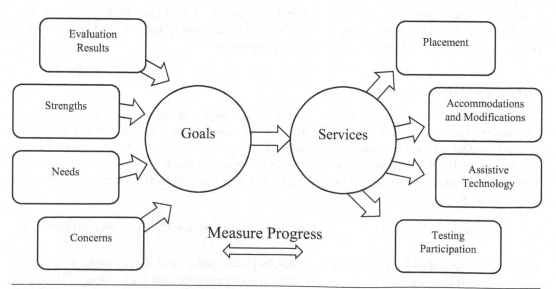

Figure 2.9 Interconnections of IEP Components

Meeting Participants

The Individuals with Disabilities Education Act (IDEA) requires that specific individuals be in attendance at the meeting, and parents must be invited and be given opportunities to participate. The facilitator must take steps to ensure that the following participants are in attendance. This includes:

- Parents/guardians of a child with a disability (must be invited)
- At least one general education teacher
- At least one special education teacher or related service provider of the child
- An administrator or designee who supervises special education services
- Other individuals with special knowledge about the child, available resources, or evaluation results
- The student with a disability, when appropriate

Parent Involvement

To take advantage of the varied expertise and perspectives of the IEP team, facilitators should consider the guidelines for leading meetings that were introduced earlier in this chapter. Parents have important knowledge to share about their child and will often make meaningful contributions to the development of the IEP. In addition, before a school can implement an IEP, parents must provide written consent.

IEP facilitators must schedule the IEP team meeting at an agreed upon time and place and provide specific information about the meeting (i.e., Prior Written Notice includes the purpose of the meeting and informs parents of their ability to invite others to the meeting). Parents may contribute by sharing information about their child's interests, strengths, and needs; suggesting learning goals for their child; and sharing ideas about what works with their child. Ways to encourage parent involvement include:

- offering choices of times to meet;
- scheduling the meeting well in advance, such as one month;
- asking for input or concerns over the phone prior to meeting; and
- having a translator available when necessary for parents with hearing impairment or native languages other than English.

Post-IEP Team Meeting

After the meeting, the IEP document needs to be available to teachers and service providers and stored in the designated location. Responsibilities for implementing the IEP should be determined by the team.

Wrap Up

Teachers have an important professional responsibility to coordinate their efforts with others to enhance students' opportunities to learn. We first reviewed effective practices for leading varied types of meetings and outlined specific guidelines for preparing, leading, and following up after meetings. Next, we focused on instructional decision-making meetings, as these are important to monitoring student performance over time and adjusting instruction in ways that impact student learning. Lastly, we showed how similar processes can be used to lead IEP team meetings. Guiding questions and checklists are helpful for keeping these meetings focused on students' learning goals, monitoring their learning, and identifying needed instructional changes.

Tips

1. **Request assistance from others**. Review local procedures for eligibility and IEP meetings and consider observing others before you lead meetings on your own. You might also ask others to provide feedback after you lead a meeting. If you anticipate a difficult meeting, ask your principal or mentor to attend.

2. **Develop an organizational system for meeting preparations**. Create templates with invitations and agendas that you can modify for the types of meetings that you lead. Keep a calendar that tracks all meetings and activities that need to be completed prior to meetings.

3. **Become knowledgeable about the meaning of assessment results.** Read literature and practitioner guides about data use in the instructional planning process and share your new learning with your colleagues as you make team decisions for program improvement. Be patient with yourself and your team, as the process of data analysis is multifaceted given the need to understand each student, his or her instructional program, and how the student is responding to instruction. Section 2 of this book provides more information about using assessment data to make instructional decisions as well as how to use multiple sources of information to understand a student's strengths and needs.

Notes

1 Newton, J. S., Horner, R. H., Todd, A. W., Algozzine, R. F., & Algozzine, K. M. (2012). A pilot study of a problem-solving model for team decision making. *Education and Treatment of Children*, *35*(1), 25–49.

2 Batsche, G. (2014). Multi-tiered system of supports for inclusive schools. In J. McLeskey, N. L. Waldron, F. Spooner, & B. Algozzine (Eds.), *Handbook of effective inclusive schools: Research and practice* (pp. 183–196). New York, NY: Routledge.

3 Fullan, M. (2008). *The six secrets of change: What the best leaders do to help their organizations survive and thrive*. San Francisco: Jossey-Bass.
  Reina, D. S., & Reina, M. L. (2006). *Trust and betrayal in the workplace: Building effective relationships in your organization* (2nd ed.). San Francisco: Berrett-Koeler.

4 Patterson, K., Grenny, J., McMillan, R., & Switzler, A. (2012). *Crucial conversations*. New York, NY: McGraw-Hill.

5 Patterson, K., Grenny, J., McMillan, R., & Switzler, A. (2012). *Crucial conversations*. New York, NY: McGraw-Hill.
  Covey, S. (2004). *The 7 habits of highly effective people: Powerful lessons in personal change*. New York, NY: Simon & Schuster.
  Knight, J. (2007). *Instructional coaching: A partnership approach to improving instruction*. Thousand Oaks, CA: Corwin Press.

6 Knight, J. (2007). *Instructional coaching: A partnership approach to improving instruction*. Thousand Oaks, CA: Corwin Press.

7 Schwartz, R. (2016). *Eight ground rules for effective meetings*. Retrieved from https://hbr.org/2016/06/8-ground-rules-for-great-meetings

8 Knight, J. (2016). *Better conversations: Coaching ourselves and each other to be more credible, caring, and connected*. Thousand Oaks, CA: Corwin Press.

9 Mandinach, E. B., Parton, B. M., Gummer, E. S., and Anderson, R. (2015). Ethical and appropriate data use requires data literacy. *Kappan*, *96*(5), 25–28.

10 Gawande, A., & Lloyd, J. B. (2010). *The checklist manifesto: How to get things right* (Vol. 200). New York, NY: Metropolitan Books.

11 Hasbrouck, J., & Tindal, G. A. (2006). Oral reading fluency norms: A valuable assessment tool for reading teachers. *The Reading Teacher, 59*(7), 636–644.

12 Brasseur, I. F., Hock, M. F., & Deshler, D. D. (2012). *The bridging strategy-revised*. Chicago, IL: McGraw-Hill Education.

13 Gawande, A., & Lloyd, J. B. (2010). *The checklist manifesto: How to get things right* (Vol. 200). New York, NY: Metropolitan Books.

14 Schumaker, J. B., & Deshler, D. D. (2006). Teaching adolescents to be strategic learners. *Teaching Adolescents with Disabilities: Accessing the General Education Curriculum*, 121–156.

Key Resources

A list of ground rules for meetings. Retrieved from http://getthepicture.ca/a-list-of-ground-rules-for-effective-meetings/

Bahr, M. W., & Kovaleski, J. F. (2006). The need for problem-solving teams: Introduction to a special issue. *Remedial and Special Education, 27*, 2–5. Entire issue.

Bocala, C., Henry, S. F., Mundry, S., & Morgan, C. (2014). *Practitioner data use in schools: Workshop toolkit* (REL 2015–043). Washington, DC: U.S. Department of Education, Institute of Education Sciences, National Center for Education Evaluation and Regional Assistance, Regional Educational Laboratory, Northeast & Islands. Retrieved from http://ies.ed.gov/ncee/edlabs.

Guidelines to Conducting Effective Meetings. http://managementhelp.org/misc/meeting-management.htm

IDEA Parent Hub. Retrieved from https://sites.ed.gov/idea/

Küpper, L. (2007). Meetings of the IEP team (Module 14). *Building the legacy: IDEA 2004 training curriculum*. Washington, DC: National Dissemination Center for Children with Disabilities. Retrieved from www.nichcy.org/training/contents.asp

Newton, J. S., Horner, R. H., Todd, A. W., Algozzine, R. F., Algozzine, K. M. (2012). A pilot study of a problem-solving model for team decision making. *Education and Treatment of Children, 35*(1), 25–49.

3

Collaborate With Families to Support Student Learning and Secure Needed Services

Mayumi Hagiwara and Karrie A. Shogren

Introduction

A critical element of effective teaching is to build collaborative relationships with families to support student learning and to enable students to access needed services and supports. The Every Student Succeeds Act (ESSA) and the Individuals with Disabilities Education Act (IDEA) recognize the importance of educators working with families to improve teaching and learning. The preamble to IDEA explicitly states that "the education of children with disabilities can be made more effective by . . . strengthening the role and responsibility of parents and ensuring that families of such children have meaningful opportunities to participate in the education of their children at school and at home."[1]

Both the ESSA and the IDEA regulations afford specific rights to parents. For example, IDEA provides for a number of mechanisms to promote parent involvement in decision-making regarding their child's education, including participation in eligibility determinations and participation in educational planning. Foundational to the enactment of these rights are collaborative relationships between parents and educators characterized by partnership principles that will be described subsequently. Although in the regulations ESSA and IDEA use the term parent to describe specific rights, the broader role of the family in supporting a child at home and at school is also recognized in the statute, and in this chapter we will focus on strategies for building family–school partnerships because of the role of the entire family system in supporting children with disabilities and their parents in achieving successful outcomes.[2]

Building collaborative relationships with families starts with educators recognizing that every family is different and has a unique culture that is influenced by a variety of factors including race/ethnicity, language, socioeconomic status, and family structure. By working to understand this unique culture, educators can build individualized communication strategies based on each family's strengths, preferences, and needs. To establish effective partnerships, seven principles play fundamental roles: communication, professional competence, respect, commitment, equality, advocacy, and trust.[3] Educators need to recognize and build on not only their expertise and resources (professional competence) but also the expertise, resources, and experiences of family members (communication and respect). This reciprocity will enable all members of the partnership to contribute (equality and advocacy) and engage in joint actions that promote student educational outcomes (trust and commitment) and lead to students' academic and social-emotional success.

Narrowing the Focus

This chapter provides specific recommendations for collaborating with families and building family-professional partnerships. We first define seven principles of effective family professional partnerships in detail and describe key elements of a collaborative process. The application of these principles can enable families and educators to work together to build on each other's expertise and use resources to make and implement decisions that promote positive student learning outcomes. After defining these principles, we highlight how partnerships can be actualized through various types of communication strategies.

Chapter Overview

1. Describe seven partnership principles that can be implemented to promote positive interactions, joint roles and responsibilities, and reciprocity to enhance student learning and access to supports and services.
2. Describe strategies to communicate effectively with families and ways to ensure communication strategies are responsive to the diverse needs of family members.
3. Describe ways that partnership principles and communication strategies can be applied to benefit all partners and enhance student learning outcomes.

Principles That Promote Positive Interactions With Educators and Families

An essential set of seven principles that define effective partnerships have emerged from research.[4] Critical to implementing the seven principles is honoring and respecting cultural diversity and differing communication styles and preferences. As an educator working to build partnerships with families, a first step is understanding each principle. We provide a definition for each partnership principle below.

- **Communication**—teachers and families communicate openly and honestly in a medium that is comfortable for the family and professional
- **Professional Competence**—teachers are highly qualified in the area they are working in, continue to learn and grow, and have and communicate high expectations for students and families
- **Respect**—teachers treat families with dignity, honor cultural diversity, and affirm strengths
- **Commitment**—teachers are available, consistent, and go above and beyond
- **Equality**—teachers recognize the strengths of every member of the team, share power with families, and focus on working together with families
- **Advocacy**—teachers focus on getting to the best solution for the student in partnership with the family
- **Trust**—teachers are reliable and act in the best interest of the student, sharing their vision and actions with the family

As teachers, it is important to use these principles and build them into ongoing interactions with families as part of educational planning and decision-making. The application of these principles can enhance student learning outcomes, as well as influence professional and family outcomes, leading to greater engagement and less stress when partnerships are stronger.[5] For example, when teachers are highly committed, they will be able to effectively share resources, identify family strengths and needs, and build trust with families. And, when teachers are professionally competent, they will be able to effectively communicate and advocate for family's rights under federal, state, and local laws.

Foundational to building partnerships is communicating with families about educational planning, its purposes, and roles and responsibilities in a meaningful way and in multiple forms that match families' preferences.

Another key aspect of building partnerships is integrating and being respectful of a family's cultural background and values. Teachers need to understand that people's cultural identity is multifaceted and highly individualized.[6] Figure 3.1 shows internal characteristics and external factors that influence individual students and their families. Students have personal characteristics such as strengths, preferences, interests, and support needs, and these factors are shaped by the people that are closest to students, which typically includes parents or caregivers (e.g., biological parents, step-parents, foster parents). Parents and caregivers share similar personal characteristics and environmental experiences with the child. Parents also adopt specific parenting styles, which influence the child with a disability. The next closest circle of support are often family members, including siblings and extended family members. They also have unique personal characteristics, but frequently share similar environments (e.g., family size and forms, religion/faith). The next circle includes people (e.g., friends, neighbors) and community supports (e.g., school, family resource center, religion/faith-based organization). The most distal circle is culture which directly or indirectly influences students, parents/caregivers, families' internal characteristics, and external factors.[7]

To successfully collaborate with families from diverse cultural and socioeconomic backgrounds and family structures, teachers first need to be aware of their own understandings toward different cultural representations and be aware that these understandings can affect their teaching.[8] Although it is nearly impossible to understand and respond to all the cultural differences that culturally diverse families bring to classroom,[9] it is important to be open to different cultural practices and values. For example, reading material about families' cultural practices or participating in cultural events in the community are ways for teachers to stay informed of cultural diversity.

Furthermore, teachers need to be aware of the resources and services available in schools and communities. For example, cultural brokers (e.g., family advocates or family partnership coordinators who experience similar cultural backgrounds as families served by the school) can be a useful resource in schools to promote respect and equality in communication between families and educators of differing cultural backgrounds. The responsibilities of cultural brokers will differ from school

Layer	Characteristics and Factors
Student	Goals, Strengths, Interests, Preferences, Support needs, Language
Parent/ Caregiver	Expectations, Parental goals, Strengths, Preferences, Support needs, Language, Parenting styles, Roles, Responsibilities, Marital status, Income
Family	Expectations, Goals, Strengths, Preferences, Support needs, Language, Roles, Responsibilities, Family size and form, Religion/Faith, Resources, Stress, Coping mechanism, Siblings, Extended families, Income, Traditions
Community	School, Neighborhood, Friends, Neighbors, Resources, Services, Family support programs, Religion/Faith
Culture	Values, Beliefs, Norms and practices, Environmental context, Beliefs about disability, Religion/Faith, Language, Traditions, View of child development, Perceptions of teaching and learning

Figure 3.1 Internal Characteristics and External Factors That Influence Students
Source: Adapted from Stoneman (2005)

to school; however, the general goal is to promote respect and communication between families and educators.[10] Cultural brokers typically support family and professional engagement and partnerships in several key ways, such as: (a) serving as a liaison for families and teachers, which can help parents to feel supported and empowered; (b) organizing support groups or mentorship programs for families to address a range of needs;[11] and (c) supporting and empowering parents as they prepare for and participate in educational planning activities. As a new teacher, it is useful to explore how cultural brokers, family liaisons, and/or family support and mentoring groups support partnerships in your school and district.

In the following sections, we provide specific strategies for how teachers can interact and communicate with parents in respectful ways. Within each communication strategy, we highlight how the partnership principles can be applied. We emphasize ways to use accessible and family-friendly language and mediums to build on family strengths.

Effective Practices That Teachers Can Use to Communicate With Parents and Families

One of the core values that should guide teachers entering into partnerships is endeavoring to understand families' strengths and goals for their children and leveraging these strengths and goals to enhance student outcomes. Teachers should focus on identifying students' and families' strengths and goals through communication. Effective communication with families allows teachers to map out the school and families' roles and resources to work together to enhance student learning outcomes. Such communication can occur in words, in pictures, or through visiting and exploring available resources. Although establishing frequent and meaningful communication takes time and effort, it will improve students' success at school and create a better classroom atmosphere. This will ultimately lead to quality of education and quality of life for families and professionals, as well as students.[12]

1. Face to Face Interactions

a) **Planned, formal, and informal meetings**. Formal face-to-face meetings, such as IEP or other educational planning meetings, are often one of the first interactions teachers have with parents. However, informal face-to-face meetings at school, in family homes, or in the community can also be an effective way to open communication channels, especially at the beginning of the school year. Teachers can individualize the style and frequency of face-to-face interactions by taking families' communication preferences into consideration. Providing resources for family members to use in preparation for the meeting, particularly for formal meetings, can help family members organize their thoughts and identify goals aligned with their strengths.[13] See Figure 3.2 for an example of a resource that can be adapted and shared with family members or used collaboratively by teachers and family members as they prepare and consider their roles prior to a meeting. This resource should be individualized to each family in terms of language, communication preferences, and accessibility.

b) **Open Houses.** Open houses (also referred to as Meet the Teacher Day) provide opportunities for parents and families to see their children's school(s) and classroom(s), interact with members of the educational team, and explore learning materials and activities that their children use. These open houses also provide family members with opportunities to talk with and build relationships with other families. Hosting open houses at different times (e.g., evenings, weekends) and providing childcare and food can be effective ways to encourage family participation and show respect for the family's needs. Family members can observe and provide feedback on aspects of their children's school experiences, like how desks and lockers are organized and how

Date:	Time:	With:
Purpose:		
How do I feel about this meeting?		Anxious, nervous, excited, hopeful, upset, frustrated. . .
What do I want to share with professionals?		1.
		2.
What questions do I have?		1.
What do I want to know?		2.
What do I want to accomplish at this meeting?		1.
What do I hope to see changes in the future?		2.
What did I actually accomplish at this meeting?		1.
		2.
How do I feel now?		Hopeful, positive, angry, successful, frustrated. . .
Next steps to take?		

Figure 3.2 Sample Resource for Use and Adaptation by Family Members and Professionals in Preparing for Formal Meeting

the classroom and school are set up. Teachers may also display samples of learning activities and student work for family members to see and touch. This helps parents understand educational practices and expectations and can promote ideas about how they can support their child's work at home. Additionally, keep in mind that families want to learn about more than academic progress, they are interested in other factors that impact quality of life, such as social relationships and well-being.[14] When preparing for open houses, ask questions like, "If I had a child in this class, what would I want to know as a parent?" Using these insights can help structure open houses and create communication materials.[15]

c) **Volunteering opportunities in classroom and at school.** Teachers can not only provide parents with opportunities to volunteer at school events and activities but also volunteer in the child's home and at community events. Such reciprocal engagement shows commitment and fosters equality among all team members. Taking pictures and sharing scenes of school and community activities, particularly for parents who are not able to participate in all activities because of other obligations, can help engage families. Researchers have found it is important for family members to feel connected to the school community and to feel like they have multiple ways to contribute.[16] Such efforts can also lead to clear opportunities to address issues that might emerge during the school year, as highlighted in Example 1.

d) **Home visits and other forms of face-to-face interactions.** One way to understand a family's preferences is for teachers to spend time in a family's home and community. If it is convenient and comfortable for families, home visits can be used to enable professionals to understand family strengths and goals and to build trust and respect.[17] Home visits can be especially useful for families who have limited time or limited transportation for school visits and families who are new to a classroom/school.[18] In addition to home visits, meeting with families at a local coffee shop or restaurant might be an option if families prefer.[19] Further, organizing class/grade/

Example 1: Building Partnerships to Promote Learning Outcomes

Ms. Peterson is a second-grade teacher at an elementary school located in a suburban area in the Midwest. She has enjoyed teaching for seven years and focuses on building strong family-professional partnerships from the beginning of the school year. She hosts a family night at the beginning of the school year in the classroom and has a classroom website that is password protected where she shares information with family members about student's learning activities. She also prints and sends copies of pages home weekly with students whose parents do not have reliable Internet access. In addition, she plans a home visit at least once during the school year with each family and tries to participate in community events where she engages with students and families outside of the school context. Recently, she noticed that one of her students, Hyun, was showing significantly decreased engagement during independent work in English Language Arts (ELAs) class. Hyun is 8 years old, and he usually engaged in reading activities, especially related to his interests of cars and airplanes, so this was a major change in his behavior. Although Ms. Peterson provided verbal, visual, and model prompts when he seemed disengaged during independent work stations, after one week, the situation had not changed. Ms. Peterson decided to reach out to Hyun's parents, leveraging their existing relationship to attempt to address this issue. Because she already collected information at the school's family night, she knew that Hyun's mother and father both routinely checked their personal emails and wanted to be informed whenever an issue came up via email for initial contact. Ms. Peterson tried to sound positive, yet direct and specific in her email.

Hello Mr. and Ms. Kim,

I hope this email finds you well. I'm emailing you to discuss how we can support Hyun's learning during English Language Arts class. He is a good reader and shows a lot of interest when reading fiction and non-fiction books, especially about cars and airplanes. During class, we have four stations where students engage in four activities: (1) read a book of their choice independently, (2) practice spelling words from a book, (3) work on a writing journal, and (4) read and practice target words in a small group with me. Hyun works very well in his small group. He reads along with others and follows directions beautifully.

However, this past week, Hyun has been more focused on his classmates than his reading when we are doing independent work. He has needed more reminders than in the past. This week we had a class discussion of expectations for independent work. Given these changes, I was wondering if you had any thoughts on what might be impacting Hyun. I am excited to work with you to figure out the best way to support Hyun to build friendships as well as engage in his English Language Arts work. Please email me back with what you think we could be doing. And, I'm happy to also set up a phone or in-person meeting, depending on your preferences.

I appreciate your time and support in identifying ways we can work together to support Hyun's learning.

Sincerely,

Meg

Hyun's father replied to Ms. Peterson's email quickly and asked if they could talk on the phone during his lunch hour. Mr. Kim began the conversation by emphasizing how important supporting Hyun's learning was to the family. He said the only change that he and his wife could think of was that one of Hyun's close neighborhood friend moved to another state recently and that this friend played an older brother role to Hyun. Ms. Peterson thanked Mr. Kim for sharing this and agreed that this could explain why Hyun was more focused on peers and less focused on his work. Mr. Kim asked if it might be okay if Ms. Kim could come and observe so they could work across home and school. He said he remembered that Ms. Peterson was open to visitors at any time. Ms. Peterson emphasized that she would be very excited to get Ms. Kim's expertise.

On the day of Ms. Kim's visit, Hyun was excited about his mother's visit and had two classmates he wanted to immediately introduce. He was also proud to show her his work, including the books he was reading. After the visit, Ms. Peterson and Ms. Kim identified two peers that could possibly become friends outside of school that Ms. Kim could contact. They both felt this might be a good way to address the loss Hyun was feeling after his friend moved. They also identified a couple of books with words that were challenging for Hyun that he could bring home for reading with his parents. Over time, Hyun both developed new relationships outside of school and became more engaged in his independent work. Having a clear communication system, an existing relationship, and an openness to the expertise of all team members enabled a positive outcome. And, this enhanced the family-professional relationships further, as Ms. Peterson emailed the Kims every week to provide updates, and the Kims began to share books from home that they were using.

school picnics in local neighborhoods where any family can easily access the event can provide an opportunity for teachers and families to informally come together and develop conversations. Being in a community setting might reduce power dynamics between teachers and family members and create a context for building partnerships.

Strategies That Can Be Used for Face-to-Face Interactions in the Community

1. Starting off a conversation with families on a positive note during home visits and carefully listening to parents' suggestions and concerns can show a teacher's openness and willingness to establish communication with families.
2. Providing options that are flexible and creative when planning home visits or other interactions to facilitate family involvement demonstrates that a teacher and family members share equal power to partner to positively influence student outcomes. Additionally, having frequent communication and following through can foster empowerment and feelings of professional competence and commitment.
3. Showing digital portfolios of students' work and classroom information on a teacher's laptop or tablet is valuable so that families who might have limited access to the Internet or technology can view them.

2. Written Correspondence

Written communication is used to share formal and informal information about school activities, parent and student rights and responsibilities, and student educational progress. Today, much more information is communicated or accessible through online tools (e.g., grades shared through online portals, or emails to share documents and outcomes of educational planning meetings). Each of these forms of communication can be used creatively to enhance partnership principles and maintain a focus on student and family strengths and effectively sharing information and resources. Despite the extensive use of technology, paper-based communication can still be valuable in the overall communication between home and school to reach out to families who have limited access to technology.[20] Further, it is a teacher's responsibility to produce written correspondence in different languages for families to stay included and informed. These actions meet the equality, respect, and advocacy partnership principles.

Written correspondence can be thought of as one-way or two-way correspondence.[21] One-way written correspondence is directed from educators to family members with limited options or expectations for response or interaction. One-way correspondence often includes things like handbooks, handouts, and newsletters. Two-way correspondence can be more interactive with options and supports for dialogue.[22] This can include on-going letters or notes and communication journals. Whether one-way or two-way communication is the focus, all communication needs to be clear, concise, and to the point. This shows respect for family member's time as well as eliminates confusion. Particularly for dense material like handbooks and newsletters, it is important to ensure readability and easily digestible information. Teachers must carefully choose a format depending on the intent of communication and should engage families as much as possible in finding the most useful format. Engaging families in this process promotes equality and leverages the strengths and knowledge of family members.

A frequently used two-way communication strategy is communication notebooks or student binders or assignment books. Such strategies can be ways for teachers, family members, and students to jointly communicate about activities at school, assignments, and other key issues. Although the focus of communication notebooks is often homework or assignment due dates, adding concrete and specific comments about students' learning can be ways to share with families the successes students are experiencing. Pictures or other mediums can also be used, based on families' communication preferences. If sending positive comments daily or weekly is challenging, start with trying to send comments a few times a month. (If students have electronic devices, teachers can send positive comments electronically as well). Teachers can also encourage students to evaluate how their days went and use this as a means to support students to communicate with family members to describe their feelings about the day.[23]

For example, students at lower elementary grades can simply choose an emoji sticker to express their feelings. For older students, teachers can model how to use highlighters to emphasize important project due dates or special events. Students' electronic devices, if used, can be used to organize assignments, special event dates, project due dates, reading logs, and other important dates and activities. Efforts to use such tools to enable student-family-professional dialogue can enable family members to feel more engaged and have more opportunities to stay touch with teachers. Teachers can also work with families when setting up such tools to leverage the strategies that families are already using at home, determining their and their child's preferences, and developing a format and shared expectations together, including how often to write and what kinds of information to share.[24]

3. Phone Calls

Another frequently used communication strategy with families is phone calls. As with all other communication strategies, building on strengths and resources of all members of the partnership should be the primary focus. Teachers should work to make sure that phone calls do not become associated with reporting on bad or negative issues. Phone calls can be a good means for quick and easy informational exchanges and emotional support.[25] One downside of phone conversations can be difficultly finding common times to talk. To avoid unnecessary frustration on both ends and "phone tag," it is critical to work to understand and establish preferences for times to call and to check in on availability on evenings and weekends and preferred phone numbers at the beginning of a school year. It is important to remember that phone calls limit access to non-verbal cues and can introduce communication barriers for some family members, particularly related to language. For example, if English is not a parents' primary language, it might be difficult for parents to convey messages without the use of body language and facial expressions, particularly if an existing relationship has not been established. Considering and planning for these factors and identifying other communication means, such as in-person conversations, can build respect.

4. Technology-Based Means of Communication

It is important to not assume that all families have ready access to the Internet or that this is a comfortable means to share personal and, at times, confidential information for all families. In the process of building relationships with families, ask them questions to find out their communication preferences about electronic forums and devices that families use most often. An individualized communication plan can also be created with each family. If your school provides a tablet or computer per student and allows students to use it at home, it is critical to make sure families also become knowledgeable and skillful with such devices. Providing face-to-face training sessions for families might be necessary, especially if families are not accustomed to such devices, so that they can have access to digital information of students' educational progress and outcomes.

a) **Emails/Texts.** When emailing and texting are parents' preferred means of communication, it is essential to check if shared parents' email addresses and phone numbers are personal or for work, how often parents check their emails/texts, and preferred times to exchange emails/texts. At the same time, teachers need to ask themselves about their comfort level with sharing their own personal email and cell phone number for text messaging. Although family members often share that having access to personal contact information is a strong reflection of commitment and builds trust,[26] this is a personal decision. Additionally, teachers also need to become familiar with any school policies and expectations and communicate these rules to families. Either way, teachers should clearly communicate with families regarding their communication preferences and establish clear boundaries from the beginning. If teachers or family members want to change the original guidelines because they did not work out for some reason, there should be a vehicle for communicating and adapting the guidelines.

b) **Course management system (e.g., Blackboard), school websites, and classroom websites/ blogs.** Course management systems (e.g., Blackboard), school websites, and classroom webpages/ blogs can also be effective means for teachers to communicate and share information with family members, share resources, and leverage strengths. Using all of these vehicles, a teacher can quickly post positive comments, announcements, highlights of a day, homework information, and whatever else that students and families can benefit from. A variety of formats can be used, including:

- **Instructional videos/Podcast.** Teachers can record their lessons and post videos on the class website so that students can refer to them when working on assignments at home. This provides an interactive way for family members to see what and how children are learning and to support homework completion. It can also be very useful to also ask families to share videos about what is happening at home and how supports are provided in the home, for teachers to learn from.
- **Audio/Video letters.** Sometimes it might be easier for teachers to audio- or video-record information about an upcoming event rather than calling or emailing parents. A video letter, for example, provides a more interactive and personalized means to communicate. A teacher can simply record her/himself or students talking and upload the recording on the website or blog. Families should also be supported to respond in the same way.
- **Photo sharing.** Sharing photos can be another way to communicate successes and accomplishments across home and school. This can be done through school websites, private Facebook pages, and other tools. It is simple to set up and easy to post and share photos of students working on projects, playing at a playground, practicing for a school band, and many other opportunities to capture moments of students' hard work. Families can share the same moments to enable teachers to understand what is occurring in the family's life.
- **Live streams.** Increasingly, teachers are setting up live streams from their classrooms. This provides an opportunity for family members to watch learning activities. This can help build trust because of open access to the classroom and can also be a means for families to learn more about what is going on and strategies they can translate at home. There can also be opportunities for families to live stream from home if they want to share something that is working well in the home environment so that educators can transfer this to the school environment.

Technology can be used to enhance the commitment, respect, and trust partnership principles. All schools will likely have protocols to ensure confidentiality when sharing information about students. As a teacher, it is necessary to be aware of these and to ensure that appropriate permissions are in place before sharing pictures or videos through any of the above mechanisms. If images are being shared publicly, then ensuring that specific faces and names are not included will be imperative. Before taking instructional videos to post publicly on the website or blog, teachers should walk around the classroom to decide which spot can capture their lesson most effectively without recording students' faces. Teachers might need to find more than one spot, especially if students are expected to move between work stations. For private sharing options, using necessary and appropriate security mechanisms and making sure these are designed to be accessible to educators and family members will be important. As mentioned above, when sharing videos or digital portfolios of students' work to families, it is important to ask families' permission and assess their comfort levels. Furthermore, for families who speak a language other than English, teachers should explore closed captions or subtitles on digital platforms. Table 3.1 shows examples of communication strategies applied to the partnership principles.

Example 2 shows how a variety of resources, including formal and informal activities and technology-based communication, can be used to support all members of a partnership to work together.

Example 2: Planning Jointly to Enhance Outcomes

Mr. Santos is a high school special education teacher who teaches social studies in an urban setting. One of his responsibilities is to organize a monthly transition planning night for students and families. In the beginning of each school year, he sends out a "Welcome Letter" that includes pictures to introduce himself, his educational background, and his plans and expectations for working with students. His welcome letter includes a QR code to his school-based website, which includes a welcome video and overview of class routines and expectations. The website also includes the syllabus and instructional videos and tips for projects and assignments, as well as links to additional transition planning resources. Because Mr. Santos speaks both English and Spanish fluently, and a large number of the families he supports speak Spanish, he works to provide as many resources as possible in both languages, as well as other languages needed by the families he supports.

For example, Mr. Santos held one of the transition nights at a local community college, where Mr. Santos introduced students and family members to options for postsecondary education and financial support. He also organized a group of young people and their families who had similar demographic characteristics to members of his classes to informally chat with students and their families. He recorded videos of stories and conversations that he made available online for families that were not able to attend for whatever reasons. He had pizza available for everyone, as well as childcare, and tried to facilitate informal but informational conversations among the participants to build community.

After this meeting, Mr. Santos sent out a modified version of a planning document, like that included in Figure 3.2, for students and their families to start identifying what they hope to do post-school and what resources they might need. He also incorporated many of these transition planning activities into social studies projects, particularly related to community mapping and developing understanding of community-based resources. A culminating activity for the social studies class was for students to make presentations to their peers and family members on what they learned about community resources. On the day of the presentation, Mr. Santos recorded the presentations so that he could send them to family members and post them on his website. He received positive comments from families who participated in the presentation or watched the videos on the website. One of the comments was, "Thank you for making me feel part of my child's education and for making our expectations for the future bigger and brighter."

Wrap Up

Building clear and open communication strategies that are welcoming to parents and families, starting all communications on a positive note, utilizing effective listening strategies, embracing frequent communication and follow-through, respecting confidentiality, and respecting the rights of families when

Table 3.1 Family–School Partnership Principles Applied to Communication With Families From Diverse Backgrounds

Principle	Teacher's Main Responsibility	Examples of Actions
Communication	Teachers create spaces for families to voice their expectations, preferences, and needs.	1. Learn about how family beliefs and values shape their goals for the child's school outcomes. 2. Ask families about ways they can maximize their involvement in educational planning. 3. Discuss and respect family preference on communication methods.
Professional Competence	Teachers continue to improve their skills and knowledge to meaningfully involve families.	1. Include students in communication to showcase growth in student learning and highlight ways skills can transfer from home to school 2. Set high expectations for school and post-school outcomes for students with disabilities. 3. Continue evaluating the progress of the partnership through conversations with family members and modify accordingly.
Respect	Teachers value family members' expectations and the role they play within their family.	1. Acknowledge that families are also experts on students' strengths, preferences, and support needs. 2. Respect family decisions. 3. Translate written products and other forms of communication into the preferred language of family members. (Although technology and online translation tools can be helpful to support translation, it is important to ensure native speakers of whatever language is being translated evaluate translations to ensure accuracy.)
Commitment	Teachers are dedicated to empowering families' and addressing families' strengths and expectations.	1. Listen to families' concerns and questions without interrupting or interpreting based on your own perspectives. 2. Remember that non-verbal communication during face-to-face interactions plays a critical role in conveying teachers' attitudes toward partnerships.
Equality	Teachers empower family members to be equal partners.	1. Make sure that families are encouraged to provide input and feedback in meaningful and interactive ways that align with communication and cultural preferences. 2. Highlight student and family accomplishments as a core part of any communication to provide a means that can build pride for and engagement with students and families. 3. Provide options for how to communicate based on each family's preferences and strengths, leading to feelings of equality and comfort in communication.
Advocacy	Teachers take action to support families' in meeting their needs.	1. Advocate for families' preferences, strengths, and support needs to the whole team. 2. Demonstrate to families that there is a team working for students' school successes and the quality of the partnerships.
Trust	Teachers act in the best interest of families.	1. Go above and beyond to locate services for families to participate in partnerships and educational planning. 2. Create a vision for students' successes at school and in the community with families and share responsibilities to support students to achieve these visions.

working with students and families will enable the development of family–professional partnerships that enhance student learning outcomes as well as family and educator outcomes. Understanding communication preferences, styles, and expectations of all partners is important to family–professional partnerships. Communicating flexibly, creatively, and in culturally responsive ways creates opportunities to advocate and show commitment, respect, equity, and competence and builds trust and reciprocity. In this chapter, we described seven principles for family–professional partnerships and highlighted practical communication strategies that can be used to build these partnerships. These strategies are meant for teachers to use with all families; however, teachers should individualize a set of communication strategies depending on each family's preferences and needs related to communication styles, language, access to technology, families' daily schedules, and family responsibilities.

Teachers can demonstrate cultural competence and responsiveness in their interactions with families and use effective strategies to translate understandings of culture into action.[27] Being culturally responsive starts with an understanding that within each of us there are multiple ways that cultural factors are expressed. It will be critical to get to know families by building partnerships and learning about cultural values and preferences. Teachers can at times serve as a translator of the communication styles and practices adopted by the education system and concurrently learn and integrate each family's unique practices, preferences, cultural beliefs, and self-identified needs into communication.[28] Teachers need to recognize the importance of collaborating to set goals in ways that are meaningful for the family rather than simply using school-based goals or protocols. This level of communication and joint responsibility has the potential to promote respect, feelings of equality, and trust across all members of the team.

Tips

1. **Promote reciprocity in partnership activities.** Recognize that family members have high levels of expertise and that many things that occur in the home and community can be highly informative for school. Exchange information with families about what has worked well and what has not worked at home and school to identify common things that work for the child and can be used across home and school.

2. **Engage all members of the school and community in classroom, school, and community events.** Invite families as well as administrators and other classes to your classroom and foster joint activities that build relationships and partnerships. Take advantage of opportunities to participate in home and community activities. And, communicate clearly and effectively with all members of the partnership using the various formats described in this chapter.

3. **Be open, positive, and not afraid of making mistakes.** Believe in your expertise, but recognize that others also have expertise. It is fine if you do not have answers for every question and situation. In these instances, reach out and draw on other members of the team such as a mentor or principal, as well as family members, to identify solutions. Working jointly can be more effective for all involved, include the student. Consider issues and problems encountered as opportunities to enhance your professional competence. Set goals jointly with families and work together to find solutions reflecting equality, respect, and your commitment.

Notes

1 Individuals with Disabilities Education Act (IDEA) of 2004, 20 U.S.C. §§ 1400 et seq. (2004).
2 Turnbull, A. P., Turnbull, H. R., Erwin, E. E., Soodak, L. C., & Shogren, K. A. (2015). *Families, professionals, and exceptionality: Positive outcomes through partnership and trust* (7th ed.). Upper Saddle River, NJ: Merrill Prentice Hall.

3 Turnbull, A. P., Turnbull, H. R., Erwin, E. E., Soodak, L. C., & Shogren, K. A. (2015). *Families, professionals, and exceptionality: Positive outcomes through partnership and trust* (7th ed.). Upper Saddle River, NJ: Merrill Prentice Hall.

4 Turnbull, A. P., Turnbull, H. R., Erwin, E. E., Soodak, L. C., & Shogren, K. A. (2015). *Families, professionals, and exceptionality: Positive outcomes through partnership and trust* (7th ed.). Upper Saddle River, NJ: Merrill Prentice Hall.

5 Burke, M. M., & Hodapp, R. M. (2014). Relating stress of mothers of children with developmental disabilities to family-school partnerships. *Intellectual and Developmental Disabilities, 52,* 13–23.

6 Kalyanpur, M., & Harry, B. (2012). *Cultural reciprocity in special education: Building family-professional relationships.* Baltimore, MD: Brookes.

7 Stoneman, Z. (2005). Siblings of children with disabilities: Research themes. *Mental Retardation, 43,* 339–350.

   Trainor, A. A. (2010). Diverse approaches to parent advocacy during special education home—school interactions: Identification and use of cultural and social capital. *Remedial and Special Education, 31*(1), 34–47.

8 Cartledge, G., & Kourea, L. (2008). Culturally responsive classrooms for culturally diverse students with and at risk for disabilities. *Exceptional Children, 74,* 351–371.

9 More, C. M., Hart, J. E., & Cheatham, G. A. (2013). Language interpretation for diverse families: Considerations for special education teachers. *Intervention in School and Clinic, 49,* 113–120.

10 Martinez-Cosio, M., & Iannacone, R. M. (2007). The tenuous role of institutional agents parent liaisons as cultural brokers. *Education and Urban Society, 39,* 349–369.

11 Graham-Clay, S. (2005). Communicating with parents: Strategies for teachers. *School Community Journal, 15,* 117–129.

12 Blue-Banning, M., Summers, J. A., Frankland, H. C., Nelson, L. L., & Beegle, G. (2004). Dimensions of family and professional partnerships: Constructive guidelines for collaboration. *Exceptional Children, 70,* 167–184.

13 Turnbull, A. P., Turnbull, H. R., Erwin, E. E., Soodak, L. C., & Shogren, K. A. (2015). *Families, professionals, and exceptionality: Positive outcomes through partnership and trust* (7th ed.). Upper Saddle River, NJ: Merrill Prentice Hall.

14 Wells, J. C., & Sheehey, P. H. (2012). Person-centered planning: Strategies to encourage participation and facilitate communication. *Teaching Exceptional Children, 44,* 32–39.

15 Ramirez, A. F. (2003). Dismay and disappointment: Parental involvement of Latino immigrant parents. *The Urban Review, 35,* 93–110.

16 Wells, J. C., & Sheehey, P. H. (2012). Person-centered planning: Strategies to encourage participation and facilitate communication. *Teaching Exceptional Children, 44,* 32–39.

17 Graham-Clay, S. (2005). Communicating with parents: Strategies for teachers. *School Community Journal, 15,* 117–129.

18 Staples, K. E., & Diliberto, J. A. (2010). Guidelines for successful parent involvement working with parents of students with disabilities. *Teaching Exceptional Children, 42,* 58–63.

19 Turnbull, A. P., Turnbull, H. R., Erwin, E. E., Soodak, L. C., & Shogren, K. A. (2015). *Families, professionals, and exceptionality: Positive outcomes through partnership and trust* (7th ed.). Upper Saddle River, NJ: Merrill Prentice Hall.

20 Ramirez, F. (2001). Technology and parent involvement. *Clearing House, 75,* 30–31.

21 Blue-Banning, M., Summers, J. A., Frankland, H. C., Nelson, L. L., & Beegle, G. (2004). Dimensions of family and professional partnerships: Constructive guidelines for collaboration. *Exceptional Children, 70,* 167–184.

22 Shogren, K. A., McCart, A., Lyon, K. J., & Sailor, W. (2015). All means all: Building knowledge for inclusive schoolwide transformation. *Research and Practice for Persons with Severe Disabilities, 40,* 173–191.

23 Staples, K. E., & Diliberto, J. A. (2010). Guidelines for successful parent involvement working with parents of students with disabilities. *Teaching Exceptional Children, 42,* 58–63.

24 Turnbull, A. P., Turnbull, H. R., Erwin, E. E., Soodak, L. C., & Shogren, K. A. (2015). *Families, professionals, and exceptionality: Positive outcomes through partnership and trust* (7th ed.). Upper Saddle River, NJ: Merrill Prentice Hall.

25 Graham-Clay, S. (2005). Communicating with parents: Strategies for teachers. *School Community Journal, 15,* 117–129.

26 Turnbull, A. P., Turnbull, H. R., Erwin, E. E., Soodak, L. C., & Shogren, K. A. (2015). *Families, professionals, and exceptionality: Positive outcomes through partnership and trust* (7th ed.). Upper Saddle River, NJ: Merrill Prentice Hall.

27 Turnbull, A. P., Turnbull, H. R., Erwin, E. E., Soodak, L. C., & Shogren, K. A. (2015). *Families, professionals, and exceptionality: Positive outcomes through partnership and trust* (7th ed.). Upper Saddle River, NJ: Merrill Prentice Hall.

28 Turnbull, A. P., Turnbull, H. R., Erwin, E. E., Soodak, L. C., & Shogren, K. A. (2015). *Families, professionals, and exceptionality: Positive outcomes through partnership and trust* (7th ed.). Upper Saddle River, NJ: Merrill Prentice Hall.

Key Resources

Beach Center on Disability. (n.d.). *Toolkit for family-professional partnerships.* Retrieved from http://beach.drupal.ku.edu/families

National Parent Teacher Association. (n.d.). *At school.* Retrieved from www.pta.org

The Center for Appropriate Dispute Resolution in Special Education. (n.d.). *The CADRE continuum.* Retrieved from www.cadreworks.org/cadre-continuum

The Iris Center. (n.d.). *IRIS resource locator.* Retrieved from https://iris.peabody.vanderbilt.edu/iris-resource-locator/

Thompson, J. R., Meadan, H., Fansler, K. W., Alber, S. B., & Balogh, P. A. (2007). Family assessment portfolios: A new way to jumpstart family/school collaboration. *Teaching Exceptional Children, 39,* 19–25.

U.S. Department of Health and Human Services. (2011). *The head start parent, family, and community engagement framework: Promoting family engagement and school readiness, from prenatal to age 8.* Washington, DC. Retrieved from www.hfrp.org/content/download/4066/109348/file/pfce-framework.pdf

Section 2
Assessment High Leverage Practices

Edited by Mary T. Brownell

Introduction to Assessment High Leverage Practices

Effective instruction for students with disabilities depends on teachers who are adept at using assessment data to inform, guide, evaluate, and adjust instruction. Most importantly, data and other assessment information (e.g., regarding a student's educational, cultural, and language experiences) are used by special education teachers to determine what a student knows regarding a content area; guide instructional planning and delivery; and determine whether instruction is effective. (Note that these assessment practices are equally applicable to addressing social and behavioral issues for students with disabilities and are further addressed in section 3 of this book). Special education teachers work with other professionals, family members, and students to collect and interpret a wide range of assessment data that are needed to understand the needs of students with disabilities, inform instructional decisions, and improve their instructional practice.

The assessment high leverage practice chapters in this section address key aspects of the roles and responsibilities of special education teachers in the assessment process. This begins with the development of a comprehensive learner profile for each student that is used to analyze and understand both a student's strengths and needs and the school-based learning environment, and determine potential supports and barriers to their educational progress. To develop a comprehensive learner profile, special education teachers work with other professionals to collect, aggregate, and interpret assessment data from a range of sources (e.g., observations, work samples, curriculum-based measures, functional behavior assessments) and ensure that these data are used in a way that is responsive to each student's language and cultural background and experiences.

Special education teachers also communicate assessment information to a range of stakeholders, including professionals, families, and the students themselves, and involve these stakeholders in the assessment process whenever possible. The role of the special education teacher includes interpreting assessment information for stakeholders and involving them in the assessment, goal development, and goal implementation process. As this occurs, it is important that special educators understand the purpose of each assessment, support key stakeholders in understanding how culture and language influence the interpretation and use of assessment data, and use data to collaboratively develop and implement an individualized education and transition plan that includes goals that are standards based, appropriate accommodations and modifications, fair grading practices, and transition goals that are aligned with student needs.

Once assessment data are used to determine educational goals for a student, special education teachers identify and implement effective instructional practices to accelerate student learning. However, even the most effective instructional practices are not effective for all students. It is thus necessary that special education teachers have skills related to monitoring the effectiveness of instruction and making adaptations as needed. These skills related to data-based decision making are at the core of effective practice for special educators. Special educators must have skills in managing and engaging in on-going data collection (or formative assessment) regarding instructional effectiveness using curriculum-based measures, informal classroom assessments, observations of student performance and behavior, self-assessment of classroom instruction, and discussions with key stakeholders (students, families, and other professionals).

4

Using Multiple Sources of Information to Develop a Comprehensive Understanding of a Student's Strengths and Needs

Amber Benedict, Kyena Cornelius, and Kelly Acosta

Introduction

Effective multi-tiered instruction that is personalized to students' needs and interests depends on high-quality, comprehensive information about individual students. Special education teachers play a critical role in developing a comprehensive learner profile that provides a deep understanding of students' strengths, areas of difficulty, interests, and home contexts. To develop such a profile, special educators must acquire skill in collecting, interpreting, and synthesizing information from a variety of assessments (formal and informal) and sources (e.g., student surveys, information from parents, general educators, and other service providers). A comprehensive learner profile depicts the student's academic and socio-emotional development and areas for growth across multiple content areas and environments (from classrooms to afterschool programs). Educational teams can use comprehensive learner profiles to make informed decisions about areas such as special education eligibility, placement in the least restrictive environment, and specially designed instruction. Additionally, special education teachers will likely serve students who are diverse in terms of culture and language.[1] Information about students' families related to home language and cultural experiences will help special education teachers and the multidisciplinary team create better instructional experiences and avoid misidentifying students for special education services.[2]

Narrowing the Focus

The Individuals with Disabilities Education Act (IDEA) and its regulations require educators to use a variety of different formal and informal assessments to develop a comprehensive learner profile that addresses students with disabilities strengths and areas of need in academics, social emotional skills, and life skills.[3] Additionally, these profiles should reflect students' interests and home and community culture, as knowledge of these aspects of students' lives can enhance the instruction educators provide. Special educators' understanding of these factors and their influence on learning is just as important as school-based information (e.g., assessment data, work samples, teacher observation) in the comprehensive learner profile. Accordingly, IDEA regulations direct schools to include information and perspectives from general and special educators, related-service providers, parents, and most importantly, students themselves.[4]

This chapter provides teachers with an overview of the formal and informal assessments used in developing a comprehensive learner profile. We provide descriptions of school-based sources and ways

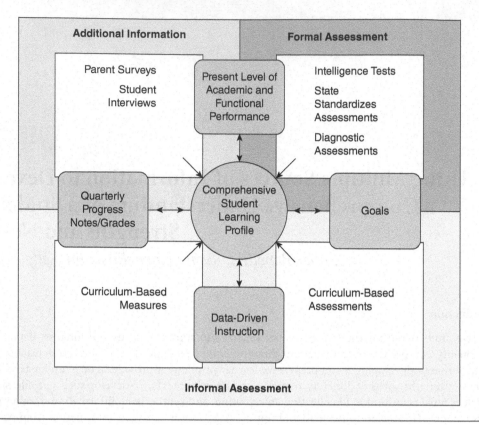

Figure 4.1 Assessment Flow Diagram

information can be solicited from students and their family members. In addition, we address how information drawn from these assessments can be used to inform the development of Individualized Education Programs (IEP). We conclude with an example of how to assemble a comprehensive learner profile.

Chapter Overview

1. Describe formal and informal assessments educators use to gather information about students' academic and behavioral strengths and needs.
2. Describe additional sources of information that educators may use (e.g., interview and survey) to develop a more comprehensive picture of a student's experience.
3. Provide a scenario to illustrate how educators may integrate information sources to create a comprehensive learner profile.

Formal and Informal Assessments

Teachers use information gleaned from formal and informal assessments to target areas where students with disabilities need more extensive educational support to promote positive outcomes. In this section, we provide an overview of school-based assessments that can be used to develop a comprehensive learner profile.

First, we review the role formal assessments play in developing a comprehensive learner profile. Second, we describe informal classroom assessments and other sources of information teachers can use to collect data. Finally, we conclude with an example of a comprehensive learner profile and tips and resources special educators can use to gather information about their students learning and social-emotional needs.

Formal Assessment

Formal assessments provide summative information about students' performance in relationship to peers in areas critical to school success (e.g., cognitive abilities, language skills, academic achievement, and social development). These assessments are used to determine students' eligibility for special education services, gather information about students' strengths and needs, and qualify students for a standard diploma.

Formal assessments are administered using standardized or uniform procedures so that students' results are comparable.[5] Formal assessments used to identify students for special education are often administered individually. Special education teachers may administer and interpret some standardized tests, such as the Woodcock-Johnson IV Tests of Achievement,[6] which are frequently used for determining eligibility for special education services. Special educators can use information from these tests to develop a profile of the students' academic and behavioral strengths and needs. They can also use information from formal assessments, such as the summative achievement tests schools give yearly, to inform decisions about grade retention and high school graduation. Examples of these summative assessments are the Regents Exam used in New York and the Florida Standards Assessment (FSA). Within the sections that follow, we provide a brief overview of several forms of formal assessments, including norm-referenced tests (NRT), criterion-referenced tests (CRT), and diagnostic assessments.

Norm-referenced Tests

NRTs compare students from specific populations in such areas as academic achievement and social-emotional development.[7] For example, a student may be compared to same-age peers to determine if the student is performing below, at, or above average in an academic content area.[8] Data garnered from NRTs can be useful in determining eligibility for special education because these measures identify students whose performance is substantially lower that of their typically developing peers and thus may require special education services.[9] Table 4.1 includes common NRTs used in making eligibility decisions for special education.

Criterion-referenced Tests

In contrast to NRTs, criterion-referenced tests (CRTs) compare student performance against a learning standard in a specific content area.[10] Schools often assess student performance on specific content standards, including the different skills needed to master the standard. For example, for the second-grade Common Core reading standard, students must determine the central idea or theme of a text.[11] However, the different skills, or benchmarks, for this standard would require the student to use word structures to decode text, orally read grade-level text fluently (e.g., 90 words per minute with 90% accuracy), and make inferences about outcomes of stories. Knowing how students perform on specific skills needed to achieve a standard can be useful in helping teachers make instructional planning decisions.[12] Criterion referenced tests are usually teacher-made tests or district-developed benchmark tests. These assessments are used to measure elementary and secondary students' academic knowledge across content areas.

NRTs and CRTs can help multidisciplinary teams identify students' general strengths and needs, but they do not provide the fine-grained information about students' specific needs. They are also

Table 4.1 Common Norm-Referenced Assessments Used in Special Education

Assessment	Processes Assessed
Wechsler Tests: WISC-V WAIS-V WPPSI-IV (usually administered by school psychologists)	• Cognition/Intelligence • Language • Auditory skills • Visual skills • Motor skills
Wechsler Individual Achievement Test – 3rd Edition (WIAT-3)	• Academic skills and achievement
Woodcock-Johnson, 4th Edition – Tests of Achievement (WJ-IV)	• Academic skills and achievement
Kaufman Tests of Educational Achievement – 3rd Edition (KTEA3)	• Academic skills and achievement
Woodcock-Johnson Scales of Independent Behavior - Revised (SIB-R)	• Social maturity and appropriateness of behavior
Vineland Adaptive Behavior Scales -II	• Social maturity and appropriateness of behavior
Behavioral Assessment System for Children – 3rd Edition (BASC-3)	• Social/emotional scales

not administered frequently enough for special educators to use them in making daily decisions about instruction. For these reasons, multi-disciplinary teams must also use diagnostic assessments to gather more fine-grained information.

Diagnostic Assessment

Diagnostic assessments are formal and informal assessments that provide teachers with detailed information about students' academic progress. Data from diagnostic assessments help teachers determine where to begin instruction and keep the comprehensive learner profile current.[13] Diagnostic assessments cover a broad range of skills across a continuum of development and content areas. Although some diagnostic assessments are more formal in nature and are administered by an expert (e.g., WJRMT-III)[14] or are computer delivered (e.g., i-Ready),[15] others can be administered by special educators. Special educators use these assessments to collect data about student's individual learning needs in a curricular area (e.g., Core Phonics Survey)[16] and design instruction.

Informal Assessment

Informal assessments align closely with instruction and are sometimes referred to as formative assessments, or assessments *for* learning. Informal assessments are often based on curricular concepts and skills. Teachers can use them to monitor progress, provide student feedback, and adjust instruction.[17] Teachers use informal assessments daily to assess students' comprehension of the lesson, look for error patterns during instruction, and observe student social interactions. Some informal assessments are summative in nature. For example, a teacher might assign a book report or a diorama at the conclusion of a unit. Chapter 6 includes more information on how to use informal assessments to systematically improve student achievement within an MTSS framework.

Curriculum-Based Assessments

Curriculum-based assessments (CBAs) are informal assessments teachers can use to create a comprehensive learner profile. Teachers can use CBAs to make instructional decisions about how to teach a particular concept, how to determine student groupings, how to alter instruction to bolster student achievement or motivation, and how to personalize instruction to student's individual needs.[18]

Curriculum-Based Measures

Curriculum-based measures (CBMs) are an example of curriculum-based assessment. CBMs, which are used to help teachers determine when to individualize instruction.[19] Time-based and administered frequently, CBMs provide teachers with a method for assessing student progress regarding basic skills in reading, math, writing, and spelling.[20] Many of these skills (e.g., oral reading fluency or number of words read correctly in a minute) are predictive of overall achievement. For students receiving intensive interventions, CBMs provide a way to collect data weekly to monitor student progress and provide teachers detailed information on a student's specific skill set, thus allowing teachers to tailor instruction. For more information on how to use CBMs to monitor student progress, please refer to Chapter 6 on assessment.

Anecdotal Seating Chart

Teachers can create observation tools to provide information about students' learning and behavior, such as an oversized seating chart to allow for anecdotal notes.[21] Teachers can use this chart to write down behaviors (e.g., "on task," "raised hand," "accurate response") next to students' names. Doing so allows teachers to quickly tally target behaviors.

Special education teachers can use anecdotal seating charts (see Figure 4.2) in general and special education classrooms to note students' engagement with peers and how students are responding to specific content demands. They then use this information to alter instruction. For example, if a teacher notices that a student has multiple "off task" tally marks when participating in a group activity, she might try to determine if the student grouping or performance expectations are inappropriate. The special education teacher can then add this information to the comprehensive learner profile.

Daily Scorecard

A second method special education teachers can use to record observation data is the daily score card. Real time data helps them recall what happened in previous lessons to inform adjustments in future lessons. The daily score card should be structured to collect data in multiple areas (e.g., accuracy of opportunities to respond (OTR), number of error corrections presented, students' affect).

We provide an example in Figure 4.3 that shows how teachers can collect information in (1) background knowledge or readiness, (2) guided practice OTR, (3) error correction/follow-up practice, (4) independent practice opportunities, and (5) physical affect. During instruction, the teacher simply circles correct responses or tallies the number of OTR and error correction provided. The teacher can also record when she provides follow-up practice and continue to record errors. Doing so helps the teacher to determine if the student's performance improved. Teachers in general education classrooms can use daily score cards to record data on multiple students and create a one-page visual summary that enables them to see how target students are performing compared to peers. Such a scorecard can provide a one-page summary of students' strengths and needs.[22] Teachers can use the scorecard to inform conversations about special education eligibility as well as placement and instructional decisions.

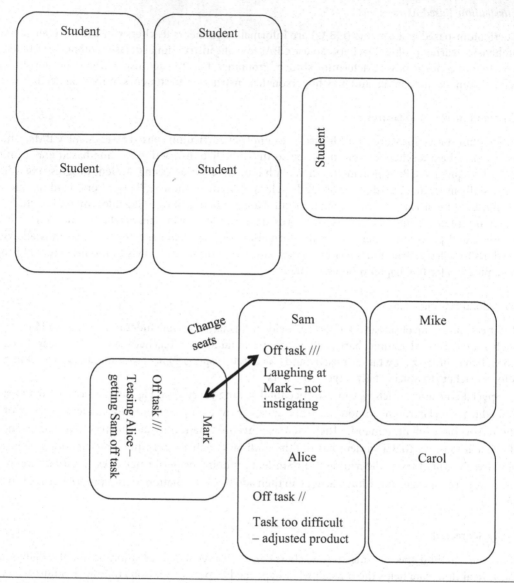

Figure 4.2 Anecdotal Seating Chart

Additional Information Sources

Special education teachers should also examine factors that improve their understanding of students' hopes and dreams, the culture of their home and community, and expectations families have for their child's education. Educators can use this information to create an educational experience that is more motivating and capitalizes on the student's background knowledge and culture. In the following section, we describe strategies teachers can use to learn more about the student as a person.

Student Voice

Students can provide teachers with valuable information about their learning.[23] Research on student voice has investigated how students' perceptions of fairness, peer and teacher relationships, motiva-

Student	Background Knowledge	G.P. OTR	Err Correct Follow-up	U.G.P. OTR	Physical Affect ☺/☹
Sam	①②③④	1 2 3 4 5 ✓ ✓ ✓ ✓ ✓	/ / / ✓ X ✓	1 2 3 4 5 ✓ ✓ ✓ ✓ ✓	☺
Mark	1 ②③④	1 2 3 4 5 ✓ X ✓ ✓ ✓	/ / / X ✓ ✓	1 2 3 4 5 ✓ ✓ X ✓ X	☹ angry, took 5 min to calm down after recess
Alice	①②③④	1 2 3 4 5 ✓ X X ✓ ✓	/ / / / ✓ X X ✓	1 2 3 4 5 ✓ ✓ ✓ X ✓	☹ became frustrated during G.P
Mike	①②③ 4	1 2 3 4 5 ✓ ✓ ✓ ✓ ✓	/ / / ✓ X ✓	1 2 3 4 5 ✓ ✓ X ✓ X	☺
Carol	①② 3 ④	1 2 3 4 5 ✓ ✓ ✓ ✓ ✓	/ / ✓ ✓	1 2 3 4 5 ✓ ✓ X ✓ ✓	☺

Figure 4.3 Daily Scorecard

Note: G.P. OTR = Guided Practice, opportunities to respond; U.G.P. OTR = Unguided practice, opportunities to respond

tion, and other aspects of schooling influence what they learn.[24]Findings from this research suggest it is critical for educators to understand how students' interests, background experiences, and culture might affect their learning. To acquire this information, special educators can interview or survey students using some of the following prompts:

- What do you do well (strengths)?
- What do you enjoy doing in your free time?
- Who do you choose to spend free time with?
- What academic or behavior areas do you need to work on (weaknesses)?
- What are your goals for learning and behavior?
- What would you like teachers to know about you?
- What helps you be successful in the classroom (accommodations, technology)?
- How can a teacher help you be successful?
- What supports do you have at home that can help you be successful at school?

Special educators can use information gathered from students to create a comprehension learner profile and then tailor instruction to students' unique needs and interests. In addition, these conversations may be the first step in fostering student self-determination and increasing student involvement in the IEP process.[25]

Family Involvement

Family members offer valuable insights about students' interests, motivations, health, language, and cultural experiences in school and at home that can be used by special educators to develop a comprehensive learner profile.[26] Special education teachers can use different techniques to gather information from families.

Teachers can use family questionnaires to gather information about students (see Figure 4.4 for an example). Questionnaires can include checklists that families use to indicate students' strengths and needs. They can also include questions related to the parents' aspirations for their child, their perceptions of their child's interests, and short- and long-term goals they have for their child. The sample questionnaire included in this chapter was developed for parents but can be modified to provide insight from other family members and friends (e.g., siblings, grandparents, or close friends).

To be used successfully, family questionnaires must be easy to complete, written in the family's home language, and appropriate for the family's literacy level. Lastly, although questionnaires may be the quickest way to obtain information from families, they are only one tool to use and should be accompanied by other strategies that provide more opportunities for families and teachers to interact.

Family stories provide another way to gather data from families.[27] By asking families to relay stories about their child, special educators help families express "their hopes, worries, successes, and questions" for their child.[28] Teachers can collect family stories by having informal conversations with families, asking family members to prepare a letter about the child, or sharing family photos and videos. Family stories can help teachers foster more authentic connections between students, their families, and their social and learning experiences in schools. Teachers should keep in mind that some families may need support in translating their story into English. Special education teachers may need to find out if translation services are available from the district office or identify a cultural broker in the community who can help communicate with the family.

Before teachers gather information from families, they need to be aware of how their students' family units are defined. Families today are more diverse than ever before, and students may have different family structures and norms than those of the teacher.[29] In addition, when working with students with special needs, teachers should realize that "all family members, not just parents, are important to the care and education of children."[30] Therefore, it is important for teachers to ask students and their parents if other family members can provide information about their child's interests and school experiences. For example, a mother might be the legal guardian of the student, but the grandmother might also be an appropriate person to interview because she also cares for the child. In this scenario, speaking with the mother and grandmother would be important. If teachers are not familiar with the culture of their students, then they should consider using a cultural broker when they first meet students' families.[31] "A cultural broker is a bilingual, bicultural advocate who purposively connects with people of different backgrounds to reduce conflict and improve collaboration."[32] Using a cultural broker can help build trusting partnerships between families and schools.

Developing a Comprehensive Student Learning Profile: Tying It All Together

Once a special educator has gathered information from various sources, this data should be assembled into an accessible comprehensive learner profile. This profile will support multidisciplinary teams in making multiple decisions, including determinations about eligibility for special education services, development of IEP goals and objectives, and in designing daily instruction. In the following section, we outline one beginning special educator's experience with using multiple formal and informal assessments and anecdotal information to create a comprehensive learning profile for Josephina, a fourth-grade student with a specific learning disability.

Student Name: _____ **Today's Date:** _____

Age: _____ **Grade:** _____ **Home Language:** _____

Parent(s)/Guardian(s) Name(s): _____

Sibling(s) Names and Ages: _____

Likes (check all that apply):

_____ Cooking   _____ Reading

_____ Playing sports   _____ Being outdoors

_____ Arts & Crafts   _____ Spending time with family/friends

_____ Music   _____ Animals

_____ Playing games   _____ Other: _____

Dislikes (check all that apply):

_____ Cooking   _____ Reading

_____ Playing sports   _____ Being outdoors

_____ Arts & Crafts   _____ Spending time with family/friends

_____ Music   _____ Animals

_____ Playing games   _____ Other: _____

Strengths:

_____ Reading/writing   _____ Playing with friends

_____ Math   _____ Listening

_____ Working with hands   _____ Being a friend

_____ Drawing/painting   _____ Sports

Weaknesses:

_____ Reading/writing   _____ Playing with friends

_____ Math   _____ Listening

_____ Working with hands   _____ Being a friend

_____ Drawing/painting   _____ Sports

What is the most important thing you want for your child in school this year? _____

_____

_____

_____

_____

In what ways do you want to see your child grow academically? _____

_____

_____

_____

_____

In what ways do you want to see your child grow socially? _____

_____

_____

_____

_____

Comments and other concerns you would like to share: _____

_____

_____

_____

_____

Figure 4.4 Parent-Generated Student Profile

Josephina moved to her school mid-year from a neighboring school in the same district. Her special education teacher is Ms. Tetrault, a fourth-grade special education co-teacher at Sunnydale Elementary School. Ms. Tetrault works closely with Mrs. Barth, the fourth-grade general education co-teacher, to facilitate the evaluation of Josephina's IEP's goals and objectives. Josephina is 10 years old and has been identified as having a specific learning disability; her parents are from Costa Rica and have limited proficiency in English. Ms. Tetrault reads Josephina's previous IEP and notes that her IEP goals are related to reading and written language; further, the present level of performance described in her IEP suggests that Josephina has needs in reading and writing. Ms. Tetrault and Mrs. Barth, however, have insufficient information for designing instruction that is personalized to Josephina's individual learning needs.

Step 1: Examine Available Data

Ms. Tetrault carefully read Josephina's previous IEP and cumulative file. Ms. Tetrault wants to learn about Josephina's learning and socio-emotional needs. Using the Comprehensive Learning Profile Checklist (see Table 4.2), Ms. Tetrault notes needs and areas of weakness documented in Josephina's IEP and cumulative file. She also notes missing data and questions she has about Josephina.

Step 2: Determine What Is Missing and Prioritize

Ms. Tetrault notes that Josephina's previous IEP is still in compliance because it is current. Her IEP incorporates general information from formal standardized achievement assessments, including Josephina's skills in relation to other typically achieving fourth-grade students. Although this information is important, it does not help Ms. Tetrault or Mrs. Barth design instruction for Josephina. They cannot determine how to differentiate and personalize Josephina's core or supplementary instruction based on information provided. Ms. Tetrault decides that to create a more complete comprehensive learner profile she needs information from Josephina's family and several informal assessments. She has Josephina's CBM data and knows that her oral reading fluency is poor. Thus, she decides to administer the Core Phonics Survey, a teacher-administered diagnostic assessment, to determine if Josephina has specific needs in the area of decoding.

While examining the checklist, Ms. Tetrault notes there is no information related to Josephina's social and emotional well-being. The lack of information makes sense to Ms. Tetrault. She has not observed Josephina exhibiting any social or emotional problems that would interfere with her work. Ms. Tetrault and Mrs. Barth agree that they will need to monitor Josephina to ensure that she is acclimating to her new environment with ease and collect additional data related to social or emotional areas if the need arises.

Step 3: Collect Missing Information

After Ms. Tetrault analyzes available data and identifies additional data needed to inform current instruction, she begins collecting it. She contacts Josephina's mother and father to ask them to complete a parental questionnaire. She arranges time to talk with Josephina individually and learn about her interests, fears, and areas of strength and challenge. She coordinates with Mrs. Barth to schedule time to administer the CORE Phonics assessment.

As Ms. Tetrault and Barth work together to develop a comprehensive learner profile, they also plan collaboratively how to support Josephina in her current fourth-grade literacy project. Josephina's class has just completed a story about a young girl, near Josephina's age, who enjoys baking with her grandmother to create a special pastry unique to her family's heritage. After reading the book, the fourth-grade

Table 4.2 Comprehensive Student Learning Profile Checklist

Area of Focus	Sources of Information
Student Perspective: Interests, hobbies, strengths and weaknesses, future plans	_____ Interview _____ Work samples _____ Checklist _____ Observations _____ Transition assessment
Family Perspective: Interests, hobbies, strengths and weaknesses, future plans, developmental history	_____ Interview _____ Medical records _____ Checklist
Cognitive: Intellectual development and skills	_____ Adaptive assessment _____ Neuropsychological _____ WISC-5 _____ Observations
Academic Skills: Reading, math, writing, expressive and receptive language	_____ Formal assessments (Ex. WIAT-3, WJ4) _____ Informal assessments (Ex. Work samples or CBM) _____ Speech and language assessments _____ Observations _____ Assistive technological assessment
Health	_____ Nurse reports _____ Doctor evaluations _____ Hospital discharge summaries
Physical	_____ Physical adaptive assessments _____ Observations _____ Physical therapy assessments _____ Occupational therapy assessments _____ Assistive technological Assessment
Social/Emotional	_____ Interview _____ Checklist _____ Standardized social/emotional rating scales (Ex. BASC-3) _____ Observations

students create dioramas documenting a family tradition. Ms. Tetrault works with Mrs. Barth to ensure Josephina has the accommodations needed to participate in this activity. Ms. Tetrault and Josephina read the book together, and Mrs. Barth and Josephina brainstorm an experience to showcase in her diorama and discuss all the materials needed to complete the diorama. Finally, Ms. Tetrault shares the project with Josephina's mother and offers to provide materials for Josephina to complete the diorama.

Step 4: Document Data Within the Comprehensive Learner Profile

Ms. Tetrault uses the Comprehensive Learner Profile (see Table 4.3) to document new information she has collected about Josephina as a learner and determines that the information provided from these various sources is comprehensive. Ms. Tetrault summarizes information for Mrs. Barth in a way that makes it accessible and then asks the school psychologist to translate the summary into Spanish.

Step 5: Share and Use to Personalize Instruction

Ms. Tetrault sets up a meeting with Josephina's parents at a time that is convenient for them. She relies on a translator to describe the information in the comprehensive learner profile and provides Joseph-

Table 4.3 Comprehensive Learner Profile (Example)

Student name: Josephina D. **Current grade:** 4
Disability: Specific Learning—Reading and Written Language **Age:** 10 years, 2 months
Home language: Spanish/English

Assessment Data

Area of Focus	Assessments Used	Strengths	Areas of Need	Notes & Additional Information Needed
Student	Interview	• Enjoys dancing and singing • Likes taking care of family dog • Enjoys drawing and writing stories	• Feels stressed reading text from science and social studies • Sometimes gets bored or loses focus when working independently for extended periods of time	Super shy, biggest fear is not having anyone to play with during recess or eat lunch with
Parent/Family (Josephina's mom)	Questionnaire	• Quiet and has several very close friends • Enjoys cooking, helping around the house, and taking care of her baby brother	• Reading and spelling is challenging and frustrating for her daughter	This is the third time that Josephina's family has had to move in the last four years due to changes in her father's employment. Her mother wants Josephina to make friends and feel confident at school
Academic Area 1: Written Language	WIAT-3; WJ-IV Writing samples	• Basic sentences with correct grammar and punctuation	• Complex sentences and paragraph formation; difficulty organizing ideas • Spelling	Do I need to give a writing prompt?
Academic Area 2: Reading	WIAT-3; WJ-IV CBM Core Phonics	• Fluency (60 CWPM at 1st grade reading level) • Alphabetic principle	• Multisyllabic words and morphemes	What types of morphemes are difficult for her? May need more data?
Academic Area 3: Reading Comprehension	WIAT-3; WJ-IV	• Explicit details	• Inferences, struggles with identifying main ideas	
Additional Informal Assessment	Window into My Family: Students in fourth-grade created shoebox dioramas to help peers in class understand a tradition unique to their family. Dioramas were shared with class in public presentation	• Very artistic, J's diorama was colorful and three-dimensional drawing from multiple different artistic mediums	• J benefited from notes and several rehearsals to help her prepare for the presentation about her diorama to her peers	J's diorama showed her mother, grandmother, and herself making a fry bread recipe unique to her family

ina's parents with an opportunity to ask questions. The comprehensive learner profile provides school staff and Josephina's family with immediate insight into her experiences as a learner. The information in the profile can be used to support Josephina's teachers in personalizing instruction to meet her individual needs and interests.

Step 6: Update as Needed

Ms. Tetrault uses this comprehensive learner profile as an introduction to Josephina's cumulative file. It provides an excellent summary of Josephina's needs across a variety of contexts. As the year progresses, Ms. Tetrault updates the comprehensive learner profile. She uses this information when she meets with Josephina's parents, when she updates Josephina's IEP with her parents, or when she sends IEP progress reports.

Wrap Up

In this chapter, we have described how special educators can create a comprehensive learner profile that helps teachers understand students' learning strengths, needs, and interests. It also helps them understand how a students' culture and life experiences might be used to support their learning. This information will be valuable for supporting educators in making eligibility determinations, developing an IEP, planning for instruction, and monitoring student learning and progress towards IEP goals.

Tips

1. Use a combination of school-based assessments to gather information about your students to create a comprehensive learner profile. The comprehensive learner profile can then be used to help make instructional decisions within an MTSS framework. For example, use standardized tests, norm-referenced tests (NRT), criterion-referenced tests (CRT), and CBM (curriculum-based assessments) to support you in understanding students' academic strengths, weaknesses, and where to begin instruction.
2. Draw from curriculum-based assessments to support you in gathering information that cannot be assessed through paper and pencil tests. The anecdotal seating chart and daily score card provide valuable observational data that can be helpful in understanding how your students interact with others and participate in unstructured time.
3. Involve the family in data collection. Teachers can gather data from families through informal checklists or the sharing of family stories.
4. Include student voice in data collection. Asking students about their preferences, strengths, and needs, as well as their perspectives, provides teachers with valuable insights; it also lays the foundation for student involvement and self-determination.

Notes

1 McFarland, J., Hussar, B., de Brey, C., Snyder, T., Wang, X., WilkinsonFlicker, S., . . . Hinz, S. (2017). *The condition of education 2017 (NCES 2017–144)*. Washington, DC: National Center for Education Statistics. Retrieved from https://nces.ed.gov/pubsearch/ pubsinfo.asp?pubid=2017144

2 Bryant, A. C., Triplett, N. P., Watson, M. J., & Lewis, C. W. (2017). The browning of American public schools: Evidence of increasing racial diversity and the implications for policy, practice, and student outcomes. *Urban Review 49*, 263–278. doi:10.1007/s11256-017-0400-6.

3 Individuals with Disabilities Education Act, 20 U.S.C. §§ 1400 *et seq.* (2006 & Supp. V. 2011). IDEA regulations, 34 C.F.R. §300 (2012).

4 IDEA regulations, 34 C.F.R. §300 (2012).

5 IDEA regulations, 34 C.F.R. §300 (2012).

6 Schrank, F. A., McGrew, K. S., & Mather, N. (2014). *Woodcock-Johnson IV*. Rolling Meadows, IL: Riverside.

7 Stiggins, R. J., Arter, J. A., Chappuis, J., & Chappuis, S. (2006). *Classroom assessment for student learning: Doing it right-using it well* (1st ed.). Portland, OR: Pearson.

8 Billingsley, B. S., Brownell, M. T., Israel, M., & Kamman, M. L. (2013). *A survival guide for new special educators.* San Francisco, CA: Jossey-Bass.

9 Terman, L. M., & Merrill, M. A. (1937). *Measuring intelligence: A guide to the administration of the new revised Stanford-Binet tests of intelligence.* Oxford, England: Houghton Mifflin.

10 McLoughlin, J. A., Lewis, R. B., & Kritikos, E. P. (2017). *Assessing students with special needs.* Boston, MA: Pearson.

11 Common Core State Standards Initiative. (2017). *English language arts standards; Reading: Literature; grade 2.* Retrieved from http://www.corestandards.org/ELA-Leteracy/RL/2
    Anastiasi, A., & Urbina, S. (1997). *Psychological Testing* (7th ed.). New York, NY: Palgrave Macmillan.

12 Common Core State Standards Initiative. (2017). *English language arts standards; Reading: Literature; grade 2.* Retrieved from http://www.corestandards.org/ELA-Leteracy/RL/2
    Anastiasi, A., & Urbina, S. (1997). *Psychological Testing* (7th ed.). New York, NY: Palgrave Macmillan.

13 Mehrens, W. A., & Lehmann, I. J. (1991). *Measurement and evaluation in education and psychology.* Fort Worth, TX: Holt, Rinehart and Winston.

14 Woodcock, R. W. (1998). *Woodcock reading mastery test-revised.* Circle Pines, MN: American Guidance Service.

15 *I-ready diagnostic and instruction.* (2013). Retrieved from www.curriculumassociates.com/products/iready/diagnostic-instruction.aspx

16 Consortium on Reading Excellence. (1999). *Core assessing reading: Multiple measures for kindergarten through eighth grade.* Novato, CA: Arena.

17 Nagro, S. A., & Cornelius, K. E. (2013). Evaluating the evidence base of video analysis: A special education teacher development tool. *Teacher Education and Special Education, 36*(4), 312–329.

18 Deno, S. L., & Fuchs, L. S. (1987). Developing curriculum-based measurement systems for data-based special education problem Solving. *Focus on Exceptional Children, 19*(8), 1–16.

19 Deno, S. L. (1985). Curriculum-based measurement: The emerging alternative. *Exceptional Children, 52*(3), 219–232.

20 Fuchs, L. S. (2003). Assessing intervention responsiveness: Conceptual and technical issues. *Learning Disabilities Research & Practice, 18*(3), 172–186.

21 Alberto, P. A., & Troutman, A. C. (20.13). *Applied behavior analysis for teachers* (9th ed.). Upper Saddle River, NJ: Prentice Hall.
    Cornelius, K. (2013). Formative assessment made easy: Templates for collecting daily data in inclusive classrooms. *Teaching Exceptional Children, 45*(5), 14–21.

22 Cornelius, K. (2013). Formative assessment made easy: Templates for collecting daily data in inclusive classrooms. *Teaching Exceptional Children, 45*(5), 14–21.

23 Cook-Sather, A. (2003). Movements of mind: The matrix, metaphors, and re-imagining education. *Teachers College Record, 105*(6), 946.

24 Cook-Sather, A. (2007). Resisting the impositional potential of student voice work: Lessons for liberatory educational research from poststructuralist feminist critiques of critical pedagogy. *Discourse: Studies in the Cultural Politics of Education, 28*(3), 389–403.

Cook-Sather, A. (2009). From traditional accountability to shared responsibility: The benefits and challenges of student consultants gathering midcourse feedback in college classrooms. *Assessment & Evaluation in Higher Education*, 34(2), 231–241.

Cook-Sather, A. (2010). Students as learners and teachers: Taking responsibility, transforming education, and redefining accountability. *Curriculum Inquiry*, 40(4), 555–575.

Duffield, J., Allan, J., Turner, E., & Morris, B. (2000). Pupils' voices on achievement: An alternative to the standards agenda. *Cambridge Journal of Education*, 30(2), 263–274.

25 Mason, C. Y., McGahee-Kovac, M., & Johnson, L. (2004). How to help students lead their IEP meetings. *Teaching Exceptional Children*, 36(3), 18–24.

Myers, A., & Eisenman, L. (2005). Student-led IEPs: Take the first step. *Teaching Exceptional Children*, 37(4), 52–58.

Hawbaker, B. W. (2007). Student-led IEP meetings: Planning and implementation strategies. *Teaching exceptional children plus*, 3(5), Article 4.

26 Turnbull, A., Turnbull, R., Erwin, E. J., Sodak, L. C., & Shogren, K. A. (2015). *Families, professionals, and exceptionality: Positive outcomes through partnerships and trust* (8th ed.). Boston, MA: Pearson.

27 Turnbull, A., Turnbull, R., Erwin, E. J., Sodak, L. C., & Shogren, K. A. (2015). *Families, professionals, and exceptionality: Positive outcomes through partnerships and trust* (8th ed.). Boston, MA: Pearson.

28 Turnbull, A., Turnbull, R., Erwin, E. J., Sodak, L. C., & Shogren, K. A. (2015). *Families, professionals, and exceptionality: Positive outcomes through partnerships and trust* (8th ed.). Boston, MA: Pearson, p. 232.

29 Sharma, R. (2013). The family and family structure classification redefined for the current times. *Journal of Family Medicine and Primary Care*, 2(4), 306–310. doi:10.4103/2249-4863. 123774.

30 Friend, M., & Cook, L. (2017). *Interactions: Collaboration skills for school professionals* (8th ed.). Boston, MA: Pearson, p. 266.

31 Rossetti, Z., Story Sauer, J., Bui, O., & Ou, S. (2017). Developing collaborative partnerships with culturally and linguistically diverse families during the IEP process. *Teaching Exceptional Children*, 49(5), 328–338.

32 Rossetti, Z., Story Sauer, J., Bui, O., & Ou, S. (2017). Developing collaborative partnerships with culturally and linguistically diverse families during the IEP process. *Teaching Exceptional Children*, 49(5), 328–338, 333.

Key Resources

- IRIS resources related to assessment and progress monitoring: https://iris.peabody.vanderbilt.edu/iris-resource-locator/ This site is designed to provide educators examples of how to select, administer, and interpret assessments within inclusive classrooms within MTSS frameworks.
- CBM Warehouse: www.interventioncentral.org/curriculum-based-measurement-reading-math-assesment-tests This free site provides teachers CBMs for reading, math, writing, and spelling. In addition, resources are provided for graphing options, norms for interpreting student performance, and manuals to support with administration.
- O*NET: www.onetonline.org Information related to careers and future interests to help students contribute to their learning profile.
- ¡Colorín colorado! www.colorincolorado.org/search-page?s=assessment Colorín colorado has resources for teachers working with students who are English Language Learners. This particular link is on assessment resources for bilingual students.

- Reading Rockets: www.readingrockets.org /search?cx=004997827699593338140%3 Anptllrzh p78&cof=FORID%3A11&ie=UTF-8&as_q=assessment Provides information on reading assessments.
- Scholastic: www.scholastic.com/teachers/articles/teaching-content/connect-kids-and-parents-different-cultures-0/ Scholastic has information and resources for teachers on working with parents from culturally and linguistically diverse backgrounds.
- Teacher Vision: www.teachervision.com/teaching-strategies/teacher-parent-collaboration Advice for teachers in working with parents.

5

Interpreting and Communicating Assessment Information With Stakeholders to Collaboratively Design and Implement Educational Programs

Margaret Kamman and Erica D. McCray

Introduction

Special education teachers interpret and communicate student assessment results for key stakeholders who help make informed decisions about students' individualized education programs (IEPs). In Chapter 4, Benedict and colleagues outlined how special educators collect assessments and use results to understand students' strengths and needs. They described how special educators should collect assessment information from a variety of sources, including families, students themselves, and general education teachers, if they want to develop a comprehensive understanding of the student. Families[1] and other key professionals must understand these assessment results if they are going to be invested in the student's education. Together, the team uses this assessment information to collaboratively design an educational plan that, when implemented, will produce maximum benefit for the student. In this chapter, we focus on strategies special educators can use to engage stakeholders more fully in interpreting assessment information and making decisions about students' IEPs.

Students with disabilities have a dedicated multidisciplinary team that works together to make decisions about their IEP. The team includes a diverse group of key stakeholders that varies in membership based on each student's needs. Key stakeholders in attendance typically include parents or caregivers, special and general education teachers, school counselors, school administrators, and other related service personnel and professionals (e.g., school nurse, speech-language pathologist, psychologist). The team cannot make student-centered decisions unless they understand assessment results and implications of those results. Special education teachers play an important role in helping the team understand a student's needs and strengths. They can interpret assessment results, develop IEP goals, choose appropriate accommodations and modifications, help general education teachers use assessment information to differentiate tier 1 instruction and focus tier 2 instruction, and identify fair grading practices. To ensure assessment is ongoing, teachers should collect data and interpret it to inform instruction.

Unfortunately, many families report feeling overwhelmed and anxious at IEP meetings.[1] Families often report they are not a valuable part of the decision-making process.[2] These feelings may be attributed to their weak understanding of information being presented.[3] Special education teachers can alleviate these concerns by involving parents and caregivers in the assessment process and

[1] The terms families, parents, and caregivers are used interchangeably throughout this chapter.

considering cultural and linguistic factors at play when selecting assessments and interpreting assessment results. Parents and caregivers also have insights into their child that can help the team develop relevant goals. Special education teachers who plan to communicate with families help to ensure that all team members understand assessment results and can collaboratively participate in the development of an educational program.[4]

Narrowing the Focus

This chapter provides specific recommendations about the process of interpreting and communicating assessment results to key stakeholders. First, we provide general information about the purpose of assessment information and how key stakeholders can use this information on an ongoing basis to guide instructional decisions. Next, we provide detailed guidance on the role of the special education teacher as a conduit of assessment results. Discussion of all potential assessments, interpretation, and communication scenarios is beyond the scope of this chapter. Instead, we discuss specific steps special education teachers can take to effectively gather assessment information, organize and interpret assessment results, consider students' strengths and needs, facilitate collaboration among team members, and monitor students' response to instructional plans. Finally, we consider the unique role and needs of each stakeholder on the IEP team and how special educators can communicate assessment results to ensure the team is ready to collaborate and make informed decisions about educational plans.

Chapter Overview

1. Describe the rationale and purposes of interpreting and communicating assessment information, with a focus on collaboration for designing educational programs.
2. Describe the specific role and steps special educators can take to interpret and communicate assessment data.
3. Describe strategies and methods in communicating assessment information with diverse key stakeholders.

The Importance and Purpose of Assessment Information

In this section, we describe the background and rationale for using and communicating assessment information. Assessment is critical for determining eligibility for special education services, determining placement in less restrictive settings, designing educational programs, and evaluating student progress, including progress in tier 1 instruction.

Legal Background

Federal legislation provides the basis for assessment. The Every Student Succeeds Act (ESSA) requires that states have a measure in place to determine student progress in the general curriculum.[5] All students, including those with disabilities, participate in statewide assessments (with some students participating in alternate assessments as designated by their IEP). The Individuals with Disabilities Education Act (IDEA) stipulates assessment as a part of eligibility determinations for disabilities and as part of the annual IEP review.[6] To determine eligibility, an IEP must provide academic and functional present levels of performance. This federal legislation ensures schools have ready access to student data that will enable special education teachers to assist in progressing towards set goals.

Initial Eligibility

Assessment results help key stakeholders make determinations about initial eligibility for special education services. As discussed in the previous chapter, multiple measures are used in initial identification of disabilities. Multidisciplinary teams use assessment data to help determine if a student responds to research-based interventions and informs the team about the need for more intensive, tier 3 supports. Special education teachers assist general education teachers in developing tier 2 interventions. Special educators can work with their general education colleagues to organize and implement assessments needed for identifying students who need more intensive services.

Present Levels of Performance

Data from assessments also provide relevant ongoing information about students' present levels of performance. It is impossible to draw accurate conclusions about students without current assessment data. Current data are critical in determining annual goals for students with disabilities and monitoring progress in meeting those goals. Without a student's present level of academic and functional performance, there is no baseline for measuring student progress.

Role of the Special Education Teacher

Special educators play a significant role in assessment. They are typically responsible for (1) collecting assessment results; (2) interpreting assessment results; (3) facilitating collaboration among team members in developing education plans; and (4) closely monitoring students' response to instructional plans.

Interpret Assessment Results

Step 1. Organize Assessment Information and Highlight Main Findings

First, special education teachers gather and organize all assessment information several weeks prior to an IEP meeting. Multiple measures are used regularly to determine present levels of student performance (see Chapter 4 for more details). Assessment data may come from a variety of sources including state standardized assessments, progress monitoring data collected on tier 1 and tier 2 interventions, interim district and school assessments, parents and caregivers, general educators, and other professionals (e.g., speech language pathologists, behavior specialists). Often assessment data are available in reports, although the writing may be technical. Special education teachers should read through all assessment information carefully and highlight/note main findings. If an assessment is unfamiliar, or data are confusing, special education teachers should seek additional counsel to interpret main findings. Professionals typically able to assist are school administrators, psychologists, and counselors. It is essential that teachers distill and summarize main findings that are related to both students' strengths and needs. Both types of data are important in the IEP team's decision-making process.

Step 2. Consider the Influence of Cultural and Linguistic Diversity

Once the special education teacher identifies key findings from assessments, the next step is to consider results in light of same-aged peers. Special education teachers should consider how language and culture might influence the interpretation of assessment results, as students who are culturally and linguistically diverse (CLD) continue to be overrepresented in some categories of special education.[7] As discussed in Chapter 4, the use of multiple measures—and accurate interpretations—is even more critical for CLD students.[8] Special education teachers should reflect carefully on results and ask themselves questions about *why* a student performed in a specific way. Such reflection helps determine the credibility of assessment data or potential factors that may be interfering with accurate representation of knowledge and ability. For instance, a teacher might ask, *Is the student struggling with comprehension because she does not know how to identify the main idea or make inferences? Or does she lack familiarity with many vocabulary words in English? Did the student struggle with oral reading because she has difficulty decoding or because her cultural background includes expectations for her to be quiet in learning environments?* Asking these types of questions can help teachers better recognize factors influencing assessment results.

Step 3. Identify Student's Strengths and Needs

The third step in interpreting data is to generate an initial list of student strengths and needs. As mentioned in the previous chapter, multiple assessments and viewpoints are beneficial for determining student proficiency. For example, results from a state-level assessment may demonstrate that a student can identify main ideas but struggles to integrate key information and ideas. Data from tier 1 and tier 2 interventions might show that the student struggles to comprehend and maintain attention when reading longer passages. Additional data from the fluency assessments and the general education teacher's anecdotal notes might show the student does not read fluently and retain details. Parents and caregivers might provide valuable information about their children's interests and perceptions of reading. This initial list of strengths and needs can be confirmed and adjusted by the IEP team or used on an ongoing basis for making instructional decisions.

Step 4. Consider How Assessment Information Impacts Accommodations, Modifications, and Fair Grading Practices

Assessment results are useful for making decisions about students' needs for accommodations, modifications, and fair grading practices. Accommodations alter *how* a student learns a particular concept or skill. Accommodations may include changing the environment, the curriculum format, or equipment that a student uses in learning and assessment. Modifications change *what* the student learns and may include altering the complexity of the material being taught or the amount of material covered. Fair grading practices typically refer to students being graded in ways that reflect their actual performance.[9]

The special education teacher, along with the team, should review assessment findings, consider identified strengths and needs, and generate potential implications for developing education plans. For example, a student who is having difficulty decoding may need an accommodation that allows for math questions to be read aloud. A student who is having difficulty answering multiple choice questions may need an accommodation that allows them to answer questions orally on class assessments. Modifications might also be recommended based on assessment data. A modification might involve teaching a concept using simpler content, such as alternate books for science or social studies that teach concepts to be learned using below grade-level material. Another modification might involve students learning two- and three-digit addition when peers are learning multiplication. Finally, assessment data may help determine fair grading practices. Again, the special education teacher can ask herself, *Will the student be able to demonstrate knowledge and skill on a specific assignment or assessment as it's designed?* For example, tier 1 and tier 2 data may help the teacher identify a student who consistently struggles on assessments that require the student to provide a written response. The IEP team may decide the student needs alternate ways to demonstrate knowledge.

Communicate Assessment Results

Step 1. Develop a Summary Sheet of Assessment Results

It may be helpful for special educators to make a guide or table that includes the different assessments, results, and interpretations to communicate assessment data effectively with key stakeholders. Special educators use data from multiple assessments and information from a variety of sources to develop a comprehensive profile (see Chapter 4) to delineate students' strengths, needs, and interests. Next, special education teachers must summarize data from these assessments to communicate effectively. Having an assessment summary sheet (see Figure 5.1 for an example) that is free of technical jargon can organize information for the comprehensive profile and make it less overwhelming.

Sally Brown, 3rd grade
Assessment Results
Date: September 25, 2017

Assessment	Main Findings	Interpretation	Strengths	Needs	Implications/ Considerations
State reading assessment	Score: 215	Below grade level. Students in third grade must score a 255 to be considered on level.	Locating main ideas	Integrating key details	State assessment not given in first language. Sally has test anxiety. Cautious interpretation of results.
State math assessment	Score: 275	Below grade level. Students in third grade must score a 282 to be considered on level.	Computation	Word problems	Possible that Sally is not reading the word problems correctly, accommodations might assist.
Dibels	Words correct: 85 Retell: 48	Below benchmarks for grade level, needs intensive support.	99% accuracy on word read, knows high-frequency words.	Decoding, Fluency and comprehension Difficulty decoding unknown words	Goals related to intervention, access to grade-level materials, considerations for accommodations in science, social studies, and math.
Parent reading record	Read independently three chapter books on festivals in last nine weeks	Interest in reading about festivals in Latin America	Likes to read about family culture.	Limited interests	Incorporation of Latin background in content increases motivation.
AR assessments and star reading assessment	Read five short stories in nine weeks, average score of 40% on AR rest. Star assessment at 2.0 grade level, same as last nine weeks.	Difficulty reading independently in class. Independent reading is not producing gains.		More structured reading opportunities	Assistance in choosing appropriate books for independent reading, or alternate plan for this time in class.

Figure 5.1 Summary Sheet Example

Step 2. Tailor the Summary Sheet Based on Key Stakeholder

Teams share assessment results at different times with a variety of people. Information might be shared at a formal IEP meeting, more informally with general education teachers to make daily instructional decisions, or with parents and caregivers to update them on their child's progress. Special educators must consider their audience when relaying assessment information. Once a summary sheet is created, it can be tailored for different audiences. For example, if a student is in tier 1 for reading instruction, the summary sheet might be changed to provide specific details relevant to reading instruction in that setting. Parents and caregivers will need brief information that is free of technical jargon and acronyms about all assessments. Assessment information should be translated into the native language of families. Families often report they understand little if any of the information that is provided in IEP meetings.[10] Being intentional about what is included can help ensure the special education teacher engages in effective communication of assessment information. More information about tailoring communication to specific stakeholders is provided in the next section.

Step 3. Create a Plan for Communication

Teams can consume information from reports and summary sheets when they have opportunities to interact with that information. Special education teachers should provide time for stakeholders to read and digest results before meeting in person. All reports should be provided according to school district confidentiality guidelines. If an IEP team is meeting, members should have assessment results and summaries a week in advance to review and consider interpretation and implications of the data. When the team has opportunities to preview and discuss information, they can make more informed decisions about educational plans in the team meeting. Special educators can include a friendly note that accompanies the reports to help ease team members', and especially families', anxieties about assessment information. The note should contain information about how results will be discussed at the upcoming meeting and how team members can contact the special educator to discuss results prior to the meeting. For families who have limited English proficiency, special education teachers should meet with the school's interpreter to discuss the translation of the assessment materials and/or the protocol for the meetings.

Facilitate Collaboration Among Team Members in Developing Educational Plans

The special education teacher plays a pivotal role in facilitating collaborative discussions among team members in meetings. When the team meets, the special education teacher can use the summary sheet to review relevant results, considerations, and implications. This structure provides a starting point for conversations about educational plans. When structuring the team meeting, it is a good idea for the special educator to stop after each assessment explanation and check in with stakeholders about their understanding, offering to answer questions. As assessment results are discussed, it is helpful to ask each member of the team to contribute their opinions at appropriate times. Special educators should also specifically solicit input from families and students by pausing periodically and asking for opinions. For example, a special education teacher could ask, "Mr. Williams, after hearing the general education teacher review the writing assessments, are you seeing similar challenges at home?" Affirming the contributions of each team member helps them feel like a valued member of the decision-making process. A statement such as, "Mrs. Gonzales, the information you provided about Tianna's reading habits and interests at home will be very helpful in designing projects for her reading group and in encouraging her participation in class," can make everyone feel their input is valued. General education teachers, parents and caregivers, students, and other professionals are more likely to participate in developing goals and objectives when they know their viewpoints contribute to the creation and evaluation of the IEP.

Closely Monitor Students' Response to Instructional Plans

Once the team develops the IEP, special education teachers must work with their general education colleagues to monitor students' response to tiered instruction, both in general and special education. To provide specially designed instruction, it is critical that teachers determine progress students are making toward their IEP goals. Teachers should use results from assessments identified in Chapters 4 and 6 to make informed decisions about instruction. Special education teachers need to collect progress data continuously to ensure that students with disabilities are responding to interventions and to make adaptations if they are not.[11] Close monitoring of student progress helps to inform the team and allows for adjustments to be made to the IEP, enabling students with disabilities access to specially designed instruction. More information about using data to inform instruction can be found in the next chapter.

Considerations for Key Stakeholders

Input from key stakeholders is essential for providing a quality, data-driven education for students. Stakeholders on the IEP team offer unique personal and professional expertise that can be used to improve students' education. The case manager, typically the special educator, should, in advance:

- request and provide relevant assessment data to each team member based on their role;
- provide a data assessment summary sheet and comprehensive learner profile that will inform the educational plan;
- share appropriate background information and contextual considerations that emphasize students' identified strengths and needs; and
- develop a plan for future data collection and use.

By taking these steps, special educators can ensure strong engagement from all key stakeholders.

Parents and Caregivers

Every student brings different background knowledge, experiences, and opportunities to learn to classrooms, and families have knowledge of their children, both at home and within the community, that schools do not. Educators must engage families to gain information about their child and community and provide them with tools to support learning at home. IDEA[12] includes procedural safeguards, such as securing caregivers' consent for assessments and encouraging participation in their child's education. Also, a parent liaison or advocate might be an important resource for caregivers, such as helping them understand assessments or seek independent assessments.

Ongoing data collection is essential for serving students with disabilities successfully. Often, data is not presented in a way that is meaningful or accessible to parents and caregivers. The summary sheet we described in this chapter provides information about assessments in a more digestible format for families, which in turn can help families understand what their child needs and participate better in collaborative team meetings, such as the IEP meeting.

Families also often view their child with a different lens than school personnel do. They bring their own experiences and expectations for the child to the table.[13] These varied understandings and experiences are crucial for non-discriminatory evaluation. They help professionals recognize cultural and linguistic differences that could be misconstrued as disability and help the team design instruction based on the students' culture and experiences.[14]

Students as Both Individuals and Extensions of Families

Culturally responsive teams understand students as individuals and extensions of their families. Students have their own ideas and goals for their future that are often impacted by their family backgrounds and culture. Teams decide when it is appropriate for students to be involved in the interpretation of their assessment data and participate in decisions about educational plans.

For example, IDEA[15] requires transition planning beginning in adolescence; however, planning for post-school outcomes should begin in early childhood. One student may have plans to live at home, but the student's family may require the student to seek employment immediately after high school to contribute to the household income. Assessing employability skills and providing on-the-job training with coaching would be appropriate. A student from a different family might view post-secondary schooling with on-campus living as ideal, which would require specific academic courses and standardized testing. Students may have individual goals that align with those of their family, or they may differ. One strategy in assisting teams with differing opinions is to focus on the results of assessment data to guide decision making. For instance, students who complete a self-directed summary of performance, which includes compiling assessment information related to transition, help both the team and themselves better understand strengths and needs in considering post-school options.[16]

General Education Teacher

The majority of students with disabilities are served in general education settings for 60 to 80 percent of the school day;[17] thus, general educators are an important source of information about students' academic, social, and behavioral skills. They also need to be able to collect information to determine if students with disabilities are doing well in their instruction, as they provide much of the core content or tier 1 instruction students with disabilities receive. Additionally, students with disabilities may participate in tier 2 instruction if they have academic needs that do not require the same intensive instruction as tier 3. For general educators to provide them with an appropriate education, they must engage in continuous instruction-assessment cycles to plan for and evaluate their instruction and ensure it is meeting their needs. The assessment information they gather can be useful in developing a more comprehensive learner profile for students with disabilities.

General educators, however, often have varying levels of skill in understanding and interpreting data and using it to inform instruction. Special educators may need to work carefully with general education teachers to assist them in identifying assessments to evaluate their instruction and implementing those assessments.[18]

School and District Leadership

School and district leaders need to understand assessment data for several reasons. One, they ultimately are responsible for ensuring that assessments are non-discriminatory and that a student's education is appropriate. Two, they should make decisions about what is "appropriate" and within the power of the school and district to provide while still protecting the best interests of students and their families. Three, they have to understand what students need to create structures and supports for general and special education teachers and related service personnel who are implementing educational plans. They must establish structures so that procedures are clear, roles are defined, and the staff (or team) is organized and functioning well. Four, they need to be well informed of students' progress in order to empower school staff and families to work together effectively. Without a good understanding of assessment results, administrators cannot fulfill their responsibilities.

The special education teacher is often the person who keeps the school leader informed. Although school leaders may not need detailed assessment information about a student's difficulties, they do need to know the implications of assessment results for securing and supporting necessary accommodations, modifications, special equipment, and other supports. Special education teachers should use summary sheets collected for the IEP team meetings and progress monitoring data to keep school leaders informed about individual students, particularly when the level of instructional supports is inappropriate to meet the student's needs.

Related Services Personnel

Related services personnel should be involved in collecting and interpreting assessments to assist the team in developing effective IEPs for students with disabilities. School psychologists, speech-language pathologists, behavior specialists and analysts, reading specialists, and other professionals often play a role in educating students with high-incidence disabilities. Each of the related service professionals bring different disciplinary expertise to assist in identifying strengths and needs. The unique perspectives of diverse personnel are key to an effective team as they share data and plan coordinated supports.

Special education teachers help to coordinate the communication of assessment data. They should ensure related service personnel share their assessment results in ways that everyone on the team can understand. Likewise, special educators should ensure that assessment results from general education teachers, students, and families are shared in clear and concise formats with related services personnel. Such sharing of information will allow related service personnel to provide input into the development of educational goals and share how their expertise might be best leveraged to assist the student. For example, a speech-language pathologist might conduct an initial evaluation that suggests a student has below average oral language skills. The general education teacher might collect assessment data that suggests the student struggles with understanding vocabulary. The family might indicate that the student seems reluctant to speak in front of less familiar adults and peers. Together, this assessment may inform strategies for core instruction, supplementary languages provided by the speech and language pathologies, and some easy strategies the family can use to engage their child in communication.

Example 1: Using Data in an IEP Meeting to Inform the Educational Plan

Mrs. Ericson, the special education teacher, is preparing for an IEP meeting. She has already completed her data assessment summary sheet and has prepared a meeting checklist to ensure (see Figure 5.2) she has requested and shared all assessment data relevant to her third-grade student, Lexi. She does this in sufficient advance of the meeting to ensure that caregivers, the general education teacher, and related services personnel have time to collect and review data. She also met with Lexi to review the assessment data and practiced with her so she would feel prepared to share in the IEP meeting. Her preparation will support the organization of the IEP team and their readiness to discuss Lexi's progress and potential goals and accommodations for the coming year.

Mrs. Ericson makes introductions and welcomes everyone to the meeting. Everyone on her preparation list is in attendance in addition to Lexi and the assistant principal, Dr. Jones. Mrs. Ericson ensures that everyone has access to data being discussed and begins the meeting by asking Lexi to use the data to talk about her strengths. Mrs. Ericson adds to Lexi's comments, indicating that she demonstrates excellent listening comprehension skills, is friendly and well-liked by peers, and has a great work ethic. Mrs. Ericson then asks for any additional thoughts on Lexi's strengths. When no

IEP Meeting Preparation Checklist

Before the Meeting

Student: Lexi Young

Meeting Date: 2/10/2020

Invitations and Assessment Data Sent To:
1. Ms. Young (parent)
2. Mr. Thompson (general education teacher)
3. Ms. Christopher (speech/language pathologist)
4. School Leader (assistant principal)

To Be Sent:
- Last statewide assessment scores with explanations
- Most recent reading test scores with summary
- Audio-recording and running records for beginning of year and most recent testing with summary
- Summary sheet of assessment results
- Blank notes and questions sheet for meeting
- Request for any assessments to be considered by team

During the Meeting

1. Introductions, welcome, share information
2. Lexi to discuss strengths first, then engage each member of team, review and agree
3. Lexi to discuss needs first, then engage each member of team, review and agree
4. Open discussion (parents and caregivers, general education teacher, speech language pathologist)
5. Develop goals
6. Close meeting with next steps
7. Follow up with school leader

To bring:
- Lexi's cumulative file
- Copies of all documents and data sent/received
- Laptop to draft e-IEP
- Printed signature page

After the Meeting

1. Send copies to parents and caregivers, records office
2. Provide updated IEP to all teachers
3. File original in cumulative file

Figure 5.2 IEP Meeting Preparation Checklist

one initially answers, Mrs. Ericson engages the other participants on the team by asking each of them individually about Lexi's strengths in their environment. She asks the general education teacher, Mr. Thompson, "What does Lexi do really well in your class?" Mr. Thompson adds that Lexi works well with her peers and likes to discuss content. He provides an example. Mrs. Ericson then asks Lexi's mom about her strengths. She shares that Lexi is very responsible and likes to keep lists of what she needs to complete. She also loves to learn about her family's history and anything to do with puppies. Dr. Jones chimes in, telling Lexi and her parents that she would love to learn more about their family. Mrs. Ericson wraps up this part of the conversation by reviewing all the strengths provided by team members, and the team provides verbal agreement.

Mrs. Ericson then discusses Lexi's needs using a similar format. Again, Lexi begins the discussion, using her data to discuss her needs. Mrs. Ericson adds to Lexi's comments by identifying that Lexi struggles with fluency and articulation. Ms. Christopher, the speech-language pathologist, indicates that Lexi is making progress but needs additional opportunities to practice her articulation exercises throughout the day and at home. There is a slight pause in the conversation, and Mrs. Ericson takes this opportunity to ask Lexi's mom if she has any insights into Lexi's needs. Lexi's mom says that Lexi often feels self-conscious about struggling academically. Lexi's mom expresses that she would help Lexi at home but doesn't really know how to help. Mrs. Ericson responds to Lexi's mom by letting her know that as they develop goals for Lexi, the team will provide her with suggestions. Mr. Thompson adds that Lexi has difficulty reading independently in class and is often distracted. Mrs. Ericson closes the conversation on needs by describing Lexi's progress in reading, including decoding, comprehension, and fluency. She indicates that Lexi still performs below grade level and would benefit from intensive interventions. Mrs. Ericson summarizes the needs conversation by reviewing areas for improvement already discussed. The team verbally agrees with the list.

Mrs. Ericson guides the team in developing appropriate goals, objectives, and accommodations for the next school year. The team frequently returns to previously generated information about strengths to leverage them in meeting Lexi's needs. For example, Mr. Thompson intends to use Lexi's interests to select reading material for her independent reading time. He will also create a self-monitoring tracking sheet to help motivate Lexi in independent reading and leverage what her mom perceives as Lexi's strong sense of responsibility. As they are creating goals, the team generates strategies that Lexi's mom can use to provide support at home. For example, Ms. Christopher provides some fun games they can play at dinner to practice conversation skills. After the group comes to consensus about Lexi's goals and accommodations, they set a plan for collecting formal and informal assessment data that would be shared quarterly so they could closely monitor Lexi's response to the educational plan. Everyone, including Lexi, felt good about the meeting, her progress, and the plan for moving forward. The next step is for the team to work together to monitor Lexi's process. See Figure 5.3 for an example of the plan that was created and notes on Lexi's progress.

After concluding the meeting, Mrs. Ericson follows up with the assistant principal, Dr. Jones. Dr. Jones said she would bring the issue of Lexi's self-esteem up with the leadership team and generate ways to help Lexi and other students struggling in this area. She wondered if other students with disabilities might be feeling the same way and thought it might be useful to garner input from some other teachers for a school-wide effort. She also encouraged Mrs. Ericson to touch base with Señora Rodriguez about an event she is coordinating for the Spanish club that might be of interest to Lexi.

Example 2: Using Data to Collaborate With Teachers and Staff to Inform Daily Instruction

Mr. Thompson, the general education teacher, noticed in the first month of school that Andre is struggling in tier 1 instruction in reading and writing. During the upcoming data team meeting, Mr. Thompson expresses his concerns to his other team members: the reading specialist, Ms. Hodge; and Mrs. Ericson, the special education teacher. He shares Andre's recent classroom assessments and writing samples. He also explains that Andre is easily distracted, always wants attention, and is often

---

3/2/2020

I increased Lexi's rate of reading goal (85wpm), and she showed some frustration. She's close, but she could use some encouragement. It would be great if you can build in some opportunities to practice in her small group or one-on-ones.—Ms. C

3/9/2020

She came in raring to go! I can tell she's motivated and practiced at home. I think in another week she'll have some confidence and be ready to increase this goal (90–95wpm).—Mr. T

Figure 5.3 Sample Shared Data/Communication Log on Lexi

off-task. Together, the team agrees to implement several tier 2 interventions to assist Andre. First, Andre will participate in a tier 2 fluency intervention group for the next 30 days that meets twice a week. Mrs. Ericson suggests teaching Andre to use a simple graphic organizer to focus his writing. Mr. Thompson will use this strategy over the next month. Finally, Mr. Thompson will implement a schedule for Andre to receive positive feedback in shorter intervals to address his need for attention and off-task behavior. Mrs. Ericson provides Mr. Thompson with a progress monitoring sheet to keep track of Andre's tier 2 interventions. The team agrees to meet in one month to review data and discuss Andre's progress.

Wrap Up

Assessment data are essential for identifying students' present levels of performance, planning effective tier 1 and individualized tier 2 instruction, and developing their IEPs. Special education teachers play a critical role in interpreting and communicating assessment results. To be effective in their roles, they must understand individual assessment tools, be able to interpret their findings, and help to consider the cultural or linguistic factors that could affect students' learning and behavior. This information helps the team identify student strengths and needs and consider appropriate accommodations, modifications, and fair grading practices. Creating a summary sheet to outline interpretations can help special education teachers organize assessment results and communicate them effectively. Doing so allows the team to provide input and create an environment where collaboration in the educational planning process is valued. Once plans are in place, the special education teacher plays an important role in helping the team monitor students' response to instruction to confirm they are progressing toward IEP goals.

Tips

1. **Take time to interpret and plan.** Successful communication of assessment results does not happen by reading results in a meeting for the first time and sharing initial thoughts. Special education teachers are busy! Effective interpretation and communication require setting aside time to review, highlight, and interpret findings. This will help you feel confident sharing assessment results and answering questions.
2. **Organize assessment results.** Consider what each team member needs to understand and organize assessment results to meet these needs. Providing a simple summary sheet can help special education teachers more comprehensively and effectively communicate with all stakeholders.
3. **Use check-ins and questioning to ensure collaboration.** Ask each member of the team simple questions throughout the meeting to solicit and ensure engagement. Affirm contributions made by stakeholders to help them feel valued for their input.

Notes

1 Hammond, H., Ingalls, L., & Trussell, R. P. (2008). Family members' involvement in the initial Individual Education Program (IEP) meeting and the IEP process: Perceptions and reactions. *International Journal about Parents in Education, 2,* 35–48.
2 Zeitlin, V. M., & Curcic, S. (2014). Parental voices on individualized education programs: 'OH, IEP meeting tomorrow? Rum tonight!'. *Disability & Society, 29*(3), 373–387.
3 Hammond, H., Ingalls, L., & Trussell, R. P. (2008). Family members' involvement in the initial Individual Education Program (IEP) meeting and the IEP process: Perceptions and reactions. *International Journal about Parents in Education, 2,* 35–48.

4 Weaver, A. D., & Ouye, J. C. (2015). A practical and research-based guide for improving IEP team meetings. *NASP Communiqué, 44*(3).

5 The Every Student Succeeds Act, Pub. L. No. 114–95 § 114 Stat. 1177 (2015).

6 Individuals With Disabilities Education Act, 20 U.S.C. § 1400 (2004).

7 Zhang, D., Katsiyannis, A., Ju, S., & Roberts, E. (2014). Minority representation in special education: 5-year trends. *Journal of Child and Family Studies, 23*(1), 118–127.

8 Linn, D., & Hemmer, L. (2011). English language learner disproportionality in special education: Implications for the scholar-practitioner. *Journal of Educational Research and Practice, 1*(1), 70–80. doi:10.5590/JERAP.2011.01.1.0.

9 Jung, L. A., & Guskey, T. R. (2011). Fair & accurate grading for exceptional learners. *Principal Leadership, 12*(3), 32–37.

10 Hammond, H., Ingalls, L., & Trussell, R. P. (2008). Family members' involvement in the initial Individual Education Program (IEP) meeting and the IEP process: Perceptions and reactions. *International Journal about Parents in Education, 2,* 35–48.

11 Danielson, L., & Rosenquist, C. (2014). Introduction to the TEC special issue on data-based individualization. *Teaching Exceptional Children, 46*(4), 6–12.

12 Individuals With Disabilities Education Act, 20 U.S.C. § 1400 (2004).

13 Harry, B., & Klingner, J. K. (2014). *Why are so many minority students in special education? Understanding race & disability in schools* (2nd ed.). New York, NY: Teachers College Press.

14 Jung, A. W. (2011). Individualized education programs (IEPs) and barriers for parents from culturally and linguistically diverse backgrounds. *Multicultural Education, 18*(3), 21.

15 Individuals With Disabilities Education Act, 20 U.S.C. § 1400 (2004).

16 Morgan, R. L., Kupferman, S., Jex, E., Preece, H., & Williams, S. (2017). Promoting student transition planning by using a self-directed summary of performance. *Teaching Exceptional Children.* doi:10.1177/0040059917734383.

17 U.S. Department of Education, Office of Special Education and Rehabilitative Services, Office of Special Education Programs, *37th Annual Report to Congress on the Implementation of the Individuals with Disabilities Education Act, 2015,* Washington, DC, 2015.

18 McCray, E. D., Butler, T. W., & Bettini, E. (2014). What are the roles of general and special educators in inclusive schools? In J. McLeskey, N. L. Waldron, F. Spooner, & B. Algozzine (Eds.), *Handbook of effective inclusive schools: Research and practice* (pp. 80–93). New York, NY: Routledge.

Key Resources

- IRIS modules for assessment and collaboration. https://iris.peabody.vanderbilt.edu/iris-resource-locator/ This site includes multiple modules, case studies and videos to assist teachers in interpreting data and communicating/collaborating with key stakeholders.
- RTI based Toolkit for SLD Identification for ELL http://rtinetwork.org/getstarted/sld-identification-toolkit/ld-identification-toolkit-considerations-for-ell While this site focuses specifically on assessments for ELL that may have disabilities, it provides useful questions the IEP team can use in considering assessment results for students from CLD backgrounds.
- Harvard Family Research Project. www.hfrp.org/var/hfrp/storage/fckeditor/File/7-DataSharing-TipSheets-HarvardFamilyResearchProject.pdf This document includes tips for administrators, teachers, and families on how to effectively share data.
- Webinar- Data Driven: Making Student and School Data Accessible and Meaningful to Families. www.nationalpirc.org/engagement_webinars/archive-webinar3.html
- Resources special education teachers can share with parents. www.parentcenterhub.org/ *and* www.ecac-parentcenter.org/media-center/the-iep-team-process-videos/

6

Using Student Assessment Data, Analyzing Instructional Practices, and Making Necessary Adjustments That Improve Student Outcomes

Erica S. Lembke, R. Alex Smith, Cathy Newman Thomas, Kristen L. McMaster, and Erica N. Mason

Introduction

One of the most important but most difficult practices for teachers to understand and implement is that of using assessment data to analyze instructional practices and make necessary adjustments that improve student outcomes. Although this practice may be known by other names, such as Data-Based Program Modification (DBPM),[1] problem solving, or data-based individualization, the basic elements are consistent. These elements include (a) identifying a 'problem' that inhibits academic or behavioral growth, (b) developing a hypothesis regarding the cause of the problem, (c) creating and implementing a plan to address the hypothesis, (d) monitoring student progress, (e) establishing decision rules about when changes in instruction or intervention should be made, (f) using these decision rules in a timely manner, (g) determining and implementing what change might be needed, and (h) persisting in continuing these steps as long as the academic or behavioral difficulty continues.[2]

Rationale

The rationale for selection of data utilization as a high leverage practice is clear. Researchers have demonstrated that when teachers utilize data to make instructional decisions, student achievement improves.[3] In addition, when teachers examine data prior to making instructional decisions, they make more frequent and appropriate decisions than when they do not use data.[4] The benefits in the form of student gains are clear when data-based decision-making is employed. A review of studies on the effectiveness of Curriculum-Based Measurement (CBM) revealed that the vast majority of studies showed positive effects for student outcomes when CBM was employed, no matter the subject area.[5] However, educators do not often apply data-based decision-making in their practice. Studies have suggested that teachers sometimes find the process too time consuming,[6] feel they do not have the necessary training, or find such assessments are not credible.[7]

Instructional Purposes

Ongoing use of student assessment data allows special education teachers to analyze their instructional practices and make necessary adjustments to improve student outcomes for each student. Such individualized decision-making based on assessment data is critical for creating instructional routines for students that are specific to individual need. Additionally, data-based decision-making aids teachers in determining when to intensify instruction for students who are not responding to typical instruction. Teachers' ability to intensify instruction is important. Approximately 3 to 5% of students do not respond to evidence-based interventions that are broadly delivered and require individualized instruction.[8]

Intended Targets

Every teacher should use data-based decision routines to answer several questions: (a) Which of my students are at-risk for reading failure? To answer this question, teachers can use universal screening of all students in a class for academic or behavioral concerns and apply cut score rules based upon published benchmarks. Screening data informs the teacher as to whether or not risk is a class-wide concern, a small-group concern, or relegated to one or two students. The prevalence of risk in a class should be used to inform how the teacher selects and implements intervention. (b) Is my student improving? Examining the ongoing academic or behavioral progress of each student using regular progress monitoring can answer this question. (c) What key skills does this student(s) need instruction on? Diagnostic data should be collected to answer this question and to generate a hypothesis as to what intervention should be selected and implemented. General education classroom teachers can work with their grade-level or content teams to discuss data and hypothesize changes in instruction or intervention that might help support more students at the class level. Special education or intervention teachers might use data to intensify instruction for small groups of students with similar skill needs, for individual students who are at risk, or to develop Individualized Education Plans (IEPs).

Narrowing the Focus

In the remainder of this chapter, we focus on the use of data-based instruction (DBI) for special education teachers. Special educators are scientists in the classroom. They are continually collecting and interpreting data, reflecting upon their practices, hypothesizing about how to improve student learning via changes in their own practices, and making changes while monitoring students' response to their instruction. Just as a scientist never stops discovering and exploring the world through the scientific method, special educators never stop systematically reflecting upon and modifying their assessment and instructional practices for students with disabilities.

Chapter Overview

1. Provide general information regarding how to use data-based instruction.
2. Describe an example of the use of data-based instruction with a fourth-grade student, Camila, in reading fluency and comprehension.
3. Describe how the DBI process can help teachers address students' behavioral needs.
4. The following sections provide more information about how teachers can use data-based decision-making, including specific examples, implications for practice, and common barriers to implementation, including how barriers can be overcome.

General Information Regarding How to Use the Practice

DBI is a type of data-based decision-making that is more intense than what general education teachers may use, as it is highly individualized. DBI is a systematic approach to teaching that uses quantified data to monitor and revise instruction according to student learning.[9] The cyclical nature of DBI allows the special educator to determine what works for whom by following several steps (see Figure 6.1): (a) establish a present level of performance, (b) set an ambitious long-term goal, (c) generate

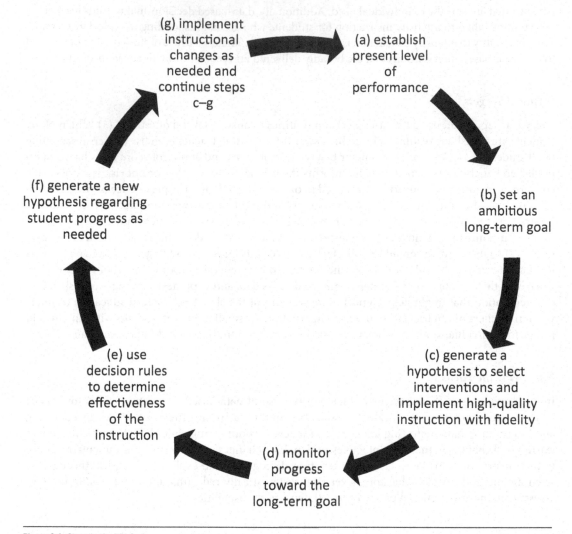

Figure 6.1 Steps in the DBI Cycle

a hypothesis to select interventions and implement high-quality instruction with fidelity, (d) monitor progress toward the long-term goal, (e) using decision rules to determine effectiveness of the instruction, (f) generate a new hypothesis regarding student progress where needed, and (g) either implement the instructional changes and repeat or continue "as is" if no change is needed. As this cyclical process suggests, special educators are continually reflecting upon their practice and making adjustments for each student.

Step A: Establishing Present Level of Performance

As a special educator begins the DBI process, the first question should be, "What is my student's present level of performance?" To answer this question, special educators need knowledge of different kinds of assessment. Curriculum-Based Measures (CBMs)[10] are quick academic assessments that are easy to administer and score. CBMs are reliable, valid, and sensitive to change. In other words, they reflect a student's academic proficiency; can be given on a regular basis, weekly or bi-weekly; and capture student learning. These characteristics allow teachers to graph the student's progress over time toward a long-term goal. There are many different types of CBMs available to assess progress in reading, spelling, writing, mathematics, and even science and social studies.

CBMs are often called global performance indicators because they indicate performance in a general skill or set of skills that are highly predictive of overall performance as opposed to measuring discrete skills. For example, number of words read correctly on grade-level passages is predictive of performance on decoding and comprehension tests,[11] although it may not measure mastery or progress in the ability to read specific letter sound patterns in decoding, such as /ant/, or measure comprehension of specific facts from the text. Thus, CBMs are a good assessment for screening, establishing a student's overall present level of performance, and setting ambitious long-term goals, but not necessarily for identifying specific strengths and weaknesses.

General and special education teachers can use CBMs to screen at the classroom level to identify the prevalence of risk within the class. For example, if over five students in a classroom of 30 students score below the 25th percentile according to published norms on the median score of three CBMs, then instruction should be addressed at the classroom level. The special education teacher may consult with the general education teacher to identify specific instructional practices they can use to address students' needs and develop a plan to implement practice and monitor class progress. If five or fewer students are identified as at-risk, then the special education teacher should consult with the general education teacher regarding small group instruction, possibly employing a collaborative teaching model. If only one or two students are identified as at-risk, then the special education teacher may consider individual or small-group pull-out instruction.

Step B: Set an Ambitious Long-Term Goal

To create an ambitious long-term goal, the teacher first administers three different grade-level CBMs, records the words read correctly per minute (WRCM) for each (when using reading CBMs), and selects the median score. This median score represents the student's baseline or present level of performance. If the student scored 18, 15, and 20 WRCM, then the baseline would be 18. Second, the teacher creates a goal that helps close the gap between the student's score and scores of same-age peers. For example, if the student's score is at the 10th percentile in the fall (i.e., 90% of students can be expected to perform better than the student), then the goal could be for the student to score in the 25th percentile by the end of the school year (i.e., 75% of students can be expected to score above the student). The teacher may also choose to use various other strategies to create a long-term goal,[12] but the predominant method is to use established benchmarks. According to reading fluency norms published by Reading Rockets (www.readingrockets.org/article/fluency-norms-chart), a third-grade student with a fall baseline performance of 18 is in the 10th percentile, and a spring performance of 78 is in the 25th percentile. These scores are represented in Figure 6.2.

Using a graphing program such as Microsoft Excel, the teacher plots the student's baseline and goal, with the vertical axis representing WRCM and the horizontal axis indicating weeks. A line is then drawn connecting the baseline to the long-term goal point in order to create a goal line by which the teacher can evaluate student growth during progress monitoring (see Figure 6.2). Once, a goal has been established for improving the students' reading fluency, the teacher should examine the student's strengths and needs to determine the focus and content of instruction as well as which intervention(s) may be the most effective.

Step C: Generate a Hypothesis, Select Interventions, and Implement With Fidelity

Continuing with the prior example, the special educator may choose to use a diagnostic measure such as the CORE Phonics Survey (2008), the Quick Phonics Screener (2001), or any of a number

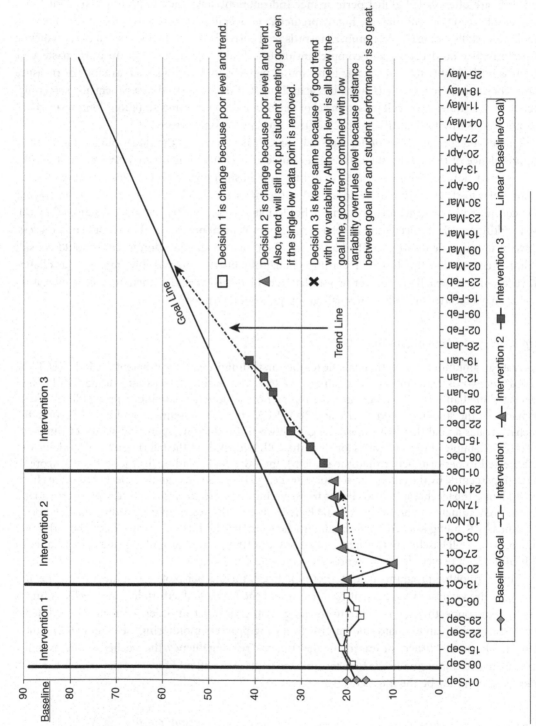

Figure 6.2 Sample Graph

of other available reading assessments. These assessments can inform the teacher about strengths and needs in decoding, vocabulary knowledge, or comprehension. Perhaps the student knows many common letter sounds and some letter combinations but struggles with words that end in silent *e*, high frequency irregular words, and multisyllabic words. The teacher would then select interventions that specifically target these skills. Additionally, analyses of writing samples and careful notes from observations of students' performance can inform the teacher's hypothesis regarding which interventions may work best. For example, perhaps the student becomes anxious when they know they are being timed. This information may influence the teacher's decision to modify certain interventions that have timed components or select interventions with fewer timed components. As another example, the student may resist reading when presented with long passages or too much text at once. The teacher may then modify selected interventions so that text is provided in shorter chunks. The teacher uses all relevant data to inform the hypothesis and select appropriate interventions. Evidence-based interventions across content areas and in behavior can be found on the What Works Clearinghouse, the Evidence-Based Intervention Network, and the National Center of Intensive Intervention (see resource section at the end of this chapter), to name a few. Once the interventions have been selected, the teacher implements them with fidelity.

Step D: Monitor Student Progress

While implementing the intervention, the teacher regularly monitors student progress to ensure growth toward the long-term goal. Using the previous example, the teacher draws a vertical line on her graph to indicate when a specific intervention began and administers a CBM-Reading (CBM-R) measure to the student once or twice a week. Each score should be plotted on the line graph (see Figure 6.2). She also tracks the percentage of words read correctly, as this can inform decision-making. As an example, a student who is not making progress in WRCM but is improving in the percentage of words read correctly (e.g., is reading fewer words but getting more of them correct) requires different instructional changes than a student not making progress in WRCM or in percentage of words read correctly. Teachers also take observational notes for each data point to inform later decision-making. For instance, it may be helpful to know that a student was ill or that a tornado drill occurred just prior to assessment, as such instances could result in unusually poor performance. Teachers should develop routines in progress monitoring assessment to ensure that CBMs are consistently administered and scored following standard procedures. Teachers may consider collaborating with other teachers to occasionally observe each other administer CBMs and check each other's scoring. This collaborative system can also serve to support teachers in decision-making and hypothesis generation. For example, if the special education teacher is collecting the progress monitoring data, sharing the graphed data with the general education teacher each week and discussing next steps for the student would be an important way to collaborate around data. Once enough data have been collected, typically six to ten weeks of data for CBM-R,[13] the teacher uses visual analysis to make a data-based decision.

Step E: Use Decision Rules to Determine Effectiveness of the Instruction

After six to ten weekly data points have been collected, the teacher evaluates the student's progress by answering these questions: (a) Are more data points above or below the goal line (level)? (b) Is there a lot of bounce in the data (variability)? (c) Does the student's trend indicate that he will meet his goal (trend)? Answers to these questions help the teacher determine whether to stay the course, increase the goal, or change instruction. Each component is addressed below and then collectively used to explain decisions indicated in Figure 6.2.

Level

If more data points are at or above the goal line than below it, students are progressing. More data points below the goal line than above indicate that instruction may need to change. Level, however, is not the sole determining factor. Teachers also consider variability and trend of data.

Variability

If the student has one or two unusually low or high data points, then teachers explore possible causes. The special education teacher analyzes the specific CBM probes aligned with outlying data points and observational notes taken in the classroom. She also speaks with the general education teacher to determine if there are any factors that may have contributed to the student's unexpected performance. Doing so might help her understand why the student did so well or poorly. If a data point seems the result of some anomaly, such as return from an extended absence, the special educator may consider eliminating that data point and recalculating the trend (e.g., slope). Alternatively, in the case of one or two unusually high data points, the special educator might look for consistencies amongst CBM probes and observational notes. For example, high data points might correspond with the topic of the CBM-R passage. As an example, the passages may be about animals, and the student likes animals. In this case, the student might have better vocabulary and sight word knowledge of words associated with animals (e.g., fur, feathers, talons, wings). Also, the teacher should evaluate errors on CBMs where the student scored high to determine if errors are consistent with other CBM forms. Finally, highly variable data across time may indicate difficulties with maintenance or issues with motivation. Perhaps the student has skills needed to perform well but is not motivated to do so on a regular basis. Again, this information should be used to inform changes in instruction.

Trend

Three decisions might be made following examination of the trend of data. First, if the trend indicates the student will exceed his goal, then the special educator raises the goal or allots more instructional time to other activities. Second, if the trend indicates the student will achieve the goal, then the special educator maintains the intervention. Third, if the trend indicates that the student will not meet the goal, then the special educator considers changing instruction. For example, in Figure 6.2, after examining trend and level, the special educator may make a change in instruction. Again, all three aspects of visual analysis (level, variability, and trend) should inform changes in instruction and/or goals.

Steps F & G: Generate a New Hypothesis and Continue the Cycle of DBI

Once visual analysis is complete and the special educator has decided whether or not to change instruction, he or she may require additional information to develop a hypothesis and inform actual changes in instruction. The special educator gains additional information about students through diagnostic assessments and then reflects on the effectiveness of her practice. Specifically, she asks the following questions: (a) Did I actually provide intervention as often and as long as I intended? (b) Did I implement the intervention with fidelity? (c) Was the student fully engaged during intervention? Conversations with the general education teacher about the student's performance on other classroom assignments would be important, as well as assessing how the student generalizes skills learned during intervention to other content instruction during the day. Once a decision regarding instruction has been made and a hypothesis is generated, the special educator draws another vertical line on the progress monitoring graph indicating a change in instruction and implements the revised intervention with fidelity. The DBI process repeats until the student meets his goal.

Figure 6.2 provides a model of how these aspects may be used in decision-making. Data for Intervention 1 is very stable and indicates a change in instruction according to both level and trend. For Intervention 2, both level and trend indicate a change in instruction. The special educator may consider the low data point and recalculate trend, but the trend, although slightly positive, still indicates that the student will not meet his goal. Data for Intervention 3 is stable and shows a positive trend that indicates the student will meet his goal. The level suggests a change of instruction, but the trend was more important because of the discrepancy between the student's current performance and goal line. This is why all three elements of visual analysis should be considered when making decisions.

The basic steps of DBI can be applied to core academic areas such as reading, writing, and mathematics, but this process is also valuable when examining data related to specific content areas, making instructional changes in content areas, and addressing behavioral changes. Teachers can also use technology for data-based decision-making processes, a point we discuss later.[14] Special educators can use DBI data to help their general education colleagues, as many students with high incidence disabilities receive much of their instruction in Tier 1 academics.

Applied Example of Data-Based Instruction in Reading

Ms. Walker, a special education teacher, serves third- through sixth-grade students who primarily have learning disabilities and/or emotional behavioral disorders. In her building, Cole Elementary, there is a diverse mix of students, with Hispanic students representing approximately 30% of the population. Ms. Walker has several Hispanic students whom she serves, and it is always challenging for her to distinguish between low achievement in reading that is possibly the result of a disability and low achievement caused by issues related to second language needs. One of the supports that Ms. Walker uses with all of her students is the DBI process. The data collected helps her make better and more frequent decisions about whether instruction is effective for each of her students. She knows that what works for one student may not work in the same way for others, so she collects ongoing progress data to determine whether instruction or intervention is meeting each individual student's needs.

Ms. Walker has been working with Camila, a fourth-grade student in her classroom, on reading fluency and comprehension. Ms. Walker has Camila for 60 minutes of reading instruction each day, during which Ms. Walker utilizes an evidence-based, structured literacy program to instruct Camila. Ms. Walker also administers a weekly, one-minute CBM oral reading measure to Camila and graphs these results. After six weeks of instruction, Ms. Walker compares Camila's data trend to the goal line that Ms. Walker set for her. At this point, Camila's data trend indicates that she is not on track to meet her long-term goal, so Ms. Walker decides to make a change in instruction. She talks with Camila's general education teacher, and they discuss recent classroom data from assignments, quizzes, and other reading activities that Camila has been completing. It seems that she is struggling with fluency due to some inefficiency in decoding and that vocabulary continues to be a struggle, particularly when Camila is trying to summarize what happened in a story. Ms. Walker and Camila's classroom teacher decide to implement some brief decoding and vocabulary practice into her reading instruction each day, and they agree that Ms. Walker will continue to collect CBM data. They will meet in four weeks to examine how the new change in instruction is working for Camila. They will also communicate this plan to Camila's parents and will include a copy of her graph. Ms. Walker feels confident that she is being responsive to Camila's needs.

Using DBI to Support Behavioral Needs

The DBI process can also help teachers identify and address students' behavioral needs; however, many schools do not use this approach.[15] We illustrate next the importance of using quantitative behavioral data in DBI and offer suggestions teachers can use.

Collect Classroom-Level Data

To get a picture of how all students within a general education classroom are doing socially, emotionally, and behaviorally, teachers can use efficient or existing measures. An efficient measure is a universal screening tool, such as The Social, Academic, and Emotional Behavior Risk Screener (SAE-BRS)[16] or the Behavior Assessment System for Children (BASC-3).[17] SAEBRS, for example, identifies students who might be at risk for social, academic, or emotional behavior problems. A general education teacher could follow the administration protocol and screen all her students. Once data are collected, the general education teacher could partner with a special education teacher, counselor, or social worker to collect additional data and then analyze results. One source of data is discipline referrals (ODRs). If a school uses a systematic ODR process that includes a universal form, operational definitions of behaviors that warrant referral (definitions that are observable and measurable), standardized procedures, staff training to promote consistency, and a system for organizing and analyzing data,[18] those data can combine with data from screening instruments to help teachers and other school personnel identify which students are at risk for continued problem behaviors.[19]

If data from a screener indicate that a large number of students require targeted (Tier 2) or intensive (Tier 3) behavioral intervention, data at the classroom level can inform general and special education teachers about aspects of the learning environment that promote or discourage appropriate behavior. For example, teachers might examine their classroom structure, students' opportunities to respond during instruction, and use of specific praise[20] to determine if they are implementing evidence-based classroom management practices sufficiently and if targeted or individualized supports are needed.

Identify the Problem and Create a Plan

Once teachers have identified students in need of targeted or individualized behavioral supports, the next step is to create a plan for addressing identified problematic behaviors. First, accurate data collection can occur when challenging behaviors are operationally defined in observable and measurable terms. Instead of describing a behavior as "rude" or "disrespectful," the teachers should use clear, objective behavioral descriptions, such as "makes off-topic comments" or "leaves classroom without permission." After operationally defining the challenging behavior, choose an intervention that addresses the underlying need (function of the behavior), and implement with fidelity.

Monitor Student Progress Toward Behavioral Goals

Once teachers or other professionals (e.g., school psychologists) operationally define undesirable behavior, they can gather direct observational data. At this point, they should determine the best approach for collecting student data. For example, for a student who "calls out" during whole-class activities, teachers or other observers may want to do a *frequency count*, tallying each time the behavior occurs, to determine how excessive the behavior is. For behaviors such as tantrums, or for students who are slow to start work, *duration* and *latency* may be more important than frequency. In these cases, the elapsed time can be captured using a stop watch.

Another common evidence-based data tool is an antecedent-behavior-consequence (ABC) chart.[21] In this case, a three-column chart is used to record the antecedent or event immediately preceding the behavior (e.g., the teacher assigned independent math work), the behavior itself (e.g., the student shouted, "I hate math!"), and the consequence or event that immediately followed (e.g., the teacher yelled, "Go to the office right now!"). After multiple observations, an ABC analysis may reveal the "function" or underlying purpose of the behavior. In this example, it is possible that the student wants to *escape* a math task, and by sending the student out of the room, the teacher may have inadvertently reinforced the behavior. Thus, the teacher may increase the likelihood that the student will misbehave during future independent math work. An ABC chart is a foundational aspect of functional behavioral analysis. Just as with academic DBI and data-based decision-making, behavioral data provides information needed to design and deliver instruction and intervention. Like academic content, behavioral skills that align with local and developmental expectations should be explicitly taught and measured.

Establish and Implement Decision Rules

While decision rules and progress monitoring tools are less developed in the area of behavior,[22] teachers are encouraged to conduct a visual analysis of level, trend, and variability of their graphically represented behavioral data[23] to determine if students are responding to interventions. Teachers should use data to continue "as is," make an instructional change, or increase students' goals. Because this process is cyclical, teachers should continue the process until students are no longer in need of targeted or individualized supports.

Using Technology to Support Data Collection and Analysis

Technology can support teachers by streamlining CBM data collection and management and producing sophisticated diagnostic reports.[24] Commercially available technology-based tools for behavioral data collection and analysis are available for use at the classroom, school, and district levels. Schools that are implementing Positive Behavior Interventions and Supports can use the School-Wide Information System (SWIS)[25] to capture ODR data. Similarly, AIMSweb can be used to record individual student scores for behavior and social skills across months and years and then compare individual scores to classroom, school, district, and national norms. For classroom-based data collection, teacher-friendly applications for smartphones, tablets, or computers are available for little or no cost. Applications can assist teachers in tracking tallies to conduct a frequency count (e.g., Tally), recording elapsed time for duration or latency information (e.g., Student/Classroom Observation and Analysis), and gathering ABC data (e.g., Behavior Snap). These applications can record, organize, store, and share information, which makes behavioral data easily accessible and usable within the DBI process.

Wrap Up

In this chapter, we discussed how special education teachers and school teams can use student assessment data to analyze instructional practices and make adjustments that improve student academic and behavioral outcomes. We described a systematic process whereby the teacher identifies a student's present level of performance, sets an ambitious long-term goal, implements research-based instruction matched to the student's needs, monitors student progress, uses decision rules to determine when instructional changes are needed, develops hypotheses to guide specific changes, and continues this process until the student reaches or exceeds the goal. This process, when implemented with fidelity using research-based assessment and instruction, shows promise for improving student outcomes.[26]

Tips

Despite its usefulness for improving instruction, teachers can find the ongoing use of formative assessment challenging to adopt and sustain in everyday practice. Current research is ongoing to determine how to ensure that teachers have the knowledge, skills, and supports needed to implement data-based decision-making. In this section, we offer recommendations and resources to support teachers' successful use of this process.

1. **Start small.** Successful data-based decision-making relies on accurate and effective implementation of a multi-component process, including administering, scoring, and graphing assessment data; implementing high-quality research-based instruction with fidelity; and making timely and appropriate instructional decisions. Each of these components takes time to learn and master. Fortunately, teachers report the process gets easier over time.[27] We recommend teachers begin with one component, allowing time for practice (with feedback from a more experienced teacher, coach, or administrator, if possible) to implement the component with fidelity. In addition, we recommend focusing data collection on one or two students at first to avoid being overwhelmed. For example, a teacher learning to collect CBM writing data might first collect and score several writing samples from one to two students. The teacher should focus on scoring accurately and reliably before starting to implement a new intervention. Once a teacher is reasonably comfortable with one component, it is important to add the next component, understanding that improvement will continue over time.

2. **Create routines and habits.** Data-based decision-making will be most effective when it is intentionally integrated into a teacher's regular practice rather than regarded as an additional responsibility. Such integration requires time. Teachers must organize systems that allow for effective and efficient data-based decision-making. This organized system might include (a) establishing schedules and procedures for collecting, scoring, graphing, and examining data on a regular basis; (b) creating systems for ensuring assessment and intervention materials are created, organized, and filed in a way that minimizes daily preparation; (c) using self-check procedures to ensure fidelity; (d) training others (e.g., educational assistants, students) to carry out these procedures as part of daily routines; and € celebrating when these routines are carried out successfully!

3. **Find collaborative supports.** Teachers need support if they are to collect and analyze data in ways that lead to improved student outcomes.[28] Teachers have reported that consistent, ongoing supports such as coaches and peers increase their sense of accountability, motivation, and likelihood of using data-based decision-making practices.[29] Coaches can provide consultation and feedback, and peers can share data and engage in problem solving that fosters decision-making.[30]

4. **Involve students.** Engaging students in the data collection process creates a shared sense of responsibility and can be a powerful motivator for students. Additionally, student outcomes improve when they engage in self-monitoring,[31] particularly when clear goals and reinforcers for appropriate behaviors are in place. Teachers need to train students in data procedures and monitor them to ensure they use procedures appropriately.

5. **Be persistent.** Interventions can take time to produce changes in students' academic or behavioral learning. It is important to be patient, systematic, and persistent in the search for "what works" for individual students. DBI decision-making should be "intensive, urgent, relentless, and goal-directed"[32] if it is to lead to improved and lasting student outcomes.

Notes

1 Deno, S. L., & Mirkin, P. K. (1977). *Data-based program modification: A manual*. Reston, VA: Council for Exceptional Children.
2 Deno, S. L. (1985). Curriculum-based measurement: The emerging alternative. *Exceptional Children, 52*(3), 219–232. Retrieved from https://doi.org/10.1177/001440298505200303

    McLeskey, J., Barringer, M-D., Billingsley, B., Brownell, M., Jackson, D., Kennedy, M., . . . Ziegler, D. (2017, January). *High leverage practices in special education*. Arlington, VA: Council for Exceptional Children & CEEDAR Center.
3 Stecker, P. M., Fuchs, L. S., & Fuchs, D. (2005). Using curriculum-based measurement to improve student achievement: Review of research. *Psychology in the Schools, 42*(8), 795–819. Retrieved from https://doi.org/10.1002/pits.20113
4 Stecker, P. M., Fuchs, L. S., & Fuchs, D. (2005). Using curriculum-based measurement to improve student achievement: Review of research. *Psychology in the Schools, 42*(8), 795–819. Retrieved from https://doi.org/10.1002/pits.20113

    Fuchs, L. S., Fuchs, D., Hamlett, C. L., & Stecker, P. (1991). Effects of curriculum-based measurement and consultation on teacher planning and student achievement in mathematics operations. *American Educational Research Journal, 28*(3), 617–641. Retrieved from https://doi.org/10.3102/00028312028003617
5 Stecker, P. M., Fuchs, L. S., & Fuchs, D. (2005). Using curriculum-based measurement to improve student achievement: Review of research. *Psychology in the Schools, 42*(8), 795–819. Retrieved from https://doi.org/10.1002/pits.20113
6 Wesson, C., King, R., & Deno, S. (1984). Direct and frequent measurement of student performance: If it's good for us, why don't we do it? *Learning Disability Quarterly, 7*(1), 45–48. Retrieved from https://doi.org/10.2307/1510260
7 Thomas, C., Allen, A., Ciullo, S., Lembke, E., Goodwin, M., & Judd, L. (under review). Exploring the perceptions of middle school administrators and teachers regarding response to intervention for struggling readers. *Journal of Learning Disabilities*.
8 Wanzek, J., & Vaughn, S. (2009). Students demonstrating persistent low response to reading intervention: Three case studies. *Learning Disabilities Research & Practice, 24*(3), 151–163.
9 Deno, S. L., & Mirkin, P. K. (1977). *Data-based program modification: A manual*. Reston, VA: Council for Exceptional Children.

    Stecker, P. M., Fuchs, L. S., & Fuchs, D. (2005). Using curriculum-based measurement to improve student achievement: Review of research. *Psychology in the Schools, 42*(8), 795–819. Retrieved from https://doi.org/10.1002/pits.20113
10 Deno, S. L. (1985). Curriculum-based measurement: The emerging alternative. *Exceptional Children, 52*(3), 219–232. Retrieved from https://doi.org/10.1177/001440298505200303
11 Wayman, M., Wallace, T., Wiley, H. I., Tichá, R., & Espin, C. A. (2007). Literature synthesis on curriculum-based measurement in reading. *The Journal of Special Education, 41*(2), 85–120. Retrieved from https://doi.org/10.1177/00224669070410020401
12 Hosp, M. K., Hosp, J. L., & Howell, K. W. (2007). *The ABCs of CBM: A practical guide to curriculum-based measurement*. New York, NY: Guilford Press.
13 Ardoin, S. P., Christ, T. J., Morena, L. S., Cormier, D. C., & Klingbeil, D. A. (2013). A systematic review and summarization of the recommendations and research surrounding curriculum-based

measurement of oral reading fluency (CBM-R) decision rules. *Journal of School Psychology*, *51*(1), 1–18. Retrieved from https://doi.org/10.1016/j.jsp.2012.09.004

14 Lembke, E., McMaster, K., & Stecker, P. (2012). Technological applications of curriculum-based measurement in elementary settings: Curriculum-based measurement in the digital age. In K. McMaster, C. Espin, S. Rose, & M. Wayman (Eds.), *A measure of success: The influence of curriculum-based measurement on education* (pp. 125–136). University of Minnesota Press. Retrieved from www.jstor.org/stable/10.5749/j.cttttxf9.14

15 Crone, D. A., Carlson, S. E., Haack, M. K., Kennedy, P. C., Baker, S. K., & Fien, H. (2016). Data-based decision-making teams in middle school: Observations and implications from the middle school intervention project. *Assessment for Effective Intervention*, *41*(2), 79–93. Retrieved from https://doi.org/10.1177/1534508415610322

16 Kilgus, S. P., Eklund, K., von der Embse, N. P., Taylor, C. N., & Sims, W. A. (2016). Psychometric defensibility of the Social, Academic, and Emotional Behavior Risk Screener (SAEBRS) teacher rating scale and multiple gating procedure within elementary and middle school samples. *Journal of School Psychology*, *58*, 21–39. Retrieved from https://doi.org/10.1016/j.jsp.2016.07.001

17 Reynolds, C. R., & Kamphaus, R. W. (2015). *Behavior Assessment System for Children-Third Edition (BASC-3)*. Circle Pines, MN: Pearson.

18 McIntosh, K., Campbell, A. L., Russell Carter, D., & Zumbo, B. D. (2009). Concurrent validity of office discipline referrals and cut points used in schoolwide positive behavior support. *Behavioral Disorders*, *34*(2), 100–113.

19 McIntosh, K., Campbell, A. L., Russell Carter, D., & Zumbo, B. D. (2009). Concurrent validity of office discipline referrals and cut points used in schoolwide positive behavior support. *Behavioral Disorders*, *34*(2), 100–113.

    Predy, L., McIntosh, K., & Frank, J. L. (2014). Utility of number and type of office discipline referrals in predicting chronic problem behavior in middle schools. *School Psychology Review*, *43*(4), 472–489. Retrieved from https://doi.org/10.17105/SPR-13-0043.1

20 Simonsen, B., Fairbanks, S., Briesch, A., Myers, D., & Sugai, G. (2008). Evidence-based practices in classroom management: Considerations for research to practice. *Education and Treatment of Children*, *31*(3), 351–380. Retrieved from https://doi.org/10.1353/etc.0.0007

21 Van Norman, R. (2008). ABC recording form. In J. O. Cooper, T. E. Heron, & W. L. Heward (Eds.), *Applied Behavior Analysis* (2nd ed.). Upper Saddle River, NJ: Pearson. Wehby, J. H., & Kern, L. (2014). Intensive behavior intervention: What is it, what is its evidence base, and why do we need to implement now? *Teaching Exceptional Children*, *46*(4), 38–44. Retrieved from https://doi.org/10.1177/0040059914523956

22 Wehby, J. H., & Kern, L. (2014). Intensive behavior intervention: What is it, what is its evidence base, and why do we need to implement now? *Teaching Exceptional Children*, *46*(4), 38–44. Retrieved from https://doi.org/10.1177/0040059914523956

23 Gage, N. A., & McDaniel, S. (2012). Creating smarter classrooms: Data-based decision-making for effective classroom management. *Beyond Behavior*, *22*(1), 48–55. Retrieved from https://doi.org/10.1177/107429561202200108

24 Fuchs, L. S. (2004). The past, present, and future of curriculum-based measurement research. *School Psychology Review*, *33*(2), 188–192.

25 May, S., Ard, W., Todd, A., Horner, R., Glasgow, A., Sugai, G., & Sprague, J. (2000). *School-wide information system*. Eugene, OR: University of Oregon.

26 Stecker, P. M., Fuchs, L. S., & Fuchs, D. (2005). Using curriculum-based measurement to improve student achievement: Review of research. *Psychology in the Schools*, *42*(8), 795–819. Retrieved from https://doi.org/10.1002/pits.20113

27 Poch, A., McMaster, K. L., & Lembke, E. (2018). *Teachers' perceptions of the usability and feasibility of data-based instruction for developing writers*. Manuscript in preparation.

28 Stecker, P. M., Fuchs, L. S., & Fuchs, D. (2005). Using curriculum-based measurement to improve student achievement: Review of research. *Psychology in the Schools*, *42*(8), 795–819. Retrieved from https://doi.org/10.1002/pits.20113

29 Poch, A., McMaster, K. L., & Lembke, E. (2017). *Teachers' perceptions of the usability and feasibility of data-based instruction for developing writers.*

30 Stecker, P. M., Fuchs, L. S., & Fuchs, D. (2005). Using curriculum-based measurement to improve student achievement: Review of research. *Psychology in the Schools*, *42*(8), 795–819. Retrieved from https://doi.org/10.1002/pits.20113

31 Shapiro, E. S., Durnan, S. L., Post, E. E., & Levinson, T. S. (2002). Self-monitoring interventions for children and adolescents. In M. R. Shinn, H. M. Walker, & G. Stoner (Eds.), *Interventions for academic and behavior problems II: Preventive and remedial approaches* (pp. 913–938). Bethesda, MD: NASP.

32 Zigmond, N. (2001). Special education at a crossroads. *Preventing School Failure*, *45*(2), 70–74.

Key Resources

- Data-Based Instruction Tools, Learning, and Collaborative Supports (DBI-TLC): www.cehd.umn.edu/edpsych/dbi-tlc/, http://education.missouri.edu/DBITLC. These sites provide information and resources for those interested in learning more about DBI and professional development, related to supporting early writing development.

- Evidence Based Intervention Network: http://ebi.missouri.edu/. This site provides guidance for selecting and implementing evidence-based interventions in classroom settings.

- IRIS Center: https://iris.peabody.vanderbilt.edu/. The IRIS Center provides in-depth modules and resources to help practitioners learn about evidence-based practices and interventions for all children, especially those with disabilities birth through age 21.

- National Center on Intensive Intervention: www.intensiveintervention.org/. NCII provides resources, tools charts that review the research base supporting progress monitoring and intervention tools, as well as implementation and instructional supports for educators to implement intensive academic and behavioral interventions.

- Research Institute for Problem Solving: www.cehd.umn.edu/EdPsych/RIPS/. RIPs provides resources, modules, and materials to guide researchers and practitioners in the process of problem solving.

Section 3
Social/Emotional/Behavioral High Leverage Practices

Edited by Timothy J. Lewis

Introduction to Social/Emotional/Behavioral High Leverage Practices

The high leverage practices in this section are foundational practices for special educators as they address social/emotional/behavioral needs of students with disabilities. These practices focus on skills that effective special education teachers use to support student success by establishing a consistent, organized, and respectful learning environment; providing feedback to guide students' behavior; explicitly teaching appropriate social behaviors; conducting functional assessments of student behavior; and developing behavior improvement plans as needed. Across each of the high leverage practices, effective special educators recognize that all behavioral supports are more effective when they are delivered in a caring, respectful, and culturally responsive manner.

As effective special educators develop consistent, organized, and respectful learning environments, they are guided by the knowledge that behavioral support strategies are more effective when delivered within the context of positive and caring teacher-student relationships. Practices that are critical in promoting student social and emotional well-being include establishing clear and consistent behavioral expectations and related rules to support a respectful, positive, predictable classroom. Special education teachers also develop consistent classroom procedures that become routine for students and develop procedures that are used to support student adherence to expectations, rules, and procedures.

To improve a student's social and behavioral learning, special education teachers provide feedback that is positive, instructive, and corrective. This feedback is specific, contingent on desired student behavior, and delivered as soon as possible after the desired behavior. It is also sincere and contextually appropriate and is responsive to the student's cultural background and experiences.

Some students with disabilities experience social/behavioral difficulties and engage in unsuccessful social interactions because they are unaware of social conventions or do not know how to respond in an acceptable way. To address this issue, special education teachers use effective instructional practices to teach students to use prosocial skills. The components of social skills instruction include developing an instructional logic, using strategies for engaging students and providing feedback, and employing strategies for providing students with opportunities for practice in natural settings.

Providing consistent learning environments and high-quality feedback, as well as teaching students social skills, are foundational practices that increase the likelihood that students with disabilities will demonstrate appropriate social behavior and enhance their ability to benefit from academic instruction. Unfortunately, foundational practices alone are not sufficient to address the behavioral needs of all students. To support these students, special education teachers must be prepared to collaborate with other professionals to conduct functional behavioral assessments of student behavior and use this information to develop a behavior support plan to address identified needs.

Finally, when using the high leverage practices that are described in this chapter, special education teachers should always keep two critical considerations in mind. First, it is always important to consider the cultural and language backgrounds and experiences of students as the social/emotional/behavioral needs of students are assessed and as strategies to address identified needs are developed and used. Second, one of the most effective approaches teachers can use to reduce problem behavior in the classroom is to provide students with well-designed, effective instruction. It is thus important that the practices in this section be used in concert with the effective instruction practices that are described later in this book to ensure that students with disabilities have the academic and behavioral supports they need to achieve success in school.

7

Consistent, Organized, Respectful Learning Environment

Talida M. State, Barbara S. Mitchell, and Joseph Wehby

Introduction

An organized, positive, and predictable environment is key to successful classroom management. A variety of evidence-based practices, such as physical arrangement, behavior management, delivery of explicit and engaging instruction, procedures to support prosocial behaviors, and procedures to discontinue inappropriate behaviors, exist to ensure student success in the classroom.[1] For example, setting up the desks to ensure visibility and mobility, having clear behavior and academic expectations, incorporating frequent opportunities to respond, providing behavior-specific praise, incorporating choice in academic tasks, and teaching predictable routines all constitute antecedents that will help students be successful in any classroom environment.[2] Effective classroom management is further enhanced when integrated with explicit instruction matched to students' needs and when teacher's efforts are supported by school and district-wide initiatives. The purpose of this chapter focuses on specific strategies teachers can use to develop and support a respectful, positive, predictable classroom.

Narrowing the Focus

Given the multitude of variables teachers should account for when considering their classroom management, it is difficult to target every single one of them. It is more effective to focus on critical variables that can make a lasting impact, such as expectations or daily routines teachers would like their students to perform independently. Teachers can create a consistent classroom environment by establishing clear expectations and rules, following predictable routines, and reinforcing students for contributing to this environment by following the established expectations and routines. Teachers and students together need to reach agreement on how the classroom should function so that everyone's needs for structure, respect, and motivation are met. Involving students in this process allows them to be the center of the learning process and to take ownership of the classroom along with the teacher.

The focus of this chapter is on establishing classroom expectations and rules that target multiple behaviors and on developing clear classroom procedures that cover critical times of the day. Having clear classroom expectations, rules, and procedures allows teachers to guide students' behaviors, as well as their own. The importance of establishing classroom expectations, rules, and procedures is frequently underestimated. Too often teachers rely on verbal conversations alone that take place with their students during the first day of class. Such brief conversations are not sufficient to establish a pattern of productive prosocial behaviors.[3] Instead, teachers have to actively engage, in a joint process, with their students to identify the classroom expectations, rules, and procedures, then explicitly teach and reinforce students for demonstrating those behaviors throughout the school year. In addition, follow-up booster teaching sessions are critical after naturally occurring transitions, such as winter break or sometimes even returning to school after a weekend.

Before addressing the specific strategies described in this chapter, we need to engage ourselves in a reflective mindset that will predispose us to be observant and respondent to our students' backgrounds. Engaging in a joint process where both teachers and students are active participants is critical. The classroom is a shared space, and the boundaries, characteristics, and interactions defining the classroom micro-community should be clear and comfortable for all.

Chapter Overview

1. Describe procedures for developing classroom expectations and related rules that support the development of a respectful, positive, predictable classroom.
2. Describe the development and use of consistent classroom procedures that become habit and routine for students and support a respectful, positive, predictable classroom.
3. Describe procedures that are used to encourage and support student adherence to expectations, rules, and procedures.

Classroom Expectations

Teachers and students alike have different personal styles and often have different perspectives about how a classroom should be run. While there is richness in being different, there is also potential for conflicts. For example, some teachers might have high levels of tolerance when it comes to background noise and movement, while other teachers are easily distracted. Similarly, some students need to be able to share ideas with a peer or move around the classroom to keep focused, while other students can be bothered by this apparent off-task behavior. Understanding one's level of tolerance and need for structure is crucial to ensuring everyone in the classroom is set up for successful interactions. One important way of managing varying tolerance levels and degrees of structure is to establish clear classroom expectations. Having clearly identified classroom expectations sets the stage for students to be successful, facilitates opportunities for teachers to have positive interactions rather than corrective exchanges with students, and may prevent a majority of minor behavior problems from ever occurring. Thus, an important first task for teachers is to be proactive by establishing classroom expectations from the first day of instruction.

Classroom expectations constitute specific guidelines for desired academic and social behaviors. Expectations define the types of behavior students should demonstrate while in the classroom. Typical expectations include behaviors such as being respectful, responsible, safe, and ready to learn. Classroom expectations are usually broad descriptors, guiding principles, or valued attitudes that direct students to success in school. Experts recommend teachers develop five or fewer expectations that are positively worded, thus informing students which behaviors they should demonstrate rather than focusing primarily on inappropriate behaviors[4] (see Figure 7.1 for example expectations).

When developing classroom expectations, teachers should decide who will have input in the development process. For example, in some cases the expectations may be defined by the teacher alone, such as in preschool or other early childhood classrooms. In other cases, such as with older children and youth, input from students and families could be included. Inviting students to participate in the development of expectations may generate greater inclination to consistently meet the expectations. In addition, when included in the development process, students may also acquire a more thorough understanding of the rationale for having clear expectations and in turn be more willing to uphold and adhere to them. However, a note of caution: when students are engaged with the development process, teachers may end up with too many expectations, expectations they don't find acceptable, or even different expectations for different sets of students. A good compromise is to develop an outline of teacher-acceptable classroom expectations ahead of time and then ask for student participation and input. When developing classroom expectations, it is important to consider anticipated or commonly experienced misbehaviors from students, daily activities taking place in the classroom, and the general makeup of the student body (e.g., grade level, number of students, functioning level, cultural background). Expectations should be broad enough to encompass multiple observable behaviors, cover different settings and activities, and enhance both behavior and academic outcomes. As examples, teachers often choose expectations such as "be respectful," "be responsible," "be safe," and "be kind." Expectations are deliberately brief, so they can be easily remembered.

Example High School Classroom Expectations & Rules

Think Responsibly Means. . .	Come Prepared Means. . .	Have Respect Means. . .	Show Self Control Means. . .
Listen	Be on time	Be courteous with each	Think before you speak or
Follow directions	Have needed materials	other	act
Be substance-free	Complete homework and	Use appropriate language	Keep hands, feet, and ob-
Adhere to the dress code	assignments	Use materials correctly	jects to self
	Move quickly and orderly to		Use controlled tone of voice
	destination		

Example Middle School Classroom Expectations & Rules

GO SAFELY Means. . .	SHOW RESPECT Means. . .	ACT RESPONSIBLY Means. . .
Keep hands, feet, and objects to self	Put belongings away when you	Actively listen and participate in class
Stay in assigned area	enter the room	activities
If someone bothers you. . .	Keep your work space clean and	Be on time
o ignore him/her or walk away	organized	Follow directions the first time asked
o say, "please stop"	Use materials for their intended	Complete your work
o get help from a teacher	purpose	

Example Elementary School Classroom Expectations & Rules

Safe Means. . .	Respectful Means. . .	Responsible Means. . .
Walk	Follow directions	Use appropriate voice level
Keep feet under desk	Listen to the speaker	Put things away
Push your chair in	Accept help	Take care of school property

Figure 7.1 Example Classroom Expectations and Rules

Classroom Rules

After three to five classroom expectations are identified, teachers can then define, with student input when appropriate, specific behaviors for meeting each expectation. For example, "be respectful" could be defined as listening to the teacher during lecture, waiting for your turn to speak during group activity, or entering the classroom quietly. These definitions are descriptions of desired behavior that leave no doubt between teacher and student about exactly what needs to be done. These behaviors are frequently referred to as "rules," which are the specific actions students do to meet the classroom expectations. When writing classroom rules, think about it as answering the question, "What does [respect, responsibility, best effort, etc.] mean or look like in this classroom?" (see Figure 7.1 for example rules). Another consideration that enhances the clarity of classroom rules is the explicitness with which they are written. To maximize understanding by all, classroom rules should be written in terms that are *observable* (behaviors we can see), *measurable* (we can count occurrences), *positively stated* (what we want students to do to be successful), *understandable* (student-friendly and age-appropriate language), and *always applicable* (the same rule is in effect every day).

Key in developing classroom rules is focusing on "what students should do instead." For example, many teachers would agree that blurting out or talking out of turn is a problem behavior that may interrupt instruction and learning. Rather than establishing a classroom rule to indicate "no shouting, talking, or blurting out," a more effective approach is to directly say what students should do in brief and clear language. In this case, "raise your hand and wait to be called on" might be an appropriate rule. A perennial challenge at the secondary level is for students to come to class on time and ready to learn. To encourage these success-oriented behaviors, the following classroom rules could be established: arrive to class on time, bring necessary materials, listen while the teacher is talking, complete assignments, and ask for help when you need it. Writing rules with this level of detail leaves little room for uncertainty about behaviors that are expected and promotes student success in school.

Classroom Procedures

In addition to clearly identified expectations and rules, student learning is enhanced when teachers develop consistent classroom procedures.[5] When students can predict the events throughout their school day, they are more likely to be engaged and less likely to display problem behavior. Predictable environments allow students to spend more time and energy actually engaged in the instructional activities rather than understanding or trying to figure out what to do. One way to increase predictability in a classroom is to establish classroom procedures early in the school year. Clear classroom expectations and rules are the basis for establishing procedures that become habit or routine among students. Specifically, classroom procedures are the method or process for how things are done in a classroom. Procedures provide students with a pattern for accomplishing particular classroom tasks such as lining up, taking attendance, making a lunch choice, sharpening pencils, having access to the restroom, or getting missed work after an absence. Clearly defined procedures create a vision of how to be a successful student. Classroom procedures allow students and teacher alike to function efficiently in an environment that is organized and predictable. Developed routines enable teachers to limit wasted instructional time due to constant interruptions required to explain procedures repeatedly. When procedures are in place, students will seamlessly complete basic tasks, such as warm-up, homework assignment and collection, bathroom breaks, group work, or dismissal, without teacher assistance. When these procedures become routine, student social and academic success quickly follows.

To create classroom procedures educators should consider all the activities they expect students to complete while in the classroom and then develop a list of steps needed for students to carry out those activities. The following is one example of an elementary level classroom procedure for using a learning position during whole group instruction.

Learning Position

1. Sit with your bottom on your chair.
2. Keep your legs under your desk.
3. Have both feet on the floor.
4. Look at the teacher while he or she is talking.
5. Keep necessary materials on top of your desk.

A second example provides explanation for lining up outside a secondary level classroom before the class period begins.

Lining Up

1. Be ready for class with pens/books.
2. Phones and hats away.
3. Store backpack correctly.
4. Stand in two quiet lines.
5. Face the front.
6. Enter the classroom and follow teacher directions.

In both examples, steps for accomplishing a common classroom task are explicitly laid out but with flexibility for individual teacher preferences and contextual fit for the specific classroom. All teachers will not have the same procedures, but all teachers should explicitly define steps within key classroom procedures and *explicitly teach* and *practice* all procedures.

To establish classroom procedures, teachers can use the following steps. First, make a list of common activities or tasks that will need to be completed in the classroom and consider particular problem areas or problem times of the day. Next, determine the desired outcome. What is it you want students to do? Third, write a list of steps that describe what students need to do to complete the task. Like classroom rules, be sure the written procedure steps are observable, measurable, positively stated, understandable, and always applicable (see Figure 7.2 for example procedures).

After establishing the classroom procedures, it can be helpful to check in with students about their knowledge and understanding of these. A teacher may have a clear vision in his or her mind of how common classroom tasks should be completed, but if this vision is not adequately taught and practiced the classroom environment may not convey consistency, organization, and respect. Checking in with students about classroom procedures can be completed in several ways. One example, for older students, is use of a self-assessment or quiz to test their knowledge of procedures (see Figure 7.3). Bonus points or other incentives could be offered for correct responses. For younger students, making a game could be fun but still also lets the teacher know how well the classroom procedures have been communicated.

Encouraging Adherence to Expectations, Rules, and Procedures

Once they are established, several simple strategies will increase the likelihood that students adhere to the classroom expectations, rules, and procedures. First, teachers should post the expectations and rules in places where they are visible to all. Procedures can also be posted visibly in parts of the room where students are likely to need them (e.g., procedures for pencil sharpening above the sharpener, procedures for lining up posted on the door). Posting the expectations, rules, and procedures is a visual reminder to students about how to demonstrate appropriate behavior but also serves as a

Example Elementary Class Procedures[6]

Room Areas/Use
- Student desks, tables, storage areas
- Learning centers, stations
- Teacher's desk, storage
- Drinking fountain, sink, bathroom

Whole-Class Activities
- Student participation
- Student attention during presentations
- Making assignments
- Passing out/collecting papers, books
- Handing back assignments
- Make-up work
- Checking class work or homework

Small Group Activities
- Student movement into and out of group
- Bringing materials to group
- Expected behavior of students in group
- Expected behavior of students out of group

Seatwork
- Talk among students
- Obtaining help
- Out-of-seat policy
- Activities after work is completed
- Turning in work

Other Procedures
- Beginning of day/class
- End of day/end of class
- When absent
- Transitions
- Substitutes
- Office referrals
- Student conduct during interruptions
- Leaving/returning to room
- Field trips

Example Secondary Class Procedures[7]

Room Areas/Use
- When you need paper and pencil
- Keeping your desk orderly
- Getting out materials
- Moving about the room
- Restroom, water fountains use

Managing Class Activities
- Getting to work immediately
- Listening to/responding to questions
- Participating in class discussions
- Passing in papers
- Exchanging papers
- Indicating whether you understand
- Coming to attention
- Working cooperatively in small group
- Changing groups/activities
- When you finish early
- Asking a question

Managing Assignments
- Returning homework
- Late or missing work
- Keeping your notebook
- Headings of papers
- Grading criteria

Other Procedures
- Entering the classroom
- End-of-period class dismissal
- When you are tardy
- When you are absent
- Going to the office
- Going to the library
- Handling disruptions
- Responding to a fire drill
- Responding to severe weather
- When visitors are in classroom
- If you are suddenly ill
- When the teacher is called away

Figure 7.2 Example Classroom Procedures

reminder to the teacher of what has been established. In addition, visibly posting the expectations, rules, and procedures will help substitute teachers, volunteers, and visitors navigate the environment. Besides posting them, effective teachers consistently use the language of the expectations, rules, and procedures to either praise students or provide corrections throughout the class. For example, if

1. What is the classroom attention signal? When does the teacher use it?
2. What is the procedure/routine for entering/exiting the classroom?
3. What is the procedure/routine for personal belongings (e.g., hats, coats)
4. What is the procedure/routine for obtaining materials/supplies?
5. What is the procedure/routine for the start of class?
6. What is the procedure/routine to gain assistance?
7. What is the procedure/routine for working in groups?
8. What is the procedure/routine for working independently?
9. What is the procedure/routine for meeting personal needs (e.g., restroom)?
10. What is the procedure/routine for turning in homework?
11. What is the procedure/routine for making up missed work?

Figure 7.3 Classroom Procedures Student Self-Assessment, Quiz, or Game

students are working quietly, the teacher could thank students by saying, "Class, thank you for being respectful" (classroom expectation). "I notice you are remembering to stay quiet during work time" (classroom rule). "This allows others to work undisturbed" (rationale for expectation and rule). Alternately, if students are becoming too noisy during group work, the teacher could point to or reiterate the posted classroom expectation and rule as a way of reminding students to be respectful by using their inside voice when working in groups.

Second, in addition to posting and consistently referring to and using the language of the expectations, rules, and procedures, teachers must also provide explicit instruction. Simply posting and discussing them is not enough. Students will need direct instruction and guided practice with the desired behaviors. Similar to teaching academic skills, a "tell, show, practice" or "I do, we do, you do" approach can be used to teach social and behavioral skills (see Chapter 9 for more information on teaching social behavior). The following steps have been recommended in the literature: a) explicitly teach classroom expectations, rules, and procedures by using examples and non-examples, providing opportunities to practice, and checking for understanding; b) actively supervise students and monitor demonstrations of behavior; and c) use immediate positive and/or corrective feedback to encourage desired behaviors or discourage problem behaviors. Note that the use of examples and non-examples should encompass not only violation of major safety issues (e.g., fighting, destroying property) but also debatable misdemeanors such as showing disrespect by facial expressions or use of sarcastic tone of voice.

Third, a menu or continuum of strategies for acknowledging student-appropriate behavior should be developed and regularly used. Strategies can be as simple as giving specific praise, such as, "Thank you for working quietly, this is a great way to be respectful and a learner." Research consistently shows teacher praise is one of the most empirically sound and influential practices for behavior change.[8] When praise is focused on positive actions, such as demonstration of classroom expectations, rules, or procedures, teachers help students develop a sense of competency and autonomy.[9] For some students whose behavior is more resistant to change, the menu of strategies may also include a token, tangible item, or access to a preferred activity. Whatever the teacher selects as a method for acknowledging students, the key message is that high rates of recognition will foster continued demonstration of desired behaviors over time and across settings (see Chapter 8 for more information on providing feedback).

Fourth, a hierarchy of response strategies that discourage problem behavior should be in place to guide students. Teachers need to decide what misbehaviors they will manage in the classroom versus those that will require administrator assistance. Once minor, moderate, and major problems are categorized, teachers can select methods of response for correcting violations. For early-stage misbehaviors (i.e., early in the behavior chain of events or low-level behavior problems) teachers can choose from a menu of simple corrective strategies such as proximity, redirect, reteach, or conferencing. For example, if a student is demonstrating off-task behavior by talking to a peer, the teacher could use proximity, make eye contact, point to the rule, give praise to a student who is engaged with the task, or provide a verbal reminder to stay focused and on task. Effective verbal reminders should be brief, delivered in proximity, and using a clear and respectful tone. In addition, all response strategies should include an instructional component—meaning identify what the student should be doing instead of the problem behavior. Some response strategies will also include additional opportunities for modeling, practice, and feedback. If the student does not conform and the misbehavior continues or escalates, the teacher can intensify the response by having a problem-solving conversation with the student after class involving the parents or administration. In Figure 7.4 an example system for responding to student problem behavior is provided. The example is organized such that as the intensity of problem behavior increases the instructional opportunity within the response strategy also increases. Teachers should adopt a response to problem behavior similar to students who demonstrate a learning error in reading, writing, or math: signal an error has occurred and provide additional instruction and re-teaching opportunities. This additional instruction will ensure

	Minor & Major Problem Behaviors	Intensity	Adult Responses
Level 1	• Refusal to follow directions • Scowling • Crossing arms • Pouting	Behavior is confined only to the focus student	• Ignore • Proximity • Nonverbal signals
Level 2	• Slamming textbook closed • Dropping book on the floor • Name calling • Inappropriate language	Behavior disrupts others in the student's immediate area	• Proximity • Redirect • Reteach • Provide choice
Level 3	• Throwing objects • Yelling • Defiance of teacher directions • Leaving the classroom	Behavior disrupts everyone in the class	• Proximity, redirect, reteach, provide choice • Student conference—may include a consequence to decrease behavior • Increase prevention strategies
Level 4	• Throwing objects • Yelling • Defiance of school personnel's directions • Leaving school campus	Behavior disrupts other classrooms or common areas of the school	• Assess child's level of escalation • Use response strategies to de-escalate
Level 5	• Display of weapons • Assault on others	Behavior causes or threatens to cause physical injury to student or others	Implement the safety plan immediately (i.e., assess safety of all involved parties to determine whether to remove student or class)

Figure 7.4 Example Hierarchy of Response Strategies for Problem Behavior

that the student understands the correct response and is given the opportunity to practice the correct response with positive feedback and acknowledgement.

Wrap Up

This chapter described key considerations for establishing a consistent, organized, respectful, culturally responsive learning environment. Recommended practices include development of three to five positively stated classroom expectations, development of rules for meeting those broad expectations, and identification of classroom procedures that will be commonly encountered across a school day. In addition to development of classroom expectations, rules, and procedures, this chapter also provided information about the need for explicit instruction that teaches students how to meet the expectations, adhere to the rules, and use the classroom procedures. Instruction alone will be adequate for many students, but some students will also need high rates of feedback about their demonstrations of behavior. The majority of feedback should be positive, noticing the student's appropriate behaviors. Attention given to problem behavior should be minimal, and when necessary the teacher should follow an established hierarchy of response that includes instructional components (e.g., maintain focus on what to do, provide practice opportunities, give feedback).

In sum, expectations, rules, and procedures are most effective when they are easy to understand and follow, commonly agreed upon, and consistently encouraged and rule breaking behaviors are promptly discouraged. Setting up predictable and supportive environments helps teachers clarify what behaviors they want to see from their students and also helps the students predict what behaviors to expect from the teacher (see the Key Resources section of this chapter for additional resources). The following tips are offered for consideration in setting up a positive and supportive classroom:

1. **Stay focused on what you want students to do.** Teachers often become bogged down in repeated reminders or responses to student problem behavior. A more effective approach is to direct a majority of attention to what it is you want students to do instead of the problem behavior. Once teachers identify what they want students to do, this becomes the foundation for a classroom expectation, rule, or procedure that can be taught.
2. **Teach classroom expectations, rules, and procedures in the same way you would teach academic skills.** Having clearly identified classroom expectations, rules, and procedures is an important first step in establishing a consistent, organized, respectful learning environment, but simply having them and telling them to students on the first day of school or including them in a syllabus is insufficient. Students need a rationale as to why expectations, rules, and procedures are important in the classroom and explicit instruction. Specifically, teachers must tell what the expectations, rules, and procedures are; show what they look like through demonstrations and modeling; provide examples and non-examples; facilitate practice opportunities; and give ongoing feedback about performance. Explicit teaching of expectations, rules, and procedures is even more important when expectations in the home and community are greatly different than in the school setting.
3. **Consistently use the language of your classroom expectations, rules, and procedures.** Substantial thought and consideration, from both the teacher and students, is required during development of the expectations, rules, and procedures. Once established, these should be the consistent language of the classroom. Teachers can regularly refer to the expectations, rules, and procedures as part of their instructional routine. Language of the expectations, rules, and procedures should also be embedded when recognizing and acknowledging student behavioral success or when correcting problem behavior.

Notes

1 Simonsen, B., Fairbanks, S., Briesch, A., Myers, D., & Sugai, G. (2008). Evidence-based practices in classroom management: Considerations for research to practice. *Education and Treatment of Children, 31*, 351–380. doi:10.1353/etc.0.0007.
2 Kern, L., & Clemens, N. H. (2007). Antecedent strategies to promote appropriate classroom behavior. *Psychology in Schools, 44*(1), 65–75. doi:10.1002/pits.20206.
3 Reinke, W. M., Herman, K. C., & Stormont, M. (2013). Classroom-level positive behavior supports in schools implementing SW-PBIS: Identify areas for enhancement. *Journal of Positive Behavior Interventions, 15*(1), 39–50. Retrieved from www.eric.ed.gov.ezproxy.lib.lehigh.edu/contentdeli very/servlet/ERICServlet?accno=ED540773
4 Sugai, G., & Horner, R. (2002). The evolution of discipline practices: School-wide positive behavior supports. *Child and Family Behavior Therapy, 24*(1–2), 23–50. doi:10.1300/J019v24 n01_03.
5 Soar, R. S., & Soar, R. M. (1979). Emotional climate and management. *Research on Teaching: Concepts, Findings, and Implications*, 97–119.
6 Evertson, C. M., Emmer, E. T., & Worsham, M. E. (2007). *Classroom management for elementary teachers* (7th ed.). New York, NY: Allyn & Bacon.
7 Wong, H., Wong, R., Rogers, K., & Brooks, A. (2012). Managing your classroom for success. *Science and Children, 49*(10), 60. Retrieved from https://search-proquest-com.ezproxy.lib. lehigh.edu/docview/1023451667/fulltextPDF/199640C68B4349EEPQ/1?accountid=12043
8 Maag, J. W. (2001). Rewarded by punishment: Reflections on the disuse of positive reinforcement in schools. *Exceptional Children, 67*(2), 173–186. doi:10.1177/001440290106700203.
9 Davis, S. (2007). *Schools where everyone belongs: Practical strategies for reducing bullying.* Champaign, IL: Research Press.

Key Resources

Classroom Management (Part 1): Learning the Components of a Comprehensive Behavior Management Plan. This module highlights the importance of establishing a classroom management system that includes expectations, rules, procedures, and consequences. Retrieved from https:// iris.peabody.vanderbilt.edu/iris-resource-locator/?term=behavior-classroom-management

Classroom Management (Part 2): Developing Your Own Comprehensive Behavior Management Plan. This module guides users through steps to create their own classroom behavior plan. Retrieved from https://iris.peabody.vanderbilt.edu/iris-resource-locator/?term=behavior-class room-management

Supporting and Responding to Behavior: Evidence-Based Classroom Strategies for Teachers. This technical brief summarizes evidence-based, positive, proactive, and responsive classroom behavior intervention and support strategies for teachers. Retrieved from www.pbis.org/resource/1016/ supporting-and-responding-to-behavior

Classroom Expectations Content Acquisition Podcast and Classroom Procedures and Routines Content Acquisition Podcast. Retrieved from http://pbismissouri.org/educators/effective-class-practice/

PBIS Technical Brief on Systems to Support Teachers' Implementation of Positive Classroom Behavior Support. This technical brief summarizes proactive, efficient, and evidence-based systems for supporting teachers' implementation of positive classroom behavior support (PCBS) practices school-wide. Retrieved from www.pbis.org/resource/1117/pbis-technical-brief-on-systems-to-support-teachers-implementation-of-positive-classroom-behavior-support

Freeman, J., & Simonsen, B. (2016). Systems to support teacher's implementation of PBIS in the classroom. Webinar www.youtube.com/watch?v=0reUiQEGhTg

8

Using Feedback to Improve Student Outcomes

Allison Bruhn, Jennifer Freeman, Regina Hirn, and Lee Kern

Introduction

Students who engage in social, emotional, and behavioral problems are a challenge to all educators, including veteran teachers. The challenge, however, is particularly formidable for beginning special education teachers who generally have little classroom experience and limited repertoires of effective management strategies.[1] These teachers find they are spending a significant portion of the school day addressing problem behavior, with little time for teaching. This leads to feelings of frustration, inadequacy, and eventually, burnout.

There are several reasons why beginning special education teachers find students' emotional and behavioral problems so challenging.[2] First, over half of special education teachers working with students with Emotional/Behavioral Disorders (EBD) lack full certification.[3] Untrained teachers lack familiarity with interventions that can successfully prevent and reduce problem behavior.[4] Further, teachers with emergency certification report lower levels of competence in many areas, including planning instruction, providing instruction, addressing behavior and social skill problems, managing their classrooms, working with families, and collaborating with others.[5]

In addition, many teachers fail to implement evidence-based practices after entry into the field, which could be a result of the aforementioned inadequate training. For instance, in a study utilizing interviews and observations, Jones found that 60% of participating special education teachers expressed doubt about the value of research, with half of those expressing open criticism, reporting "disdain" and "lack of trust."[6] Further, few evidence-based practices were seen during classroom observations, even among the teachers who reported extensive use.

Finally, because of the significant needs of students with EBD, paraprofessionals are frequently hired to offer support inside and outside of the classroom.[7] Such positions typically are not associated with educational training requirements.[8] As a result, individuals in school settings with the least amount of training are often responsible for both instruction and behavior management of students who are often the most challenging.

Regrettably, effective management skills are not quickly acquired while teaching. For example, the majority of in-service teachers are not familiar with common universal strategies that prevent problem behavior and teach school expectations[9] nor are they aware of common programs with substantive evidence for successfully reducing problem behavior.[10] It is also concerning that nearly half of general educators view common evidence-based practices for preventing and reducing problem behavior (e.g., behavior support or management plans, choice making opportunities, curricular modifications, social skills instruction) as far less important than special educators.[11] The frequent and unfortunate consequence of having inadequate skills to reduce problem behaviors is high teacher turnover.[12]

Narrowing the Focus

Although the foregoing data portend poorly for both students with challenges as well as teacher longevity, teachers can use high leverage practices to incur pervasive and positive effects on student behavior and academic performance. One such practice is teacher-provided feedback to students to reinforce pro-social skills.

Chapter Overview

1. Describe the effective use of feedback to support students' pro-social skills.
2. Describe examples and non-examples of applications of feedback across a range of grade levels and instructional contexts.
3. Describe strategies that teachers can use to implement high rates of specific, positive feedback throughout each school day.

Feedback: Positive, Instructive, Corrective

Feedback is a high leverage practice often cited as one of the most powerful influences on students' academic, social, and behavioral learning.[13] Although feedback can take many forms (e.g., spoken, written, gesture), by its most general definition, it is simply information provided to someone that improves or maintains performance. Teachers use several types of feedback, including positive, instructive, and corrective.

Positive Feedback

Positive feedback is explicitly defined as a statement demonstrating approval of a behavior. When the positive acknowledgment describes a specific behavior, it is called behavior-specific feedback. For instance, a teacher may see that rather than blurting out an answer in class, Izzy raises her hand and waits to be called on. When using behavior-specific feedback, the teacher might say, "Great job raising your hand, Izzy. I appreciate you waiting to be called on!" In this scenario, the teacher has provided positive feedback (i.e., great job) for a specific behavior (i.e., raising your hand), which helps the student connect the positive acknowledgement to her behavior.[14] Not only can this help increase the likelihood Izzy will raise her hand in the future, but the behavior-specific feedback can serve as a prompt to other students in the classroom to do the same. Had the teacher simply said, "Good job," then Izzy and her classmates may not know what behavior the teacher was acknowledging. In this case, the lack of specificity would not have the same reinforcing effect. Instead, the specificity of the feedback helps describe the desired and expected behavior to Izzy and her classmates. Beyond fostering desirable academic and social behaviors, positive feedback can help nurture a healthy and welcoming classroom climate, particularly when delivered at a higher rate when compared to reprimands. Conventional wisdom is that for every one reprimand or corrective, four specific positive feedback statements to that student are desirable.[15]

There is research evidence suggesting positive feedback is most effective when it is descriptive, that is, behavior-specific.[16] Behavior-specific feedback has been linked to increases in on-task behavior, task completion, work accuracy, and decreases in problem behavior among students with a range of ages and abilities, including those with EBD and learning disabilities.[17] Further, as students encounter various academic and social challenges, research has shown that process-centered feedback, rather than person-centered feedback, is more effective in fostering engagement, motivation, and perseverance.[18] Person-centered feedback sounds like, "You are so smart!" or "You are such a good boy!" This type of feedback alludes to intelligence or behavior being fixed within the student, which can be detrimental because students learn their achievement or behavior is not something they can change—it just is what it is. On the other hand, process-centered feedback sounds like, "You really worked hard on your math assignment. I like the strategies you used to solve those problems," or "You did a great job working quietly and waiting for help patiently when you were frustrated." This type of feedback indicates what students did well and provides a cue for what they can do in the future in similar situations.[19] It also implies that students can exercise control over their own behavior, and in fact it is not fixed (as implied by person-centered feedback). By using behavior-specific, process-centered feedback, teachers can facilitate motivation, resilience, and learning, which are critical for achievement in and out of school.

Instructive Feedback

Instructive feedback is a technique designed to make learning more efficient for students by providing additional information about student responses or behavior.[20] The goal is to teach more in the same amount of time. Typically, instructive feedback has been used to teach an academic skill by confirming and repeating correct student responses, emphasizing previously learned concepts, or adding new information. In practice, a teacher might ask students, "What is 2 + 3?" A student may respond, "Five." A teacher may deliver instructive feedback by saying, "That's right! 2 + 3 is 5. And, 3 + 2 is also 5. You can put the addends in any order and get the same answer!" Instructive feedback does not require the student to respond to the additional information.

Although this type of feedback is most often associated with academic learning, it also can be used for social and behavioral learning. First, teachers must explicitly teach the behaviors they expect students to display. While they are teaching these behaviors through concrete examples, they can provide instructive feedback throughout the learning process. For example, a teacher may be teaching students what it means to be respectful during whole group instruction by describing and modeling respect. Then, the teacher may ask students, "What are some things you can do to show respect while I am teaching the whole class?" A student may raise his hand and say, "You can raise your hand when you want to speak." The teacher can provide instructive feedback by saying, "That's right, Michael, you can raise your hand to speak exactly like you did just now. It is also important to wait to be called on while you are raising your hand just like you did." The idea is that students' positive behavior will be acknowledged, and this helps them acquire information about desired behaviors. Like positive feedback, instructive feedback has evidenced success across a range of ages and learners, including those with mild, moderate, and severe disabilities, and across a range of skills and behaviors.[21] When teachers provide instructional and emotional support in the form of feedback, they help foster a positive classroom climate and, in turn, enhance academic achievement—particularly for young students with high academic and behavioral risk.[22]

Corrective Feedback

Unlike positive and instructive feedback, corrective feedback is used to correct social or academic behavior errors by highlighting the error and then providing information on how to correct it. This is differentiated from a reprimand, which is a correction that is delivered harshly with little to no information on how to correct the behavior. Although reprimands may result in an immediate reduction of problem behavior, they may not produce long-lasting behavioral change because no positive behaviors are taught to replace the problem behavior being reprimanded. Hence, corrective feedback is preferred over reprimands, as it is more likely to result in sustained behavioral change.

When using corrective feedback as a strategy for responding to inappropriate behavior, a teacher briefly describes the incorrect behavior and then offers a suggestion for what can be done differently.[23] In this way, the teacher is helping the student to acquire the desired behavior much like s/he would do when a student makes an academic error. If a student is asked to come to the white board to write the answer to a math problem, the teacher is not going to admonish the student by saying, "No! That's not the answer. You should know that!" Instead, the teacher is going to look for the source of the error and provide a gentle prompt on how to correct the error. Similarly, when students make low-level behavioral errors such as blurting out an answer in class or being off-task, a teacher can calmly, immediately, and specifically provide corrective feedback by focusing on what the student needs to do instead. For instance, if Silas is talking to other students when he should be doing independent reading, the teacher may (in a calm tone) say, "Silas, instead of talking to your neighbor, please work quietly on your independent reading." This differs from a reprimand that might sound more like, "Silas, stop talking!" In other words, corrective feedback focuses on what the teacher wants students to do, not what s/he does not want them to do. Again, like other types of feedback and as opposed to harsh reprimands, corrective feedback contributes to creating a safe, positive, and productive learning environment that results in higher rates of academic and behavioral learning.[24]

Characteristics of Effective Feedback Strategies

Effective feedback, whether positive, instructional, or corrective, exhibits several key characteristics. Effective feedback is specific,[25] contingent,[26] timely,[27] sincere,[28] contextually and culturally relevant,[29] and applied appropriately within the phases of learning.[30]

Specific

Specific feedback directly names the targeted behavior. For example, rather than saying "good job" or "please stop," a teacher says "thank you for working quietly" or "please remember to stay in your seat during independent work time." By specifically naming the behavior when providing feedback, the teacher ensures the student is able to fully understand the expected behavior.[31]

Contingent

Effective feedback also must be contingent on a target behavior. That is, feedback is delivered only when the target behavior is observed and not delivered in the absence of a target behavior.[32] For example, when an eighth-grade class is working effectively in cooperative groups, a teacher may provide positive feedback to the class, noting they are meeting expectations. However, if the whole class is not working effectively in groups the teacher should not offer feedback on effective cooperative work to the whole class. Otherwise, the class may misconstrue what is expected of them.

Timely

Feedback should be delivered immediately or as soon as possible following a target behavior.[33] Timely feedback facilitates learning by (a) making sure students connect the behavior with the feedback and

(b) allowing students to maintain or adjust their behavior as quickly as possible. This is particularly important for younger children who may not clearly remember engaging in a target behavior later in the day or on subsequent days. However, even for older students' timely feedback provides them with the opportunity to adjust their behavior in order to maximize learning potential. For example, if Arika does not put away her lab equipment properly and the teacher waits until the end of class to provide corrective feedback she is likely to continue to put the lab equipment away incorrectly. She then practices the incorrect behavior rather than having an opportunity to learn the appropriate way to put lab equipment away. Similarly, consider Jonas, who is just learning to ask a teacher for help when he is struggling with an assignment. He raises his hand and the teacher helps him. However, the teacher does not acknowledge his hand-raising behavior until later in the afternoon when she sees him in the hallway. Although the teacher provides feedback to Jonas, it is not timely, and Jonas may have forgotten he even raised his hand. If Jonas does not make the connection between his behavior earlier in the day to the delayed feedback, he is less likely to raise his hand to ask for help in the future and may revert to previous more efficient behaviors for getting help (e.g., calling out) or avoiding difficult work (e.g., putting head down). Timely feedback that occurs in close proximity to the desired behavior maximizes instructional time by ensuring students do not waste time engaging in incorrect behaviors and increases the rate at which they practice desired behaviors.

Sincere, Contextually and Culturally Relevant

Feedback, as a key component of effective instruction, should always be delivered in a sincere tone of voice, void of sarcasm or joking.[34] For example, if the teacher says, "Thanks a lot for getting started on your work right away," in a sarcastic tone of voice, students may not perceive this as sincere or reinforcing and may be less likely to get started on their work quickly in the future. Additionally, different students may not respond similarly to the same feedback. To maximize the effectiveness of feedback, teachers must ensure that their feedback takes individual student characteristics and learning histories into account. For example, Jasper and Quincy cleaned up their art materials neatly. The teacher provides verbal feedback to them in front of the class. Quincy, who loves public attention, finds the feedback in front of his peers highly reinforcing and is more likely to clean up neatly in the future. However, Jasper is shy and finds that exact same feedback "punishing" rather than reinforcing. In order to deliver effective feedback teachers must understand that the way in which students' ages, learning histories, cultural backgrounds, and preferences, as well as classroom dynamics, all impact the way feedback is received.[35] For example, some adolescents, who tend to be peer focused, may prefer private feedback from the teacher rather than public feedback in front of their peers. Similarly, a student whose learning history or culture includes values centered in communal responsibility may respond more positively to group rather than individual feedback. Teachers should monitor student's response to feedback to ensure they are delivering feedback effectively and that students are receiving it and responding as expected.

Applied Within Phases of Learning

Finally, the type and frequency of feedback should be adjusted to facilitate students' progression through the phases of learning.[36] When learning new skills, students progress through five basic stages of learning: basic acquisition of a skill (ability to do something accurately), fluency (ability to perform the skill at a functional rate), maintenance (ability to perform the skill across time without re-teaching), generalization (ability to perform a skill across settings, teachers, formats), and adaptation (ability to modify skill use across contexts or purposes).[37] In order to maximize the effectiveness of feedback, teachers must consider the student's phase of learning.

When students are first learning a new skill (acquisition), feedback should be delivered frequently and focus on shaping and supporting students' accuracy with a particular behavior. When students are able to perform a skill accurately but are working to improve fluency, teachers should continue to provide high rates of feedback, but it should now focus on the rate of performance. In this way, as students progress through the phases of learning, teachers continue to modify the focus of the feedback to match the students' learning needs. For example, Ms. Robbie taught her first graders to play rock-paper-scissors as a strategy to use for settling peer disagreements such as who should go first. After initially teaching her students how to play, Ms. Robbie focused on providing frequent specific feedback to students who were able to play accurately and frequent instructional feedback to students who still needed support. As students mastered playing accurately, Ms. Robbie altered the focus of her feedback to helping students use the strategy efficiently. That is, she faded the frequency with which she provided feedback focused on accuracy and increased her feedback related to things like quickly deciding to use the strategy, playing rock-paper-scissors, determining the winner, and deciding who should go first and moving on with the activity. As students began to use the strategy accurately and fluently, she modified her feedback again to focus on encouraging students to use the strategy over time and in new contexts. In this way, Ms. Robbie was able to maximize the effectiveness of her feedback by aligning it with her students' learning needs and phases. Additionally, by fading rates of feedback, naturally occurring reinforcers (e.g., getting to start the activity without arguing with peers) began to take over, which allowed her to ensure students did not become dependent on her for prompting or feedback.

In sum, teachers can maximize the effectiveness of their feedback by using specific, contingent, timely, sincere, and contextually and culturally relevant feedback that is modified based on students' learning phases. Tables 8.1 and 8.2 provide examples and non-examples of academic and behavioral feedback statements that can be used in elementary and secondary instructional settings, respectively.

Strategies to Increase Rates of Specific Positive Feedback

Unfortunately, simply knowing the characteristics of effective feedback is insufficient for most teachers to improve their practice. Evidence consistently shows that training (or knowledge) alone is unlikely to lead to sustained changes in teachers' behaviors in the classrooms.[38] Teachers may need to use coaching, peer support strategies, or prompting/self-monitoring strategies to increase feedback rates.

Coaching. The use of coaching that includes performance feedback makes it far more likely that teachers will successfully use effective practices such as specific positive feedback.[39] Coaching can be defined as the active and repeated delivery of reminders, encouragement, and corrections designed to increase successful implementation and decrease errors.[40] Coaching is typically provided (a) by someone with credibility and experience with the target skill(s), (b) in real time (in person or virtually),[41] (c) after initial training, and (d) repeatedly (e.g., monthly) until a skill is solidly in place. For example, after Mr. Newman attended an in-service training about specific positive behavioral feedback, the school coach provided a number of follow-up supports. First the coach checked in with Mr. Newman to ensure that he understood what positive specific feedback was and how to apply it in his classroom. The coach also worked with Mr. Newman to set a specific goal for the number of times positive specific feedback would be used. Then the coach provided regular (e.g., weekly) reminders to Mr. Newman about his goal and of the critical features of positive specific feedback. Finally, the coach observed in Mr. Newman's classroom once each month and provided specific positive feedback about his implementation, offering suggestions for continued improvement. After three months, Mr. Newman was accurately providing feedback that was specific and positive and was meeting the frequency goal. These coaching supports assured Mr. Newman improved his practice.

Table 8.1 Elementary School Examples and Non-Examples of Feedback

Type of Feedback	Academic/ Behavioral	Example	Non-Example
Positive General	Academic	"Nice Job!"	"No, that's wrong."
Positive General	Behavioral	"Way to go!"	"Stop it!"
Positive Behavior-Specific	Academic	"Yes, 3 times 4 is 12."	"Yes, that is right."
Positive Behavior-Specific	Behavioral	"Great job putting the art materials into the cabinet table six."	"Thanks for your help."
Positive Process-Centered	Academic	"Oliver, you worked really hard on your model. You used each problem-solving step."	"Oliver, I like your model."
Positive Process-Centered	Behavioral	"I like the way you asked your friend for the glue, Marco. You used please and thank you"	"Nice job, Marco."
Instructive	Academic	"Yes, class, this is a quadrilateral. A flat shape with four sides and four angles."	"Good, a quadrilateral."
Instructive	Behavioral	"That's correct Thomas. You place all the silverware in the bucket before putting the tray in the window."	"Thanks, Thomas."
Corrective	Academic	"There is one more step to the water cycle. Where would the clouds go on our poster, class? "	"We are missing a step."
Corrective	Behavioral	"Caroline, instead of pushing to get into line, please wait for the next open floor square to stand on."	"Stop pushing, Caroline."

Although formal coaching supports may be limited in some schools, many districts and states provide beginning teachers with mentors who may be able to provide this type of coaching support. For beginning teachers who are not paired with a mentor or for whom their mentor is not able to provide this type of coaching support, they may consider recruiting peer support or utilizing the prompting and self-monitoring strategies described below.

Peer Support Strategies

Although effective, formal coaching supports may not be readily available to all teachers who are looking to improve their classroom practices. Fortunately, researchers have found that coaching can be effectively provided by peers as a part of a grade-level team or professional learning community.[42] For example, the ninth-grade team of teachers at Northeast High School is working together to help each other increase their rates of positive specific feedback. First, they met together to set goals and to share ideas about how to apply the practice to their classrooms. The team members then agreed to help remind each other of their goals and to check in weekly to share how it was going. Finally, the team members agreed to observe each other teaching and simply count the number of positive specific feedback events given. In some cases, schedules allowed team members to observe in person;

Table 8.2 Secondary School Examples and Non-Examples of Feedback

Type of Feedback	Academic/ Behavioral	Example	Non-Example
Positive General	Academic	"Nice job!"	"No!" (with a sigh and sarcasm)
Positive General	Behavioral	"Good class today."	"Wrong answer."
Positive Behavior-Specific	Academic	"Correct, each side is 11 meters, and 11 times 4 is 44. "	"Yes, right."
Positive Behavior-Specific	Behavioral	"Thank you for cleaning up the trash from the bleachers after the game."	"Kate, I appreciate that."
Positive Process-Centered	Academic	"Correct, the hypotenuse is 11 when using the Pythagorean Theorem."	"Yes, the answer is 11."
Positive Process-Centered	Behavioral	"Compromising on a title for the poster is tough. Using a pro/con list was a great idea."	"Nice poster title."
Instructive	Academic	"Your essay is great. The use of imagery is very specific in the character development."	"Good essay, Sid."
Instructive	Behavioral	"The presentation was informative. You used visuals to support the thesis. You could also share the key points similar to the handout you provided."	"Good presentation."
Corrective	Academic	"Paul, instead of working on your homework, please take group notes."	"Paul, put the homework away."
Corrective	Behavioral	"Ladies, you may be familiar with this presentation, but please sit quietly during the assembly so others can hear."	"Ladies, stop talking."

in other cases, team members videotaped themselves teaching and shared the recording with their teammates for feedback. These peer coaching supports allowed the ninth-grade team to improve their practice without the need for a designated school-based coach.

Prompting/Self-Monitoring Strategies

For beginning special educators who are not able to find coaching or peer support, prompting and/or self-monitoring strategies may be an effective way to support implementation. Prompting strategies involve physical or audio cues as reminders to teachers to provide feedback. An example of an audio cue is a mobile app timer that beeps at pre-set times. The beep cues the teacher to look around the room for students exhibiting desired behaviors and then acknowledge them with behavior-specific feedback. An example of a physical prompt is the use of a pager-like device called a MotivAider™. This device can be set to vibrate on a pre-determined interval schedule. The teacher wears the device and the vibration cues the teacher to provide feedback. Research has shown this sort of physical, or tactile, prompting can increase rates of teachers' positive feedback while simultaneously increasing students' rates of on-task behavior.[43]

If prompting is not enough support, teachers can add self-monitoring to the prompting strategy. When using these combined strategies, after teachers are prompted to provide feedback via a physical or audio cue, they record (on a form or electronically) whether or not they provided the feedback. This notation serves as an additional reminder and tracking procedure. For instance, Mr. Landrew set the MotivAider ™ to vibrate every two minutes. After he received the physical prompt, he spotted Paige working quietly on her math assignment. He said, "Paige, I like how you are working quietly and independently. Keep up the good work." On a form consisting of ten rows labeled "2 min., 4 min., 6 min., up to 20 min." and accompanying boxes to check "yes" or "no," he marked "yes" at the 2-minute row indicating that he delivered positive, specific feedback. At the end of 20 minutes, he counted the number of intervals marked "yes" to determine how many times he delivered feedback as intended. Not only does this combined prompting and self-monitoring strategy increase the likelihood he will provide feedback, it also serves as a strategy for keeping track of his implementation fidelity.[44]

Wrap Up

The prevalence of challenging behaviors in the classroom and the lack of teacher preparation in managing these behaviors, in conjunction with the need for teachers to implement evidence-based instructional and intervention strategies, underscores the importance of using positive, instructive, and corrective feedback in the classroom. Research has shown consistently that teacher-delivered feedback can improve students' academic and behavioral performance significantly. Central to accurate implementation of this strategy are considering the types of feedback and the characteristics of effective feedback. Additional information and resources can be found in the Key Resources section of this chapter. In closing, the following tips are offered regarding feedback.

1. **Feedback should be specific, positive, and delivered contingently**. A wide range of feedback strategies should be considered that are age, developmentally, and contextually appropriate. Feedback should be delivered in a genuine and carrying manner. Rate of feedback should also be matched to learning phase with high rates during the acquisition phase of learning new skills.
2. **Use corrective feedback to "teach," not "punish."** Social challenging behavior at times can feel personal. However, it is important that you simply view problem behavior similar to a math error. That is, you wouldn't punish or threaten or react harshly to a math error; you would re-teach, provide an opportunity to practice, and reinforce when the student performs the math problem correctly. Use the exact same set of steps for social behavior "errors."
3. **Build in professional development opportunities that include performance feedback**. Just like our students, educators also need to learn effective strategies and receive feedback on our use. Seek out simple strategies such as peer coaching or self-monitoring to count the number of positive, corrective, and reprimand statements you make within a targeted instructional period. Strive for a high ratio of positive to negative statements to promote student success.

Notes

1 Beam, H. D., & Mueller, T. G. (2017). What do educators know, do, and think about behavior? An analysis of special and general educators' knowledge of evidence-based behavioral interventions. *Preventing School Failure: Alternative Education for Children and Youth, 61*, 1–13. doi:10.1080/10 45988X.2016.1164118.

2 Beam, H. D., & Mueller, T. G. (2017). What do educators know, do, and think about behavior? An analysis of special and general educators' knowledge of evidence-based behavioral interventions. *Preventing School Failure: Alternative Education for Children and Youth, 61*, 1–13. doi:10.1080/10 45988X.2016.1164118.

3 Cook, B. G., Landrum, T. J., Tankersley, M., & Kauffman, J. M. (2003). Bringing research to bear on practice: Effecting evidence-based instruction for students with emotional or behavioral disorders. *Education and Treatment of Children, 26*(4), 345–361.

4 Cheney, D., & Barringer, C. (1995). Teacher competence, student diversity, and staff training for the inclusion of middle school students with emotional and behavioral disorders. *Journal of Emotional and Behavioral Disorders, 3*(3), 174–182.

5 Sutherland, K. S., Denny, R. K., & Gunter, P. L. (2005). Teachers of students with emotional and behavioral disorders reported professional development needs: Differences between fully licensed and emergency-licensed teachers. *Preventing School Failure: Alternative Education for Children and Youth, 49*(2), 41–46.

6 Jones, M. L. (2009). A study of novice special educators' views of evidence-based practices. *Teacher and Teacher Education, 32*(2), 101–120.

7 Bradley, R., Doolittle, J., & Bartolotta, R. (2008). Building on the data and adding to the discussion: The experiences and outcomes of students with emotional disturbance. *Journal of Behavioral Education, 17*(1), 4–23.

8 Carroll, T. G., Fulton, K., & Doerr, H. (2010). *Team up for 21st century teaching and learning: What research and practice reveal about professional learning.* Washington, DC: National Commission on Teaching and America's Future (NCTAF). Retrieved from http://nctaf.org/wp-con tent/uploads/2012/01/TeamUp-CE-Web.pdf

9 Beam, H. D., & Mueller, T. G. (2017). What do educators know, do, and think about behavior? An analysis of special and general educators' knowledge of evidence-based behavioral interventions. *Preventing School Failure: Alternative Education for Children and Youth, 61*, 1–13. doi:10.1080/10 45988X.2016.1164118.

10 Stormont, M., Reinke, W., & Herman, K. (2011). Teachers' knowledge of evidence-based interventions and available school resources for children with emotional and behavioral problems. *Journal of Behavioral Education, 20*(2), 138–147.

11 Gable, R. A., Tonelson, S. W., Sheth, M., Wilson, C., & Park, K. L. (2012). Importance, usage, and preparedness to implement evidence-based practices for students with emotional disabilities: A comparison of knowledge and skills of special education and general education teachers. *Education and Treatment of Children, 35*, 499–519.

12 Billingsley, B., Carlson, E., & Klein, S. (2004). The working conditions and induction support of early career special educators. *Exceptional Children, 70*(3), 333–347.
    Harrell, P., Leavell, A., van Tassel, F., & McKee, K. (2004). No teacher left behind: Results of a five-year study of teacher attrition. *Action in Teacher Education, 26*(2), 47–59.

13 Hattie, J., & Timperley, H. (2007). The power of feedback. *Review of Educational Research, 77*(1), 81–112.

14 Simonsen, B., & Myers, D. (2015). *Classwide positive behavior interventions and supports: A guide to proactive classroom management.* New York, NY: Guilford Press.

15 Conroy, M. A., Sutherland, K. S., Snyder, A. L., & Marsh, S. (2008). Classwide interventions effective instruction makes a difference. *Teaching Exceptional Children, 40*(6), 24–30.

16 Brophy, J. (1981). Teacher praise: A functional analysis. *Review of Educational Research, 51*(1), 5–32.
    Chalk, K., & Bizo, L. A. (2004). Specific praise improves on-task behaviour and numeracy enjoyment: A study of year four pupils engaged in the numeracy hour. *Educational Psychology in Practice, 20*(4), 335–351.

17 Bruhn, A. L., Balint-Langel, K., Troughton, L., Langan, S., Lodge, K., & Kortemeyer, S. (2015). Assessing and treating stereotypical behaviors using a functional approach. *Behavioral Disorders, 41*(1), 21–37.
    Sutherland, K., & Wehby, J. H. (2001). The effect of self-evaluation on teaching behavior in classrooms for students with emotional and behavioral disorders. *The Journal of Special Education, 35*, 161–171.

Sutherland, K. S., Wehby, J. H., & Copeland, S. R. (2000). Effect of varying rates of behavior-specific praise on the on-task behavior of students with emotional and behavioral disorders. *Journal of Emotional and Behavioral Disorders, 8*(1), 2–8.

18 Hattie, J., & Timperley, H. (2007). The power of feedback. *Review of Educational Research, 77*(1), 81–112.

Dweck, C. (2007). The perils and promises of praise. *Educational Leadership, 65*(2), 34–39.

19 Dweck, C. (2007). The perils and promises of praise. *Educational Leadership, 65*(2), 34–39.

20 Werts, M. G., Wolery, M., Holcombe, A., & Gast, D. L. (1995). Instructive feedback: Review of parameters and effects. *Journal of Behavioral Education, 5*, 55–75.

21 Werts, M. G., Wolery, M., Holcombe, A., & Gast, D. L. (1995). Instructive feedback: Review of parameters and effects. *Journal of Behavioral Education, 5*, 55–75.

22 Hamre, B. K., & Pianta, R. C. (2005). Can instructional and emotional support in the first-grade classroom make a difference for children at risk of school failure? *Society for Research in Child Development, 76*, 949–967.

23 Simonsen, B., Fairbanks, S., Briesch, A., Myers, D., & Sugai, G. (2008). Evidence-based practices in classroom management: Considerations for research to practice. *Education and Treatment of Children, 31*, 351–380.

24 Singh, J., & Singh, N. N. (1986). Increasing oral reading proficiency. *Behavior Modification, 10*, 115–130.

O'Leary, K. D., & Becker, W. C. (1968). The effects of the intensity of a teacher's reprimands on children's behavior. *Journal of School Psychology, 7*(1), 8–11.

25 Chalk, K., & Bizo, L. A. (2004). Specific praise improves on-task behaviour and numeracy enjoyment: A study of year four pupils engaged in the numeracy hour. *Educational Psychology in Practice, 20*(4), 335–351.

Sutherland, K. S., Wehby, J. H., & Copeland, S. R. (2000). Effect of varying rates of behavior-specific praise on the on-task behavior of students with emotional and behavioral disorders. *Journal of Emotional and Behavioral Disorders, 8*(1), 2–8.

26 Brophy, J. (1986). Teacher influences on student achievement. *American Psychologist, 41*, 1069–1077.

Shute, V. J. (2008). Focus on formative feedback. *Review of Educational Research, 78*, 153–189.

27 Brookhart, S. M. (2008). *How to give effective feedback to your students.* Alexandria, VA: Association for Supervision and Curriculum Development.

28 Conroy, M. A., Sutherland, K. S., Snyder, A., Al-Hendawi, M., & Vo, A. (2009). Creating a positive classroom atmosphere: Teachers' use of effective praise and feedback. *Beyond Behavior, 18*(2), 18–26.

29 Henderlong, J., & Lepper, M. R. (2002). The effects of praise on children's intrinsic motivation: A review and synthesis. *Psychological Bulletin, 128*, 774–795.

Hitz, R., & Driscoll, A. (1988, July). Praise or encouragement? New insights into praise: Implication for early childhood teachers. *Young Children, 43*, 6–13.

30 Conroy, M. A., Sutherland, K. S., Snyder, A., Al-Hendawi, M., & Vo, A. (2009). Creating a positive classroom atmosphere: Teachers' use of effective praise and feedback. *Beyond Behavior, 18*(2), 18–26.

31 Chalk, K., & Bizo, L. A. (2004). Specific praise improves on-task behaviour and numeracy enjoyment: A study of year four pupils engaged in the numeracy hour. *Educational Psychology in Practice, 20*(4), 335–351.

Sutherland, K. S., Wehby, J. H., & Copeland, S. R. (2000).Effect of varying rates of behavior-specific praise on the on-task behavior of students with emotional and behavioral disorders. *Journal of Emotional and Behavioral Disorders, 8*(1), 2–8.

32 Brophy, J. (1986). Teacher influences on student achievement. *American Psychologist, 41*, 1069–1077.

Shute, V. J. (2008). Focus on formative feedback. *Review of Educational Research, 78*, 153–189.

33 Brookhart, S. M. (2008). *How to give effective feedback to your students.* Alexandria, VA: Association for Supervision and Curriculum Development.

34 Conroy, M. A., Sutherland, K. S., Snyder, A., Al-Hendawi, M., & Vo, A. (2009). Creating a positive classroom atmosphere: Teachers' use of effective praise and feedback. *Beyond Behavior, 18*(2), 18–26.

35 Henderlong, J., & Lepper, M. R. (2002). The effects of praise on children's intrinsic motivation: A review and synthesis. *Psychological Bulletin, 128,* 774–795.

  Hitz, R., & Driscoll, A. (1988, July). Praise or encouragement? New insights into praise: Implication for early childhood teachers. *Young Children, 43,* 6–13.

36 Conroy, M. A., Sutherland, K. S., Snyder, A., Al-Hendawi, M., & Vo, A. (2009). Creating a positive classroom atmosphere: Teachers' use of effective praise and feedback. *Beyond Behavior, 18*(2), 18–26.

37 White, O. R., & Haring, N. G. (1980). *Exceptional teaching.* Columbus, OH: Merrill.

38 Fixsen, D. L., Naoom, S. F., Blase, K. A., Friedman, R. M., & Wallace, F. (2005). *Implementation research: A synthesis of the literature.* Tampa, FL: University of South Florida, Louis de la Parte Florida Mental Health Institute, The National Implementation Research Network (FMHI Publication #231).

  Joyce, B., & Showers, B. (2002). *Student achievement through staff development.* Alexandria, VA: ASCD.

  Oliver, R. M., & Reschly, D. J. (2007). *Effective classroom management: Teacher preparation and professional development.* Washington, DC: National Comprehensive Center for Teacher Quality. Retrieved from www.tqsource.org/topics/effectiveClassroom Management.pdf

39 Fixsen, D. L., Naoom, S. F., Blase, K. A., Friedman, R. M., & Wallace, F. (2005). *Implementation research: A synthesis of the literature.* Tampa, FL: University of South Florida, Louis de la Parte Florida Mental Health Institute, The National Implementation Research Network (FMHI Publication #231).

  Joyce, B., & Showers, B. (2002). *Student achievement through staff development.* Alexandria, VA: ASCD.

  Sutherland, K. S., Wehby, J. H., & Copeland, S. R. (2000). Effect of varying rates of behavior-specific praise on the on-task behavior of students with emotional and behavioral disorders. *Journal of Emotional and Behavioral Disorders, 8*(1), 2–8.

40 Fixsen, D. L., Naoom, S. F., Blase, K. A., Friedman, R. M., & Wallace, F. (2005). *Implementation research: A synthesis of the literature.* Tampa, FL: University of South Florida, Louis de la Parte Florida Mental Health Institute, The National Implementation Research Network (FMHI Publication #231).

  Freeman, J., Sugai, G., Simonsen, B., & Everett, S. (2016). Multi-tiered support systems coaching: Bridging knowing to doing. *Theory into Practice, 56*(1), 29–37.

  Joyce, B., & Showers, B. (2002). *Student achievement through staff development.* Alexandria, VA: ASCD.

41 Rock, M. L., Schoenfeld, N., Zigmond, N., Gable, R. A., Gregg, M., Ploessl, D. M., & Salter, A. (2013). Can you Skype me now? Developing teachers' classroom management practices through virtual coaching. *Beyond Behavior, 22*(3), 15–23.

42 Duchaine, E., Jolivette, K., & Fredrick, L. (2011). The effect of teacher coaching with performance feedback on behavior-specific praise in inclusion classrooms. *Education & Treatment of Children, 34*(2), 209.

43 Hatton, H. (2017). *Improving classroom management and reducing referrals for targeted interventions with tactile prompting.* A study presented at The 2017 International Association for Positive Behavior Support Conference.

44 Bruhn, A. L., Balint-Langel, K., Troughton, L., Langan, S., Lodge, K., & Kortemeyer, S. (2015). Assessing and treating stereotypical behaviors using a functional approach. *Behavioral Disorders*, *41*(1), 21–37.

OSEP Technical Assistance Center on Positive Behavioral Interventions and Supports. (2017). *Positive behavioral interventions & supports [Website]*. Retrieved from http://www.pbis.org/ Common/Cms/files/pbisresources/PBIS%20Technical%20Brief%20on%20Systems%20to%20 Support%20Teachers%20Implementation%20of%20Positive%20Classroom%20Behavior%20 Support.pdf

Key Resources

IRIS Center (2017). *Providing Positive Feedback [Website]*. Retrieved from: https://iris.peabody.vanderbilt.edu/module/ecbm/cresource/q2/p06/.
- This website offers modules with detailed examples and directions for providing behavior specific praise and acknowledging student success.

OSEP Technical Assistance Center on Positive Behavioral Interventions and Supports (2017). *Positive Behavioral Interventions & Supports [Website]*. Retrieved from www.pbis.org/common/cms/ files/pbisresources/Supporting%20and%20Responding%20to%20Behavior.pdf.
- This document provides an overview of evidence-based classroom management practices. Each practice, including specific praise, is described in terms of the critical features, elementary and secondary examples of implementation, and non-examples.

Simonsen, B., & Myers, D. (2015). *Classwide positive behavior interventions and supports: A guide to proactive classroom management*. New York, NY: Guilford Press.
- Throughout this guide, authors emphasize the importance of feedback in the learning process. Additionally, specific and contingent praise is discussed as a strategy for reinforcing appropriate behaviors.

University of Louisville (2017). *Academic and Behavioral Response to Intervention [Website]* Retrieved from:*http://louisville.edu/education/abri/primarylevel/praise/group*
- On this site, users can read about using specific praise during group instruction and then watch video exemplars demonstrating how to implement the strategy.

9
Teaching Social Skills
Sara McDaniel, Imad Zaheer, and Terrance M. Scott

Introduction

The ability to successfully interact with others and to navigate difficult social interactions in a manner that predicts continued success is the essence of social skills.[1] Effective social skill use is important not only for students. Social skill is a broad term that encompasses categories of critical skills across various social situations (e.g., on a soccer team, passing someone in the hallway, participating in instruction). Major categories of social skills include communication (e.g., appropriate voice tone, eye contact), problem solving (e.g., disagreeing appropriately, accepting feedback), resolving conflict (e.g., perspective taking, negotiating), and working cooperatively (e.g., taking turns, coming to consensus). Effective social skill use should be displayed across peer and adult interactions, which require different sets of skills.

Problems with social skills result in difficulties at school and beyond. Specifically, social skills deficits at school can result in missed instruction, exclusionary discipline, and limited social opportunities for improvement. In the home and community, poor social skills can result in coercive relationships, disengagement with others, and a general lack of crucial social support. Students who do not master appropriate social skills during their school years can demonstrate difficulty with obtaining and maintaining employment, getting along with others at work, and having difficulties with social relationships outside of work as well.

The exact nature of social skill deficits can vary in type and intensity across grade and developmental levels and can predict a range of poor school outcomes. Although effective schools teach, encourage, and reinforce appropriate social behavior across all students (i.e., universal supports), it's likely that some students will demonstrate repeated errors and failures in the social realm, resulting in frequent conflict or isolation. These students will require additional targeted interventions consisting of direct, explicit, and intensive instruction in key social skills. Further, a small number of students will require highly intensive and individualized interventions. For example, students who qualify for special education services under categories such as autism, other health impairments, and intellectual disabilities often demonstrate deficits specific to social communication or other social skills domains. Among those most frequently requiring direct instruction in social skills are students identified as having an emotional disturbance (ED).[2] By definition, students with ED manifest an inability to maintain successful interpersonal peer relationships and suffer from conflict with teachers and parents.[3]

Narrowing the Focus

Oftentimes students engage in unsuccessful social interactions because they are not aware of the accepted social convention, they do not know a better way, or inappropriate social behavior is more effective in meeting the student's need. Instruction for social behavior is neither conceptually nor practically different from typical academic instruction. Effectively teaching the use of prosocial skills begins with consideration of effective instructional practices.[4] That is, the tenets of effective instruction offer the highest likelihood of success.[5] The focus of this chapter is to outline a process for developing an instructional logic, using engagement strategies for students during instruction, and facilitating practice to mastery. Using explicit case examples, this process will be described in the context of eight key components of effective social skills instruction.

Chapter Overview

1. Describe the components of effective instruction for social skills that address a) developing a logic for social skill instruction; b) developing strategies for engaging students and providing positive and corrective feedback; and c) developing strategies for providing students with naturalistic practice.
2. Describe additional considerations for teachers when teaching students social skills in the classroom.
3. Describe an example of the development of a social skill group that focuses on resolving peer conflicts.

The Components of Effective Instruction for Social Skills

The key features of effective instruction are empirically well-established regardless of the lesson content.[6] Social skills can and should be taught using the same logic and principles that have been identified for effectively teaching academics. Components of effective instruction can generally be considered within three broad planning considerations often referred to as teach (e.g., "I do"), model (e.g., "we do"), and practice (e.g., "you do").

Develop an Instructional Logic

Developing an instructional logic refers to applying basic effective instruction procedures during the planning and initial teaching steps. Planning for effective instruction begins with assessing for deficit type and intensity, or identifying students and defining necessary skill instruction. Once students and specific skills are identified, teachers must break expected prosocial behaviors into smaller, teachable steps for instruction. Coupled with step instruction, relevant examples and non-examples with rationales must be provided for maximum understanding. These four steps in developing an instructional logic for teaching social skills are further described below (see planning tool in Figure 9.1).

Step 1: Identify Students and Define Targeted Skills

The first step of developing an instructional logic combines information across three critical areas: (a) systematically, and proactively identifying students with social skills deficits, (b) identifying specific social skills areas for instruction, and (c) determining social skills group membership designation. Social skills deficits can be identified by varying assessment procedures. First, schools that utilize systematic screeners such as the Strengths and Difficulties Questionnaire (SDQ) or the Social

Social Skill Lesson Planning Checklist

Targeted Social Skill: _____

Group Members: _____

Lesson Scheduling (Day/Time/# weeks): _____

Guidelines	Planned	Completed

Instructional Logic

1. Define key rule for the skill being taught—how would one know if it was being done correctly?

2. Break skill into teachable component steps—set students up for high rates of success.

3. Select examples that sample the range of circumstances, settings, and contexts under which the skill is appropriate across the student's environments.

4. Sequence examples to show full range and to help the learner discriminate appropriate vs. inappropriate skills.

Engage Students

5. Facilitate student engagement within each lesson—provide opportunities to respond.

6. Provide frequent and immediate feedback on student performance.

Practice to Mastery

7. Guide student practice to facilitate high levels of success and continue to mastery.

8. Facilitate generalization—prompt and reinforce skill use across environments.

Figure 9.1 Social Skill Lesson Planning Checklist

Skills Improvement System (SSIS) Rating Scale can identify students with social skills deficits proactively and systematically through teacher ratings.[7] A less systematic and proactive procedure for identifying students with social skills deficits is to analyze schoolwide office discipline referral (ODR) data. Students who demonstrate disruptive interactions with others (e.g., physical aggression, inappropriate language) and who are given ODRs as a result of their deficits can be identified through regular inspection of schoolwide discipline data. Similarly, if your classroom contains a data collection system on social behaviors, the data can also be used to identify students in need of social skills instruction.

After reliably identifying students with social skills deficits, it is important next to determine the specific type of deficit. Deficits may be categorized by general characteristics, such as problem solving, conflict management, communication, and by whom the students typically display poor social skills with, peers or adults. Because social skills encompass a broad category of interaction deficits, it is important to identify what specific skills should be addressed through instruction. Some students may demonstrate social skills deficits in multiple areas or with both peers and adults. In these cases, it is important to prioritize prosocial expected behaviors that can increase success in school. For example, a student may demonstrate difficulty accepting feedback from adults, resulting in limited positive interactions with teachers, and difficulty negotiating with peers, resulting in verbal and physical altercations between peers.

Social skills groups are most effective when developed based on a commonality among student deficits. While schools often create a social skills group with a consistent group of students throughout the year (e.g., groups from the same classroom, groups from the same grade), it makes more sense to create groups based on specific skill deficits. In this manner, instructional delivery is targeted to specific skill deficits common across students. Once mastery is achieved, a new group can be formed focusing on a new set of skills as needed. While it is likely that many students would attend multiple groups throughout the year to receive instruction on an array of skills, each group is developed to focus on a set of related skills.

Step 2: Break Skills Into Teachable Steps

Due to the complexity of some social skills, teachers should break complex skills (e.g., resolving peer conflict) into smaller, sequenced teachable steps (e.g., check for understanding, offer your opinion, identify areas for compromise, and check for agreement on a compromise) that facilitate high rates of student success at every step. In general, the rule of thumb is to make the steps no larger than what would be considered to provide a high probability of student success. That is, consider the largest possible steps in which there is reasonable confidence the student will be successful and receive high rates of positive acknowledgement. When breaking down complex skills, it is important to start with the end in mind, considering what the skill would look like when correctly performed. Oftentimes we think of what typical social behavior looks like for same- or similar-aged peers and set that as the mastery criteria. Working backwards, individual skills can be developed to create a logical set of lessons leading from current levels of performance to the desired end result.

Step 3: Use Relevant Examples

This step extends explicit step-by-step instruction to constructed examples, non-examples, and role-playing scenarios. The student's ability to use a skill in the natural environment will, in large part, be dependent upon the degree to which examples used during training include the full range of settings, contexts, and circumstances the student is likely to encounter. Instruction that uses only published curricula or other generic or non-relevant examples is unlikely to provide sufficient content to promote high rates of success. For example, teaching a student to shake hands and say "good morning, friend" is unlikely to facilitate successful outcomes for a teenage high school student and may even make success in this setting less likely, as shaking hands is not a socially valid behavior for most teenagers and repeating the phrase "good morning, friend" is not generally age appropriate for teenagers. Consideration of effective examples must take into account culture, age, and a range of individual differences that make up the natural environment for a given student or classroom.

As part of the effective selection of examples for any particular student or students, a teacher should consider what are the locations and circumstances under which these skills will be required. Effective instruction should vary examples across the natural environment to maximize the likelihood of generalization. Clearly, including every possible natural example is not feasible, as the number of potential examples may be endless. But it is possible to group similar circumstances for instruction. In so doing, examples of each of the different circumstances from the instructional universe can be represented. For example, we might break greeting behaviors into formal contexts (e.g., business-related handshakes), informal contexts (e.g., verbal greetings for casual acquaintances), and close friends (e.g., fist bumps). While there may be a wide range of variation within each of these groupings, including examples from each enhances discrimination for the student and promotes the likelihood of generalization. Considerations of culture, age, and individual differences play an important role in determining which of these examples best represent the range of what the student is likely to encounter in the natural environment, including school (e.g., classroom, non-classroom contexts), home (e.g., inside the home, in the front yard), and community (e.g., church, youth group, part-time job, the mall).

Step 4: Sequence Examples

Once examples have been selected, they must be organized and sequenced for presentation during instruction. As a general rule, examples from each of the relevant groupings identified in the last step (e.g., school, home, community) should be equally weighted and purposefully sequenced during instruction based on prioritizing where the social skill deficit is most likely to result in negative out-comes first. The teacher can continually call attention to key features of the natural environments and use those to prompt students as to the correct response variation across environments. For example, if a young student demonstrates an inability to share materials, toys, and attention with peers, the teacher can sequence examples of sharing materials during group work in the classroom first, then provide examples of sharing toys during free time and build towards teaching sharing of teacher's attention during centers and playground time based on prioritizing where the deficit results in the most disruption to instruction. Although the explicit steps to sharing with others remains the same across these examples and the relevant examples were identified, this step increases high rates of success by prioritizing and building variations in different contexts.

Engage Students

The next set of steps in effective social skills instruction highlight the importance of engaging students in instruction and providing timely positive and corrective feedback. These two steps are especially important in ensuring that the well-planned lessons from Steps 1–4 are delivered to maximize high rates of success during instruction and prior to naturalistic practice.

Step 5: Facilitate Student Engagement

During social skills instruction, it is important to continue effective teaching practices by developing engaging lessons that are well-paced in delivery.[8] Oftentimes social skills lesson plans mirror academic lesson plans with their core components (e.g., teach, model, practice). Within each lesson, teachers should plan for numerous and various opportunities to respond by asking students to answer simple questions, demonstrate skills, discuss thoughts, and indicate understanding through gestures such as hand raising or using response cards. Further, teachers can foster engagement by using authentic or relevant examples that students are likely to encounter on a regular basis. For example, after introducing a new social skill such as giving compliments, a teacher may engage the students by tying the lesson in with a recent book club text read by the class, or popular movie. The teacher could also ask students to provide examples and non-examples that they have seen across school, home, and community. Additionally, teachers may engage students with the use of technology such as creating video examples of key skills. Using effective teaching practices to engage students increases participation and learning, which promotes high rates of success across academic, behavioral, and social contexts.

During group instruction, oftentimes only one student at a time is actively involved in a role-play example, and as a result, teachers find it challenging to maintain engagement of all students during practice. To address this issue, all role-play and practice opportunities should involve tasks for all students—even those not directly involved. For example, while one student demonstrates an appropriate response to a difficult scenario, other students can be asked to identify specific skills, watch for signals, or judge the overall success of the attempt. At the end of each demonstration, students can be asked to report on their thoughts. Providing every student with a task during practice opportunities increases engagement and helps to minimize possible disruptive behaviors.

Step 6: Provide Performance Feedback

High levels of student engagement provide teachers with critical opportunities for performance feedback during lessons (See Chapter 8 for more information on feedback).[9] Two types of feedback critical to promoting mastery for social skills are positive and corrective feedback. Both types of feedback should be immediate, consistent, and specific. Positive, behavior-specific praise should explicitly describe the positive skill or steps demonstrated, a statement of approval indicating desired behavior, and a rationale of why it is desired. Similarly, immediate, corrective feedback should describe any steps that were completed correctly along with the exact steps where error occurred, followed by encouragement and an opportunity to practice the skill correctly. Ongoing, consistent feedback can also include a range of verbal and gestural signals (e.g., high fives, thumbs up) and can be tied to an existing reinforcement system.

Naturalistic Practice to Mastery

Naturalistic practice, teaching, and practicing social skills in the settings in which they are expected to occur (e.g., hallway, bus, cafeteria) is an essential component of the instructional sequence following the planning and delivery of explicit instruction and constructed modeling scenarios. Like the other instructional components, high levels of success with naturalistic practice is critical. Repetition, particularly in the naturalistic setting with feedback helps to build the fluency that is necessary to facilitate high rates of success.

Step 7: Guided Practice

As with any lesson content, social skills instruction requires ongoing feedback, re-teaching, and numerous naturalistic practice opportunities. To facilitate mastery, teachers begin with instruction that sets students up to experience high rates of success and positive acknowledgement. As students demonstrate mastery during instruction, the teacher will gradually remove the structures within instruction that have been used to facilitate student success. However, prior to expecting students to demonstrate behaviors in a totally independent manner the teacher should consider how to guide practice opportunities early and gradually fade as the student continues to be successful. Guiding practice can involve various strategies, such as (a) asking the student to think aloud and move slowly during initial practice, (b) prompting the student prior to a practice opportunity to use the explicit steps, or (c) reminding the student of a missed step during the naturalistic practice scenario.

Despite the fact that repetition builds fluency, teachers must be careful to consider that practice is not overdone to the point of boredom. Generally, practice should occur in small bursts with facilitation of high rates of success through the use of scaffolded support strategies mentioned above and repetition over time.[10]

Step 8: Facilitate Maintenance and Generalization

After multiple trials with natural practice in a single setting or context on a specific skill, it is important that teachers promote generalization of the newly mastered skill by providing opportunities to practice the same skill in various authentic situations outside of the learned context. For instance, consider that a student's targeted skill is accepting consequences and that she has demonstrated success with one classroom teacher. As a next step, the teacher must enlist the help of other adults to assess the student's ability to successfully use that new skill under other conditions with different classroom teachers or adults. It might be important to ensure generalizability of the same steps across varying contexts such as during physical education class, at lunch in the cafeteria, and during hallway transitions. In addition, plans for generalization should include all faculty and staff. Social skills deficits may be problematic in a single context; however, they should be taught as larger skill sets that can be applied in a full range of reasonably predictable situations. Helping students to use their new skills in different contexts will deepen their knowledge and mastery of that skill.

Finally, high rates of success in the "real world" will also depend on continually using the new social skills across all contexts over time. This concept is known as maintenance. It is important to promote maintenance of prosocial skills after initial lessons and generalization practice occurs. Although students may not continue to receive small group social skills instruction and frequent feedback, it is important to systematically fade support and intermittently assess whether the new skills are still in place.

Additional Considerations in Teaching Social Skills

Acquisition Versus Performance Deficits

Instruction and assessment differ as instruction progresses across the various stages of learning. At the initial acquisition stage of learning, students are simply learning the new skill, and assessment is focused on a student's ability to demonstrate all of the required steps of the skill as defined in a constructed scenario. Once this is established, the focus shifts to increasing the student's fluency or automaticity with the skill or the ability to use it without undue effort. Social skills instruction must eventually improve performance deficits past constructed scenarios, in naturalistic settings. It is important to know whether the skill deficit is truly a skill deficit (and requires explicit step-by-step instruction) or a performance deficit where knowledge of the appropriate steps is already known, but the skill is not performed accurately. For example, consider the student who knows what constitutes appropriate and inappropriate language in school but often uses inappropriate language because she receives laughter and attention from peers for being rude. Clearly, simply teaching what appropriate language is won't change the problem behavior, but instruction will still be important for teaching the student when to use the skill and what the consequences are related to appropriate and inappropriate language. Because the function or purpose of the behavior appears to be to access peer attention, intervention may involve manipulating the environment to remove peer laughter while simultaneously developing conditions under which the student can receive peer attention for an appropriate behavior (see Chapter 10 for more information on teaching "functionally" equivalent social skills). Instruction involves both practice with the desired social skill and clear definitions regarding these consequences. Initial assessment of the skill deficit (i.e., Step 1) should provide information regarding the baseline of social skill deficit and whether a skill and/or performance problem exists.

Progress Monitoring

A concrete, observable definition of each skill provides guidance for all adults in a setting to evaluate student progress. Throughout skill instruction, role play, and naturalistic practice, student progress should be monitored and analyzed for responsiveness. During instruction, progress monitoring may require direct observation of step completion, accuracy of step identification, or instances requiring corrective feedback. Similarly, progress monitoring during naturalistic practice may require daily progress reports, self-rating, or notations of displayed deficits. Monitoring progress will inform the need for remediation, additional repetition, different examples, practice in different contexts, or the readiness for fading and maintenance (see Figure 9.2).

Weekly Social Skill Progress Monitoring Checklist

	Prosocial Use of Skill (record tally mark for each incident)	Social Error of Skill (record tally mark for each incident)	Context (record location and consequence)
Date:			
Date:			
Date:			
Date:			
Date:			

Figure 9.2 Weekly Social Skill Progress Monitoring Checklist

Student Involvement

Because social skills are pertinent to successful interactions with others, it is important to include student involvement in all possible aspects of instruction and practice. Students can co-create examples and non-examples, promoting open discussion regarding positive and negative social choices. This allows students to be active participants in the process and makes the content more relevant by bringing up examples and non-examples from their own daily experience. This can also lead to necessary discussions for addressing barriers to using prosocial skills and the social acceptability of skills we are expecting students to use in varying contexts. Students can also co-create role-play scenarios for their teacher and/or peers to act out and solve.

Home–School Collaboration

A final consideration is to promote home–school collaboration through common social skill instruction. Although social skill demonstration may vary across the school, home, and community contexts, the foundational steps and rationales for utilizing prosocial skills remains consistent. It is important to promote collaboration with the home around teaching and reinforcing key skills at home and in the community. For example, teachers and parents may discuss certain social skills that are important across both school and home settings, reinforce successful instances of social skills, and provide corrective feedback as necessary.

Example Development of a Social Skill Group

Resolving Peer Conflict
Portville Elementary School is an urban, Title I, K–5 neighborhood school that serves students in a high-poverty, high-mobility community. Portville Elementary uses SOAR (Solve problems peacefully, Own your own actions, Accept responsibility, Respect others) to denote their school-wide expectations and has a family liaison who focuses on home–school collaboration with regard to attendance and social/emotional/behavior supports. Overall, most students consistently display social skills related to the school-wide expectations. However, the special education teacher noted that several fifth-grade boys on his caseload were not using the skills and repeatedly being sent out of their general education classrooms for non-compliance. In response to the noted challenges, the special education teacher met with the fifth-grade teachers to design a small group social skills intervention to increase the likelihood the students demonstrate the appropriate skills across all of their classrooms.

In accordance with Step 1, the teachers prioritized important skills for the target students to work on first. They identified ignoring others and handling peer teasing as high-priority skills to alleviate the peer conflict among the small group of fifth-grade students. The team created explicit lessons across these core social skills. The special education teacher along with one of the fifth-grade teachers decided to co-teach a small group weekly social skill lesson.

Next, the teachers completed Step 2 by breaking the three prioritized social skills into smaller, sequenced steps for instruction. Handling peer teasing was broken down into the following steps: (a) let the student know that they are not being kind, (b) take a breath and be calm, and (c) choose an activity to escape the unkind behavior (e.g., walk away, tell an adult, simply ignore, talk to someone else).

The developed lessons provided explicit steps for completing the prosocial skill. Explicit instruction for teachers to teach the new skill, model examples and non-examples, facilitate role playing, provide performance feedback, and apply the skill in naturalistic settings throughout the day with ongoing feedback was planned in advance. Specific to Step 3, teachers decided to preplan two examples and non-examples for each skill (i.e., ignoring others and handling peer teasing) and to allow each student to create one example and non-example after the teacher examples were used. In accordance with Step 4, the teachers decided that it was important to sequence the two teacher examples and non-examples as hallway examples, given that the hallway presented the biggest challenge for the group of students involved. The teachers would then allow students to create examples that pertained to other non-classroom settings.

During the first session, the teachers introduced the social skills lesson procedures and introduced handling peer teasing as the skill that would be the first focus of instruction. To address cultural responsiveness for the group of students involved in this instruction, the teachers discussed ways in which peers, family, and community members addressed peer conflict outside of school and how those strategies are similar and dissimilar to what is expected at school. Additionally, the teachers asked students for their own examples during role-play practice and allowed students to create phrases for skill steps and choices that they found acceptable.

During each lesson the teachers presented preplanned, sequenced examples pulled from the natural environment with engaging discussions (i.e., Step 5). For example, the students discussed a situation in which friends were talking about another student's old backpack having holes in it and saying that the student was poor. The teachers asked the students to consider what they would do if they were the student with the backpack, and students generated a range of examples of appropriate behavior to respond to the teasing.

In Step 6, teachers provided feedback during role-play situations so that students had an opportunity to practice the new steps. Because some students were less inclined to demonstrate the skills effectively according to the progress monitoring checklist of step completion, the teachers provided prompts and reminders to all as role plays began. For one student with additional challenges, the teachers added a think-aloud walk-through of the role play prior to asking the student to demonstrate independently. Instruction continued until all students were able to demonstrate effective and appropriate responses to a range of teasing situations using multiple strategies.

After initial small group instruction, all of the fifth-grade classroom teachers were involved with Steps 7 and 8, practicing to mastery. The classroom teachers monitored and corrected unkind behavior but also monitored student's responses to unkind behavior by counting the number of incidences when students used positive, prosocial resolution strategies and when their reactions were inappropriate. The checklist had a column for recording positive demonstrations and another column for recording errors in naturalistic contexts. The final column prompted the teacher to record where the incident took place and the resulting consequence (see Figure 9.2). Throughout the day, the teachers also provided feedback to the students regarding their performance. After ten weeks, the teachers completed the initial lessons across both social skills with sufficient opportunities for practice and decided that further lessons were not needed as a whole group based on overall responsiveness as documented on the daily checklists. Teachers continued to provide behavior specific praise and corrective feedback when necessary across all school contexts.

Wrap Up

In summary, social skill development, specifically the ability to interact appropriately with peers and adults, has long been considered a crucial aspect in students' development. Social skills are more than simply the teacher's preference for behavior. They are the critical student behaviors that predict success during interaction with others. Because they are a critical pre-requisite for student success, social skills must be taught as part of a basic and foundational curriculum throughout the school, including special education settings.

Teaching social skills is conceptually no different than instruction for any other content. That is, lesson plans for social skills instruction are structurally similar to teaching math, reading, or any other critical skill. Steps for effective social skills instruction include: (1) identify students who require similar skill instruction, (2) explicitly define the expected social skill, (3) break the social skill down into teachable steps, (4) provide relative examples and non-examples, (5) sequence instruction to meet the needs of students, (6) engage students in instruction, (7) provide corrective feedback and practice, and (8) promote generalizability of the new skill across all contexts. These eight steps can be modified and applied across grade levels and school contexts and carefully constructed to be developmentally appropriate and culturally responsive to student needs and interests. See the Key Resources section of this chapter for additional resources. The following tips should be consideration in teaching social skills:

1. **Follow effective instruction strategies to teach social skills**. Similar to teaching math or U.S. history, social skill lessons should incorporate effective instructional strategies. A basic format of "tell-show-practice" should be used where you describe the skill and when to use it (tell), demonstrate the skill using examples and non-examples taken from the student's environment (show), and have the students use the appropriate skill during role play (practice).
2. **Organize groups around common social skills**. Though tempting to simply group all struggling students together, common or related social skill groupings will allow the individualized and intensive practice often needed among students with disabilities. Grouping around common skills also allows for more sustained and targeted guided practice.
3. **Tie small group social skills to school-wide or classroom expectations**. An on-going challenge in teaching social skills is to promote generalized and maintained skills use, especially for students whose problem behavior is maintained by the environment. If you are working in a school with a common set of school-wide expectations, make sure each lesson is linked and uses the same language (e.g., "stopping" when you get angry shows "respect" for others). If common school-wide expectations are not in place, then link all lessons to your classroom expectations.

Notes

1 Cook, C. R., Gresham, F. M., Kern, L., Barreras, R. B., Thornton, S., & Crews, S. D. (2008). Social skills training for secondary students with emotional and/or behavioral disorders a review and analysis of the meta-analytic literature. *Journal of Emotional and Behavioral Disorders, 16*(3), 131–144.

2 Individuals with Disabilities Education Act, 20 U.S.C. § 1400 (2004).

    Gresham, F. M., Van, M. B., & Cook, C. C. (2006). Social skills training for teaching replacement behaviors: Remediating acquisition deficits in at-risk students. *Behavioral Disorders, 31*(4), 363–377.

3 Marcus, R. F. (1996). The friendships of delinquents, *Adolescence, 31*, 145–159.

    Walker, H. M., Ramsey, E., & Gresham, F. M. (2004). *Antisocial behavior in school: Evidence-based practices* (2nd ed.). Belmont, CA: Thomson/ Wadsworth Learning.

    McLaughlin, D. M., & Carr, E. G. (2005). Quality of rapport as a setting event for problem behavior: Assessment and intervention. *Journal of Positive Behavior Interventions, 7*(2), 68–91.

4 Scott, T. M. (2016). *Teaching behavior: Managing classroom behavior with effective instruction.* New York, NY: Corwin Press.

5 Engelmann, S. (2007) Student-program alignment and teaching to mastery. *Journal of Direct Instruction, 7*(1), 45–66.

    Hattie, J. A. C. (2009). *Visible learning: A synthesis of over 800 meta-analyses relating to achievement.* New York, NY: Routledge.

6 Engelmann, S. (2007) Student-program alignment and teaching to mastery. *Journal of Direct Instruction, 7*(1), 45–66.

7 Goodman, R. (1997) The strengths and difficulties questionnaire: A research note. *Journal of Child Psychology and Psychiatry, 38*, 581–586.

    Gresham, F., & Elliott, S. N. (2008). *Social skills improvement system rating scales.* Minneapolis, MN: Pearson.

8 Christenson, S. L., Reschly, A. L., & Wylie, C. (Eds.). (2012). *Handbook of research on student engagement.* New York, NY: Springer Science & Business Media.

9 Hattie, J. A. C., & Timperley, H. (2007). The power of feedback. *Review of Educational Research, 77*(1), 81–112.

10 McDaniel, M. A., Fadler, C. L., & Pashler, H. (2013). Effects of spaced versus massed training in function learning. *Journal of Experimental Psychology: Learning, Memory, and Cognition, 39*(5), 1417.

Key Resources

Author (2017). *Tier 1 Positive Behavior Interventions and Supports.* Retrieved from: www.pbisworld.com/tier-1/

Author (2017). *Social Skill Instruction Lesson Plans.* Retrieved from: www.boystowntraining.org/lesson-plans.html

Gresham, F. M., & Elliott, S. N. (2017). Social Skills Improvement System Overview. Retrieved from: www.pearsonclinical.com/therapy/RelatedInfo/ssis-overview.html

McGinnis, E. (2011) Skillstreaming the Elementary School Child: A Guide for Teaching Prosocial Skills (3rd Ed). Research Press: Champaign, IL.

10
Conducting Functional Behavior Assessments to Develop Individualized Behavior Support Plans

Blair P. Lloyd, Howard P. Wills, and Timothy J. Lewis

Introduction

Building consistent learning environments, providing high rates of positive specific feedback, and explicitly teaching social skills are all necessary pre-requisites to promote academic and social success in the classroom. However, children and youth receiving special education may continue to engage in problem behaviors inhibiting their progress. Beginning special educators must prepare to support *all* students, including those who do not respond to class-wide or more targeted supports. These students will need individualized behavior support plans (BSPs). Because effective BSPs are based on results of a functional behavior assessment (FBA), knowing when and how to complete FBAs to develop individualized BSPs is a critical role for all special educators.

During an FBA, educators use a systematic process to identify a student's problem behaviors, the events or conditions predicting the occurrence of the behaviors, and the events or conditions maintaining the behaviors over time.[1] The process focuses on interactions between a student's behavior and his or her environment. Just as features of the classroom environment can impact student behavior, student behavior can impact the classroom environment. For example, during independent seatwork, a student's environment may be lacking in social interactions with peers. In response to this set of conditions, a student might throw an eraser at a classmate, immediately changing the environment: the classmate turns around, and other students laugh. Of course, each student is unique in how they respond to different features of their environments and how their behavior impacts those features. As a result, the FBA and development of BSPs is a highly individualized process.

Evidence supporting the FBA process as a means to guide individualized BSPs has been accumulating since the early 1980s, with the earliest research focusing on individuals with severe cognitive deficits in clinical settings.[2] Over time, however, the evidence base has spread to educational settings, including public schools;[3] across implementers, including teachers and other classroom staff;[4] and across student populations, including students with mild disabilities and those at-risk for disabilities.[5] In fact, the What Works Clearinghouse (WWC) recently published a report summarizing the findings of high-quality research on FBA-based interventions for K–12 students with or at risk for an emotional disturbance. The report documented conclusive evidence of positive effects across two domains: problem behavior and school engagement.[6] Moreover, for students with disabilities and those at high risk, research suggests that interventions based on FBA results are more effective and efficient at decreasing problem behavior relative to interventions that are not function-based.[7]

Equally important, federal law (i.e., Individuals with Disabilities Education Act) stipulates conditions that require FBAs and individualized BSPs. FBA guided behavior plans are mandated for students with disabilities who have been suspended from school for ten or more days due to problem behavior or whose problem behavior is determined to be a manifestation of their disability.[8] However, such guidelines have been described as an "absolute minimum by legal standards" and "ineffective and inefficient by best practice standards."[9] Rather than basing the decision to conduct an FBA on a student's disability status or exclusionary discipline practices, this decision should be based on the extent to which a student's problem behavior (1) persists despite the presence of evidence-based instruction and behavior management practices and (2) impacts the student's academic and social progress at school.[10]

Narrowing the Focus

In this chapter, we address beginning special educators and focus on their roles and responsibilities when it comes to students who need individualized behavior support. We do not mean to imply, however, that special educators are solely responsible for conducting FBAs and developing individualized BSPs. In fact, high-quality FBAs are not done in isolation but should be a collaborative effort in which teams carefully consider information from multiple sources to identify when and why a student is engaging in problem behavior. Including multiple school staff members who support the student in different contexts can help shed light on a student's varied strengths and needs. In addition to special educators, behavior specialists, school psychologists, counselors, or general education teachers may be included and play active roles in the FBA process. Furthermore, for schools that are implementing multi-tiered systems of behavior support, special educators may collaborate with members of a designated student support team (e.g., Tier 3 team) who have experience with intensive intervention, data-based individualization, and progress monitoring.[11]

While a wide range of assessment and intervention methods exist and have been evaluated in school-based research,[12] the focus of this chapter is on the *essential* components of FBAs and individualized BSPs that beginning special educators should know.

Chapter Overview

1. Describe a functional approach to understanding behavior.
2. Describe critical components of FBAs, hypothesis statements generated from FBA results, and individualized BSPs.
3. Describe two examples to illustrate how results of FBAs are used to generate hypothesis statements and how hypothesis statements are then used to develop individualized BSPs.

The A-B-C Model

The FBA process requires special educators to apply an Antecedent-Behavior-Consequence or "A-B-C" model to understand student behavior. This model assumes that *every* behavior—whether appropriate or inappropriate—serves some function or purpose in a student's environment. By taking a closer look at consequences, or what happens *after* problem behavior, teachers can get ideas about what purpose the behavior is serving for that student. For example, the student who threw the eraser at a classmate might have done so to get attention from his peers. Considering antecedents, or what happens *before* problem behavior, is also important. This is because the presence of certain events or conditions can affect the value of consequences. When a teacher assigns independent seatwork, a student has few opportunities to interact with peers. This context might make peer attention more valuable. In this case, the student might be more likely to engage in disruptive behaviors that result in peer attention. Instead of focusing solely on the problem behavior, considering problem behavior as one part of an A-B-C sequence can help teachers identify when and why the behavior is occurring.

Essential Components

Functional Behavior Assessments

In the critical first step of an FBA, educators must identify and define the targeted problem behavior(s). The goal here should be to describe the problem behavior in specific, observable terms, such that someone unfamiliar with the student could easily recognize the target behavior when it happens. While teachers often describe students' problem behavior in general terms such as "getting worked up" or "shutting down," this is the time to define what "shutting down" looks like. Perhaps the student verbally refuses to complete work by saying things like "I'm done" or "You can't make me." Perhaps he puts his head down on his desk and does not respond to teacher prompts or redirections. Specific, observable descriptions of behavior will help a team objectively and consistently document how frequently these behaviors occur.

After defining the target behavior(s), the next step involves collecting data on the behaviors and variables potentially impacting their occurrence. Two main types of assessment data inform the FBA process, indirect and direct. Indirect assessments involve collecting information on people's perceptions of the student's problem behavior, including when and why it happens. Indirect assessments include interviews, checklists, questionnaires, and rating scales. Adults who know the student best (e.g., parents, teachers) typically complete these assessments. However, the students themselves also may complete the assessments depending on the student's age, communication skills, and willingness to participate.[13] Direct assessment involves observing the student in the contexts in which problem behaviors reportedly occur and collecting data on what they see. Direct observation data can range from informal note-taking to completing highly structured observation forms in which antecedents and consequences are coded for each occurrence of problem behavior and summarized quantitatively.[14] While informal observations can be helpful initially, structured forms of direct observation—especially when completed by trained observers with behavioral expertise—are better suited for reliably documenting patterns of problem behavior.

In some cases, another form of direct assessment known as functional analysis may be warranted. In a functional analysis, a student's problem behavior is measured as one or more features of the environment is systematically increased or decreased (e.g., easy vs. difficult tasks, low vs. high rates of peer attention). This type of assessment is more intensive than indirect assessments and direct observations and typically requires supervision from a behavior specialist. Functional analysis is not required for all FBAs and is beyond the scope of this chapter. However, it is a powerful tool for directly testing hypotheses about when and why problem behavior is occurring.[15]

Hypothesis Statements

Results of both indirect and direct assessments are summarized and considered together to generate a hypothesis statement, that is, the team's best guess of when and why a student engages in the targeted problem behavior. Hypothesis statements should therefore include three critical components: (1) *when* the problem behavior occurs (Antecedent); (2) *what* problem behavior occurs (Behavior); and (3) the outcome, or *why*, the problem behavior occurs (Consequence). It is important to keep in mind that various aspects of a student's classroom environment can impact the behaviors. Some students' behavior may be particularly sensitive to aspects of instruction (e.g., task type, task difficulty, level of prompting, instructional materials); others may be sensitive to aspects of their social context (e.g., proximity to specific peers or adults, instructional groupings) or other physical features of their environment (e.g., noise level, crowded spaces).

Just as the targeted problem behaviors (*what*) should be defined in observable and specific terms, so too should the environmental conditions that are hypothesized to contribute to problem behavior (*when* and *why*). Instead of referring to internal states or emotions such as "winning a power struggle," the focus should be on observable events that happen before and after problem behavior. The antecedent component of the hypothesis statement (*when*) should identify specific conditions that trigger problem behavior. These antecedents include events that immediately precede problem behavior, such as when a teacher assigns a difficult math task. In addition to immediate antecedents, earlier events or conditions that set the stage for problem behavior can also be identified in hypothesis statements, such as when a student has not gotten enough sleep the night before or was bullied on the bus that morning.

The last component of the hypothesis statement (*why*) should identify a relevant consequence the student experiences after engaging in the target behavior. This component will involve either something added to the student's environment or something removed from the student's environment and is intended to explain why the student continues to engage in these behaviors. For example, some students engage in problem behavior to *get* attention from teachers or peers, while other students engage in problem behavior to *escape* such attention. Some students engage in problem behavior to *gain* access to preferred activities or materials (e.g., time on the computer), whereas others do so to *avoid* non-preferred events, activities, or settings (e.g., difficult math tasks, a crowded cafeteria). While interactions between the student and his/her environment can be complex, all behavior either serves to "get" or to "avoid" something in that student's environment.

As shown in the following examples, a hypothesis statement should include all three of these critical components and may include both immediate and distant antecedent events:

(A)   During independent seatwork, Sidney (B) calls out (C) to get attention from her teacher.

(A_1)   When prompted to take turns during free play, Alex (B) drops to the floor and screams (C) to maintain access to preferred toys. (A_2) The less sleep Alex gets the night before, the more likely this pattern is to happen.

Behavior Support Plans

Generating a hypothesis statement provides the foundation for developing a BSP. A BSP has five critical components. First, the team must identify an appropriate behavior to *replace* the targeted problem behavior. To effectively replace the problem behavior, this appropriate behavior must result in the same or similar outcome as the problem behavior. For example, consider the following hypothesis statement: "When prompted by his teacher to read aloud, Jeremiah pushes instructional materials off his desk to *avoid completing the task*." In this case, an appropriate replacement behavior might be *asking for a break*, as this behavior is a more acceptable way to obtain the same consequence (temporary escape from tasks). Similar methods to those described in Chapter 9 (Teach Social Behaviors) may be used to introduce, teach, and reinforce replacement behaviors.

After identifying an appropriate replacement behavior, the next critical components of BSPs involve modifying the student's environment. The second step is to modify antecedent variables to reduce the likelihood of problem behavior. For example, if reading aloud is a difficult or non-preferred activity for Jeremiah, his teacher might try to make the task easier or more preferred. Perhaps the teacher asks him to first follow along in the text while she reads aloud, or she allows Jeremiah to choose the text to read from, or she is careful to introduce this task between activities that are easier for Jeremiah. The goal of any of these antecedent modifications is to decrease the value of the consequence—in this case, decreasing Jeremiah's motivation to avoid the task. Of course, the motivation to avoid tasks cannot be completely eliminated without also removing expectations to complete the task. This brings us to the third step, which is to make the replacement behavior more effective and efficient than the problem behavior. For example, if all Jeremiah has to do to get a break from reading aloud is to ask for one, he will be more likely to ask appropriately instead of pushing his materials off the desk. To arrange an environment that supports the replacement behavior, teachers must consistently provide the consequence when the replacement behavior occurs (e.g., honoring Jeremiah's appropriate requests for breaks). The fourth step, which can be the most difficult one to implement consistently, is to prevent or minimize the same consequence from happening when the student engages in problem behavior. For Jeremiah, this means that if he resorts to pushing materials off his desk again, he should not be allowed to avoid the task. Even if it takes a moment for teachers to re-present the task to follow along in the book, this brief delay to task completion would be shorter than a break he could earn by asking appropriately. A fifth and final critical component of BSPs is to collect progress monitoring data on targeted problem and replacement behaviors. Without this information, special educators have no way of determining when to continue, modify, or discontinue the BSP (see Table 10.1 for essential component summaries).

Example 1: Kyree

Kyree was a third-grade student with attention-deficit/hyperactivity disorder. He spent most of the school day in his third-grade general education classroom and received instructional support for

Table 10.1 Critical Components of Functional Behavior Assessments, Hypothesis Statements, and Behavior Support Plans

Functional Behavior Assessments	Hypothesis Statements	Behavior Support Plans
1. Define problem behavior in observable terms	1. *What*: Targeted problem behavior	1. Teach appropriate replacement behavior
2. Collect indirect data from those who know the student best	2. *When*: Conditions that trigger problem behavior	2. Modify environment to prevent the occurrence of problem behavior
3. Collect direct observation data in relevant classroom contexts	3. *Why*: Consequences that explain why problem behavior continues to happen	3. Modify environment to make replacement behavior more effective and efficient than problem behavior
		4. Modify environment to prevent problem behavior from producing the previous consequence or outcome
		5. Collect progress monitoring data for continued intervention planning

reading from Ms. Howell, the special education teacher. The third-grade teacher had several class-wide behavior management practices in place. She regularly reviewed behavioral expectations and provided frequent praise and corrective feedback to students based on whether they were meeting expectations. Despite these strategies, however, Kyree continued to engage in frequent disruptive behaviors. The disruptive behaviors occurred across settings but were more frequent in the general education classroom. Kyree's teachers became increasingly concerned that these behaviors were affecting his academic progress. They decided he needed an individualized BSP to address these behaviors before they worsened and required more extreme disciplinary action.

Functional Behavior Assessment

Kyree's teachers began by defining the disruptive behaviors based on what they looked like in the classroom. They agreed to define Kyree's disruptive behavior as any time he (a) left his seat without permission, (b) talked out above a conversational volume when a teacher was providing instruction, or (c) touched or took a peer's materials without asking. Because these behaviors were reported to occur more often in the general education setting, Ms. Howell asked the third-grade teacher to complete a 16-item questionnaire about the situations in which Kyree's disruptive behavior typically occurred and what usually happened after he became disruptive. Ms. Howell summarized the responses, which suggested Kyree may be engaging in the targeted disruptive behaviors to get attention from teachers or peers.

Ms. Howell then offered to collect direct observation data on Kyree's disruptive behaviors in the third-grade general education classroom. She wanted to document whether the patterns described on the questionnaire were happening in the classroom. She used a structured data collection form, with rows to mark each occurrence of disruptive behavior and several possible antecedents and consequences to check off based on what happened immediately before and after the disruptive behavior. She completed two 20-minute observations during independent seatwork—a routine in which the third-grade teacher reported Kyree's disruptive behavior happened most often. By the end of the second observation, Ms. Howell had recorded 13 instances of disruption. She found that all thirteen (100%) occurred when Kyree was in close proximity to peers and that most instances of disruptive behavior (10 of 13; 77%) were followed by some type of peer response (e.g., eye contact, laughter, comments). Because these patterns were consistent with results of the questionnaire, the teachers quickly reached consensus on the following hypothesis statement: *When independent seatwork is assigned and Kyree is in close proximity to peers, he engages in disruptive behavior to access peer attention.*

Behavior Support Plan

Kyree's teachers then used their hypothesis statement to develop an individualized BSP. They began by identifying an appropriate behavior to replace Kyree's disruptions. Based on their understanding that to replace the disruptive behavior, this new behavior would have to lead to the same consequence, they decided to focus on appropriate peer initiations. When teaching this replacement behavior to Kyree, they not only reviewed *how* to recruit attention from peers (e.g., tapping a classmate on the shoulder, saying their name or "Excuse me") but *when* it was appropriate to do so (e.g., during free time, on the playground, at the lunch table). Together, they reviewed examples and non-examples of appropriate peer initiations and invited one of Kyree's preferred peers to help practice these behaviors using role play.

Next, the teachers focused on modifying Kyree's environment in ways that supported the use of appropriate peer initiations while minimizing the payoff of peer attention following disruptive behavior. To make the replacement behavior more effective and efficient than disruptive behavior, they set up frequent opportunities for Kyree to initiate high-quality social interactions with peers at times of day that allowed for these activities (e.g., running a class errand with a peer, playing a game with a group of peers on the playground). To minimize disruptive behavior during independent seatwork, as well as the likelihood that peers would respond to it, they modified the seating arrangement to increase Kyree's proximity to the teacher and decrease his proximity to preferred peers.

Before and after initiating the BSP, the teachers collected data on the frequency of Kyree's disruptive behavior during the independent seatwork routine. They found that while the frequency of disruptive behavior had decreased since beginning the intervention, these behaviors still occurred intermittently during independent seatwork. Based on their progress monitoring data, they decided to add a component to the plan. They introduced a reward system to the independent seatwork routine in which Kyree could earn time to work with a preferred peer in Ms. Howell's classroom for staying on task. They reviewed expectations for staying on task with Kyree and began by requiring him to remain on task without engaging in disruptive behavior for only a brief portion of the independent seatwork routine (e.g., five minutes) to earn partner work time. As Kyree successfully earned the reward, they gradually increased the criterion from five to 20 minutes (the duration of the independent seatwork routine).

Example 2: Mila

Mila was a seventh-grade student with a label of emotional disturbance. She attended a school with a multi-tiered system of behavior support in place and received instruction in both the general education setting and a classroom for students with behavior problems. She also met weekly with the school counselor. While Mila had struggled with off-task behaviors in the past, she had recently become more noncompliant in the classroom, actively refusing to do work and even verbally lashing out at her teachers when they tried redirecting her to the task. These behaviors had continued even after a targeted (Tier 2) intervention was attempted in which Mila had daily check-ins with her special education teacher, Mr. Martinez. When Mila's behavior still did not improve, Mr. Martinez reached out to the school's Tier 3 team for assistance in conducting an FBA and developing an individualized BSP.

Functional Behavior Assessment

Mr. Martinez met with two members of the Tier 3 team—the school counselor and school psychologist—to define the behaviors to target for Mila's FBA. They defined noncompliance as any time Mila did not initiate a teacher-directed task within 30 seconds; put her head down on her desk; or verbally refused to complete a task (e.g., "No!" or "I don't want to!"). They also decided to target inappropriate language, which they defined as any instance of audible profanity or any time she yelled at a teacher (above conversational volume).

Once the target behaviors were identified and defined, the school psychologist recommended Mr. Martinez use a structured, student-directed interview with Mila to collect information on her likes and dislikes at school. During the student interview, Mila indicated her least favorite subject was English/Language Arts (ELA), and she especially didn't like writing tasks because she was "no good at it." Based on what Mila shared about her struggles in ELA, Mr. Martinez used a structured interview form to collect information from her ELA teacher on what usually happens before and after Mila's problem behavior. The ELA teacher indicated Mila commonly asked to go to the bathroom or the nurse's office during writing assignments. When her requests were denied, she would get visibly upset, refuse to complete her work (e.g., "I don't want to do this stupid assignment!") and stop responding to teacher prompts or redirections. The ELA teacher reported she would sometimes send Mila to the office when she started using profanity in front of the other students.

Based on information collected from the interviews, the school psychologist observed Mila during ELA. He used a narrative-recording method on three separate occasions to document the pattern and sequence of antecedents, problem behaviors, and consequences. Across three different school days, the school psychologist was able to document the pattern described in the interview. Noncompliance occurred following prompts to begin writing tasks, and inappropriate language occurred when the teacher redirected Mila or denied her request to change activities. In addition, despite the teacher's best intentions, Mila successfully avoided completing the writing task by conversing with her teacher or being sent to the office. Mr. Martinez met with the Tier 3 team to review all the assessment data together. They reached consensus on the following hypothesis: *When Mila is assigned writing tasks, she engages in noncompliance and inappropriate language to avoid completing the task.*

Behavior Support Plan

The team used the hypothesis statement to collaboratively develop a multi-component BSP for Mila. First, even before identifying a replacement behavior, they determined that Mila needed additional instructional support in writing to make these tasks less difficult (e.g., breaking each writing task into discrete steps, incorporating visual supports). They reasoned that if writing tasks were less difficult for Mila, she would be less motivated to avoid them in the first place. Then, the team identified a replacement behavior that provided a more appropriate way for Mila to temporarily escape the task, exchanging a hall pass card that represented a five-minute break (e.g., trip to bathroom, getting a drink of water).

During the planning process, both the ELA teacher and Mr. Martinez expressed concerns about allowing Mila to avoid writing tasks whenever she asked to use a hall pass. To address this concern, the team decided to set up a reward system in which Mila earned hall passes for initiating writing tasks independently and asking for assistance from a teacher when she got stuck. An important component of the plan was that Mila would no longer be allowed to leave the classroom if she was noncompliant or used inappropriate language. To set Mila up for success, they began by allowing her to earn up to three 5-minute breaks within the 30-minute writing period. Mr. Martinez and the ELA teacher collaborated to collect progress monitoring data on Mila's compliance and inappropriate language. After initiating the BSP, her inappropriate language immediately decreased, and compliance gradually increased. As Mila's compliance continued to increase, they allowed her greater independence in this routine and incorporated choice-making opportunities within the reward system. For example, as she earned her hall passes, she could choose whether to exchange them immediately or save them to exchange for longer breaks at a later time.

Wrap Up

When students engage in problem behavior, teachers should interpret their behavior as a signal that there is a mismatch between the student's needs and their current environment.[16] The FBA process provides a pathway to find and address this mismatch. Kyree had a need for quality social interactions with his peers but required individualized support on how and when it was appropriate to initiate these interactions. For Mila, there was a mismatch between the difficulty level of her writing assignments and her current skill level. With additional instructional supports, and an avenue to request breaks when she needed them, Mila had more opportunities to experience success with writing tasks and was no longer motivated to avoid them.

In this chapter, we introduced FBAs as a high leverage practice to develop individualized BSPs. In describing when and how to use this practice, it should be clear why FBAs are reserved for the few students who do not respond to less intensive strategies. Namely, FBAs and BSPs require time, careful planning, and active collaboration between special educators and other school staff. Fortunately, a growing body of evidence suggests these efforts are worthwhile. We hope this chapter communicates the value of FBAs and BSPs for students with the most intensive needs and provides beginning special educators a starting point to develop these important skillsets.

Tips

The following tips should assist beginning special educators in conducting effective FBAs and developing function-based BSPs (see also the Key Resources section of this chapter for additional resources):

1. **Seek support from a team.** Special educators can play critical roles in conducting FBAs and developing individualized BSPs, but not without support from other school staff. We encourage special educators to solicit support from other team members when conducting FBAs. Depending on the district and school, support might come from a pre-established student support team or less formal partnerships (e.g., consulting with a behavior specialist, school psychologist, or another teacher who supports the student in a different setting).

2. **Collect progress monitoring data regularly.** Collecting ongoing progress monitoring data is essential for students who have individualized BSPs. Sometimes, teachers may be tempted to skip or discontinue data collection, especially on a student's "best" or "worst" days. On good days, they might consider progress monitoring unnecessary; on bad days, the prospect of collecting data on top of everything else they must do may be too overwhelming. However, both pieces of information—when the plan is working and when the plan is *not* working—are critical for continued intervention planning. These data can help teachers determine when it is time to fade out a component of support based on a student's success, or when it is time to add or adapt a component to meet the student's changing needs.

3. **Focus on the parts of a student's environment you can control.** Special educators must acknowledge their students' behavior is impacted both by what they encounter within and outside of their classroom.[17] While teachers cannot control what their students encounter at home, in the community, or even in other classrooms in the school building, they must not discount what they can offer these students: a safe and reliable learning environment in which adults clearly communicate expectations, follow through on planned consequences, celebrate major and minor successes, and address problem behaviors as new opportunities to learn.

Notes

1 Sugai, G., Horner, R. H., Dunlap, G., Hieneman, M., Lewis, T. J., Nelson, C. M., . . . Ruef, M. (2000). Applying positive behavior support and functional behavior assessment in school. *Journal of Positive Behavior Interventions*, *2*, 131–143.

2 Carr, E. G., & Durand, M. V. (1985). Reducing behavior problems through functional communication training. *Journal of Applied Behavior Analysis*, *18*, 111–126.
    Iwata, B. A., Dorsey, M. F., Slifer, K. J., Bauman, K. E., & Richman, G. S. (1982). Toward a functional analysis of self injury. *Analysis and Intervention in Developmental Disabilities*, *2*, 3–20. Reprinted in *Journal of Applied Behavior Analysis*, *27*, 197–209.

3 Lloyd, B. P., Weaver, E. S., & Staubitz, J. L. (2016). A review of experimental functional assessment methods conducted in public school classroom settings. *Journal of Behavioral Education*, *25*, 324–356.

4 Lewis, T. J., Mitchell, B. S., Harvey, K., Green, A., & McKenzie, J. (2015). A comparison of functional behavioral assessment and functional analysis methodology among students with mild disabilities. *Behavioral Disorders, 41*(1), 5–20.

Lloyd, B. P., Wehby, J. H., Weaver, E. S., Goldman, S. E., Harvey, M. N., & Sherlock, D. R. (2015). Implementation and validation of trial-based functional analyses in public elementary school settings. *Journal of Behavioral Education, 24,* 167–195.

5 Shumate, E. D., & Wills, H. P. (2010). Classroom-based functional analysis and intervention for disruptive and off-task behaviors. *Education and Treatment of Children, 33*(1), 23–48.

Kern, L., Childs, K. E., Dunlap, G., Clarke, S., & Falk, G. D. (1994). Using assessment-based curricular intervention to improve the classroom behavior of a student with emotional and behavioral challenges. *Journal of Applied Behavior Analysis, 27,* 7–19.

Lewis, T. J., & Sugai, G. (1996a). Functional assessment of problem behavior: A pilot investigation of the comparative and interactive effects of teacher and peer social attention on students in general education settings. *School Psychology Quarterly, 11,* 1–19.

Lewis, T. J., & Sugai, G. (1996b). Descriptive and experimental analysis of teacher and peer attention and the use of assessment based intervention to improve the pro-social behavior of a student in a general education setting. *Journal of Behavioral Education, 6,* 7–24.

Umbreit, J. (1995). Functional assessment and intervention in a regular classroom setting for the disruptive behavior of a student with attention deficit hyperactivity disorder. *Behavioral Disorders, 20,* 267–278.

6 What Works Clearinghouse. (2016). *Functional behavioral assessment-based interventions.* What Works Clearinghouse Intervention Report, Institue of Education Sciences. Retrieved from https://ies.ed.gov/ncee/wwc/EvidenceSnapshot/667

7 Ingram, K., Lewis-Palmer, T., & Sugai, G. (2005). Function-based intervention planning: Comparing the effectiveness of FBA indicated and contra-indicated intervention plans. *Journal of Positive Behavior Interventions, 7,* 224–236.

Newcomer, L. L., & Lewis, T. J. (2004). Functional behavioral assessment: An investigation of assessment reliability and effectiveness of function-based interventions. *Journal of Emotional and Behavioral Disorders, 12,* 168–181.

Payne, L. D., Scott, T. M., & Conroy, M. (2007). A school-based examination of the efficacy of function-based intervention. *Behavioral Disorders, 32,* 158–174.

8 Individuals with Disabilities Education Act, 20 U.S.C. §§ 1400 *et seq.*

9 von Ravensberg, H., & Blakely, A. (2014). When to use functional behavior assessment? Best practice vs. legal guidance. *Positive Behavioral Interventions & Supports Newsletter.* Retrieved from www.pbis.org/evaluation/evaluation-briefs/when-to-use-fba

10 von Ravensberg, H., & Blakely, A. (2014). When to use functional behavior assessment? Best practice vs. legal guidance. *Positive Behavioral Interventions & Supports Newsletter.* Retrieved from www.pbis.org/evaluation/evaluation-briefs/when-to-use-fba

11 Crone, D. A., & Horner, R. H. (2003). *Building positive behavior support systems in schools: Functional behavioral assessment.* New York, NY: Guilford Press.

12 Lloyd, B. P., Wehby, J. H., Weaver, E. S., Goldman, S. E., Harvey, M. N., & Sherlock, D. R. (2015). Implementation and validation of trial-based functional analyses in public elementary school settings. *Journal of Behavioral Education, 24,* 167–195.

Lloyd, B. P., Weaver, E. S., & Staubitz, J. L. (2017). Classroom-based strategies for incorporating hypothesis testing in functional behavior assessments. *Beyond Behavior, 26,* 48–56.

13 O'Neill, R. E., Albin, R. W., Storey, K., Horner, R. H., & Sprague, J. R. (2015). *Functional assessment and program development for problem behavior: A practical handbook.* Stanford, CT: Cengage Learning.

14 O'Neill, R. E., Albin, R. W., Storey, K., Horner, R. H., & Sprague, J. R. (2015). *Functional assessment and program development for problem behavior: A practical handbook.* Stanford, CT: Cengage Learning.

Staubitz, J. L., & Lloyd, B. P. (2016). Beyond ABC data: A tutorial for measuring contingencies in the classroom. *Beyond Behavior, 25,* 17–26.

15 Lloyd, B. P., Weaver, E. S., & Staubitz, J. L. (2016). A review of experimental functional assessment methods conducted in public school classroom settings. *Journal of Behavioral Education, 25,* 324–356.

Lloyd, B. P., Weaver, E. S., & Staubitz, J. L. (2017). Classroom-based strategies for incorporating hypothesis testing in functional behavior assessments. *Beyond Behavior, 26,* 48–56.

16 Dunlap, G., Harrower, J., & Fox, L. (2005). Understanding the environmental determinants of problem behaviors. In L. M. Bambara & L. Kern (Eds.), *Individualized supports for students with problem behaviors* (pp. 25–46). New York, NY: Guilford Press.

17 Lewis, T. J., Hatton, H. L., Jorgenson, C., & Maynard, D. (2017). What beginning special educators need to know about conducting functional behavior assessments. *Teaching Exceptional Children, 49,* 231–238.

Key Resources

- Alberto, P. A., & Troutman, A. C. (2013). *Applied behavior analysis for teachers* (9th ed.). Upper Saddle River, NJ: Pearson. *This textbook provides a thorough and accessible introduction to the principles of applied behavior analysis (ABA) and their application in classroom settings. It is written for teachers who are new to ABA. Chapters are organized in a way that presents all critical components of a behavior plan, and include several tools for data collection and intervention planning.*

- Hirsch, S. E., Bruhn, A. L., Lloyd, J. W., & Katsiyannis, A. (2017). FBAs and BIPs: Avoiding and addressing four common challenges related to fidelity. *TEACHING Exceptional Children, 49,* 369–379. *This article offers practitioners a guide to avoid potential pitfalls of the FBA and BSP process. It includes a list of helpful resources for completing FBAs and BSPs (Table 1) and an accompanying checklist for troubleshooting and action planning (Figure 1).*

- O'Neill, R. E., Albin, R. W., Storey, K., Horner, R. H., & Sprague, J. R. (2015). *Functional assessment and program development for problem behavior: A practical handbook.* Stanford, CT: Cengage Learning.

- Umbreit, J., Ferro, J. B., Liaupsin, C. J., & Lane, K. L. (2007). *Functional behavioral assessment and function-based intervention. An effective, practical approach.* New York, NY: Pearson. *Both of these handbooks are written for teachers who have some experience with FBAs and BSPs. Each provides a hands-on approach, uses case summaries to apply content, and offers a variety of tools and templates for data collection and intervention planning.*

- What Works Clearinghouse (2016). *Functional behavioral assessment-based interventions.* What Works Clearinghouse Intervention Report, Institute of Education Sciences. Retrieved from https://ies.ed.gov/ncee/wwc/EvidenceSnapshot/667 *This report summarizes the existing evidence for FBA-based interventions for students with or at risk for emotional disturbance. The report includes intervention descriptions, summary ratings of effectiveness, and procedural details on studies contributing to the evidence base.*

- www.basicfba.com *This website provides free access to a variety of professional developmental materials (e.g., online trainings, data collection forms, graphing templates) used to train school teams to conduct 'basic' FBAs to develop BSPs for students with mild to moderate problem behavior.*

Section 4
Instruction High Leverage Practices

Edited by Lawrence Maheady

Co-edited by Lisa A. Rafferty, Angela L. Patti,
and Shannon Budin

Introduction to Instruction High Leverage Practices

Teaching students with disabilities is a strategic, flexible, and recursive process. Effective special education teachers use content and pedagogical knowledge, as well as formative assessment data on student learning, to design, deliver, and evaluate their instructional effectiveness. Furthermore, these teachers base their instruction on the use of effective practices in combination with their professional wisdom and a thorough understanding of individual student needs and contextual restraints. Special education teachers value diversity and infuse knowledge of student backgrounds, culture, and language into instructional planning and decision-making. They apply this knowledge and decision-making competence to improve student outcomes across varied curricula and in multiple educational settings.

The process of developing and delivering effective instruction begins with well-designed lessons. To plan instruction, effective special education teachers integrate their knowledge of general education and other contextually relevant curricula (e.g., culturally responsive and universally designed); link these understandings to appropriate learning standards, progressions, and benchmarks; and align them with specific IEP requirements to prioritize long- and short-term learning goals. Based on student learning goals, special educators systematically design instruction and adapt curriculum tasks and materials as needed to support student learning.

Once goals are identified and lessons are designed, effective special educators have the pedagogical skills to deliver well-planned instruction. This instruction is designed to actively engage all students in meaningful learning activities, provide scaffolded supports to assist those in need, guide student learning using constructive feedback, and plan instruction that promotes generalization of learning across time and settings. Special educators also use instructional technology and a Universal Design for Learning framework to plan, deliver, and differentiate instruction that addresses a range of important student learning goals.

To meet the range of instructional needs of students with disabilities, effective special educators use a variety of flexible grouping arrangements and instructional strategies to deliver instruction that varies in intensity level and is differentiated based on student learning needs. This includes the use of teacher-led practices such as explicit instruction to increase the intensity of instruction for small groups of students with similar learning needs or for larger groups at varied skill levels. Effective special educators augment teacher-led instruction with a variety of peer-assisted teaching practices that enhance learning and promote prosocial interactions. They also teach students to use strategies to support their own learning, as well as to function independently of others' support.

Effective special education teachers use teacher-led, peer-assisted, student-regulated, and technology-assisted practices and know when and where to apply them to improve student learning. They monitor individual, small group, and whole-class progress using appropriate formative assessment measures and adapt and/or discard instructional practices that do not sufficiently improve student learning. Ultimately, effective instructional practices are defined by their impact on student learning. If students do not make acceptable academic progress, then their teacher must "try another way."

11
Identify and Prioritize Long- and Short-Term Learning Goals

*Sheila R. Alber-Morgan, Moira Konrad, Terri Hessler,
Maria R. Helton, and Alana Oif Telesman*

Introduction

Setting appropriate instructional goals is critical for student success, but how does a teacher know what an "appropriate" goal is? When identifying goals, teachers must consider grade-level standards determined by local, state, and federal agencies; individual learning needs specified in individualized education programs (IEPs); and content and skill priorities within academic disciplines. In consideration of these factors, goals must be designed to produce the most meaningful student outcomes.

Not all goals are of equal importance, so it is imperative to prioritize which knowledge and skills should be addressed immediately and which can be targeted later. Prioritizing includes setting goals around critical content, linking goals to each student's present level of performance,[1] and using data on an ongoing basis. Well-designed goals, derived from instructional standards, are written from the student's point of view,[2] so students can understand what is expected of them and take ownership of their goal planning, which can then motivate them to reach their goals.

It is essential that students with diverse learning needs have specific learning plans and measurable objectives to allow for measurement to determine adequate progress toward their goals. In addition to adhering to IEP goals, teachers must incorporate academic goals based on content standards.[3] IEPs should also provide long-range academic plans that guide students throughout their academic careers toward appropriate postsecondary outcomes. Annual goals that are composed of short-term learning targets serve as stepping stones toward mastering the ultimate goal. For example, a teacher might set monthly reading targets that incrementally lead to grade-level reading benchmarks (see Hasbrouck and Tindal[4] for an example of grade-level benchmarks/norms).

Arguably, recent implementation of Common Core State Standards (CCSS) has increased the rigor of current classroom curriculum and led to more robust academic expectations for all students. Teachers are responsible for adapting their instruction to ensure each student's individual needs are being met while simultaneously ensuring that students are accessing grade-level standards. Effective systematic instruction is customized to each student's present level of performance and is frequently monitored until the goal is met. In addition to examining grade-level standards, IEP goals and benchmarks, and student assessment data, effective teachers also consider essential curriculum components, prerequisites, and foundations when developing appropriate goals. With appropriate accommodations (see HLP 13), students with diverse learning needs can reach ambitious goals and maximize their success in a rigorous general education curriculum.

Narrowing the Focus

Teachers are required to develop appropriate instructional goals that are aligned with grade-level standards and design instruction that enables all students to reach those goals regardless of their learning challenges.[5] In this chapter, we discuss considerations that influence selection of learning goals, including grade-level standards, student assessment data, IEPs, and research-based instructional priorities within academic disciplines. Additionally, we describe a process for identifying instructional goals that are aligned with grade-level standards and individual needs.

Chapter Overview

1. Identify considerations that influence selection of learning goals.
2. Describe instructional and individualized priorities across academic content areas.
3. Describe a process for identifying instructional goals that are aligned with grade-level standards and individual needs.

Considerations That Influence Identification of Learning Goals

When deciding what to teach, there are two major considerations: the general curriculum and the individualized curriculum. The general curriculum is what all students are expected to know and be able to do in each content area, in each grade. Teachers must consider this first. Therefore, the first source teachers must consult is the grade-level standards. All 50 states have standards that outline the knowledge and skills students need to attain in each grade level.[6] Many of these are based on the CCSS; however, individual schools and districts may have local standards as well. In addition, teachers should consult standards that have been developed by professional organizations or advisory panels in their disciplines (e.g., National Reading Panel, National Mathematics Advisory Panel, National Council for the Social Studies).

Next, teachers must keep in mind the individual needs of students in order to inform the development of an individualized curriculum. An individualized curriculum requires teachers to customize the general curriculum based on the individual's learning needs. Teachers will have diverse groups of students with a range of background knowledge, skills, and abilities. Although all students should have access to the general curriculum, many students will need to meet specialized learning goals in order to be successful. These goals should be based on individual assessment data, IEP goals and benchmarks, and family input.

Instructional Priorities

Because not all goals are of equal importance, it is necessary to prioritize goals around critical content and skills. Again, there are two major considerations: the general curriculum and the individualized curriculum.

Identifying General Curriculum Standards

The following are examples of priorities in the general education curriculum that have been identified through research (e.g., meta-analyses) and recommendations by experts in their respective content areas: reading, writing, math, science, and social studies.

Reading

The National Reading Panel identifies phonemic awareness, alphabetic principle, fluency, vocabulary, and comprehension as instructional priorities to increase reading achievement.[7]

- **Phonemic awareness.** Phonemic awareness includes phoneme manipulation, segmenting, and blending. Rhyming, syllable manipulations, and identifying onsets and rimes are important stepping stones on the path to phonemic awareness.[8]
- **Alphabetic principle.** Students must learn the correspondence between phonemes and printed letters in order to decode words. Goals for this component include decoding phonetically spelled words (e.g., cat), reading irregular words (e.g., done), and reading words in context. As students master basic letter-sound correspondence, they should begin to learn to use structural analysis to decode words, which requires instruction on root words, prefixes, suffixes, compound words, and syllabication.[9]
- **Fluency.** Fluent reading is critical for helping students to understand what they read. Fluency is not just reading quickly and accurately; it also includes prosody. Teachers should consult grade-level reading fluency norms to help them determine individual students' reading fluency goals. For example, second graders reading at the 50th percentile should be correctly reading 89 words per minute by the end of the school year with an average weekly improvement of 1.2 words per week.[10]
- **Vocabulary.** According to the National Reading Panel, the most effective vocabulary instruction incorporates both receptive (listening, reading) and expressive (speaking, writing) modes of communication. Teachers should group vocabulary words in three tiers for instruction.[11] Tier 1 words are high-frequency, everyday words (e.g., *restaurant, play, huge*) that generally do not require instruction. In contrast, Tier 3 words are specialized for specific content areas (e.g., *convection, totalitarianism*) and will likely require explicit instruction by a content area teacher. Tier 2 consists of words that are high frequency, but also advanced (e.g., *collaboration, analyze, aggressive*). Because Tier 2 words are important for language and literacy and are not likely to be learned incidentally by all students, teachers should focus their efforts on these words. In other words, Tier 2 words are instructional priorities. Ultimately, vocabulary instruction should target words that are relevant to understanding specific expository and narrative reading passages, their meanings, and their use in context.
- **Comprehension.** Given that comprehension is the ultimate goal of reading, teachers should view comprehension as a high priority skill. The Institute of Education Sciences (IES) practice guide for improving reading comprehension identifies goals for students.[12] Specifically, students should learn, practice, and consistently implement reading comprehension strategies (e.g., self-questioning, summarizing) and how to identify and use the text's organizational structure to comprehend, learn, and remember content.

Writing

Writing Next, a meta-analysis of research for teaching written expression, identified evidence-based goals for writing achievement.[13] These goals include students learning the writing process and strategies for pre-writing, planning, revising, and editing. Sentence combining, summary writing, writing for content learning, writing collaboratively with peers, and using the computer to write are also important goals for improving writing skills. Additionally, students need to have basic transcription skills that include spelling, handwriting, and keyboarding to be successful writers.

Math

The National Mathematics Advisory Panel identified the following critical foundational math goals for students through seventh grade: fluency with whole numbers, fluency with fractions, and geometry and measurement.[14] Under each critical foundation is a list of benchmarks. For example, the end of fifth-grade benchmark, "*solving problems involving perimeter and area of triangles*," is nested under the geometry and measurement goal.

The following is a list of priorities for elementary and middle school mathematics.[15]

- base ten numeration system
- equivalence, comparison, operation meanings and relationships
- properties
- basic facts and algorithms
- estimation
- patterns
- variables
- proportionality
- relations and functions
- equations and inequalities
- shapes and solids
- orientation and location
- transformations
- measurement
- data collection
- data representation
- data distribution
- chance

For each topic, a corresponding list of mathematical understandings that are foundational to understanding that topic is provided. For example under "Chance," the following are examples of mathematical understandings: "probability can provide a basis for making predictions; some probabilities can only be determined through experimental trials; an event that is certain to happen will always happen (The probability is 1.) and an event that is impossible will never happen (The probability is 0.)."[16]

Science

The National Committee on Science Education Standards and Assessment developed the National Science Education Standards (NSCS) around the following themes:[17]

- unifying concepts and processes in science
- science as inquiry
- physical science
- life science
- earth and space science
- science and technology
- science in personal and social perspectives
- history and nature of science

The goals for each theme are broken down by grade level. For example, under the physical science standards, the goals for students in K–4 include understanding properties of objects and materials; position and motion of objects; and light, heat, electricity, and magnetism. For grades 5–8, the goals include understanding properties and changes of properties in matter, motions and forces, and transfer of energy. For high school students, the goals include understanding the structure of atoms, structure of properties of matter, chemical reactions, conservation of energy, and interactions of energy and matter.

Social Studies

The National Council for the Social Studies (NCSS) identified standards that are organized around the following ten themes.[18]

- culture
- time, continuity, and change
- people, places, and environments
- individual development and identity
- individuals, groups, and institutions
- power, authority, and governance
- production, distribution, and consumption
- science, technology, and society
- global connections
- civic ideals and practices

Within each of the ten themes, the NCSS identifies a series of goals. For example, under the theme "Culture," one of the goals is, "Through experience, observation, and reflection, students will identify elements of culture as well as similarities and differences among cultural groups across time and place."[19]

Identifying Individualized Priorities

Once teachers have set instructional goals based on the standards and academic content priorities, they must complete another step for some of their students—differentiating goals as determined by individual students' needs. The first place to start in this process is each individual student's IEP, if one has been drafted. Teachers should keep in mind the lack of an identifying label does not preclude a student's need for an individualized goal, especially in early grades, when the referral process for special education may not have begun. In some cases, this process is initiated by the classroom teacher's monitoring of a student's progress and resulting need for individualization.

Student Assessment Data

There are two types of assessments teachers can use to obtain data on a student's progress: formative and summative. The major distinction between formative and summative assessments is related to how the data will be used. When the data are used to inform teaching decisions, it is formative; when they are used to evaluate students or assign grades, they are summative.

Formative assessments are formal or informal practices that teachers utilize to collect data on student progress in order to improve instruction.[20] These assessments should occur during and immediately following all lessons.[21] For example, during a mathematics lesson covering operations, the teacher could assess her students' understanding by presenting eight to ten practice problems on the SmartBoard one at a time as the students provide their answers in unison on write-on white boards from their desks. Without having to grade papers, the teacher can recognize immediately if her students are "getting it" or if operations need to be reviewed or retaught. The teacher can also note if any students (and which ones) are still struggling with the content. Record-keeping of data can be done with a simple roster document and checkmark system (see Figure 11.1). At the end of the lesson, the teacher can administer a brief assessment (e.g., exit slip with one or two problems) that can be quickly graded to guide the next day's instruction. Teachers may find that technology is an efficient way to assist with assessment of student progress. Apps such as Socrative, NearPod, Plickers, Kahoot, and Goformative can be useful for conducting formative assessment (see Key Resources for web addresses).

The second type of assessment is summative, which usually occurs at the end of an instructional unit and may also be cumulative.[22] Permanent products, such as quizzes, tests, writing products, and portfolios, are typical summative assessment tools.

Administering assessments that align with instructional objectives provides teachers with information that can guide instructional decisions and inform progress towards goals.[23] Therefore, formal and informal assessments are continuously used to assess student progress, as teachers cannot wait until the end of a grading period to make adjustments to instruction.[24] Additionally, continued assessment of student progress leads to more time-efficient instructional practices instead of spending instructional time on a skill a student has already mastered.[25]

General and special education teachers can use formal and informal assessment procedures regularly to assess student progress and modify instruction based on student needs.[26] Once assessment data have been collected, teachers should analyze the data in order to identify students who may need extra support or instruction.[27] Using assessment data effectively requires the teacher to provide immediate feedback to students. Thus, the teacher must review the data quickly and make meaningful changes to address student needs.[28] Data derived from the assessments should inform what comes next for each student.[29] This assessment process determines instructional priorities for individual students.

Assessment is not always about evaluating the effects of current instruction; it also includes identifying prior knowledge. Before embarking upon a unit, teachers can increase their efficiency by assessing what students already know about the topic. The long-standing KWL chart (K: what we *k*now; W: what we *w*ant to find out; L: what we *l*earned and still need to learn)[30] is still the standard. Even though it has undergone a 21st-century renovation (i.e., KWHLAQ: What do I know? What do I want to know? How do I find out? What have I learned? What action will I take? What new questions do I have?),[31] the first step to this process has remained the same: Find out what the students think they know. This serves as an important starting point as well as a chance to identify and prioritize goals. During this process of asking what students already know, the teacher can prepare and organize the information for efficient delivery, especially for those students with the greatest needs. The following are recommendations for prioritizing instruction for students with disabilities: (a) emphasize connections between content items that are important; (b) assist students in organizing and categorizing information; and (c) make a connection between newly taught information and information already learned.[32] Teachers must be cautious when activating background knowledge. Spending too much time on activating prior knowledge may take away time from instruction and may allow students to practice errors. Teachers may also consider using formal assessments of background knowledge, such as pretesting, collecting baseline data, and directly observing performance.

4th Period Math— End of Lesson Checks—— Operations

√ = frequent incorrect answers

Name: Last, First	11/12	11/13	11/14	11/15	11/16	11/19	11/20	11/21	11/22	11/23	11/26	11/27	11/28
1. Balks, Tobias													
2. Burken, Demetri													
3. Dowling, Arastelle		√											
4. Elvesh, Denisha													
5. Earhart, Shalaya		√	√	√		√	√						
6. Farmon, Payton		√											
7. Geiffish, Zander													
8. Haskell, Edith													
9. Horton, Emitt		√	√		√	√							
10. Jones, Savanna													
11. Kelly, Emmitt		√			√								
12. Magier, Cashia													
13. Maxell, Jordana	√	√											
14. Novak, Kern				√									
15. O'Leary, Quinn		√											
16. Thomas, Xander		√											
17. West, Vance													
18. Warner, Lomax													
19. Yellen, Nash													
20. Young, Betty	√												
21. Zang, Carmen													
22. Ziff, Bailey		√											

Figure 11.1 Simple Roster Document and Checkmark System

Individualized Education Programs (IEPs)

Teachers are expected to make sure that all standards are accessible for all students regardless of learning challenges.[33] For students receiving special education services, the goals and objectives included in their IEPs should be the skills that are absolutely critical for student success and their ability to access grade-level curriculum. IEP teams must identify present levels of performance and develop instructional goals that will help students make progress toward reaching grade-level standards.

When identifying goals that will allow students with disabilities to access and succeed in inclusive classrooms, teachers must consider individual student strengths and needs and select goals that are ambitious, attainable, and socially significant. Ambitious goals are meant to challenge, but not overwhelm, the learner. Attainable goals can be reasonably accomplished within the time frame of the school year. Socially significant goals are age appropriate, are likely to produce reinforcement for the learner, are necessary prerequisite skills for more complex skills, increase accessibility to other important environments, and predispose others to interact with the learner.[34]

Family Input

Sometimes there are instructional priorities that teachers are only aware of because of family concerns. Examples of common priorities for families may include the student's behavior management needs, physical needs, and emotional needs. For instance, a student who has social anxiety may not participate in class. The teacher may view this as defiance or a lack of communication skills and may then develop goals that focus on compliance or participation. Working with the family may help the teacher identify a goal area that addresses the underlying reasons for lack of participation. A more appropriate goal, for example, might be related to learning anxiety-management strategies or self-advocacy. It is important that professionals collaborate with families in identifying these priorities, as families know their children best and are highly invested in the success of their children. Suggestions for working effectively with families are discussed with HLP 2 and HLP 3.

Using Instructional Priorities to Identify Instructional Goals

Instructional priorities, once identified, are not usable until the teacher has turned them into instructional goals. It is these goals that ultimately drive instruction. The following sections describe a process for identifying instructional goals.

Identify Big Ideas Related to Grade-Level Standards

Learning standards are broad statements about what students should know and be able to do. Teachers should become familiar with the grade-level standards for the content area(s) they are teaching and identify the "big ideas" for the subject(s) they teach. Big ideas are "highly selected concepts, principles, rules, strategies, or heuristics that facilitate the most efficient and broadest acquisition of knowledge." [35] Given their importance and their foundational nature, teachers should teach big ideas first. This makes teaching of subsequent knowledge and skills more efficient. In order to identify the big ideas, teachers should ask themselves, "What skills and knowledge will have the broadest application? If my students could only learn a handful of concepts and skills in my class, what would those be?"

Most curriculum areas will have both content-based big ideas and skill-based big ideas. A content-based big idea can be thought of as an umbrella of knowledge under which many other details fall. For example, in history, the idea of problem-solution-effect[36] can be applied to all history and social studies content. The *problem* of taxation without representation led to the *solution* of the Declaration of Independence, which led to the *effect* of the Revolutionary War. This effect led to several other problems, solutions, and subsequent effects. If teachers "frontload" content-based big ideas from the beginning (e.g., explicitly teach on the first day of class the idea that all history can be viewed from this heuristic), they give their students an instructional anchor and a way for them to self-assess understanding of all new concepts. Students can then approach all content information with this structure to guide them through new content.

A skill-based big idea is a foundation upon which to build more advanced skills. For instance, phonemic awareness is a big idea because learning to read becomes easier when students have an understanding of the structure of language (i.e., words are made from sounds). When printed text is introduced, mapping phonemes to graphemes makes sense to the learner, and the learner can begin to generalize to new printed text. As the learner becomes more fluent, he or she becomes capable of decoding and comprehending increasingly more complex text. In written expression, a big idea is the writing process—strong writers approach writing as a process that is recursive and collaborative.[37] When students learn this skill-based big idea, they can apply it to a range of writing tasks, across all curricular areas, and over their academic careers.

Identify Knowledge and Skills Needed to Reach Standards

Given that learning standards are broad and sometimes vague, they must be deconstructed—unpacked—before they can be useful in planning instruction. Although there are many ways to approach deconstructing a standard, the goal is the same: to break it down into teachable components. This involves determining what students need to know and to be able to do to reach the standard, which includes not only component skills (i.e., the skills and knowledge that make up the standard) but also prerequisite skills and access skills. Prerequisite skills are those that students should know *before* beginning to work toward a specific standard; these are often skills that should have been mastered in a previous grade. Access skills—skills that allow students to *access* the content— are those that may or may not be directly linked to the standard's content; however, without these skills, the student would not be able to meet the standard. They include, but are not limited to self-management, attention, social skills, functional communication, and foundational academic skills. Identifying gaps in these access skills is critical for individualizing instruction and is particularly important for students with disabilities.

Once the knowledge and skills needed for mastery of a standard have been identified, the teacher should develop clear learning goals or targets and order those targets into logical learning progressions. These ideas are discussed further in the chapter on HLP 12.

Wrap Up

Although state standards provide guidance on what to teach, they are often vague, overwhelming, and lacking in individualization. Effective teachers understand these standards as a starting point, but good curriculum design should not rely on a one-size-fits-all approach.

The process described in this chapter assists teachers in finding the balance between the general curriculum standards and the individual needs of their students. Developing long- and short-term goals based on prioritized knowledge and skills serves as a foundation for robust instructional design.

Tips

1. **Rely on others who have already done the work.** Content area experts have been working on unpacking the standards since the adoption of the Common Core State Standards.[38] Several of the websites in the "Key Resources" section of this chapter provide guidance and examples of deconstructed standards as well as resources for teaching to the standards.

2. **Go high tech.** Take advantage of mobile applications that can help make goal setting, planning, assessment, data collection, and data analysis easier. Several of the websites in the "Key Resources" section of this chapter provide suggestions for high-tech help.

3. **Find creative ways to get more bang for your buck.** Educators are tasked with the challenge of closing the gaps between students with and without disabilities. This means they must teach more efficiently! When identifying lesson objectives, always strive to teach at least one academic (general curriculum) goal *and* one access goal. Try to strategically align them with one another by identifying natural overlaps when possible. For instance, when teaching students to self-graph their math fact fluency, this part of your lesson may include three mini-objectives: (a) a math fluency goal, which may be individualized for each student; (b) a graphing goal, such as identifying the x- and y-axis, if that is part of the general curriculum standards; and (c) a self-management goal that may target goal setting, self-evaluation, and/or self-reinforcement. In science class, when conducting a lab, you will, of course, set goals related to the science content. However, you might also set goals for social skills (e.g., working with lab partners), writing skills (e.g., writing a summary of findings from the experiment), and self-management (e.g., checking off completed tasks on a lab self-monitoring checklist, self-evaluating written summary with a student-friendly rubric). Finding this overlap will be more challenging for some lessons, but always be on the lookout for opportunities to maximize your instructional time.

Notes

1 Doabler, C. T., Cary, M. S., Junghohann, K., Clarke, B., Fien, H., Baker, S, Smolkowski, K., & Chard, D. (2012). Enhancing core mathematics instruction for students at risk for mathematics disabilities. *Teaching Exceptional Children*, *44*(4), 48–57.

2 Moss, C. M., Brookhart, S. M., & Long, B. A. (2011). Knowing your learning target: The first thing students need to learn is what they're supposed to be learning. *Educational Leadership*, *68*, 66–69.

3 Konrad, M., Keesey, S., Ressa, V. A., Alexeeff, M., Chan, P. E., & Peters, M. T. (2014). Setting clear learning targets to guide instruction for all students. *Intervention in School and Clinic*, *50*(2), 76–85.

4 Hasbrouck, J., & Tindal, G. (2006). *Oral reading fluency: 90 years of measurement* (Technical Report No. 33). Eugene, OR: Behavioral Research and Teaching.

5 Konrad, M., Keesey, S., Ressa, V. A., Alexeeff, M., Chan, P. E., & Peters, M. T. (2014). Setting clear learning targets to guide instruction for all students. *Intervention in School and Clinic*, *50*(2), 76–85.

6 Chard, D. (n.d.). *Differentiating instruction for students with special needs*. Houghton-Mifflin Harcourt Journeys. Retrieved from www.doe.in.gov/sites/default/files/curriculum/chard-special-education-paper.pdf

7 National Reading Panel. (2000). *Teaching children to read: An evidence-based assessment of the scientific research literature on reading and its implications for reading instruction* (National Institute of Health Pub. No. 00-4769). Washington, DC: National Institute of Child Health and Human Development.

8 Yopp, H. K., & Yopp, R. H. (2000). Supporting phonemic awareness development in the classroom. *The Reading Teacher*, *54*, 130–144.

9 Alber-Morgan, S. R. (2010). *Using RTI to teach literacy to diverse learners, K-8: Strategies for the inclusive classroom*. Thousand Oaks, CA: Corwin Press.

10 Hasbrouck, J., & Tindal, G. (2006). *Oral reading fluency: 90 years of measurement* (Technical Report No. 33). Eugene, OR: Behavioral Research and Teaching.

11 Beck, I., McKeown, M., & Kucan, L. (2002). *Bringing words to life: Robust vocabulary instruction*. New York, NY: Guilford Press.

12 Shanahan, T., Callison, K., Carriere, C., Duke, N. K., Pearson, P. D., Schatschneider, C., & Torgesen, J. (2010). *Improving reading comprehension in kindergarten through 3rd grade: A practice guide (NCEE 2010-4038)*. Washington, DC: National Center for Education Evaluation and Regional Assistance, Institute of Education Sciences, U.S. Department of Education. Retrieved from what-works.ed.gov/publications/practiceguides

13 Graham, S., & Perin, D. (2007). *Writing next: Effective strategies to improve writing of adolescents in middle and high school*. Washington, DC: Alliance for Excellence in Education.

14 National Mathematics Advisory Panel. (2008). *Foundations for success: The final report of the National Mathematics Advisory Panel*. Washington, DC: U.S. Department of Education.

15 Charles, R. I. (2005). Big ideas and understandings as the foundation for elementary and middle school mathematics. *Journal of Mathematics Education Leadership, 7*(3), 9–24.

16 Charles, R. I. (2005). Big ideas and understandings as the foundation for elementary and middle school mathematics. *Journal of Mathematics Education Leadership, 7*(3), 9–24, 21.

17 National Committee on Science Education Standards and Assessment. (1996). *National research council*. Retrieved from www.nap.edu/catalog/4962.html

18 National Council for the Social Studies. (2010). *National curriculum standards for social studies: A framework for teaching, learning, and assessment*. Retrieved from www.socialstudies.org/standard

19 National Council for the Social Studies. (2010). *National curriculum standards for social studies: A framework for teaching, learning, and assessment*. Retrieved from www.socialstudies.org/standard

20 Shepard, L. (2008). Formative assessment: Caveat emptor. In C. A. Dwyer (Ed.), *The future of assessment: Shaping teaching and learning* (pp. 279–304). New York, NY: Routledge.

21 Graham-Day, K. J., Fishley, K. M., Konrad, M., Peters, M. T., & Ressa, V. A. (2014). Formative instructional practices: How core connect teachers can borrow ideas from IDEA. *Intervention in School and Clinic, 50*(2), 69–75.

22 Chappuis, S., & Chappuis, J. (2008). The best value in formative assessment. *Educational Leadership, 65*, 14–19.

23 Chard, D. (n.d.). *Differentiating instruction for students with special needs*. Houghton-Mifflin Harcourt Journeys. Retrieved from www.doe.in.gov/sites/default/files/curriculum/chard-special-education-paper.pdf
    Graham, S., & Perin, D. (2007). *Writing next: Effective strategies to improve writing of adolescents in middle and high school*. Washington, DC: Alliance for Excellence in Education.
    Graham-Day, K. J., Fishley, K. M., Konrad, M., Peters, M. T., & Ressa, V. A. (2014). Formative instructional practices: How core connect teachers can borrow ideas from IDEA. *Intervention in School and Clinic, 50*(2), 69–75.

24 Graham, S., & Perin, D. (2007). *Writing next: Effective strategies to improve writing of adolescents in middle and high school*. Washington, DC: Alliance for Excellence in Education.
    Graham-Day, K. J., Fishley, K. M., Konrad, M., Peters, M. T., & Ressa, V. A. (2014). Formative instructional practices: How core connect teachers can borrow ideas from IDEA. *Intervention in School and Clinic, 50*(2), 69–75.

25 Joseph, L. M. (2014). Planning interventions for students with reading problems. In A. Thomas & P. Harrison (Eds.), *Best Practices in School Psychology* (Vol. VI.). Bethesda, MD: National Association of School Psychologists.

26 Graham-Day, K. J., Fishley, K. M., Konrad, M., Peters, M. T., & Ressa, V. A. (2014). Formative instructional practices: How core connect teachers can borrow ideas from IDEA. *Intervention in School and Clinic, 50*(2), 69–75.

27 Graham-Day, K. J., Fishley, K. M., Konrad, M., Peters, M. T., & Ressa, V. A. (2014). Formative instructional practices: How core connect teachers can borrow ideas from IDEA. *Intervention in School and Clinic, 50*(2), 69–75.

28 Graham-Day, K. J., Fishley, K. M., Konrad, M., Peters, M. T., & Ressa, V. A. (2014). Formative instructional practices: How core connect teachers can borrow ideas from IDEA. *Intervention in School and Clinic, 50*(2), 69–75.

29 Graham-Day, K. J., Fishley, K. M., Konrad, M., Peters, M. T., & Ressa, V. A. (2014). Formative instructional practices: How core connect teachers can borrow ideas from IDEA. *Intervention in School and Clinic, 50*(2), 69–75.

30 Ogle, D. M. (1986). K-W-L: A teaching model that develops active reading of expository text. *The Reading Teacher, 39*(6), 564–570.

31 Tolisano, S. (2011, July 21). *Upgrade your KWL chart to the 21st century.* [Web log post]. Retrieved from http://langwitches.org/blog/2011/07/21/upgrade-your-kwl-chart-to-the-21st-century/

32 Chard, D. (n.d.). *Differentiating instruction for students with special needs.* Houghton-Mifflin Harcourt Journeys. Retrieved from www.doe.in.gov/sites/default/files/curriculum/chard-special-education-paper.pdf

33 Konrad, M., Keesey, S., Ressa, V. A., Alexeeff, M., Chan, P. E., & Peters, M. T. (2014). Setting clear learning targets to guide instruction for all students. *Intervention in School and Clinic, 50*(2), 76–85.

34 Cooper, J. O., Heron, T. E., & Heward, W. L. (2007) *Applied behavior analysis* (2nd ed.). Upper Saddle River, NJ: Merrill/Prentice Hall.

35 Kame'enui, E. J., Carnine, D. W., Dixon, R. C., Simmons, D. C., & Coyne, M. D. (2002). *Effective teaching strategies that accommodate diverse learners* (2nd ed.). Upper Saddle River, NJ: Merrill Prentice Hall, p. 9.

36 Kinder, D., & Bursuck, W. (1993). History strategy instruction: Problem-solution-effect analysis, timeline, and vocabulary instruction. *Exceptional Children, 59*, 324–335.

37 Graham, S., & Perin, D. (2007). *Writing next: Effective strategies to improve writing of adolescents in middle and high school.* Washington, DC: Alliance for Excellence in Education.

38 Charles, R. I. (2005). Big ideas and understandings as the foundation for elementary and middle school mathematics. *Journal of Mathematics Education Leadership, 7*(3), 9–24.

Key Resources

Achieve the Core: www.achievethecore.org/

Apps for Educators: www.masteryconnect.com/goodies.html

Socrative: www.socrative.com/apps.html

NearPod: https://nearpod.com/

Plickers: www.plickers.com/

Kahoot: https://kahoot.it/

Goformative: https://goformative.com/

Konrad, M., Keesey, S., Ressa, V. A., Alexeeff, M., Chan, P. E., & Peters, M. T. (2014). Setting clear learning targets to guide instruction for all students. *Intervention in School and Clinic, 50*(2), 76–85.

National Association of Special Education Teachers, IEP Goals and Objectives app. Retrieved from www.naset.org/3636.0.html

North Carolina Department of Public Instruction. Retrieved from www.dpi.state.nc.us/

Virginia Department of Education Retrieved from www.doe.virginia.gov/special_ed/iep_instruct_svcs/stds-based_iep/stds_based_iep_guidance.pdf

12
Systematically Design Instruction Toward a Specific Learning Goal

Moira Konrad, Terri Hessler, Sheila R. Alber-Morgan, Carrie A. Davenport, and Maria R. Helton

Introduction

Effective instructional strategies are necessary but not sufficient for producing optimum academic outcomes. Choosing *what to teach*, including depth and breadth, and *when to teach it*, including instructional sequence, are just as important as *how to teach*. This emphasis on systematically designed instruction is particularly important for students with disabilities[1] in general education classrooms who may struggle to learn when instruction has not been tailored to their specific needs. In this chapter, the term *systematically designed instruction* refers to instruction that is carefully and logically sequenced toward a specific goal. This chapter will focus on three critical elements of such instruction: clear instructional goals, logical sequencing of knowledge and skills, and teaching students to organize content.

Narrowing the Focus

In this chapter, we will help teachers answer questions that will guide them in setting goals, prioritizing content, and sequencing instruction: (a) is my learning goal clear; (b) what skills and knowledge are most important; (c) what should I teach first; (d) how do I sequence instruction; (e) how do I help students make connections; and (f) how do I know I'm on track?

Chapter Overview

1. Describe the importance and characteristics of clear learning goals.
2. List and describe elements of instructional design that help teachers prioritize and sequence learning goals.
3. Describe strategies teachers can use to help students make connections.

Setting Clear Goals

Prior to systematically designing instruction toward specific goals, it is first necessary to identify and prioritize long- and short-term goals centered on individual learning needs in the context of the general education curriculum and classroom. See Chapter 11 for a description and discussion of how to identify students' learning needs based on grade-level standards, assessment data, learning progressions, students' prior knowledge, and IEP goals. Once teachers have identified and prioritized learning goals, they must turn them into learning targets that are clear, measurable, ambitious, attainable, and actionable.

Establishing and communicating clear learning goals gives teachers and students direction for planning.[2] Clear learning goals help teachers know what to teach and assess, students understand what they are expected to learn, and parents better understand student progress to become more engaged in student learning.[3] Most importantly, when teachers are clear about their learning targets, student achievement is positively affected.[4] Specifically, findings from a large meta-meta-analysis revealed that when teachers set *specific* goals, results were better than when they set generic goals such as "do your best."[5]

Developing clear learning goals can be challenging for teachers. It requires them to deconstruct curriculum standards, clearly articulate the conditions under which they hope learning will occur, develop mastery criteria, and ensure the goals are appropriate for the learners. As such, Graham-Day and Konrad developed a mnemonic, ACCOMPLISH (see Figure 12.1), to assist beginning teachers as they learn to write and evaluate their students' learning goals.[6] Each letter in the mnemonic reminds teachers to include a specific component. The first three letters (ACC) refer to the three parts of a goal: *A*ntecedent condition, *C*onspicuous behavior, and *C*lear criteria. The remaining letters are refining features that provide teachers with direction for evaluating and polishing the goal to make it most appropriate: *O*bservable, *M*easurable, *P*ositive, *L*inked to the general curriculum, *I*ndividualized, *S*ocially valid, and *H*igh-reaching. Table 12.1 provides examples of goals that do not meet these standards (i.e., "Un-ACCOMPLISHED-ed Goals") with critiques and revised goals that may serve as models of well-developed goals (i.e., "ACCOMPLISH-ed Goals").

Antecedent Condition

Teachers should be clear about the conditions under which the desired learning will occur. In other words, what are the instructional stimuli learners are responding to? One way to help teachers clarify the antecedent conditions is to know exactly how the learners will be assessed. Antecedent condi-

Help Students

ACCOMPLISH
Their Goals

*A*ntecedent condition
*C*onspicuous behavior
*C*lear criteria
*O*bservable
*M*easurable
*P*ositive
*L*inked to the general curriculum
*I*ndividualized
*S*ocially valid
*H*igh-reaching

Figure 12.1 ACCOMPLISH: A Mnemonic for Setting Goals

Table 12.1 Examples and Non-Examples of Clear Goals

Un-ACCOMPLISH-ed Goal	Critique	ACCOMPLISH-ed Goal
Students will write a paragraph.	• No antecedent condition • No mastery criteria	*Given a descriptive writing prompt*, students will write a paragraph *consisting of a topic sentence, three to four supporting detail sentences, and no more than three transcription errors.*
Given a reading passage from a history textbook, students will identify three causes of the Civil War.	• Target behavior not conspicuous (not observable, not measurable)	Given a reading passage from a history textbook, students will *write* three causes of the Civil War.
Given a specific task during cooperative learning group activities, students will decrease their interruptions.	• Not positively stated	Given a specific task during cooperative learning group activities, students *will take turns speaking.*
Students will read a passage twice each session for five weeks.	• Not linked to general curriculum and/or IEP goals • No mastery criteria	*Given two attempts reading an expository third grade–level passage each session, students will improve their first read fluency by 100% over five weeks.*
Students will write the weekly 20 spelling words correctly three times each.	• Not individualized	*Given feedback on their performance on a spelling pretest*, students will write the weekly words they *spelled incorrectly* three times each.
When presented with a Word Find of 20 science terms, students will locate and circle each term (horizontally, vertically, diagonally, and backwards).	• Not socially valid	When presented with a *reading passage with ten highlighted science terms*, students will refer to a list of *defined morphemes* and *write the definitions of the terms with 80% accuracy.*
Given 20 multiplication facts, students will write the products with 50% accuracy.	• Not high reaching	Given 20 multiplication facts, students will write the products *within 25 seconds with 90% accuracy.*

tions may include, but are not limited to, the following: (a) environmental settings and situations, (b) instructional/assessment materials, (c) level of material, (d) task directions, (e) prompts, (f) assignments, and (g) time limitations. For example, if my goal is related to writing an essay, under what conditions would I expect the student to write this essay? Consider how the expected behavior/goal would differ under these two different antecedent conditions:

1. When given an expository writing prompt, a graphic organizer, access to a computer with word processing software, and 45 minutes to write, the student will . . .
2. When given a list of story elements, directions to "write a story," paper and pen/pencil, a self-monitoring checklist, and 30 minutes to write, the student will . . .

Teachers should evaluate their antecedent conditions to ensure they meet the appropriate refining features: *M*easurable, *I*ndividualized, *S*ocially valid, and *H*igh-reaching. Specifically, the antecedent conditions delineate exactly how the skills and knowledge will be measured. Although teachers often will set a goal that is generally appropriate for a group of students, they must recognize that some students will need individualized conditions to be successful (e.g., more prompting, more time to complete an assignment, different level reading passage). Teachers should recognize that socially valid antecedent conditions are authentic and meaningful learning situations. Although systematic instruction sometimes requires skills to be taught in isolation, the ultimate goal is for students to combine skills and perform them under natural conditions in a range of settings. For instance, students may learn to decode words in isolation before independently reading in a text. Contrived antecedent conditions should be considered temporary and as intentional steps toward the ultimate goal of performing in natural settings and situations. In fact, these natural settings help define high-reaching outcomes.

Conspicuous Behavior

Teachers should develop goals that clearly define what the student will do to demonstrate learning. Teachers will know a behavior is conspicuous if they can see or hear students emitting it. Conspicuous behaviors may include, but are not limited to, writing, speaking, reading aloud, pointing or gesturing, and keyboarding or touching a screen. Teachers should evaluate conspicuous behaviors to ensure they meet the other refining features: Observable (Can you see it or hear it?), Measurable (Can you count it or time it?), Positive (Does it state what the students will do rather than what they will not do?), Linked to the general curriculum (Is there a standard for it?), Individualized (Do individual students need to work on a variation of or a prerequisite for the skill to meet an IEP goal?), Socially valid (Does it pass the "who cares?" test? Will meeting this goal help students move toward meaningful outcomes?), and High-reaching (Is the goal ambitious, yet realistic?).

Clear Criteria

Teachers must set clear criteria in order to determine if the student has achieved the goal. Criteria should be ambitious, but attainable. Criteria may focus on accuracy (e.g., number correct), fluency (e.g., number correct per minute), duration (e.g., amount of time engaged in a task), latency (e.g., length of time needed to start a task), and magnitude (e.g., intensity needed to accomplish a task, such as pressing down hard enough with a pencil to make writing legible). Teachers should evaluate criteria to ensure they meet the appropriate refining features: Observable (Can you see it or hear it?), Measurable (Can you count it or time it?), Individualized (Do individual students need to work toward a different level of mastery?), Socially valid (Is the skill important or valued by others?), and High-reaching (Are the criteria set high enough to allow meaningful access to natural reinforcement and/or future learning?).

Determining ambitious but attainable criteria is challenging and requires teachers to consider a myriad of factors, including the individual student's present level of performance and grade- or age-level expectations (e.g., published norms or performance of typical classmates). For some goals, there may be published expected rates of improvement (i.e., expected weekly gains in fluency); for most, though, there is no formula. Establishing appropriate criteria takes practice, experience, and the realization that criteria may need to be adjusted based on student performance. It is important to note, however, that if a student is not reaching a goal, the teacher's last assumption should be that the goal is too high. Rather, the teacher should examine instructional practices, intensity of instruction, and need for accommodations *before* deciding the goal is too ambitious. After these factors have been addressed, revising the criteria may be warranted. On the other hand, if a student is progressing more quickly than expected, teachers should not hesitate to raise expectations.

Systematically Sequencing Instruction

Once goals have been set, educators must work toward accomplishing them in the most efficient way. Clear learning goals provide teachers and students with direction so they know *where* they are going. Systematically sequenced instruction helps them get there. Direct instruction is one example of an evidence-based teaching model in which learning is systematically sequenced through careful planning. Students attain mastery of concepts incrementally and generalize skills to new content with gradually reduced guidance.[7] The literature is replete with support for direct instruction. Indeed, several meta-analyses and meta-meta-analyses have identified direct instruction (including commercial Direct Instruction [DI] programs and teacher-designed explicit instruction) as quite effective, especially for struggling learners.[8] Although there are many instructional features of DI/explicit instruction programs (e.g., active student responding, frequent feedback, progress monitoring) that contribute to their effectiveness, mastery learning, and systematic sequencing of knowledge and skills are cornerstones. (Explicit instruction and some of its features are discussed in other chapters of this book.) When planning instruction, teachers should keep in mind the importance of ensuring that students master basic knowledge and skills before moving on to more advanced learning.[9] Specifically, they should consider the following when sequencing instruction:

- Teach big ideas and main ideas before details.[10]
- Teach according to a logical hierarchy: less complex skills before more complex ones; prerequisites before requisites; and unambiguous information before ambiguous information.[11]
- Separate skills and concepts that are similar before requiring discrimination.[12]
- Teach commonly encountered content before lower-frequency content.[13]

Teach Big Ideas and Main Ideas Before Details

Big ideas are "concepts, principles, rules, strategies, or heuristics that facilitate the most efficient and broadest acquisition of knowledge."[14] They are foundational and thus should be taught first in order to facilitate learning of subsequent knowledge and skills. For example, when students understand the big idea of *cycles*, they can then more easily learn about the water cycle, the life cycle of a star, the food chain, the rock cycle, and so on. Understanding the idea that many phenomena in science are cyclical is an instructional anchor that helps students make connections between and among concepts. If teachers start their instruction on a topic by introducing big ideas, they give their students a foundation and a tool for understanding subsequent information. Big ideas are discussed in more depth in the chapter on HLP 11.

Just as big ideas should be taught before delving into unit concepts, it is important to teach *main ideas* prior to teaching detailed information.[15] A big idea is an umbrella under which many topics and concepts may be organized, whereas main ideas are learning targets or topics within a lesson or unit. For instance, within a lesson or unit, the big idea of *cycles* may include a *main idea* of the stages of the life cycle of a butterfly. These stages are the main ideas, and the *details* are what happens during each stage. Students will learn more if they understand the main ideas first.

Understanding the distinction among big ideas, main ideas, and details can help educators differentiate curriculum. It may be appropriate to go into more detail with some students than with others. However, it is important to note that differentiating instruction in this manner should not result in diluting the curriculum. The integrity of the curriculum should remain intact no matter the level of detail. With this in mind, teachers should ask themselves the following questions:

- Does future learning rely on acquisition of the knowledge or skill? In other words, is it a prerequisite skill?

- Is the skill needed for independent living? In other words, is it a life skill?
- Will the skill help students in other content areas or classes?
- Is the skill a standard or goal on the student's IEP?
- Does the skill help the student contact reinforcement in the community or future environments? In other words, is it a skill that is valued by others in the "real world"?
- What is the cost-benefit ratio? In other words, is the amount of time required to teach this skill or content commensurate with the expected outcomes?

Answering "yes" to any of these questions helps teachers discern the importance and thus the necessity of the content for all students.

Teach According to a Logical Hierarchy

Relatedly, teachers should order content from simpler information to more complex information. For example, students must have mastered multiplication facts before learning about fractions. Before learning multiplication facts, students must master addition. This hierarchy of skills must be identified, and students must master prerequisite skills before moving on to higher-order skills. When teaching phonological awareness, word-level awareness and rhyming should be incorporated into instruction before the more difficult phonemic awareness skills (i.e., segmenting, blending, and manipulating phonemes). Consider prerequisite skills the building blocks needed to lay the foundation for higher-level information.

Similarly, teachers should teach unambiguous information before ambiguous information. Teaching information that students can easily grasp will lay the foundation and build momentum for attacking more challenging information that might confuse students. For example, when teaching spelling, teachers should teach the rules first before teaching the exceptions to the rules. In elementary science, when classifying animals, students should learn unambiguous examples of mammals, such as horse, dog, and human, before being introduced to those confusing members of the class Mammalia, such as the platypus, the bat, and the dolphin.

Separate Skills and Concepts That are Similar Before Requiring Discrimination

When students are first learning a new concept, teachers should keep in mind that simplicity and clarity are more important than meticulous discrimination. For this reason, students should master concepts that are quite distinct from each other (e.g., circle and square) before those that are more similar (e.g., square and rectangle). As a general rule, teachers should teach the distinct content and skills well—teach to mastery—before introducing concepts that have subtle differences. For instance, teach the difference between a democracy and an absolute monarchy first. Then, introduce dictatorship and ensure students understand the distinctions among all three before then introducing ideas requiring finer discrimination, such as oligarchy, representative democracy, and parliamentary democracy.

Teach Commonly Encountered Content Before Lower-Frequency Content

Content or skills should be prioritized so that the most frequently encountered, and thus most useful, should be taught first (e.g., sight words, morphemic analysis, vocabulary). If students know high-frequency morphemes, they can decode and comprehend more multisyllabic words even if those words have not been directly taught. For higher-performing students, teachers can introduce lower-frequency content as a way to differentiate. As students become more proficient with high-frequency content and skills, they can be gradually introduced to lower-frequency content and skills.

Teaching Students to Make Connections

Once teachers have identified appropriate sequencing of content and skills, they should strategically design instruction in a way that helps students make connections. There are six principles of effective instruction that can be helpful when communicating to students how their new learning fits with background knowledge, previously learned content and skills, and upcoming learning targets.[16] Teachers can use these principles to design instruction that may be easier to access and lead to increased academic success. The strategies discussed could also promote generalization and maintenance of the learned material and thereby increase instructional efficiency. These six principles are: (a) big ideas, (b) conspicuous strategies, (c) mediated scaffolding, (d) strategic integration, (e) primed background knowledge, and (f) judicious review.

Big Ideas

Big ideas, as discussed in the chapter on HLP 11 and earlier in this chapter, help students make connections because they are broad enough to encompass a range of new topics and skills. Teachers can use this concept to teach students to ask themselves, "How does this new information relate to the big ideas for the unit or the course?" In this way, the teacher is explicitly helping students make connections to concepts that are broader than just the current day's target skill or topic.

Conspicuous Strategies

Another design element teachers should incorporate is conspicuous strategies. Because they are explicit and unambiguous, conspicuous strategies help students make connections by providing them with rules that have broad application and promote generalization. Good strategies are directly related to one or more big ideas. For example, one big idea is that letter-sound correspondence is generally reliable. A related conspicuous strategy is sounding out words and blending when coming across an unknown word. Students can count on this strategy and apply it when they are reading new words. The key here is to make the connection explicit to learners so they are cognizant of the idea that they are learning an applicable strategy, not an isolated concept.

Mediated Scaffolding

The third principle of effective instruction is mediated scaffolding. Teachers can provide mediated scaffolding by using a model-lead-test sequence (e.g., my turn, our turn, your turn) until the student is able to do the skill or learn the content independently. Mediated scaffolding helps students make connections by gradually moving from teacher-supported to more independent performance. Again, particularly for older students, teachers can be overt with students about the fading of their support. For instance, after a teacher provides several models with think-alouds for writing paragraph summaries, she may then provide a structured worksheet for students to write their own paragraph summaries. To help students make connections, she may explicitly state, "Yesterday, I modeled these for you. Today, I gave you a template to follow. Once you're able to do it with the template, we'll move to writing your own paragraph summaries without a template."

Primed Background Knowledge

Another principle of effective instruction is primed background knowledge, which connects students to content via their prior experiences with the topic and hooks the new learning onto their previous knowledge. Teachers prime student background knowledge by guiding them to identify information they already know through probing questions and discussion. For example, if students are learning about magnets, the teacher can have students identify times they have used a magnet (e.g., to hang something on the fridge) and then have students identify what a magnet does (i.e., attracts metal). This helps students connect new learning to their previous experience. When activating background knowledge, teachers should keep in mind that students will have differing levels of background knowledge and should use caution not to spend too much time "activating" it, particularly when students have minimal background knowledge. Further, they should not hesitate to correct mistakes or erroneous information. Again, when activating background knowledge, it is important for teachers to explicitly acknowledge connections.

Strategic Integration

Strategic integration involves combining new information with what the learner already knows in order to produce a higher-order skill. This includes background knowledge learners bring to the classroom but also requires teachers to design lessons that systematically build upon one another. Each time they introduce a new skill or concept, teachers can maximize their instruction if they make explicit connections to previous and future learning. For instance, when teaching animal classification, after students have learned the characteristics of mammals and are not being introduced to ambiguous exceptions (e.g., dolphins), teachers can refer students to the knowledge attained earlier in the classification unit (e.g., mammals have hair, give live birth, breathe air) to build on what students know.

Judicious Review

Judicious review is carefully designed instruction that helps students maintain skills and knowledge they learned so they can build on it and continue to make connections to enhance future learning. Review activities should be distributed across time rather than lumped into one review period (e.g., right before the big test), as distributed practice has been shown to be more effective than massed practice.[17] Teachers should contextualize review within the big idea framework to help students make connections, and they should be strategic to be sure they are reviewing the highest-priority content sufficiently and systematically.

Teaching Students to Organize Content

In addition to designing and delivering instruction that systematically and explicitly introduces, reviews, and integrates new learning, teachers should provide students with tools to help them organize content with visual displays. Visually presenting information helps students see and understand relationships between and among topics. The chapter on HLP 13 provides more detail about graphic organizers that may be used to help students organize content.

Ongoing Changes Guided by Student Performance

Even the most strategically, systematically sequenced instruction will require adjustments to meet the needs of all learners. This requires that teachers monitor student progress to ensure their instruction is effective. In fact, Fuchs and Fuchs found that students with high-incidence disabilities whose individualized education programs were "monitored systematically and developed formatively" have better academic outcomes than those whose programs were not.[18]

Ongoing data collection should reveal student progress, or lack thereof, and thus allow teachers to determine what changes in their instruction might yield better outcomes. If several students are not making adequate progress, it is likely not a reflection of a need to individualize instruction. Rather it likely indicates instruction has not been designed or delivered effectively. Teachers who find that more than a handful of students are not meeting goals should examine their instructional design to identify possible issues with goals, sequencing, or connections. See chapters related to HLPs 4 and 6 for more information about collecting and using student data to guide instruction.

Example

The following example illustrates how one teacher, Mrs. Kalambaya, systematically designs her instruction to meet the needs of her Tier 2 (small group) struggling readers. Here is a list of questions she thinks about: (a) Have I prioritized the skills and knowledge most critical for my students' progress and sequenced my instruction logically? (b) Are my goals clear? (c) How do I help my students connect new knowledge to what I already taught? (d) How will I monitor their progress so that I know they are on track to meet their goals?

Prioritizing Knowledge and Skills

Mrs. Kalambaya uses a structured literacy approach to remediate her students' language and reading deficits. Fortunately for her, the National Reading Panel has determined what knowledge and skills she should prioritize; hence, each of her lessons contain these essential elements: phonemic awareness, phonics, fluency, vocabulary, and comprehension.[19]

Setting Clear Goals

Mrs. Kalambaya's students have been identified as needing remediation based on reading fluency data that all classroom teachers collect in Tier 1. She uses the ACCOMPLISH mnemonic to help her set two types of goals. First, as a long-term goal for all of her students, she wants them to reach grade-level benchmarks. Goal: *When given a second-grade reading passage, each student will read aloud at a rate of 87 or more words per minute.* See Figure 12.2 for a breakdown of how this goal addresses each component of the mnemonic.

Second, before each lesson, Mrs. Kalambaya creates daily objectives, one for each component of her lesson. For instance, for a phonics portion of her lesson, she might set the following goal: *When presented with the letter* k, *each student will state aloud the /k/ sound on five out of six trials while maintaining letter-sounds already acquired in previous lessons with a minimum of 90% accuracy.* Further, she will need to think about how to individualize goals and instruction for students struggling with specific letters or letter-sounds.

Systematically Sequencing Instruction

As she plans her lessons, she must think about the best way to sequence her instruction for the most robust learning outcomes. Using the phonics section again as an example, she has a scope and sequence to refer to that presents the phonemes from simple (e.g., *a, t, b, l, f,* and *h*) to complex (e.g., *qu, sh, tion, augh*). In addition, when she teaches graphemes that have more than one sound, she teaches the more common sound first. She also recognizes that struggling readers tend to confuse *b* and *d* longer than typical students, so she will separate these skills before requiring discrimination (i.e., teach one to mastery well before teaching the other).

Teaching Students to Make Connections

To help students make connections, Mrs. Kalambaya teaches students a big idea related to alphabetic principle: There are predictable patterns and rules in reading and spelling words. This provides an instructional anchor each time she introduces a new sound, pattern, or rule. Having this anchor gives

Goal: When given a second-grade reading passage, students will read aloud at a rate of 87 or more words per minute.	
ACCOMPLISH Components	Illustration from Mrs. Kalambaya's Class
Antecedent condition	Goal states, "When given a second-grade reading passage . . ."
Conspicuous behavior	Goal states students will "read aloud."
Clear criteria	Goal states students will reach a "rate of 87 words per minute."
Observable	Goal specifies students will "read aloud," as opposed to silently.
Measurable	Criterion is provided (rate of 87 words per minute), which is countable and, therefore, measurable.
Positive	Goal focuses on what student will do rather than what they will not do.
Linked to the general curriculum	Goal focuses on reading fluency, one of the state's curriculum standards.
Individualized	Students assigned to Mrs. Kalambaya's small group are heterogeneously grouped based on their specific needs; she also sets individualized goals within each lesson.
Socially valid	Reading fluency is an excellent predictor of reading comprehension, so focusing on it will help students achieve success across the curriculum.
High-reaching	Minimum goal represents "benchmark" for the end of the school year for students in the same grade, indicating ambition to catch students up to same-age peers.

Figure 12.2 ACCOMPLISH: An Illustration

students a reliable and effective approach to reading and spelling, which helps them feel less overwhelmed and more empowered to take on literacy-related challenges. To maximize effectiveness of this big idea, Mrs. Kalambaya recognizes the importance of being explicit and helping students make connections. For example, initially students are confused when spelling *c* words after learning this spelling rule: When *c* is followed by an *a*, *o*, or *u* it says /k/ as in *cat*, and when *c* is followed by *e*, *i*, or *y* it says /s/ as in *city*. To help them make the connection between the sounds *c* makes and the spelling rules, she teaches them *It's icy in Center City.*

Monitoring Progress

Mrs. Kalambaya wants to be sure her students are on track to meet the grade-level fluency goal she set for each of them, so she assesses them weekly to be sure they are progressing, even if only incrementally. In addition, she collects data daily on other lesson elements. For example, in the phonics section, in which they learn and practice letter-sound correspondence, she uses a simple chart of all the phonemes followed by columns and daily checks to indicate *proficient*, *emerging*, or *not introduced* yet. The same matrix has columns with headings of other skills they practice throughout the lesson (e.g., comprehension, grapheme spelling) for her to track individual progress. Data collection like this enables her to determine, who, if anyone, needs more individualized instruction, such as more time on a concept or skill, enriching content, or one-on-one time.

Wrap Up

This chapter has focused on what teachers should do in between identifying instructional priorities and teaching those priorities to their students. Specifically, after teachers have established their instructional priorities, they need to break these curricular priorities into learning goals that are clear, meaningful, and ambitious. These learning goals should drive the next step of systematically sequencing instruction. Sequencing requires teachers to identify big ideas that reach across and beyond their focus curricular area and main ideas that target the most essential skills and knowledge all students must master. This then allows teachers to arrange instruction in the most logical hierarchies: main ideas before details, less complex skills before more complex ones, prerequisites before requisites, unambiguous information before ambiguous information, and commonly encountered content before lower-frequency content.

Again, implementing a collection of evidence-based instructional techniques does not necessarily yield optimum outcomes. Teachers must strategically and systematically identify what to teach and in what order to teach it before they start teaching. Additionally, they must be explicit in helping students make connections between what they know, what they are learning, and what they will learn in the future. This knowledge empowers students to take ownership of their learning and "helps them respond to feedback, self-monitor and reflect on their progress, and develop a sense of responsibility."[20] Only then will teachers be able to get the most out of the techniques addressed throughout the other chapters in this book.

Tips

1. **Don't reinvent the wheel.** When available, use commercial direct-instruction programs; the work of systematically sequencing instruction is already done, which allows you to focus on delivery of instruction. When well-designed commercial programs are not available, use the key resources below to help you sequence your instruction.
2. **Collaborate with others when designing instruction.** Breaking down standards into manageable learning goals and then logically sequencing those goals is challenging and tedious work and requires expertise in content and pedagogy. Special educators should reach out to general educators for their content knowledge, and general educators should reach out to special educators for their expertise in task analysis and mastery learning. Working with others harnesses the power of teamwork while making the task more fun.
3. **Organize to optimize.** If you are charged with developing your own scope and sequence, be sure to have in place a system for keeping track of the work you are doing. A quick web search will yield many templates that might be used to organize and document your planning, and web-based planning tools, such as Google Sheets or Google Docs, make it easy to share and collaborate.

Notes

1 Archer, A. L., & Hughes, C. A. (2011). *Explicit instruction: Effective and efficient teaching*. New York, NY: Guilford Press.
2 Marzano, R. J. (2007). *Art and science of teaching*. Alexandria, VA: Association for Supervision and Curriculum Development.
3 Chappuis, J., Stiggins, R., Chappuis, S., & Arter, J. (2012). *Classroom assessment for student learning* (2nd ed.). Upper Saddle River, NJ: Pearson.
4 Hattie, J. (2009). *Visible learning: A synthesis of over 800 meta-analyses relating to achievement*. London: Routledge.

5 Hattie, J. (2009). *Visible learning: A synthesis of over 800 meta-analyses relating to achievement.* London: Routledge.

6 Graham-Day, K. J., & Konrad, M. (2014). *Accomplish: Writing meaningful learning goals.* Unpublished manuscript.

7 Adams, G., & Engelmann, S. (1996). *Research on direct instruction: 25 years beyond DISTAR.* Seattle, WA: Educational Achievement Systems.

8 Forness, S. R., Kavale, K. A., Blum, I. M., & Lloyd, J. W. (1997). Mega-analysis of meta-analysis. *Teaching Exceptional Children, 29*(6), 4–9.
    Hattie, J. (2009). *Visible learning: A synthesis of over 800 meta-analyses relating to achievement.* London: Routledge.
    Swanson, H. L., & Hoskyn, M. (1998). Experimental intervention research on students with learning disabilities: A meta-analysis of treatment outcomes. *Review of Educational Research, 68,* 277–321.

9 Hattie, J. (2009). *Visible learning: A synthesis of over 800 meta-analyses relating to achievement.* London: Routledge.

10 Hattie, J. (2009). *Visible learning: A synthesis of over 800 meta-analyses relating to achievement.* London: Routledge.

11 Archer, A. L., & Hughes, C. A. (2011). *Explicit instruction: Effective and efficient teaching.* New York, NY: Guilford Press.

12 Archer, A. L., & Hughes, C. A. (2011). *Explicit instruction: Effective and efficient teaching.* New York, NY: Guilford Press.

13 Archer, A. L., & Hughes, C. A. (2011). *Explicit instruction: Effective and efficient teaching.* New York, NY: Guilford Press.

14 Kame'enui, E., J., Carnine, D. W., Dixon, R. C., Simmons, D. C., & Coyne, M. D. (2002). *Effective teaching strategies that accommodate diverse learners* (2nd ed.). Boston, MA: Pearson, p. 9.

15 Hattie, J. (2009). *Visible learning: A synthesis of over 800 meta-analyses relating to achievement.* London: Routledge.

16 Coyne, M. D., Kame'enui, E. J., & Carnine, D. W. (2007). *Effective teaching strategies that accommodate diverse learners.* Upper Saddle River, NJ: Pearson Merrill Prentice Hall.

17 Hattie, J. (2009). *Visible learning: A synthesis of over 800 meta-analyses relating to achievement.* London: Routledge.

18 Fuchs, L. S., & Fuchs, D. S. (1986). Effects of systematic formative evaluation: A meta-analysis. *Exceptional Children, 53,* 199–208, 205.

19 National Reading Panel. (2000). *Report of the National Reading Panel: Teaching children to read.* Retrieved from www.nichd.nih.gov/publications/pubs/nrp/Documents/report.pdf

20 Konrad., M., Keesey, S., Ressa, V. A., Alexeeff, M., Chan, P. E., & Peters, M. T. (2014). Setting clear learning targets to guide instruction for all students. *Intervention in School and Clinic, 50,* 76–85, 77.

Key Resources

Archer, A. L., & Hughes, C. A. (2011). *Explicit instruction: Effective and efficient teaching.* New York, NY: Guilford Press.

Bursuck, W. D., & Damer, M. (2014). *Teaching reading to students who are at risk or have disabilities* (3rd ed.). Boston: Pearson.

Carnine, D. W., Silbert, J., Kame'enui, E. J., Slocum, T. A., & Tarver, S. G. (2016). *Direct instruction reading* (6th ed.). Boston: Pearson.

Coyne, M. D., Kame'enui, E. J., & Carnine, D. W. (2007). *Effective teaching strategies that accommodate diverse learners.* Upper Saddle River, NJ: Pearson Merrill Prentice Hall.

"GO FOR IT" Practice Alerts. Retrieved from www.teachingld.org/alerts

Hattie, J. (2009). *Visible learning: A synthesis of over 800 meta-analyses relating to achievement.* London: Routledge.

Heward, W. L. (2003). Ten faulty notions about teaching and learning that hinder the effectiveness of special education. *The Journal of Special Education, 36,* 186–205.

IRIS Center Resources, Content Instruction Retrieved from https://iris.peabody.vanderbilt.edu/iris-resource-locator/?term=content-instruction

Stein, M., Kinder, D., Silbert, J., & Carnine, D. W. (2005). *Designing effective mathematics instruction: A direct instruction approach.* Boston: Pearson.

Waack, S. (2017). *Visible learning: What works best for learning.* Retrieved from https://visible-learning.org/

13
Adapt Curriculum Tasks and Materials for Specific Learning Goals

Sheila R. Alber-Morgan, Maria R. Helton, Alana Oif Telesman, and Moira Konrad

Introduction

Students in inclusive classrooms represent a wide range of diverse abilities and learning needs that require teachers to adapt curriculum materials and tasks to facilitate student achievement. Like their peers, students with disabilities are expected to make progress toward challenging and rigorous standards. The individualized education programs (IEPs) that are written for students with disabilities delineate accommodations and supports, but teachers must be equipped with the necessary tools and practices to implement such supports so all students are successful.

Chapters on HLPs 11 and 12 include information about identifying, prioritizing, and sequencing long- and short-term goals. However, well-selected and well-sequenced learning goals are meaningless if students cannot access them. When designing instructional tasks and materials, teachers must realize their decisions can either promote or inhibit student access; they must understand that barriers to learning may arise when individual students interact with the materials and tasks. So, this chapter will focus on adapting curriculum tasks and materials to help all learners achieve ambitious academic goals. Adaptations include any changes teachers make to materials and tasks in order to better meet students' needs. They may include designing materials from the onset in a way that takes learner needs into consideration (e.g., materials designed in the context of Universal Design for Learning; see HLP 19) or may be accommodations that are provided to support access to existing materials (e.g., highlighted text, larger font, fewer choices on multiple choice tests). Although many of the adaptations in this chapter are designed to make content accessible to struggling learners, they all have the added benefit of improving outcomes for the full range of learners represented in today's classrooms.

Narrowing the Focus

This chapter provides practitioners with specific strategies, procedures, and examples for adapting curriculum tasks and materials and enhancing content to make learning accessible for a range of diverse learners. Adaptations described in this chapter include: (a) simplifying task directions, (b) altering the difficulty level of material, (c) altering the amount of material provided to students, and (d) highlighting relevant information. Each of these types of adaptations may be specified in students' IEPs.

Teachers can also supplement the curriculum with content enhancements. Content enhancements are techniques that enable students to access, understand, and remember the information presented in the curriculum.[1] The content enhancements described in this chapter include: (a) guided notes, (b) graphic organizers, and (c) mnemonic strategies. Students who have difficulty taking notes during lectures because of listening and/or writing deficits may benefit greatly from using guided notes, which are "teacher-prepared handouts that 'guide' a student through a lecture with standard cues and prepared space in which to write the key facts, concepts, and/or relationships."[2] Similar to guided notes, graphic organizers also provide visual representations that are instrumental for understanding and studying relationships among concepts. For example, a graphic organizer representing the water cycle illustrates water evaporating from oceans, lakes, and rivers; water vapor condensing to form clouds; and clouds producing precipitation that sends water back to the oceans, lakes, and rivers. See Figure 13.1.

Mnemonics are memory strategies that help students retain complex information and vocabulary. For example, learning the sentence "Kids Prefer Cheese Over Fried Green Spinach" can help students remember the order of taxonomy by the first letter of each word in the sentence (i.e., Kingdom, Phylum, Class, Order, Family, Genus, Species). These content enhancements can be combined to make instruction even more effective. For instance, a graphic organizer showing the water cycle can be embedded within guided notes, and students can develop a mnemonic to help them remember the stages of the cycle. Combining various adaptations—such as guided notes, visual representations, and mnemonics—can be very useful for enabling access to instructional materials for a wide range of learners.

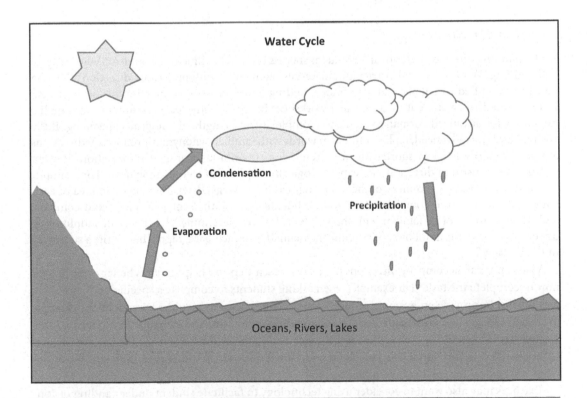

Figure 13.1 Example of a Graphic Organizer Representing the Water Cycle

Chapter Overview

1. Describe various ways to make adaptations to curriculum tasks and materials, including simplifying task directions, altering the level of difficulty and amount of material, and highlighting relevant material.
2. Describe the design and implementation of content enhancements, including guided notes, graphic organizers, and mnemonic strategies.

Making Adaptations for Specific Goals

Teachers are expected to provide instruction that meets each student's individual needs. This can be a daunting task for teachers who have large classes and students with a wide range of needs. Differentiating classroom materials has been emphasized as a practice for teachers to ensure that each student is receiving appropriate instruction, and although differentiation requires intentional planning, it is critical for student success. Fortunately, there are many relatively easy options for integrating elements of differentiation into instructional planning and delivery.

Material and Task Adaptations

As previously noted, some simple strategies for providing material adaptations include: (a) simplifying task directions, (b) altering the difficulty level of material, (c) altering the amount of material provided to students, and (d) highlighting relevant information. Each of these strategies benefits not only students with disabilities but others in the class as well. It is not surprising that many of these material adaptations have overlapping characteristics and can be incorporated simultaneously.

Simplify Task Directions

Understanding directions is critical for student success but can be difficult for students who struggle with reading. Worksheets and curriculum materials often come with prewritten directions that can be easily modified to enhance student understanding and successful completion of assignments.[3] Prior to requiring a student to complete a worksheet independently, teachers should examine the directions for advanced vocabulary, sentence complexity and length, and logical sequencing. If the vocabulary is too advanced, replace unknown words with familiar synonyms or phrases. If directions are unnecessarily lengthy, shorten them by removing superfluous words or information. Prevent confusion by ensuring directions are explicit, logically sequenced, and unambiguous. For example, "Prior to composing a summary of the following reading passage, determine the main idea of each paragraph" may be too complicated for some students because the sentence is long and complex, and students may not be familiar with the words "prior" or "determine." Teachers can simplify task directions by revising as follows: "Underline the main idea in each paragraph. Then, write a summary of the passage."

Visual aids can accompany directions to illustrate each step and help students better comprehend how to complete the task.[4] For example, when asking students to complete a specific math problem, it is helpful to provide an example problem for students to use as a guide. Directions for example problems can include visual aids such as color coding, bold font, and symbols. In Figure 13.2, the teacher has broken down each critical step for calculating the arithmetic mean of a data set. She has highlighted key information using bold and underlined font to help students identify which components are critical for solving the problem.

Teachers may also want to consider using technology to facilitate student understanding of concepts. For example, teachers can use text-to-speech software such as NaturalReader (www.natu-

Directions: Find the **arithmetic mean** of a data set. Use the model below to help you.

Example data set: 5, 3, 1, 2, 4

Step one: **Add** up all of the numbers in the data set to find the **total**.

$$5 + 3 + 1 + 2 + 4 = \textbf{15}$$

Step two: Count **how many** numbers there are in the data set.

5, 3, 1, 2, 4 5
1   2   3   4 5

Step three: **Divide** the **total** you calculated (from Step one) by **how many** numbers are in the set (from Step two).

$$\frac{15}{5} = 3$$

Answer: The **mean** of the data set is **3**.

Figure 13.2 Example of Simplifying the Directions

ralreaders.com) to help students who struggle with decoding text. Video technology can also be used to supplement text as a way to demonstrate concepts. Teachers should examine various ways adaptations can be used to facilitate understanding of specific concepts and consider using a combination of these types of supports. Combining adaptations may increase the likelihood of student success.

Alter Amount of Material

Students may become overwhelmed if a worksheet contains too much information or too many tasks to complete. When deciding how to reduce the amount of material on a worksheet, examine *why* each piece of specific information is critical for understanding and what text or illustrations can be removed without impeding student learning. Teachers can also adapt materials by requiring the completion of fewer items (e.g., comprehension questions, math problems) than typically required or altering the presentation of questions. For example, multiple choice questions can be adapted by reducing the number of choices.

Alter Difficulty Level of Material

Teachers may create multiple worksheets with varying difficulty levels to accommodate their individual students, but creating multiple worksheets can be time consuming. Additionally, providing modified worksheets for lower performing students reduces their access to advanced material and may stigmatize them as being "different" and less competent than their peers.[5] Providing a single worksheet that builds from easier to more challenging content is an efficient way to provide this differentiation.[6] This type of material adaptation enables lower performing students to access challenging content while simultaneously providing a warm up for the higher performing students. See Figure 13.3 for an example of such a worksheet.

Another way to alter the level of material is to simplify reading passages. First, teachers should analyze the vocabulary and sentence structure of the text to determine its level of difficulty. There are many helpful technological tools that can assist with this analysis. Computer software programs such as Readability Calculations, Readability PLUS, or Microsoft Word's Readability Program are some beneficial tools. Additionally, Lexile levels can be calculated and analyzed through various websites (e.g., https://lexile.com/tools/lexile-analyzer/step-1-what-texts-can-be-measured).

If the analysis reveals that reading material is too advanced for some learners, teachers should rewrite the passages using simpler vocabulary and sentence structure. Fortunately, there is software available to assist teachers in this process (e.g., Achieve3000, Rewordify). These programs assist in the process by rewriting the passages so that students with less advanced reading levels are able to understand them. However, it is critical that teachers carefully examine each revised passage to ensure it is coherent and conveys the original passage's purpose, main idea, and important details. Alternatively, teachers may pair challenging texts with other supplemental materials (e.g., magazine or website articles, trade books, graphics/pictures, video/audio recordings) that can aid students in understanding more complex topics.

Highlight Relevant Material

It is difficult for some students to distinguish the important ideas and concepts within a text from the other surrounding content. Teachers can help students acquire important concepts by highlighting

---

Multiplication Practice

Directions: Complete a whole row before going to the next row. Follow the arrows!

Solve the multiplication problems.   Highlight the **key** math words. Then solve the problem. Show your work!

1	5	6
×3	×7	×5

Max has 7 boxes. Each box has 5 hats. How many hats does Max have?

41	86	38
× 5	× 5	× 5

Kim has 6 boxes of pens. Each box has 21 pens. How many pens does Kim have?

16	22	47
×13	×11	×52

Joshua got paid $12 for each lawn he mowed last summer. He mowed a total of 14 lawns. How much money did Joshua earn?

Figure 13.3 Example of Altering the Difficulty Level of a Worksheet

relevant information within a text, lecture, or worksheet. Teaching students strategies to decipher the important features of the text can significantly enhance learning and reduce frustration. Teachers should preview the text and highlight any key ideas helpful for student knowledge.[7] These key concepts can be bolded, highlighted, or underlined to alert students to the critical information. (Figure 13.4 shows an example of a highlighted reading passage.) Once a passage has been highlighted, teachers should be explicit about how students can benefit from the highlighting. For example, teachers may begin a lesson by stating, "Before you read this passage, look at the highlighted words and phrases, and consider what this passage will be about." This may lead to a brief discussion wherein students share what they already know about the topic, teachers correct any misconceptions, students make predictions about what they will learn, and students ask themselves questions they hope will be answered by reading the text. As a follow-up to reading a highlighted passage, teachers might assess comprehension by having students write brief summaries using the highlighted words and phrases. As students become stronger readers, teachers can adjust the amount of highlighting or the type of highlighting (e.g., use bold font for new vocabulary words and underline font for main ideas). Teachers can create this supported text for use by all students and gradually remove these supports as students become more proficient readers.

Content Enhancements

Content enhancements are used to support students who have difficulty reading grade-level textbooks, understanding curriculum vocabulary, listening to lectures, and/or taking notes. The following three content enhancements are described next: (a) guided notes, (b) graphic organizers, and (c) mnemonics.

Guided Notes

Guided notes are content enhancements that provide students with active responding opportunities and an accurate set of notes to study. They are handouts that accompany teacher-led instruction and contain background information and visual prompts for students to write key facts and concepts as they follow along with the teacher.[8] Guided notes can assist students with the retention of information related to the course content and may improve independent note-taking skills. Cues such as blank lines or bullet points in guided notes help students identify the important information they need to write down, thus providing students with a complete study guide for future tests and assignments. In order to increase independent note-taking skills, teachers can gradually fade guided notes as students become more proficient with identifying and writing down key points. For example, teachers can fade the cues (i.e., bullet points, blank lines) and/or gradually require students to write more content information.

Alexander Graham Bell is famously known for his **invention of the telephone**. Both his mother and his wife were deaf, so he developed a fascination with sound. This fascination and study of sound resulted in Alexander Bell learning how to send voice signals through a telegraph wire. After this discovery, **Alexander Bell hired his famous assistant Thomas Watson**, and they worked together to come up with the idea of the telephone. It is widely reported that the first words spoken on the telephone occurred on March 10, 1876. Many other scientists at this time were also working on similar inventions, so Alexander Bell worked quickly so that his name would be on the original patent. He and Watson formed the **Bell Telephone Company in 1877**. Today, the telephone is used throughout the world. It is difficult to think about what life would be like without this form of **communication**.

Figure 13.4 Example of Passage With Relevant Material Highlighted

Additionally, guided notes have been demonstrated to increase active responding during lectures and increase academic achievement on tests and quizzes.[9] When instructors use guided notes, students are more likely to ask questions and remain on-task throughout the lecture.[10] Figure 13.5 shows an example of guided notes.

The following are recommended guidelines for creating and using guided notes:[11]

- Develop a lecture using presentation software (e.g., PowerPoint, Prezi).
- Create an outline that contains the most important content from that presentation.
- Delete from the outline key facts, concepts, and relationships and replace with cues such as asterisks, lines, and bullets to indicate when, where, and how many concepts the students have to write (refer to Figure 13.5 for sample symbols to use).
- Leave enough space for students to write, but keep in mind that requiring students to write too much information may undermine some of the benefits of guided notes.
- Include supporting information and supplemental resources within the guided notes.
- Allow students to have access to guided notes prior to class.
- Teach students how to complete guided notes before expecting them to use them independently.
- Combine guided notes with other effective practices. For instance, embed additional response opportunities (e.g., choral response, response cards; see HLP 18), graphic organizers (see below), and mnemonic instruction (see below).
- Monitor students' completion of guided notes and provide feedback to encourage their continued use.

Abraham Lincoln

✱ Abraham Lincoln was the 16th _____ of the United States.
- Prior to being president, Abraham Lincoln served a single term in the _____.
✱ During his presidency, Abraham Lincoln was best known for his fight against _____.
- Abraham Lincoln's goal was to keep the _____ together.
- Tragically, Abraham Lincoln was _____ while watching a play in 1865.

✓ Take out your true/false response cards and be ready to respond on Ms. May's signal. Tally your correct responses in the box below.

📖 **Read pages 65–68 in your textbook, and write three more details about Abraham Lincoln.**
1.
2.
3.

🐟 When everyone is ready, Ms. May will give you instructions to share your details with a neighbor. Work silently until you receive these instructions.

✓ Take out your true/false response cards and be ready to respond on Ms. May's signal. Tally your correct responses in the box below.

Figure 13.5 Example of Guided Notes

Graphic Organizers

Graphic organizers are visual displays that present information in a manner that makes it easy for students to understand relationships between, and organization of, concepts.[12] Lines, arrows, circles, and boxes may be used to illustrate conceptual relationships. These relationships may be hierarchical, cause/effect, compare/contrast, cyclical, or linear.[13] The following steps are recommended for creating graphic organizers:[14]

- Step 1: Identify the information or content you wish to share with students.
- Step 2: Identify key components from the content.
- Step 3: Create a graphic representation of the information. (See Figure 13.6 for an example.) The chart should represent key ideas and components of the content and show relationships among them.
- Step 4: Assist students with identifying the connections within the material by examining the information given.

Graphic organizers are most effective when instruction is informed, explicit, intentional, and scaffolded.[15] Specifically, the teacher *informs* the students by explaining what graphic organizers are and how they are used. The teacher is *explicit* and *intentional* by overtly modeling how the graphic organizer is used. After the students have demonstrated basic abilities to complete the graphic organizers, the teacher can switch to more implicit forms of instruction and allow the students to adapt and create their own.[16] Finally, the teacher may *scaffold* use of graphic organizers in two ways. First, the teacher can coach students as they are learning how to use graphic organizers. Second, the teacher

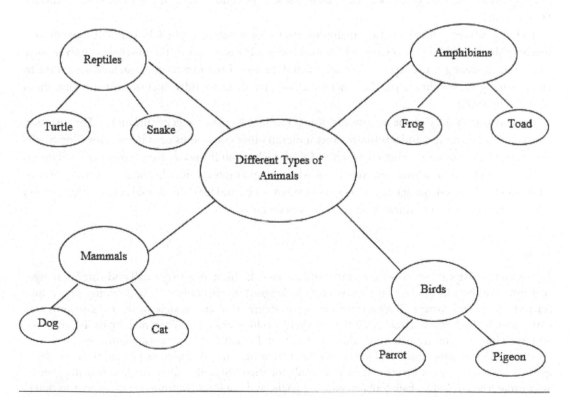

Figure 13.6 Example of Concept Map Graphic Organizer

can start with simpler versions of graphic organizers, and as students develop an understanding of how to use them, he can introduce more complex versions.[17]

Mnemonic Strategies

Mnemonic strategies are used to increase students' abilities to remember important aspects of lessons and content.[18] Two helpful mnemonic strategies are the keyword strategy and the letter strategy.[19] The keyword method has been identified as the most effective mnemonic strategy.[20] The three-step process for using the keyword mnemonic for remembering new vocabulary is recoding, relating, and retrieving.[21] *Recoding* is identifying a similar sounding familiar word to associate with the new vocabulary word. For example, "apex" means the top or highest point of something, so the image can be an ape at the top of mountain.[22] *Relating* is having the student illustrate the image with the meaning of the vocabulary word. *Retrieving* is when the student thinks of the keyword and image in order to remember the meaning of the vocabulary. The keyword strategy can be instrumental for learning vocabulary across academic areas such as science, social studies, and literature.

The letter strategy is another mnemonic strategy that requires the student to create an acronym or a sentence mnemonic. An acronym is a word formed from the first letters of the key words students are trying to remember. An example of a common acronym is HOMES, which is used to remember the five great lakes (Huron, Ontario, Michigan, Erie, and Superior). A sentence mnemonic is a sentence formed from words beginning with the first letters of the key words students are trying to remember. Sentence mnemonics are particularly helpful when information needs to be remembered in order. For example, "Please Excuse My Dear Aunt Sally" stands for the order of operations for simplifying mathematical expressions (i.e., Parentheses, Exponents, Multiplication/Division, Addition/Subtraction).

Helping students learn to use mnemonic strategies requires explicit instruction. Specifically, teachers should model the strategy, which may include breaking down the mnemonic into smaller steps and modeling those steps.[23] To scaffold student use of the mnemonic, teachers may want to create cueing sheets illustrating the mnemonic and give them to individual students or hang them in the classroom.

To maximize utility of the mnemonic, it is important to plan for generalization.[24] For instance, teachers can encourage students to use mnemonics in other classrooms or at home. However, teachers should help students recognize when and under what conditions a given mnemonic will apply. When students come across new situations where a mnemonic can help them (but none exists), students should be encouraged to develop new mnemonics, and teachers should support this process with scaffolded instruction that is as explicit as necessary.

Wrap Up

Instructional adaptations are essential for student success. Implementing small and simple changes will not only benefit students with learning challenges but also enhance the learning experience for a diversity of learners. Teachers can choose strategies that are feasible in their classrooms and can gradually build more strategies into their daily teaching practice. When making decisions about which adaptations to use with individual students (and when and how to use them), teachers must consider the students' individual goals and determine the kind of supports needed to reach those goals. Effective teachers identify ambitious goals for their students, pinpoint their learning needs, adapt materials in light of students' needs and goals, and conduct continuous assessment to determine the effectiveness of the adaptations.

Tips

1. **Start small.** Do not overwhelm students or yourself attempting to implement too many adaptations all at once. Start with the adaptations required by the individual students' IEPs, then gradually build more adaptations across curriculum and skill areas so that all students may benefit.

2. **Share the work.** Be creative in identifying collaborators who share the goal of adapting materials and tasks. For instance, special education and general education co-teachers can take turns adapting worksheets alternating every other week. Grade-level teams might divide the task of developing content enhancement such as guided notes and graphic organizers. Consider forming a district-wide grade-level team with teachers who teach the same content and exchange materials using a shared drive such as Google Docs. As teams develop more materials, they might consider building a website to share them with larger audiences.

3. **Reflect on your successes (and challenges).** After each lesson and instructional unit, use data collected during and following instruction to evaluate the effectiveness of your teaching. If students have not mastered the material, one of your first assumptions should be that there were insufficient adaptations and content enhancements in place. Use this information to develop a plan for remediation/re-teaching and to inform your planning for the next time you teach the lesson. Once you find something that works and that students like, keep it!

Notes

1 Bulgren, J. A., Deshler, D. D., & Lenz, B. K. (2007). Engaging adolescents with LD in higher order thinking about history concepts using integrated content enhancement routines. *Journal of Learning Disabilities, 40*(2), 121–133.

2 Heward, W. L. (1994). Three "low-tech" strategies for increasing the frequency of active student response during group instruction. In R. Gardner, D. M. Sainato, J. O. Cooper, T. E. Heron, W. L. Heward, J. Eshleman, & T. A. Grossi (Eds.), *Behavior analysis in education: Focus on measurably superior instruction* (pp. 283–320). Monterey, CA: Brooks/Cole, p. 304.

3 Westwood, P. (2013). *Inclusive and adaptive teaching: Meeting the challenge of diversity in the classroom.* New York, NY: Routledge.

4 Singleton, S. M., & Filce, H. G. (2015). Graphic organizers for secondary students with learning disabilities. *Teaching Exceptional Children, 48*(2), 110–117.

5 Hall, S. (1997). The problem with differentiation. *School Science Review, 78*(284), 95–98.

6 Westwood, P. (2013). *Inclusive and adaptive teaching: Meeting the challenge of diversity in the classroom.* New York, NY: Routledge.

7 Schumm, J. S., Vaughn, S., & Saumell, L. (1992). What teachers do when the textbook is tough: Students speak out. *Journal of Reading Behavior, 24*(4), 481–503.

8 Heward, W. L., Alber-Morgan, S. R., & Konrad, M. (2017). *Exceptional children: An introduction to special education* (11th ed.). Upper Saddle River, NJ: Pearson.

9 Konrad, M., Joseph. L. M., & Eveleigh, E. (2009). A meta-analytic review of guided notes. *Education and Treatment of Children, 32,* 421–444.

10 Heward, W. L., Alber-Morgan, S. R., & Konrad, M. (2017). *Exceptional children: An introduction to special education* (11th ed.). Upper Saddle River, NJ: Pearson.

11 Heward, W. L., Alber-Morgan, S. R., & Konrad, M. (2017). *Exceptional children: An introduction to special education* (11th ed.). Upper Saddle River, NJ: Pearson.

12 Ives, B. (2007). Graphic organizers applied to secondary algebra instruction for students with learning disabilities. *Learning Disabilities Research & Practice, 22,* 110–118.

13 Ellis, E., & Howard, P. (2007). Graphic organizers. *Current Practice Alerts, 1*(13), 1–4.

14 Dye, G. A. (2000). Graphic organizers to the rescue! Helping student link-and remember-information. *Teaching Exceptional Children, 32*(3), 72–76.

15 Ellis, E., & Howard, P. (2007). Graphic organizers. *Current Practice Alerts, 1*(13), 1–4.

16 Ellis, E., & Howard, P. (2007). Graphic organizers. *Current Practice Alerts, 1*(13), 1–4.

17 Ellis, E., & Howard, P. (2007). Graphic organizers. *Current Practice Alerts, 1*(13), 1–4.

18 Mastropieri, M. A., Sweda, J., & Scruggs, T. E. (2000). Teacher use of mnemonic strategy instruction. *Learning Disabilities Research and Practice, 15*, 69–74.

19 Kleinheksel, K. A., & Summy, S. E. (2003). Enhancing student learning and social behavior through mnemonic strategies. *Teaching Exceptional Children, 36*(2), 30–35.

20 Scruggs, T. E., & Mastropieri, M. A. (1991). Classroom applications of mnemonic instruction: Acquisition, maintenance, and generalization. *Exceptional Children, 58*(3), 219–229.

21 Levin, J. R. (1988). Elaboration-based learning strategies: Powerful theory—Powerful application. *Contemporary Educational Psychology, 13*, 191–205.

22 Mastropieri, M. A, Scruggs, T. E., & Fulk, B. J. M. (1990). Teaching abstract vocabulary with the keyword method: Effects on recall and comprehension. *Journal of Learning Disabilities, 23*, 293–296.

23 Kleinheksel, K. A., & Summy, S. E. (2003). Enhancing student learning and social behavior through mnemonic strategies. *Teaching Exceptional Children, 36*(2), 30–35.

24 Kleinheksel, K. A., & Summy, S. E. (2003). Enhancing student learning and social behavior through mnemonic strategies. *Teaching Exceptional Children, 36*(2), 30–35.

Key Resources

Alber-Morgan, S. (2010). *Using RTI to teach literacy to diverse learners, K–8: Strategies for the inclusive classroom.* Thousand Oaks, CA: Corwin Press.

"GO FOR IT" Practice Alerts. Retrieved from www.teachingld.org/alerts

Guided Notes: Increasing Student Engagement During Lecture and Assigned Readings. Retrieved from www.interventioncentral.org/academic-interventions/study-organization/guided-notes-increasing-student-engagement-during-lecture-

Hattie, J. (2009). *Visible learning: A synthesis of over 800 meta-analyses relating to achievement.* London: Routledge.

Heward, W. L., Alber-Morgan, S. R., & Konrad, M. (2017). *Exceptional children: An introduction to special education* (11th ed.). Upper Saddle River, NJ: Pearson.

Main Idea Maps. Retrieved from www.interventioncentral.org/academic-interventions/reading-comprehension/main-idea-maps

Smith, T. E., Polloway, E. A., Patton, J. R., & Dowdy, C. A. (2011). *Teaching students with special needs in inclusive settings with what every teacher should know about: Adaptations and accommodations for students with mild to moderate disabilities* (6th ed.). Upper Saddle River, NJ: Pearson.

14

Teaching Cognitive and Metacognitive Strategies to Support Learning and Independence

Shannon Budin, Angela L. Patti, and Lisa A. Rafferty

Introduction

A primary role for special educators is to help their students find success in terms of their social, academic, physical, and management needs. An effective special educator is one who engages in practices that facilitate students' abilities to be more self-directed and strategic learners who are eventually able to independently identify and reach their learning and behavioral goals. Educators often accomplish this by teaching students cognitive and metacognitive strategies they can use across settings and content areas to solve problems, regulate attention, organize thoughts and materials, and monitor their own thinking.

Researchers have described strategy instruction as teaching students *how* to learn and perform.[1] Learning and performance outcomes can include, but are not limited to: monitoring one's attention to a task, writing an essay, reading for meaning, knowing how to work with a peer, or knowing what to do if lost in the community. Educators can teach these strategies to the whole class (i.e., as core curriculum at Tier 1 in a multi-tiered system of support) or small group (i.e., Tier 2) levels, or they can modify the strategies to meet the unique needs of one or two students in the class (i.e., Tier 3).

Equally important, a student must also be explicitly taught the metacognitive skills of how to:[2] (a) determine which strategy to use to work through a task, (b) develop a learning goal, (c) monitor the effects of the strategy, (d) determine if the use of the strategy is helping to meet the learning goal, and (e) change or "fix up" the approach as needed in order to experience success. A teacher's role in this process is key. Therefore, in this chapter, we will emphasize what a teacher must *do* in order to facilitate learning and successful use of cognitive and metacognitive strategies worthy of the title "high leverage practice."

Narrowing the Focus

The high leverage practice (HLP) "teach cognitive and metacognitive strategies to support learning and independence" is unique because both the teacher and student have significant responsibilities. The teacher teaches the student the steps within a cognitive strategy, supports the development of the metacognitive skills needed to use the strategy effectively, and provides examples and non-examples of when to use the strategy. It is then the goal of instruction that the student will master the strategy and use it independently and correctly, as needed.

With strategy instruction, a successful student (i.e., strategic learner) utilizes strategies that have been taught and is systematic in the approach. That is, the student recognizes the task or problem, makes a plan to address it, and carries out the plan (with changes to the plan, as needed) using the cognitive strategy.

A non-strategic learner may need more initial support from a teacher to identify appropriate strategies and how to implement them. Therefore, teacher expertise is needed to act as a conduit between the task and the goal of achieving it. In other words, although a strategy can be defined as an *individual's* approach to a task,[3] it is often the *teacher* who is vital to student success. A student's familiarity with a strategy will not lead to improved learning and performance unless a skilled teacher has taught him/her when and how to use it.[4]

Chapter Overview

1. Describe the reciprocal relationship between teacher and student in strategy instruction.
2. Describe the critical role of the teacher in strategy instruction.
3. Provide resources for strategy instruction and classroom scenarios as a means of illustration.

The Reciprocal Relationship Between Teacher and Student in Strategy Instruction

There is a reciprocal relationship between teaching and learning in all areas of instruction, but as illustrated in Figure 14.1, this is especially true when it comes to teaching and independently using cognitive and metacognitive strategies. The teacher is responsible for teaching the strategies, which includes: (a) identifying areas of student need, (b) selecting or developing appropriate strategies, (c) teaching when and how to use the strategies, and (d) monitoring the effectiveness of strategy use. The student is responsible for learning and applying the strategies when needed, which includes monitoring the appropriate selection, use, and effectiveness of the strategies towards meeting learning or behavioral goals. Thus, both teacher and student are responsible for the implementation and success of this HLP. Given the complex nature of describing cognitive and metacognitive strategies and how they work, as well as the relationship between teacher and student roles when using these strategies, we will first provide a classroom example to illustrate the key points.

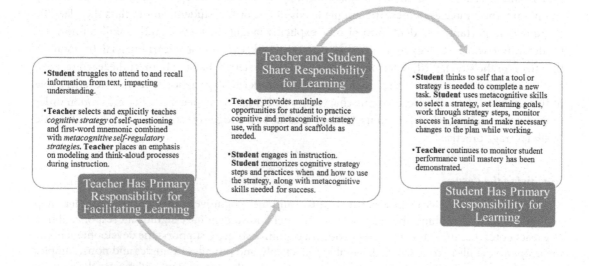

Figure 14.1 Example of Reciprocal Role of Teacher and Student in Cognitive and Metacognitive Strategy Learning and Use

A student is presented with grade-level text about a specific topic, such as the structure of the solar system and universe. She may be interested in this content and is able to decode the written text, but she cannot remember and recall information about the solar system days, hours, or even minutes after reading. As a result, her understanding about the solar system is negatively affected. This sample student may be considered a *nonstrategic learner* in that she is unaware of how to approach the challenge of remembering and understanding material she is otherwise capable of reading and interested in learning. This student may experience frustration, readily give up, or wait for a teacher or peer to provide the answers.

An effective teacher may recognize the nature of the breakdown or areas of challenge for the student and implement certain instructional techniques to facilitate attention, understanding, and recall. By teaching the student to be "more actively involved" in her reading by using a self-questioning strategy,[5] for example, increased independence can be achieved. The teacher could also teach the student a memory-enhancing mnemonic strategy to assist in recalling the order of the planets (e.g., *My Very Excellent Mother Just Sent Us Noodles* to represent Mercury, Venus, Earth, Mars, Jupiter, Saturn, Uranus, and Neptune). It is important to note that both the self-questioning strategy and mnemonic strategy must be taught explicitly. This includes modeling with think-alouds, guided practice, and independent practice, with many opportunities for student engagement and performance feedback.

Assuming these techniques are taught skillfully by the teacher and thus understood by the student, the responsibility is now shared. The student must now recognize when she needs a strategy, select which strategy to use, and engage in using the strategy as intended while continually monitoring her own progress to determine if she is experiencing success.

In the above scenario, we see a classic combination of cognitive and metacognitive strategy use with involvement of both teacher and student. In this example, cognitive strategies are used to help the student achieve the goal of attending to and understanding the text, while metacognitive strategies are used to ensure that the goal has been reached. Recognizing a common challenge, the teacher selects evidence-based strategies that facilitate the reader's attention, understanding, and recall (i.e., cognitive strategies of self-questioning and first-letter mnemonic). Once the teacher explicitly teaches how and when to use the strategy, she must also teach the student how to monitor the effects of the strategy. After initial instruction and practice opportunities, some students may be prepared to use strategies independently, while others may need additional practice opportunities with support. The teacher must continue to provide supports until the student is able to recognize challenges and use that strategy when needed (see Figure 14.1).

In the example, if the student first recognizes her challenge of attending to and recalling information, and then makes a conscious decision to use a series of steps she has been taught to help her attend to and recall ideas from her reading, she illustrates metacognition in action. That is, she is able to monitor and assess her ongoing performance in accomplishing her cognitive goal of attending to and recalling information about the solar system.

The student's metacognitive strategy use continues as we see her erroneously attempt to use a tool like a story structure elements questioning cue card (a tool for a self-questioning strategy for narrative text) as a prompt when she tries to answer the questions on the cue card: "Who is the main character?" and "Where does the story take place?" A student who is strategic quickly notices a mismatch between the tool and/or strategy she selected (story structure cue card) and the type of text she is engaged with (informational text about the solar system). Her awareness that she must select a *different* self-questioning strategy to match the informational text about the solar system shows her ability to use metacognitive strategies to self-regulate her behavior. In other words, the student uses metacognitive strategies to ensure that her goal of attending to and recalling information about the solar system through text is met by appropriately using the cognitive strategies (i.e., self-questioning and mnemonic strategies). If she determines she is not making progress towards meeting her goal, she will redirect and change her approach.

Through the use of metacognitive strategies, the sample student is aware of her own thought processes and is taking a more active role in her learning. An effective teacher is one who not only teaches a student when and how to use the appropriate cognitive strategy but also helps the student develop self-regulatory skills to monitor her strategy use and its effectiveness during the learning process by using metacognitive strategies such as self-monitoring.

As we explore later, it is not enough for a teacher to select an appropriate cognitive strategy and teach it explicitly. Rather, as this scenario illustrates, self-regulation also plays an important role. Even an appropriately selected, well-designed, and skillfully taught cognitive strategy may not lead to the desired outcome if a student does not know and/or use metacognitive strategies as well. A student who knows the steps of an effective notetaking strategy may find herself daydreaming during a lecture, leaning over to chat to a peer, forgetting the key ideas before she records them on the specially formatted notetaking paper, or perhaps being unable to identify which strategy to use in this situation. Therefore, to be effective in supporting learning and independence, a teacher must integrate the explicit teaching of the appropriate metacognitive strategies and routines as well.

The Critical Role of the Teacher in Strategy Instruction

Many factors influence the success of cognitive and metacognitive strategy use—of primary importance is the teacher's role. In the following section, we explore practices related to explicit strategy instruction and the ways in which teachers can prepare students to solve problems, regulate attention, organize thoughts and materials, and monitor their own thinking.[6] It is important to note that we will not cover all components of explicit instruction in this chapter, as they are discussed in more depth in the chapter focused on HLP 16: *Use Explicit Instruction*. HLPs that influence strategy instruction include (but are not limited to): (a) systematically design instruction toward a specific learning goal (HLP 12), (b) provide scaffolded supports (HLP 15), (c) use explicit instruction (HLP 16), (d) teach students to maintain and generalize new learning across time and settings (HLP 21), and I provide positive and constructive feedback to guide students' learning and behavior (HLP 22). Each of these practices is described in more depth in other chapters throughout this book and should be considered when designing effective strategy instruction.

Selecting or Designing Appropriate Strategies Based on Student Needs

Ideally, an effective teacher is one who is able to recognize learning or behavior difficulties and then facilitate students' abilities to become more self-directed and independent learners via the evidence-based approach of cognitive strategy instruction (CSI).[7] Essentially, CSI teaches students how to learn.[8] Through CSI, strategies can be taught as mental routines or procedures that students can use to accomplish their cognitive goals.[9] A teacher can use CSI to teach students "specific and general cognitive strategies to improve learning and performance."[10] Teachers should consider CSI as a flexible framework that can be used to teach *any* strategy, whether it is a teacher-created tool used to address a specific problem or a larger instructional package with multiple strategies embedded within (e.g., Collaborative Strategic Reading).[11]

Once an area of student need is recognized, a teacher has at least two options when identifying appropriate strategies for her students. One option is to examine sources of evidence-based practices that already exist. She does not need to "reinvent the wheel" to meet a specific student need. She can examine the professional research literature for strategies and tools that may benefit her students. Educational databases provide access to numerous empirical, peer-reviewed studies that evaluate a particular strategy's effectiveness with students from various age and grade levels and from various disability groups in a range of settings.

While examining the research literature for high-quality, empirical studies may be the most rigorous manner in which to identify strategies, it may also have the least practicality for busy practitioners. A more realistic approach might be to explore expertly curated clearinghouses, online professional development resources, websites from educational organization and research institutes, or peer-reviewed books which offer a range of strategies that can be selected based on a student's unique needs. A sample of resources that have already been expertly vetted can be found in Figure 14.2.

Resource	Brief Description
Center on Instruction www.centeroninstruction.org	Collection of research-based resources on K–12 instruction in reading, math, science, special education, and English language learning.
Center on Positive Behavioral Interventions and Supports www.pbis.org	Provides resources related to research-based school-wide and individualized positive behavior interventions and supports.
Effective School Interventions: Evidence-Based Strategies for Improving Student Outcomes Second Edition Book by Natalie Rathvon Guilford Press, ISBN: 9781572309678	Includes 70 evidence-based interventions, presented in step-by-step format, that are aimed to improve student outcomes in a variety of areas.
Evidence Based Intervention Network http://ebi.missouri.edu	Provides a sampling of evidence-based interventions and associated resources that provide guidance in the selection and implementation of interventions.
Intervention Central www.interventioncentral.org	Collection of academic and behavioral intervention and assessment resources and tools for educators in grades K–12.
IRIS Center https://iris.peabody.vanderbilt.edu	Provides resources about evidence-based practices for use in preservice preparation and professional development. Online tutorial modules and step-by-step guides provided.
National Center on Intensive Intervention www.intensiveintervention.org	Provides reviews and description of tools and strategies appropriate for intensive intervention in reading, mathematics, and behavior for students with severe and persistent learning and/or behavioral needs.
University of Nebraska Department of Special Education and Communication Disorders http://cehs.unl.edu/csi	Provides a curated list of research validated learning strategies as a professional development resource on cognitive strategy instruction.
What Works Clearinghouse https://ies.ed.gov/ncee/wwc	Reviews the existing research on different programs, products, practices, and policies in education. Provides intervention reports, practice guides and reviews of individual studies.

Figure 14.2 Sample Resources for Research Validated Strategies

A second option a teacher can employ for identifying appropriate strategies is gathering evidence on teacher-developed strategies or procedures. That is, a teacher does not have to rely on a "menu" of cognitive strategies from which to choose. Rather, she can develop strategies by studying what strategic learners do to accomplish the goal of interest. A teacher must start with a task analysis of what is needed to accomplish the learning or behavioral goal, create a series of steps or procedures to help meet that goal, and explicitly teach it to the student.[12] The teacher can then gather data from within her own classroom to influence everyday practice.

For example, a teacher notices that students are struggling to take notes in content area classes such as science or social studies. The students either write nothing or tend to write every little detail and get overwhelmed when they cannot keep pace with the content area teacher. The teacher knows it is important to help students determine the best way to take notes but has little time to conduct a literature review to find a formal notetaking strategy. Therefore, the teacher can easily study how strategic learners take good notes, identify the underlying skills needed, and design a strategy to accomplish those steps.[13] Although note taking can be highly individualized based on personal preference, all good note takers must possess a few key prerequisite skills. In order to help the students gear up for successful notetaking, the teacher analyzes the most important aspects and creates a strategy with design features that include short sequential steps that form a mnemonic device. Since good note takers must first be free of distraction and actively listen, a first step is to "attend" to the instructor. Students learn that "attend" means to look, listen, and generally focus on only the teacher. Good note takers must also have some familiarity with the content. Prior subject knowledge and overall context of what is being taught is key. Therefore, the next step is to teach students to "activate" background knowledge. This may include completing readings prior to class; having a discussion about what they know about the topic; previewing content by examining illustrations or textbook images, timelines, or other graphic representations in the text; or perhaps watching a video in advance. Finally, students are encouraged to "ask" clarifying questions when needed by communicating and engaging with the teacher, including asking for repetition, or statement of key ideas. These three key ideas—*attending*, *activating*, and *asking*—lead to the act of choosing the preferred form of note taking. Students should be taught explicitly—and have an opportunity to practice—a range of note-taking tools, which may include the use of outlines, mind maps, t-charts, or other preferred methods. Thus, the teacher with struggling note takers created the "Triple A then Choose" strategy (Attend, Activate, Ask then Choose tool) based on key skills needed in the successful note-taking process. This strategy illustrates useful content features that include both the cognitive and metacognitive processes and overt actions required to reach their goal. The strategy "Triple A then Choose" includes sequential steps, as recommended by Hughes,[14] that require specific mental and physical actions in order to take better notes.

Identifying and Implementing a Model for Strategy Instruction

Researchers have studied different models of strategy instruction that fit into a larger CSI framework,[15] including those embedded into strategy instructional programs aimed to improve student outcomes in specific areas. One example is Solve It!,[16] which is an instructional program used to help students acquire and apply cognitive and metacognitive strategies to solve math word problems. In specific and general implementation models, there are slight variations, but both are designed to help students think, plan, and execute the task demands for academic, social, and/or behavioral success. Two commonly implemented instructional models that can be used to teach a variety of strategies are the Self-Regulated Strategy Development[17] (SRSD) model and Strategic Instruction Model™ (SIM).[18]

Self-Regulated Strategy Development

Using the SRSD model, the teacher emphasizes teaching specific cognitive strategies to meet a task demand while simultaneously teaching students the metacognitive strategies needed for success.[19] As summarized in Figure 14.3, it is a comprehensive and flexible model, with sequential steps, that allows the teacher to use professional judgment while implementing it with students. Steps are designed to be recursive, and they can be reordered or combined if the teacher considers it appropriate when making data-based decisions.

Embedded in the SRSD model is the essential need to help students develop the metacognitive skills that make strategy use effective. In other words, to be useful to the learner, it is not enough for a student

---

Overview

SRSD is a scientifically validated framework for explicitly teaching learning strategies to students. Within this framework, teachers also provide explicit instruction on self-regulation strategies, helping students to learn self-monitoring, self-instruction, goal-setting, and self-reinforcement.

Procedures

* **Develop Background Knowledge**
  * Identify the requisite skills students will need to use a particular strategy
  * Assess whether the students possess these skills
  * Help students develop the necessary skills (e.g., vocabulary) they may need to learn the academic and self-regulation strategies
* **Discuss the Strategy**
  * Help the students to understand the benefits of using a strategy
  * Teach the students how and when to use a particular strategy
  * Emphasize the importance of student effort, motivation, and self-instruction
  * Explain to the students that once they learn a strategy, they can use it during different kinds of activities and in different situations
  * Describe ways to self-monitor
* **Model the Strategy**
  * Expose the students to the thought processes used by skilled learners while performing the task
  * Show the students how to perform the steps in a strategy
  * Explain the reasons the steps in a strategy are necessary
* **Memorize the Strategy**
  * Require the students to learn the steps of the strategy and what action is performed during each step
  * Encourage the students to become fluent in the steps of a strategy so that they can use them without having to stop and think about what step comes next
* **Support the Strategy**
  * Collaboratively use the writing and self-regulation strategies with students
  * Use strategy charts and graphic organizers
  * Make sure students work toward attaining their initial goals
  * Increase students' goals gradually until their final goals have been reached
  * Offer constructive feedback guidance and positive reinforcement
  * "Fade" (or modulate) support based on students' individual needs
  * Discuss with students ways to maintain or continue to use the strategy
  * Support students so that they are able to use the strategy in other settings
* **Establish Independent Practice**
  * Monitor and support student performance, as needed

Figure 14.3 Summarized SRSD Steps From IRIS Center

Source: The IRIS Center. (2013). Study Skills Strategies (Part 1): Foundations for Effectively Teaching Study Skills. Retrieved from https://iris.peabody.vanderbilt.edu/wp-content/uploads/modules/ss/pdfs/ss_03_link_SRSD.pdf#content Used with permission.

to know how to implement strategy steps under the close guidance of a teacher. If a student is going to independently implement a strategy to successfully meet an academic, social, or behavioral goal, s/he must also understand why each step is implemented, when and where to use the strategy, how to monitor and assess if the strategy is working, and what to do if the strategy is not helping to meet identified goals. This is accomplished by explicitly teaching the student to simultaneously use self-regulation procedures (e.g., goal-setting, self-monitoring, self-talk, self-reinforcement) during each step in the process.

Strategic Instruction Model

As illustrated in Figure 14.4, characteristics of SRSD are also evident in the SIM Learning Strategies instructional approach developed by researchers from the University of Kansas' Center for Research on Learning.[20] SIM Learning Strategies address areas such as writing, reading, math, test taking, and study skills. This model of strategy instruction is designed to tackle challenges faced by students while ensuring fidelity, generalization, and maintenance of the strategy. The curriculum focuses on three broad areas of learning: (a) acquisition (i.e., Word Identification, Paraphrasing, Self-questioning); (b) storage (i.e., FIRST-Letter Mnemonic, Listening and Notetaking); and/or (c) expression/demonstration (i.e., Sentence Writing, Paragraph Writing). Each area is composed of "a complex set of cognitive strategies used in sequence to successfully complete a generic academic task."[21] Based on this implementation model, critical features of successful strategy instruction include: (a) daily and sustained instruction, (b) multiple opportunities to practice the strategy in a variety of situations, (c) individualized feedback, and (d) required mastery of the strategy.[22]

Regardless of the specific cognitive or metacognitive skills taught using SRSD or SIM, both implementation models contain common design features. Hughes states that design features "relate to the way the strategy is packaged for presentation to the students" as well as how it "is organized and arranged for instruction . . . to lead to optimal student learning and use."[23] Common design features that enhance student memory and recall include components such as use of steps, mnemonic devices, and short action-oriented words that help cue the student for the action needed to complete the strategy's step (e.g., Attend, Activate, etc.).

As demonstrated by the significant research evidence supporting both SRSD[25] and SIM,[26] once a strategy is selected or created, *how* it is taught to students may be equally, if not more, vital in ensuring the understanding, use, and generalization of the tool. Swanson determined that a combined direct instruction and strategy instruction model may be more effective than many other instructional approaches, particularly for students with learning disabilities.[27]

Elements of explicit instruction are vital to ensure learning and use of specific cognitive and metacognitive strategies. Based on the two implementation models summarized above, knowledge and use of additional high leverage practices (HLPs) is required.

Effective Instruction of Cognitive and Metacognitive Strategies

A formal instructional model such as SRSD or SIM is not required to be successful in teaching students when and how to use cognitive and metacognitive strategies. Rather, emphasizing the foundations of explicit instruction and underlying principles of effective instruction is key.

Therefore, to effectively teach strategies of any kind, the following instructional components should be considered:[28]

- Pre-teaching of necessary pre-requisite skills
- Instruction of how, when, where, and why to use the strategy, including the importance and purpose of each step

---

Overview

SIM is based on a set of instructional guidelines that can be used to effectively teach students a variety of learning strategies. Though each stage of the model focuses on different instructional practices (noted below), each also involves the use of advance organizers, post organizers, and goal-setting.

Procedures

* Pretest and Make Commitments
  * Motivate students to learn the strategy
  * Assess the current performance level of the students in regard to the skill
* **Describe**
  * Provide an overview of the strategy
  * Discuss how this strategy will benefit students
  * Describe how the students will use self-instruction to regulate their use of the strategy
* **Model**
  * Provide instruction on how to use the strategy
  * Use "think alouds" to demonstrate how to use the strategy
  * Demonstrate self-instruction
* **Verbal Practice**
  * Make sure students can describe in their own words the strategy and the steps involved
  * Ensure that students can describe how to use self-instruction when applying the strategy
  * Make sure that students are fluent in naming the steps
* **Controlled Practice and Feedback**
  * Provide ample opportunity for the students to practice using the strategy with easy materials until they can apply the strategy with fluency and confidence
  * Increase the level of difficulty until the students can effectively use the strategy with grade-level tasks
  * Decrease the level of teacher support across time
  * Provide corrective feedback
* **Advanced Practice and Feedback**
  * Assign grade-level tasks in which the students independently apply the strategy
  * Provide assignments that remind the student to adapt the strategy24
  * Decrease the use of prompts
  * Monitor student performance and provide corrective feedback
* **Posttest and Make Commitments**
  * Determine whether the students have mastered the strategy
  * Provide additional practice opportunities for students who have not mastered the strategy
  * Encourage the students to review their goals and provide self-reinforcement for achieving them
  * Explain the importance of using the strategy in other settings (i.e., generalization)
* **Generalization**
  * Discuss the benefits of using the strategy in other settings
  * Encourage students to use the strategy outside of class (e.g., for assignments in other classes, at home)
  * Encourage students to set goals to increase their use of the strategy
  * Discuss the cognitive processes taking place when using a strategy and practice adapting the strategy for novel tasks
  * Promote maintenance of the strategy across time

Figure 14.4 Summarized SIM steps From IRIS Center

Source: Ellis. E., Deshler, D., & Lenz. K. (1991). An instructional model for teaching learning strategies. *Focus on Exceptional Children. 23(6)*, 1–24.

For more information about SIM®, please visit kucrl.org/sim. Most SIM instructional materials are available only in conjunction with professional development provided by certified SIM Professional Developers.

The IRIS Center. (2013). Study Skills Strategies (Part 1): Foundations for Effectively Teaching Study Skills. Retrieved from https://iris.peabody.vanderbilt.edu/wp-content/uploads/modules/ss/pdfs/ss_03_link_SIM.pdf#content Used with permission.

- Breaking the strategy down into logical and manageable pieces or chunks
- Clear, step-by-step strategy demonstrations while scaffolding the level of support from a high to low level
- Modeling of self-talk and "inner language" through the use of teacher think-alouds, which are important for students to monitor effective strategy use
- Numerous opportunities for practice that include monitoring, feedback, and positive reinforcement
- Opportunities to use the strategy in different contexts and over time to promote generalization and maintenance

In the following classroom scenario, examples of these important instructional components can be found as we look at a description of how two co-teachers might provide effective strategy instruction in an inclusive classroom.

A Classroom Scenario

Ms. Hernandez, a special education teacher, and Mr. Powell, a general education teacher, are co-teaching in a fourth-grade classroom. In math class, they spend a great deal of time focusing on the skills needed to solve mathematical problems across a variety of topical areas such as basic operations (addition, subtraction, multiplication, division) with whole numbers, basic operations with fractions, and geometry. They recognize the skills and strategies associated with math problem solving extend beyond their grade level; the students will need to solve math problems as they move through math curriculum in upper grade levels and utilize math in their everyday lives. Therefore, the teachers decide to take the time to teach their students a math problem-solving strategy.

At a conference she attended recently, Ms. Hernandez learned of a mnemonic strategy for solving math word problems, UPSC. The steps in the strategy are understand, plan, solve, and check. In the first step, students read and analyze the problem to *understand* what is being asked. In the second step, students develop a *plan* for solving the problem. This plan may include the use of a variety of approaches for solving problems such as drawing a picture, working backwards, guessing and checking, and looking for patterns. In the third strategy step, students work through their plan to *solve* the problem. Finally, in the fourth step, they *check* their work for accuracy and to ensure it makes sense.

Ms. Hernandez shares this strategy with Mr. Powell, who agrees it would be a great strategy to teach their entire fourth-grade class. The co-teachers develop a series of lessons in which they teach the UPSC strategy to their class using an explicit instruction approach including modeling, guided practice, and independent practice.

Before instruction, they tell students about the strategy and provide a rationale for learning it. They state:

- *Over the next few days, we are going to learn a strategy in math class. A strategy is a tool that helps you accomplish a task. In this case, our strategy is going to help us solve math word problems. We will be able to use this strategy for all different types of math word problems this year in fourth-grade. This strategy will also be helpful in solving math problems in higher grade levels and in real life!*

Next, they name the strategy and describe each of the strategy steps using a strategy poster as a visual. (See example in Figure 14.5.) They tell students that each step is important in the process, so it is necessary to memorize the four steps and always use each step when solving problems. They provide structured time for students to practice memorizing the steps.

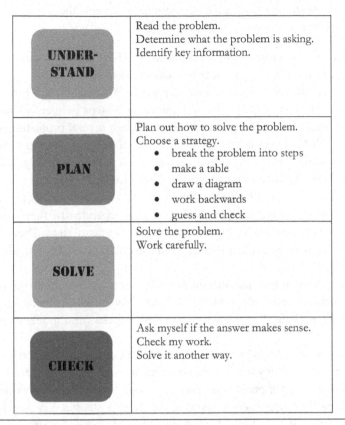

UNDER-STAND	Read the problem. Determine what the problem is asking. Identify key information.
PLAN	Plan out how to solve the problem. Choose a strategy. • break the problem into steps • make a table • draw a diagram • work backwards • guess and check
SOLVE	Solve the problem. Work carefully.
CHECK	Ask myself if the answer makes sense. Check my work. Solve it another way.

Figure 14.5 Poster: Steps for the UPSC Strategy

In the modeling phase of instruction, Mr. Powell and Ms. Hernandez demonstrate the strategy steps using several different math word problems. In their modeling, they also incorporate the metacognitive skills needed to work through the strategy. For example, they demonstrate frequent self-talk and self-questioning in the form of think-alouds to make their thinking processes visible to the students. Examples include:

- *It looks like this assignment requires me to solve math word problems. Where do I even start? Oh, I know. We learned a strategy for this—the UPSC strategy! I will use that strategy to help me!*
- *Now it is time for me to plan how I will solve this problem. I know there are many different approaches I can use. Hmm . . . which approach seems like a good fit for this problem?*

With their self-talk, they also include self-monitoring. They demonstrate that problem solvers monitor their use of strategy steps. They also demonstrate what they do when they get stuck on a strategy step. Examples include:

- *I completed the "solve" step of my problem. I have my answer, but I know I am not done yet. I know it is important to do all strategy steps, so I need to do the "check" step to make sure my answer makes sense and that I did my calculations correctly.*
- *Oh no! I just checked my answer, and it does not seem correct. What do I do? Well, first, I am going to do my calculations one more time to see if I can figure out my mistake. If not, I think I'll go back*

to the beginning of the strategy to reread the problem and examine the plan I developed. Hopefully, I can figure out where I went wrong.

In addition to modeling these metacognitive skills, the teachers explicitly name them for students and explain that these are skills effective learners and problem solvers use.

The teachers do two different phases of guided practice. First, they work through several more problems using the strategy but ask for student input on next steps frequently throughout the process. Next, they put students in small groups to work through several problems using the strategy. During this phase, both teachers circulate around the room, stopping into groups to discuss their problem solving and strategy use. They closely monitor student understanding and use of the strategy and provide additional practice and support to those students who need it.

Finally, in an independent practice phase, Mr. Powell and Ms. Hernandez provide several word problems for each student to solve using the strategy steps independently. They collect the work and provide feedback to students on their implementation of the strategy steps. They also use this work as data to determine if any re-teaching is required and can differentiate this remediation based upon student need.

To promote generalization and maintenance of the strategy, throughout the remainder of the school year, the teachers remind students to use the UPSC strategy when solving word problems with new math topics. They periodically review the steps with the class and model them when working with new topics.

It is important to note that this is just an example of the instructional components that Mr. Powell and Ms. Hernandez provide. They teach these components over the course of several lessons/days and based on student mastery of pre-determined lesson objectives (e.g., identifying when the strategy is needed, naming the strategy steps, applying the strategy steps at a certain level of accuracy, self-monitoring of strategy steps). While they set out with a rough plan for strategy instruction, they regularly assess student progress towards these objectives and make changes to their instruction as needed.

Wrap Up

Teachers strive to support student learning and independence in the classroom. One way to achieve that goal is to teach students specific cognitive strategies they can use to address typical academic, social, and/or behavioral challenges (e.g., being attentive and active in class, making predictions, summarizing, etc.). Teachers must also teach metacognitive strategies to assist students in selecting appropriate strategies and monitoring their effects; it is not enough to be aware of a problem-solving strategy, a student must also know when to apply it, how to use it, and whether or not it is working. Teachers should rely on their expertise and experience to identify appropriate evidence-based strategies either through professional resources or by examining student outcomes within their own classrooms to develop tools. Cognitive and metacognitive strategies must be taught explicitly using evidence-based instructional practices and routines. Various models of strategy instruction offer insight into the procedures needed to effectively teach independent use of these tools. Through modeling and guided practice with feedback, students can gradually gain fluency in using cognitive and metacognitive strategies, leading to independence and classroom success.

Tips

1. Ensure the target skills that are the focus of strategy instruction are in an area students need to improve upon and they are developmentally appropriate.

2. Develop a plan to help pace and scaffold instruction of the strategy. Stages of instruction should be criterion-based, not time-based, to ensure that students acquire and gain proficiency with the use of a strategy prior to being expected to use it independently.[29] This is likely to take multiple lessons over the course of days or even weeks.

3. Ensure that students understand *how, when, where,* and *why* to implement a particular strategy. If students only understand *how* to implement it during a teacher-controlled context, without understanding *when, where,* and *why* to use it, then it is not possible to develop independent and self-regulated strategy use.

4. Integrate the teaching of cognitive and metacognitive strategies. Help students to understand how the metacognitive strategies support their use of cognitive strategies.

5. Teach academic strategies during typical class instruction on the target skill, during one subject area at a time, when possible. This ensures that students have many meaningful opportunities to practice.

6. Provide students with multiple practice opportunities to use the strategy with teacher feedback, especially for those students who are less strategic learners and do not develop their own strategies naturally.[30] For these students, they may need additional examples and practice opportunities to become more proficient.

7. Periodically monitor student strategy use to ensure fidelity and that any procedural changes do not influence strategy effectiveness. In other words, it is okay for students to modify strategies as they become more proficient in using them, such as combining or skipping unnecessary steps, as long as the strategy continues to help them meet their learning goals.[31]

Notes

1 Hughes, C. (2011). Effective instructional design and delivery for teaching task-specific learning strategies to students with learning disabilities. *Focus on Exceptional Children, 44*(2), 1–16.

2 Luke, S. D. (2006). The power of strategy instruction. In *Evidence for Education,* (Vol. 1, pp. 1–11). Washington, DC: National Dissemination Center for Children with Disabilities.
   Hughes, C. (2011). Effective instructional design and delivery for teaching task-specific learning strategies to students with learning disabilities. *Focus on Exceptional Children, 44*(2), 1–16.

3 Schumaker, J. B., & Deshler, D. D. (2006). Teaching adolescents to be strategic learners. In D. D. Deshler & J. B. Schumaker (Eds.), *Teaching adolescents with disabilities: Accessing the general education curriculum* (pp. 121–156). Thousand Oaks, CA: Corwin Press.

4 Jones, B. F., Palincsar, A. S., Ogle, D. S., & Carr, E. G. (1987). *Strategic teaching and learning: Cognitive instruction in the content areas.* Alexandria, VA: Association for Supervision and Curriculum Development, in cooperation with North Central Regional Educational Laboratory.

5 Joseph, L. M., Alber-Morgan, S., Cullen, J., & Rouse, C. (2016). The effects of self-questioning on reading comprehension: A literature review. *Reading & Writing Quarterly, 32*(2), 152–173.

6 Council for Exceptional Children & CEEDAR Center. (2017). *High-leverage practices in special education.* Arlington, VA: Council for Exceptional Children.

7 Dole, J. A., Nokes, J. D., & Drits, D. (2009). Cognitive strategy instruction. In G. G. Duffy & S. E. Israel (Eds.), *Handbook of research on reading comprehension.* Mahwah, NJ: Erlbaum.
   Harris, K. R., & Pressley, M. (1991). The nature of cognitive strategy instruction: Interactive strategy construction. *Exceptional Children, 57*(5), 392–404.
   Krawec, J., & Montague, M. (2012). A focus on cognitive strategy instruction. *Current Practice Alerts, 19,* 1–4. Retrieved from http://TeachingLD.org/alerts

8 Jitendra, A. K., Burgess, C., & Gajria, M. (2011). Cognitive strategy instruction for improving expository text comprehension of students with learning disabilities: The quality of evidence. *Exceptional Children, 77*(2), 135–159.

9 Dole, J. A., Nokes, J. D., & Drits, D. (2009). Cognitive strategy instruction. In G. G. Duffy & S. E. Israel (Eds.), *Handbook of research on reading comprehension*. Mahwah, NJ: Erlbaum.

10 Krawec, J., & Montague, M. (2012). A focus on cognitive strategy instruction. *Current Practice Alerts, 19*, 1–4, 1. Retrieved from http://TeachingLD.org/alerts

11 Vaughn, S., & Klingner, J. K. (1999). Teaching reading comprehension through collaborative strategic reading. *Intervention in School & Clinic, 34*(5), 284–292.

12 Harris, K. R., & Pressley, M. (1991). The nature of cognitive strategy instruction: Interactive strategy construction. *Exceptional Children, 57*(5), 392–404.

13 Harris, K. R., & Pressley, M. (1991). The nature of cognitive strategy instruction: Interactive strategy construction. *Exceptional Children, 57*(5), 392–404.

14 Hughes, C. (2011). Effective instructional design and delivery for teaching task-specific learning strategies to students with learning disabilities. *Focus on Exceptional Children, 44*(2), 1–16.

15 Deshler, D. D., & Schumaker, J. B. (2006). *High school students with disabilities: Strategies for accessing the curriculum*. New York, NY: Corwin Press.

Ellis, E. S., Deshler, D. D., Lenz, B. K., Schumaker, J. B., & Clark, F. L. (1991). An instructional methodology for teaching learning strategies. *Focus on Exceptional Children, 23*, 1–24.

Graham, S., & Harris, K. R. (2003). Students with learning disabilities and the process of writing: A meta-analysis of SRSD studies. In H. L. Swanson, K. R. Harris, & S. Graham (Eds.), *Handbook of learning disabilities* (pp. 323–344). New York, NY: Guilford Press.

16 Krawec, J., Huang, J., Montague, M., Kressler, B., & de Alba, A. M. (2013). The effects of cognitive strategy instruction on knowledge of math problem-solving processes of middle-school students with disabilities. *Learning Disability Quarterly, 36*, 80–92.

Montague, M., Warger, C., & Morgan, T. H. (2000). Solve it! Strategy instruction to improve mathematical problem solving. *Learning Disabilities Research & Practice, 15*(2), 110–116.

Montague, M., & Dietz, S. (2009). Evaluating the evidence base for cognitive strategy instruction and mathematical problem solving. *Exceptional Children, 75*, 285–302.

17 Graham, S., & Harris, K. R. (2003). Students with learning disabilities and the process of writing: A meta-analysis of SRSD studies. In H. L. Swanson, K. R. Harris, & S. Graham (Eds.), *Handbook of learning disabilities* (pp. 323–344). New York, NY: Guilford Press.

18 Deshler, D. D., & Schumaker, J. B. (1988). An instructional model for teaching students how to learn. In J. L. Graden, J. E. Zins, & M. J. Curtis (Eds.), *Alternative educational delivery systems: Enhancing instructional options for all students* (pp. 391–411). Washington, DC: National Association of School Psychologists.

Ellis, E., Deshler, D., & Lenz, K. (1991). An instructional model for teaching learning strategies. *Focus on Exceptional Children, 23*(6), 1–24.

19 Harris, K. R., & Graham, S. (1996). *Making the writing process work: Strategies for composition and self-regulation*. Brookline, MA: Brookline Books.

Harris, K. R., Graham, S., Brindle, M., & Sandmel, K. (2009). Metacognition and children's writing. In D. J. Hacker, J. Dunlosky, & A. C. Graesser (Eds.), *Handbook of meta-cognition in education* (pp. 131–153). New York, NY: Routledge.

20 Deshler, D. D., & Schumaker, J. B. (1988). An instructional model for teaching students how to learn. In J. L. Graden, J. E. Zins, & M. J. Curtis (Eds.), *Alternative educational delivery systems: Enhancing instructional options for all students* (pp. 391–411). Washington, DC: National Association of School Psychologists.

Ellis, E., Deshler, D., & Lenz, K. (1991). An instructional model for teaching learning strategies. *Focus on Exceptional Children, 23*(6), 1–24.

Fritschmann, S. N., Deshler, D. D., & Schumaker, J. B. (2007). The effects of instruction in an inference strategy on the reading comprehension skills of adolescents with disabilities. *Learning Disability Quarterly, 30*, 245–262.

21 Tralli, R., Colombo, B., Deschler, D. D., & Schumaker, J. B. (1996). The strategies intervention odel: A model for supported inclusion at the secondary level. *Remedial and Special Education, 17*, 204–216, 205.

22 Ellis, E. S., Deshler, D. D., Lenz, B. K., Schumaker, J. B., & Clark, F. L. (1991). An instructional methodology for teaching learning strategies. *Focus on Exceptional Children, 23*, 1–24.

Ellis, E., Deshler, D., & Lenz, K. (1991). An instructional model for teaching learning strategies. *Focus on Exceptional Children, 23*(6), 1–24.

23 Hughes, C. (2011). Effective instructional design and delivery for teaching task-specific learning strategies to students with learning disabilities. *Focus on Exceptional Children, 44*(2), 1–16, 3.

24 Hughes, C. (2011). Effective instructional design and delivery for teaching task-specific learning strategies to students with learning disabilities. *Focus on Exceptional Children, 44*(2), 1–16.

25 Graham, S., & Harris, K. R. (2003). Students with learning disabilities and the process of writing: A meta-analysis of SRSD studies. In H. L. Swanson, K. R. Harris, & S. Graham (Eds.), *Handbook of learning disabilities* (pp. 323–344). New York, NY: Guilford Press.

26 Tralli, R., Colombo, B., Deschler, D. D., & Schumaker, J. B. (1996). The strategies intervention model: A model for supported inclusion at the secondary level. *Remedial and Special Education, 17*, 204–216.

Deshler, D. D., & Schumaker, J. B. (2006). *High school students with disabilities: Strategies for accessing the curriculum*. New York, NY: Corwin Press.

27 Swanson, H. L. (1999). Reading research for students with LD: A meta-analysis of intervention outcomes. *Journal of Learning Disabilities, 32*, 504–532.

28 Hughes, C. (2011). Effective instructional design and delivery for teaching task-specific learning strategies to students with learning disabilities. *Focus on Exceptional Children, 44*(2), 1–16.

Luke, S. D. (2006). The power of strategy instruction. In *Evidence for Education* (Vol. 1, pp. 1–11). Washington, DC: National Dissemination Center for Children with Disabilities.

Schumaker, J. B., & Deshler, D. D. (2006). Teaching adolescents to be strategic learners. In D. D. Deshler & J. B. Schumaker (Eds.), *Teaching adolescents with disabilities: Accessing the general education curriculum* (pp. 121–156). Thousand Oaks, CA: Corwin Press.

Dole, J. A., Nokes, J. D., & Drits, D. (2009). Cognitive strategy instruction. In G. G. Duffy & S. E. Israel (Eds.), *Handbook of research on reading comprehension*. Mahwah, NJ: Erlbaum.

Harris, K. R., & Pressley, M. (1991). The nature of cognitive strategy instruction: Interactive strategy construction. *Exceptional Children, 57*(5), 392–404.

Archer, A., & Hughes, C. (2011). *Explicit instruction: Effective and efficient teaching*. New York, NY: Guilford Press.

Kiewra, K. A. (2002). How classroom teachers can help students learn and teach them how to learn. *Theory into Practice 41*(2), 71–80.

29 Deshler, D. D., & Schumaker, J. B. (2006). *High school students with disabilities: Strategies for accessing the curriculum*. New York, NY: Corwin Press.

30 Deshler, D. D., & Schumaker, J. B. (1988). An instructional model for teaching students how to learn. In J. L. Graden, J. E. Zins, & M. J. Curtis (Eds.), *Alternative educational delivery systems: Enhancing instructional options for all students* (pp. 391–411). Washington, DC: National Association of School Psychologists.

31 Harris, K. R., & Pressley, M. (1991). The nature of cognitive strategy instruction: Interactive strategy construction. *Exceptional Children, 57*(5), 392–404.

Kiewra, K. A. (2002). How classroom teachers can help students learn and teach them how to learn. *Theory into Practice 41*(2), 71–80.

Jones, B. F., Palincsar, A. S., Ogle, D. S., & Carr, E. G. (1987). *Strategic teaching and learning: Cognitive instruction in the content areas*. Alexandria, VA: Association for Supervision and Curriculum Development, in cooperation with North Central Regional Educational Laboratory.

Key Resources

IRIS Module: This module provides step-by-step instructions on how to implement the Self-Regulated Strategy Development Model. *SRSD: Using Learning Strategies to Enhance Student Learning.* Retrieved from: https://iris.peabody.vanderbilt.edu/module/srs/challenge/#content

University of Nebraska Department of Special Education and Communication Disorders: Cognitive Strategy Instruction. http://cehs.unl.edu/csi

Kansas University's Strategic Intervention Model. https://sim.drupal.ku.edu/sim-curricula

Pressley, M. (1990). *Cognitive strategy instruction that really improves children's academic performance.* Cambridge, MA: Brookline Books.

15
Provide Scaffolded Supports

Troy Mariage, Judith Winn, and Arfang Dabo

Introduction

Picture a scaffold outside of a building under construction. The scaffold is necessary for the workers to get the job done—they could not complete their work without it. The scaffold is sometimes many stories high and sometimes not, varying with the workers' task and what they need. It can be seen as a tool for job completion.[1] Additionally, it is temporary, disassembled when not needed. Now picture an adult helping a child learn to float. The adult may model, floating herself while the child watches and explaining how she did it; she may hold the child so he floats; may keep her arms under the child without touching him while he floats; may hold the child again if needed; may praise the child, describing what he is doing correctly. Before long, the child is floating independently!

Similar to the scaffold by the building, the adult's support is necessary to get the job done; the child is not ready to float on his own. The support varies as the child gains or temporarily loses confidence or forgets what to do, varies as the water becomes choppier or calmer, and is removed once the child can float independently. This kind of support—scaffolded support—is provided to students by effective special education teachers during instruction to help the students move towards independence.

What do we mean by scaffolded supports during instruction? As in the example above, the supports are termed "scaffolded" as they allow the students to be successful on tasks they are not ready to do alone, are tailored to an analysis of the task requirements, and are adjusted flexibly to what the students understand and can do. There is also an eye towards the instructional goal or performance objective, so removing scaffolded support facilitates independent and self-regulated learning.[2]

What and when do we scaffold? Teachers are responsible for teaching specific skills, thinking strategies, processes, and performances. A co-teacher in high school biology may teach key vocabulary words related to a unit on single-cell organisms, demonstrate how to take notes, and discuss the scientific method as part of a unit on water quality in a local stream. An elementary teacher of students with autism may be teaching her students how to ask questions and talk to their peers about a text they have just read to increase their comprehension. The teacher understands that if she can help students to ask questions and engage in discussion, this will make visible her students' ideas and allow her to scaffold their thinking. In both of the examples, the learning process starts with either formal or informal assessment of what students understand and can do. In some instances, the students may have already mastered the skill or strategy, so instruction is designed to firm and reinforce what they already know. Scaffolded supports are not needed. If the students have some understanding, but cannot yet perform the task alone, then scaffolded supports from the teacher may be needed for them to become independent.

The scaffolded supports can be planned; they also may be unplanned or delivered "on the spot" in response to students. The scaffolding process happens in what Vygotsky called the zone of proximal development,[3] or with tasks that are between what a child can understand and do independently and what s/he can do with assistance (not too easy, not too difficult). This is where supports are needed and can be most effective. Scaffolded supports are associated with the gradual release of responsibility,[4] or the *I DO, WE DO, YOU DO* framework.[5] The supports change as students assume more and more of the "work" over time and become more competent.

The field of special education has been responsible for creating many of the most effective examples of scaffolded supports, particularly through cognitive strategy instruction in reading,[6] written expression,[7] and math.[8] Although difficult to separate the impact of the scaffolded supports from other features of the instruction, research has shown gains in reading comprehension, written recalls, many aspects of the writing process, and factual and conceptual comprehension through instruction incorporating scaffolded supports.[9]

Narrowing the Focus

Many kinds of scaffolded supports have been identified: providing more familiar examples;[10] helping students use tools such as graphic organizers, cue cards, semantic maps, and manipulatives;[11] the use of technology responses and prompts;[12] and scaffolding through dialogue—modeling, thinking aloud, focusing students' attention, partially completing the task, prompting, questioning, and providing informative feedback.[13] Sometimes what the teacher says or her "talk moves,"[14] both planned and on-the-spot, are the prominent scaffolded support. However, teachers also use these "talk moves" in conjunction with content, material, or technology supports, which we refer to as tools. The focus of this chapter is on scaffolded support through dialogue both as the prominent support and used in conjunction with other supports or tools.

Chapter Overview

1. Describe principles to guide the provision of scaffolded support.
2. Describe the ways teachers can use dialogue, or interactions with students, as scaffolded support during the *I DO, WE DO,* and *YOU DO* phases of the gradual release of responsibility.
3. Provide an example of a teacher using dialogue and tools as scaffolded support in planning and providing instruction.

Principles of Scaffolded Support

Decisions about supports are made; they are not random and arbitrary but rather stem from knowing the students, the goals for them, and how to achieve the goals with those students. Teachers who use scaffolded supports value and are guided by the following four principles:

1. **Dynamic assessment.** Providing scaffolded supports is responsive to what a student, a group of students, or an entire class understands or does not understand about a particular skill, strategy, concept, or process. This means that, first, teachers must have a deep understanding of what students already know and are able to do. Teachers can quickly assess a student's understanding

of and proficiency with specific skills. This is necessary, but not sufficient; finding out what students can already do independently informs scaffolding, but what about how they do with help? Dynamic assessment is characterized by the teacher learning what a student can do with support and requires that the teacher have access to the thinking, language, writing, or performance of students in order to make visible the student's understanding.[15] When a teacher can hear a student's thinking or watch him perform a task, then she has information that can inform what kind of support is needed.

2. **Knowledge of curriculum.** Teachers who are effective in scaffolding performance must also have an eye towards the horizon of complete performance. What are we scaffolding toward? What is the outcome we expect to see from our students? Teachers must have a good knowledge of curriculum standards and benchmarks, a general knowledge of the scope and sequence of curriculum, and clarity about prerequisite skills and understandings. Teachers who know more about their content are able to structure the task difficulty more carefully for their students, focusing on essential knowledge and skills. This tells teachers what is the most critical to assess, teach, and support.

3. **Motivation, purpose, and engagement.** Scaffolding always has a bi-directional[16] and relational quality. Teachers can increase their chances of creating the conditions where students feel comfortable by creating an environment in which they understand and act on what is culturally relevant[17] and motivating to students. Effective teachers in special education are attentive to the learner's motivation and engagement and whether students understand and value the purpose of learning a particular concept or strategy. Teachers need to be prepared to provide additional support at any time in order to maximize learning.

4. **Varying levels of support.** Effective teachers provide only the amount of scaffolded support necessary to allow a student or group of students to perform at a level they could not have performed at independently. If teachers provide too little support, the students are not successful and may become frustrated. If teachers provide too much support, the students can become dependent upon external supports and may not internalize the skill, concept, or strategy as efficiently. Teachers are constantly assessing their students' learning zones and moving the students towards more complex thinking and performances.

Gradual Release of Responsibility

Gradual release of responsibility[18] is an instructional framework applicable across content areas. Within the framework, teachers purposefully move students to independent understanding and competence by first assuming much of the responsibility for the learning task and then gradually relinquishing this responsibility. The framework is also referred to as *I DO, WE DO, YOU DO,*[19] in which the teacher is "I" and the students "YOU." *I DO* involves the teacher selecting the goal and task(s) and then explicitly explaining, modeling, and thinking aloud. As the students develop competence and understanding, the teacher can "back off" and help them but not do as much of the work as she did in the *I DO* phase. Rather, she guides and supports the students as necessary (*WE DO*). Then, as the students become even more competent, they do even more of the task (*YOU DO*). The teacher's work is not done at this point, however. She can continue to draw attention to what is being done well and link how the students' efforts are moving them toward their goal. She may need to refocus students or encourage them to use a tool. Students have the major responsibility for the thinking, but the teacher still is available as a sounding board or to step in to provide support if necessary.

How do scaffolded supports relate to this framework? To us, the concepts are almost synonymous and are guided by the four principles of scaffolding discussed above. Teachers create opportunities to provide scaffolded supports when they choose skills and strategies that are in students' zones of proximal development and are guided by **knowledge of curriculum**. They provide the "just right" amount of support, often starting as quite planned, explicit, and directive (*I DO*) and then moving to the "on the spot" provision of varying levels of support as they **dynamically assess** what the students need when they assume more responsibility but are not totally on their own (*WE DO*). Finally, in the *YOU DO* phase, when teachers provide students with many opportunities to practice skills or strategies independently or with peers to firm up their understanding, the teacher may continue to support, but the support is generally minimal.

It has been pointed out that gradual release of responsibility is not necessarily rigid (e.g., no student input in *I DO*) and completely linear;[20] neither is the provision of scaffolded supports: **varying levels of support** will need to be added based on student **motivation, purpose, and engagement** and/or task factors. Recall the adult teaching the child to float having to move in with more support as the child became tired or the water choppy. A student may become distracted or discouraged. Likewise, he may need more support in solving a mathematics problem with unnecessary information than one in which all stated information is relevant.

We believe using the gradual release of responsibility framework provides an organized way to think about providing scaffolded supports. In Table 15.1, we provide examples of planned and on-the-spot supports within the *I DO, WE DO, YOU DO* components as well as indicate which principles are likely to be driving decisions.

In the following section we provide a classroom example of a teacher using scaffolded supports over time.

Classroom Example: Scaffolded Supports in Reading Comprehension

In this section we illustrate with actual classroom transcripts the way Joan, a special education teacher, used planned and unplanned supports in a scaffolded manner when working with seven third graders in reading.[21] You will notice several things: (1) Joan used both tools (e.g., posters, sticky notes for particular strategies, question stems) and "talk moves" together to support the students in a gradual way rather than having them use the tools on their own when they were not ready; (2) the *I DO, WE DO, YOU DO* phases are not totally linear—although Joan gradually releases responsibility, she and her students both take responsibility to some degree in all of the phases; and (3) providing scaffolded supports in well thought-out instruction, although difficult with its on-the-spot decision making, can be very powerful, as evidenced by the sophisticated student discussion you will see at the end of the example.

This example is a "Thinking Apprenticeship,"[22] as it shows teaching as a form of apprenticing students into the thinking and actions of more able learners. These interactions have the feel of joint problem-solving, where the teacher and/or peers work with one another to move towards a solution. In their problem-solving dialogues, Joan and her students "make visible the invisible" thinking, so that it can be made public, shared, and co-edited. Thinking apprenticeship recognizes that students may not originally have the language skills, thinking strategies, or background knowledge to perform a task independently, so the teacher creates activities for co-participation with them. In this example, we will see Joan use both planned and moment-to-moment scaffolds to support a thinking apprenticeship over a six-week unit on learning how to discuss informational text.

The seven third-graders were all struggling with reading comprehension and in an intervention group. Each student's reading scores placed them in the lowest 25th percentile in their grade. Joan's instructional goal was for these students to be self-regulated and strategic readers who could use tools for marking and annotating text to help remember key information that they could discuss with

Table 15.1 Examples of Scaffolded Supports in *I Do*, *We Do*, and *You Do*

Instructional Phase	Example of Scaffolded Supports	Guiding Principles	Notes
I DO	**Planning:** Consider the need to understand place value before comparing three-digit numbers. **Planning:** Decide to introduce an editing checklist to keep students focused on what they are to look for in their papers. **Planning:** Decide to use a math game in which students have to explain their strategies to the opposing team. **Purpose:** *We are learning how to use headings to help us predict what we will learn in each section. This will help us pay attention to what is important and not get bogged down in all of the details* **Modeling:** *I am writing down reasons that the law benefits people who are sick and reasons it is not beneficial. These are what I am going to use to make my argument. Writing would help you too.* **Thinking aloud:** *When I see a fraction like ¾, I always say to myself that the figure is divided into four equal parts, and this number is three of those parts. I picture that in my mind.*	✓ Knowledge of curriculum ✓ Motivation, purpose, engagement ✓ Varying levels of support	Many of the supports in this phase are planned through considerations of the students' prior knowledge (place value) and interests (explaining strategies through games) along with considerations of the curriculum and ultimate goals. The teacher makes clear what students are learning and why (*to help us predict what we will learn in each section*) to help them begin to understand the goal of their upcoming activities. She has to think about the level of support they will need to be successful. Modeling and thinking-aloud, while engaging the students, is almost all the responsibility of the teacher. However, she is continually watching for signs of student understanding or confusion and where she can involve them.
WE DO	**Prompting:** *See if there is a sentence starter on your list that might grab the reader's attention.* **Questioning:** *Why did you choose this formula, and how did it help you?* **Prompting:** *Try the other sound of "c" and see if that word makes sense.* **Prompting:** *Let's try it with the number line.* **Focusing attention:** *Look at the prefix "re." It means "again." Now what do you think the word means?* **Thinking aloud:** *That reminds me of the book we read about the rain forest. What do you think of?* **Partial completion of the task:** *We need three pieces of evidence for our statement that Jacob is a loner. I found one on page 12 in the description of what Jacob does after school and one on page 13 when he shares his thoughts about games. Can you find a third one?*	✓ Dynamic assessment ✓ Varying levels of support ✓ Motivation, purpose, engagement	The teacher is alert to students' developing understanding and competence (*might grab the reader's attention*) and provides support that takes these into account (sentence starters). The supports differ in several ways. They always involve dialogue but sometimes also a tool (number line, sentence starter). Sometimes the teacher is actually doing some of the task (identifying evidence) and sometimes giving hints to the student so they can do it more (*try the other sound of "c"*) independently. Finally, she may ask the students to justify their actions (*how did it help you?*). These supports have different levels of student responsibility but much more than in the I DO phase. Based on dynamic assessment, teachers provide different supports for different students at different times.
YOU DO	**Supported independence:** *I want you and your partner to use the rubric to create the PowerPoint presentation on the invasive species you researched.* **Supported independence:** *We are going to spend 10 minutes discussing in our Book Club group. You can use any of the literature response strategies we have talked about this semester.* **Informative feedback:** *You did great—made a t-chart first and used that to identify the pros and cons.* **Encouragement:** *You read this so much more fluently than you did yesterday. Your reading today really sounds like talking.*	✓ Varying levels of support ✓ Motivation, purpose, engagement ✓ Application of new skills or strategies	The students are taking all or most of the responsibility for the work; the teacher continues to scaffold by providing some support (peers, reminding to use literature strategies), pointing out what is being done well (*made a t-chart first*) and why (*sounds like talking*).

their peers to deepen their comprehension. To meet the goal, the students had to learn strategies for annotating text as well as strategies to participate in discussions.

Preparing for Instruction: Pre-Planned Scaffolds

Joan recognized that there were explicit core curriculum standards in the areas of third-grade reading, speaking, and listening that could be directly addressed through a long-term focus on building discussion skills. She also knew how important close reading is throughout the grades. She needed to assess her students to identify what they could do without support. To do this, on three successive days, Joan read aloud a high-interest passage, directed the students to read the passage silently, gave them highlighters to use as they wished, and then asked them to discuss the passage. During the discussion, Joan observed that the students used their highlighters to underline whole sentences in the texts. Then, when asked to discuss the passage, they fell into a round-robin reading of their highlighted sentences, thinking that this was what was meant as discussion.

Joan decided to plan scaffolded support in the area of social and communication skills, knowing that challenges with these could be behind students' difficulty holding a discussion. She identified an evidenced-based language and social skill strategy framework developed by Vernon, Schumaker, and Deschler (1996)[23] called "SCORE." In the original SCORE research, students were taught five strategies, including Share ideas, Compliment others, Offer help or encouragement, Recommend changes nicely, and Exercise self-control. To make the SCORE strategies more explicit, Joan created three pre-planned scaffolds: (1) a 3' x 4' SCORE poster, (2) a SCORE self-evaluation checklist, and (3) a SCORE laminated cue card—composed of the SCORE poster content but put on a key ring with other pre-planned scaffolds (see Figure 15.1). With these pre-planned supports, she then taught the SCORE strategies through an apprenticeship process including defining the strategy, explaining why the strategy is important, modeling the strategy, and practicing the strategy.

A second set of pre-planned scaffolded supports that Joan prepared for instruction was designed to directly teach students to take notes using four thinking strategies (question, clarify, comment, connect). Joan called this the "Note It" strategy and explained to her students that good readers jot down notes as they read, especially to help them get ready to discuss what they have read with their peers. To teach this strategy to her students, Joan created a laminated cue card with each of the four thinking strategies, a different colored sticky note for each strategy, and a series of sentence stems to help the students write their notes on either the passage or the sticky notes (see Figure 15.1). The following example shows the students learning to use the Note It strategy. Joan has an eye towards gradually releasing more responsibility to her students through an *I DO, WE DO,* and *YOU DO* model. She uses a combination of both the pre-planned scaffolds and on-the-spot scaffolds to help respond to students in their learning zones. For clarity, we refer to Joan as "Teacher."

I Do

To start the process, Joan engages her students in goal setting by explaining what she called "good reading" tips. She provides a direct explanation with a PowerPoint image of the four Note It strategies she wanted students use:

Teacher: *Alright, so today, we are going to do something a little bit different. We are not going to use highlighters because sometimes we highlight everything we read, and we are so busy highlighting, I am not sure we are thinking about what we are reading. So today, we are going to read the passage together, then you are going to read it again on your own and use these sticky notes to help with your thinking.*

Ashton: *Different colors?*

Teacher: *Yes. Okay, so after I read, I will take a sticky note and write a question on it. Here are some ideas for what it could say (pointing to image on screen):*

I have a question about . . .

My question is . . .

I am wondering whether . . .

Okay everyone, now that you've read the passage, it is time to take that sticky note and write something you have a question about. Then, take your sticky note with the question and put it right on your text.

Joan repeats this with each of the four Note It strategies the students will be using and shows students several sentence stems they could use under each sticky note. Notice below that she begins, even this early on, to transfer control to students by engaging them in reading the sentence stems for the third and fourth strategies from the PowerPoint.

Teacher: *Okay, the third would be a comment. What could you use to make a comment, Allen? What sentence starters could you use?*

Allen: *I could use (reading from the PowerPoint) "A comment I have is . . .", "I think that . . .", "I learned that . . .", "I would like to share . . .", "My opinion is that . . .", "I think an important detail is . . ."*

We Do

Joan then shifts the lesson slightly by creating a model that illustrates to students what using sticky notes for responding to text might look and sound like. She has created a slide for students that includes a single paragraph about how a blue whale breathes and placed sticky note icons with each of the four strategies above the notes. Within each note is an example response that represents that strategy.

Teacher: *Okay, so this is an example of what we might do.* (Teacher reads aloud paragraph about how a blue whale breathes.)

Alright, so a question you might ask is what, Allen? Can you look at the note up there? What is a question you could ask?

Allen: (reading) *My question is how long can blue whales hold their breath under water?*

Teacher: *Perfect. And you would write that on your note and put that on your passage.*

Teacher: *What is a clarification you could make, Jalen?*

Jalen: (reading) *I did not know whales had two blow holes. I thought they had one! Why do they have two?*

Joan could have elected to have the students come up with their own questions, but because this was the very first lesson on these four discussion strategies, she decides to have students read the example strategies and practice what it would feel like and sound like in an actual discussion. She provides students with a *partially completed task*, so that students could tackle a smaller chunk of the process before taking on more complex thinking.

Next, Joan gives students more responsibility (moving beyond reading the model questions). She responds to Jalen, who asks for clarification about the task. Then she suggests how to use the sticky notes and models. We now have more of a sense that Joan and the students are working together.

Teacher: *Okay, does this make sense to you? Thumbs up if it makes sense. We are going to keep this up here, because this is the one I want you to look at when you are writing your comments. Today, I want you to choose two or three sticky notes. You don't have to do all four. These are the things you will use for your discussion.*

Teacher: *Okay, so Jalen needs some clarification. Jalen, I am glad you asked me before we went ahead.*

Teacher: *Okay, so we are going to read the passage together today. It is about fossils. I am going to read it. Then you're going to read it. On the sticky note, you are going to write, based upon what you read here, a comment about what you read; if there was something you didn't understand . . . like there's a big word you didn't understand, you could put that here (pointing directly to sticky note with the word "clarification" across top). You could look up there and say, "What does . . ."*

Ashton: *. . . Paleontologist mean.*

Teacher: *Exactly. You could ask a question, you could look up there again, you can see that there are sentence starters up there. "My question is . . ." might be the easiest. Or a connection you have. Okay? Do the best that you can.*

Teacher: *Alright, are you ready team? (Teacher reads passage, "Fossils," about paleontologists.)*

Teacher: *Alright, I am going to put this up here again (image of four sticky notes with sentence starters below each note). Okay, I want you to read to yourself. Do your sticky notes. Put them on your passage. And then we'll discuss. Make sure you re-read first.*

Joan gives the students more responsibility but is "right there with them" when they need support.

You Do

The following snippet represents the very first discussion that was planned without the teacher's support. It is evident that there is still some confusion about what discussion looks like, as Allen thinks that they are supposed to copy down others' strategies on their sticky notes. They all seem to think they are to take turns presenting their sticky notes rather than responding to each other's notes. Joan needs to step in.

Teacher: *Okay, I think we are going to go ahead and start our discussion. Remember, the idea is that these are things you can use to start your discussion, what you read with your peers. I am not going to be in on this one, I'll talk about it when you are done. Who would like to start? And you can have your papers any way you would like. I think that is a good strategy, so you can see all of the sticky notes at once. That is a good start.*

Allen: *Paleontologists have the coolest job (pause). That's a comment.*

Jalen: *What does "amber" mean?*

Allen: *Do we write each other's [ideas down on our note] . . . (confusion about what to do)*

Teacher: *No. I am just noticing—Jalen asked a question. So, Ashton, can you just leave your notes? Jalen, can you ask the question again and see if someone in the group can answer it for you?*

Joan notices that, even with the tools, the students were not having an actual discussion. So, on the spot, she had to step in and become more directive. In fact, in subsequent days, Joan conducted a very brief mini-lesson about following up on another's idea in discussion, so students understood that discussion involves listening to, supporting, adding on, or even challenging ideas. Once students began to internalize how to follow up and respond to their peer's ideas, they began to have more productive discussions.

Several weeks later, the students held an 8 minute, 4 second, discussion of a text they were reading on their own. As you look at examples from that discussion, notice the progress the students have made. They have used two pre-planned scaffolded supports in their discussion, including a laminated cue-card listing the four strategies with sentence stems and the colored-sticky notes with the strategy listed on top of the note. Joan's participation and responsibility is much less and seems to be mainly to keep the conversation going and to make sure students were not overlooked. Unlike the first discussion, students routinely follow-up with one another, recognize other members' ideas, and use others' ideas as a scaffold for their own responses. They use all four strategies and ask questions, clarifications, comments, and make connections.

Devin:	*Why don't they make . . . why don't they make a levee . . . like when the lava explodes on volcanoes, so it won't ruin people's houses and stuff?*
Ashton:	*Well I think . . . If you made a levee, I bet the lava would melt it.*
Devin:	*I am talking like made out of bricks.*
Barbara:	*Probably not, probably not do much damage, but for like one house, it probably might catch on fire because of how hot it is.*

. . .

Barbara:	*I have a question.*
Teacher:	*Barbara's turn.*
Barbara:	*How does pressure grow?*
Ashton and others:	*Pressure?*
Barbara:	*Like how does pressure grow in like the volcano?*
George:	*It grows like like, um, the pressure from the ground, um, like possibly pressure, shoots up pressure from the ground, like left over pressure shoots . . . and makes it explode?*
Ashton:	*It probably pushes it up, like when I, my hands are the lava . . . and, if, if like I am pushing the table up, that's putting, that's putting pressure on it. I think that's what lava is.*
Devin:	*This is like how volcanoes explode* (motioning with hands upward) *. . . "spoosh."*
Allen:	*It's like, like when, like in a volcano, like in a lot of spray, if you shake it up . . . it will, if it is closed, it will get really huge, and if you open it it will explode.*

. . .

Jalen:	*Clarification.*
Teacher:	*Clarification, Jalen?*
Jalen:	*Why does it explode?*
Teacher:	*Why does it explode?*
Barbara:	*Probably because of the pressure of the lava.*
George:	*Yeah. Maybe the pressure is so much . . . that it is just like . . . Maybe the lava is like the lava is trying to hold it in but then it is just stable. The pressure of the lava . . .*
Allen:	*The lava is like in the center of the earth. Like if the lava gets so hot, it creates more and more pressure, so eventually it has to come up somewhere.*
Devin:	*Like especially in the cold water. It will go "sh, sh."*

George: *And also, I forgot who said the, "How does the rock form?" Yeah, it is exactly like Allen said. It's like, like basically like wax, it falls over and it kind of, without other hot stuff it is not that hot and kind of just freezes?*

This type of rich discussion was made possible because of Joan's conscientious use of both pre-planned and moment-to-moment scaffolded supports within an apprenticeship process that lasted over a six-week period of instruction. The SCORE poster, Note It cue-card, and sticky notes were planned scaffolded supports that had multiple purposes, including: (1) serving as a *social/behavioral scaffold* in discussion; (2) providing a *language scaffold* for supporting discussions (e.g., sentence stems); (3) serving as a *memory scaffold* by allowing students to write ideas on sticky notes as they were reading for future discussion; and (4) serving as a *visual scaffold* for what one's passage might look like with sticky notes (e.g., PowerPoint model).

To further reinforce the SCORE strategies, Joan had students occasionally complete a SCORE card after the conclusion of the discussion (see Figure 15.1). Having students reflect on their own discussion performance provided them with another opportunity to focus on the behaviors used in good discussions and move towards self-regulation of their use of the strategies.

I DO, WE DO, YOU DO was Joan's overriding framework in helping her students become able to mark and annotate text to support discussion. Joan knew that the ultimate goal was to have her students engage in rich discussion to help them comprehend what they were reading and then to internalize the use of the thinking strategies to increase comprehension. She thought carefully about all that might need to be supported, especially given that discussion was a new skill for her young third-grade students. But even Joan, an experienced teacher, could not anticipate all that she had to scaffold. When Joan's students could not hold an effective discussion, even with the tools of the SCORE poster, Note It cue card, and labeled color-coded sticky notes all available, she knew she had to provide more scaffolded support. Thus, she added a mini-lesson on the importance of "following up" on another's idea; only then did the students begin to engage in authentic discussion. Joan added support where and when needed. This flexibility, her provision of a motivating task in the students' zone of proximal development, and her careful analysis of student understanding and competence helped Joan's students move towards their instructional goal.

Wrap Up

Identifying and using scaffolded supports is one of the most powerful practices for moving students to higher levels of understanding and competence. By the teacher providing tools and interacting through modeling, thinking aloud, prompting, cueing, and highlighting, students can complete tasks they are not yet ready to do on their own. Providing students with only "just enough" and "just in time" support to move them from where they are currently functioning to being independent is the domain of the high leverage practice of providing scaffolded supports.

Scaffolded supports can be powerful in promoting learning when working with students in whole classes, small intensive groups, or individually. Students within groups can be provided different levels of support within the same lesson. For example, during a co-taught writing lesson, the special education teacher could provide modeling for all students and also give students who are struggling to organize their writing a paragraph frame. She can fill in parts of the frame for those who need even further support. The flexibility and responsiveness of scaffolded supports make them appropriate for use across and within instructional tiers in a multi-tiered system of instruction support.

Teaching and learning in a student's zone of proximal development is a bi-directional relationship. We need to engage students in motivating and responsive learning activities where they can

SCORE Poster

THINK	DO	SOUNDS LIKE	LOOKS LIKE
Share ideas	Everyone contributing	I think that... / I wonder about... / One idea I had is...	
Compliment others	Everyone supporting	I really like that idea... / I agree with ___ because... / That's a good point.	
Offer help or encouragement	Everyone giving and accepting encouragement	Can I help? / You are doing great / You are really thinking hard	
Recommend changes nicely	Everyone respecting and building on each others ideas	Another idea I had was... / Can you tell us more? / Why do you think that? / Do have evidence for that idea?	
Exercise self-control	Everyone listening	I need to think before I speak / I don't want to interrupt / I need to wait my turn / I keep my eyes on speaker / I am a good listener	

SCORE Self-Monitoring Checklist

How Did I SCORE Today?

Name _____
Date _____

SCORE Card	Few		Some		Often	
Did I...Share ideas:	0	1	2	3	4	5
Did I...Compliment others:	0	1	2	3	4	5
Did I...Offer help and encouragement	0	1	2	3	4	5
Did I...Recommend changes nicely	0	1	2	3	4	5
Did I...Exercise self-control	0	1	2	3	4	5

Note It Strategies Cue-Card

Note It Strategy

A Question

Question

I have a question about...
My question is...
I am wondering whether...

A Clarification

Clarification

What does ___ mean?
I don't think I understood...
The word ___ was unclear
Can you explain what they mean by ___?

A Comment

Comment

A comment I have is...
I think that...
I learned that...
I would like to share that...
My opinion is that...
I think an important detail was.

A Connection

Connection

This made me think about...
A connection for me was...
This was like...

Note It Example

Let's Practice!

Why are snakeheads thought to be a dangerous invasive species? Invasive species are animals or other living things, like plants, that are introduced to a new environment where they do not normally exist. Invasive species compete with the native species for food and habitat. If the invasive species eats the food in the environment and uses materials, this can take away these things from other living things. For example, the young snakehead eats zooplankton, insect larvae, small crustaceans, and baby fish of other species. This means that the snakehead impacts the food chain at many different points.

A Question
My question is how do they get rid of invasive species from the environment?

A Clarification
I don't think I understood what they meant by a food chain at a different points. That part was confusing.

A Comment
A comment I have is, if snakeheads are good eating, maybe they can be used to feed people who are hungry.

A Connection
A connection for me was my grandpa. My grandpa said that he used to fish for snakeheads in the canals when he went to Florida for the winter. He said they are very good fighters.

Figure 15.1 Planned Tools Used to Support Third-Grade Students' Apprenticeship in Discussion

share their thinking. Students must understand the purpose of what they are learning, be engaged with relevant content, and feel supported in sharing what they know.

A powerful and very important high leverage practice? Yes! A challenging one? Absolutely! Assessment, both prior to instruction and on-going, provides the teacher access to students' understanding and reveals a zone of proximal development.[24] It can be difficult to accurately assess students with language, social, or communication difficulties to determine what is interfering with understanding and competence,[25] especially in more complex learning tasks. Another challenge is that the on-the-spot assessment and provision of support cannot always be planned; sometimes it is difficult to "think on our feet." Withdrawing the supports at the right time—not too early or too late, can be a challenge.[26] Some supports never need to go away. Nearly all of us can attest to using our phones to gain information and skills to guide and support us each day. But how tempting to continue to use a tool or teacher assistance when we truly do not need it.

To help increase your repertoire of tools and talk moves to use in a scaffolded manner, we present examples of each, along with what can be accomplished with them, in Tables 15.2 and 15.3.

A key goal for all of us as teachers is for students with and without disabilities to become as independent, self-regulated and self-determined as possible. Accomplishing this goal means that we need to be conscientious in making sure that we are transferring control of the thinking or tools to the students over time. Effective scaffolding provides students with just enough support to accomplish a task they could not do independently but with a goal of moving towards internalizing the knowledge, skills, strategies, or processes as necessary. The more you know about standards, curriculum sequences, your students, and the variety of tools to support learning, the more confident you become in providing effective and efficient scaffolded support. Providing scaffolded supports is nuanced, unpredictable, and ever-changing but, in the end, allows students to be successful in tasks with which they have not experienced success. We need special education teachers who have specialized knowledge in providing scaffolded supports.

Reminders and Tips

Below are several reminders and tips to consider. We present these in an attempt to scaffold your use of scaffolded supports.

- Scaffolded supports can be planned or applied moment to moment.

  - Planned supports often include things like posters, rubrics, checklists cue cards, graphic organizers, think-sheets, and other visual supports. These can be introduced and taught through a gradual release of responsibility framework.
  - Moment by moment supports are often talk moves, where a teacher "steps in" to provide support or "steps back" to encourage students to continue thinking.[27] Note that the tools also could be used on an as-needed basis in the moment. Alternatively, at times a teacher plans her talk moves prior to instruction.

- Technology can provide scaffolded support and make it possible for students to perform successfully on tasks they cannot yet do alone.
- Scaffolded supports can occur not only in academics but also in language, behavior, motivation, attention, social skills, and communication.

Table 15.2 Talk Moves to Scaffold Learning in Moment-to-Moment Interaction

FUNCTION OF TALK MOVES		TALK MOVES	SOUNDS LIKE	PURPOSE
		Thinking aloud	*I am thinking that I need to. . .*	• Provide new information
	Talk Moves to Provide More Support	Modeling inner thoughts	*This makes me think that I. . .*	• Make visible the task
		Self-instructions	*First, I need to . . . then . . . next . . . finally*	• Clarify directions
		Direct explanation	*Let me show you an example*	• Attach thinking to actions
		Cueing	*I am going to point out a few things that I think are important. . .*	• Model language, actions, thoughts
		Invitation to participate	*Tell us more about that. . .*	• Elicit student thinking
		Adding on	*Can someone add to that idea?*	• Give control of talk to group
Talk as Scaffolded Support	**Talk Moves to Invite Thinking and Participation**	wait time	*Your idea is important. Take your time.*	• Move beyond teacher-student-teacher turns
		Prompting	*You are on the right track. . .*	• Foster problem-solving
		Questioning	*I have a question. Can you help answer that?*	
		Seeking clarification	*I am still unclear about . . . Can you help me understand. . .*	
		Revoicing	*So what Latrice is saying is that. . .*	• Support individual students
	Talk Moves to Support Participation	Repeating	*Darnell, can you repeat that? That is an important idea.*	• Build trust
		Direct call	*Sarah, I want to hear from you. You have a lot of experience. . .*	• Model equity
		Supporting	*You took a chance with your thinking. Thank you.*	• Ensure students know that each voice is capable of adding
		Floor holding	*Hold on. Duane, you wanted to say something. . .*	
		Managing conversation	*We benefit when everyone participates.*	

Table 15.3 Examples of Planned Tools That Can Scaffold Performance

	FUNCTION OF TOOLS	TOOLS	EXAMPLES	PURPOSE
	Tools to Structure Information, Strategies, or Processes	Graphic Organizers Anchor Charts Strategy Posters Tables/Maps Rubrics/Checklists Vocabulary Maps		• Structures learning tasks • Provides reminders • Allows for self-monitoring • Allows students to focus on essential components
Tools as Scaffolded Supports	**Tools to Allow Students to Interact with Information or Perform Tasks**	Sentence Starters Paragraph Frames Partially Completed Tasks Highlighters Routines with Sticky Notes		• Fosters "conversation" with text • Highlights key information • Preserves thinking in memory • Models language of the discipline
	Tools to Facilitate Thinking by Reducing Memory Load	Word Wall Calculators Spell Checkers Mnemonics Text Generation		• Allows students to memorize mnemonics that represent multiple step strategies • Makes the abstract more concrete • Allows students to focus on the needed thinking

- In providing supports:

    - Work to create a safe environment in which students feel respected and comfortable sharing their thinking and in which you provide many opportunities for them to do so.
    - Watch and listen to students carefully to make sure they understand the goal rather than only "carry out the motions."
    - Remove a support once it is not needed; put it back when it is.
    - Practice what you could say to students and remember that you may have to try again with a different prompt.
    - Be positive and patient and caring, as it can be discouraging if your first attempts to provide scaffolded supports are not effective.
    - Throughout your career, keep abreast of technology that provides scaffolded support for students with and without disabilities.
    - Take advantage of resources on providing scaffolded instruction, including the video examples listed in this chapter under resources.

Notes

1 Putambecker, S., & Hübscher, R. (2005). Tools for scaffolding students in a complex learning environment: What have we gained and what have we missed? *Educational Psychologist, 40*(1), 1–12.

2 Wood, D., Bruner, J., & Ross, G. (1976). The role of tutoring in problem solving. *Journal of Child Psychology and Child Psychiatry, 17*, 89–100.

3 Vygotsky, L. S. (1978). *Mind in society: The development of higher psychological processes.* Cambridge, MA: Harvard University Press.

4 Pearson, P. D., & Gallagher, M. C. (1983). The instruction of reading comprehension. *Contemporary Educational Psychology, 8*, 317–344.

5 Archer, A. L., & Hughes, C. A. (2011). *Explicit instruction: Effective and efficient teaching.* New York, NY: Guilford Press.

6 Boardman, A. G., Swanson, E., Klingner, J. K., & Vaughn, S. (2013). Using collaborative strategic reading to improve reading comprehension. In B. B. Cook & M. Tankersley (Eds.), *Research-based practices in special education* (pp. 33–46). Upper Saddle River, NJ: Pearson.
    Englert, C. S., Tarrant, L. K., Mariage, T. V., Oxer, T. (1994). Lesson talk as the work of reading groups: The effectiveness of two interventions. *Journal of Learning Disabilities, 27*(3), 165–185.
    Palincsar, A. S., & Brown, A. L. (1984). Reciprocal teaching of comprehension-fostering and comprehension-monitoring activities. *Cognition and Instruction, 1*, 117–175.

7 Englert, C. S., Mariage, T. V., & Dunsmore, K. (2006). Sociocultural perspectives of writing instruction. In Graham MacArthur & Fitzgerald (Eds.), *Handbook of writing research* (pp. 208–221). New York, NY: Guilford Press.
    Graham, S., Harris, K. R., & Mason, L. (2005). Improving the writing performance, knowledge, and self-efficacy of struggling young writers: The effects of self-regulated strategy development. *Contemporary Educational Psychology, 30*, 207–241.

8 Jitendra, A. K. (2007). *Solving math word problems: Teaching students with learning disabilities using schema-based instruction.* Austin, TX: PRO-ED.
    Montague, M. (2008). Self-regulation strategies for improving the mathematical problem solving for students with learning disabilities. *Learning Disabilities Quarterly, 31*(1), 37–44.

9 *High leverage practices in special education: The final report of the HLP writing team.* (CEC, 2017).

10 The IRIS Center. (2017). *What is instructional scaffolding?* Retrieved on 10/23/2017 from https://iris.peabody.vandertilb.edu/module/sca/

11 The IRIS Center. (2017). *What is instructional scaffolding?* Retrieved on 10/23/2017 from https://iris.peabody.vandertilb.edu/module/sca/

   Dexter, D., & Hughes, C. A. (2011). Graphic organizers and students with learning disabilities: A meta-analysis. *Learning Disabilities Quarterly, 34*(1), 51–72.

   Rosenshine, B. (2012). Principles of instruction: Research-based strategies that all teachers should know. *American Educator, 39*, 12–19.

   Rosenshine, B., & Meister, C. (1992). The use of scaffolds for teaching higher-level cognitive strategies. *Educational Leadership*, 26–33.

12 Sherman, C. K., & De La Paz, S. (2012). Technology to facilitate the general education curriculum. In J. E. Aitken, J. P. Fairley, & J. K. Carlson (Eds.), *Communication technology for students in special education and gifted programs* (pp. 26–33). Hershey, PA: Information Science Reference (an imprint of IGI Global).

13 Englert, C. S., & Mariage, T. V. (1996). A sociocultural perspective: Teaching ways-of-thinking and ways-of-talking in a literacy community. *Learning Disability Research and Practice, 11*(3), 157–167.

   Fisher, D., & Frey, N. (2010). *Guided instruction: How to develop confident and successful learners.* Alexandria, VA: ASCD.

   Palincsar, A. S. (1986). The role of dialogue in providing scaffolded instruction. *Educational Psychologist, 21*, 73–98.

14 Chapin, S., O'Connor, C., & Anderson, N. (2013). *Classroom discussions in Math: A teacher's guide for using talk moves to support the common core and more, grades K-6: A multimedia professional learning resource* (3rd ed.). Sausalito, CA: Math Solutions Publications.

   van der Veen, C., van der Wilt, F., van Kruistum, C., van Oers, B., & Michaels, S. (2017). MODEL-2TALK: An intervention to promote productive classroom talk. *The Reading Teacher, 70*(6), 689–700.

15 Minick, N., & Lidz, C. S. (Ed). (1987). *Dynamic assessment: An interactional approach to evaluating learning potential* (pp. 116–140). New York, NY: Guilford Press.

16 Reid, D. K. (1998). Scaffolding: A broader view. *Journal of Learning Disabilities, 31*(4), 386–396.

17 Gay, G. (2010). *Culturally responsive teaching: Theory, research, and practice.* New York, NY: Teachers College Press.

18 Pearson, P. D., & Gallagher, M. C. (1983). The instruction of reading comprehension. *Contemporary Educational Psychology, 8*, 317–344.

19 Archer, A. L., & Hughes, C. A. (2011). *Explicit instruction: Effective and efficient teaching.* New York, NY: Guilford Press.

20 Reid, D. K. (1998). Scaffolding: A broader view. *Journal of Learning Disabilities, 31*(4), 386–396.

21 Dabo, A., & Mariage, T. V. (2017, April). *Close reading for 3rd grade struggling readers: Discourse and comprehension strategies.* A presentation at the National Council for Exceptional Children Conference. Boston, MA.

22 Rogoff, B. (1991). *Apprenticeship in thinking: Cognitive development in social context.* Oxford, UK: Oxford University Press.

23 Vernon, D. S., Schumaker, J. B., & Deshler, D. D. (1996). *The SCORE skills: Social skills for cooperative groups.* Lawrence, KS: Edge Enterprises.

24 Minick, N., & Lidz, C. S. (Ed). (1987). *Dynamic assessment: An interactional approach to evaluating learning potential* (pp. 116–140). New York, NY: Guilford Press.

25 Larkin, M. (2002). *Using scaffolded instruction to optimize learning.* Retrieved on 4/9/2007 from www.vtaide.com/png/ERIC/Scaffolding.htm

26 Grant, M., Lapp, D., Fisher, D., Johnson, K., & Frey, N. (2012). Purposeful instruction: Mixing up the "I," "We," and "You." *Journal of Adolescent and Adult Literacy, 56*(1), 45–55.

27 Englert, C. S., & Dunsmore, K. (2002). A diversity of teaching and learning paths: Teaching writing in situated activity. In J. Brophy (Ed.), *Social constructivist teaching: Affordances and constraints* (Advanced in research on teaching, Vol. 9, pp. 81–130). United Kingdom: Emerald Group Publishing Limited.

Resources

Videos

The videos provide examples of general and special education teachers providing scaffolded supports while teaching.

Teaching Channel Videos

Gradual Release of Responsibility

www.teachingchannel.org/videos/gradual-release-of-responsibility
A ninth-grade English teacher helps students assume more responsibility in writing about Shakespeare.

I Do, We Do, You Do

www.teachingchannel.org/videos/modeling-strategy-getty/?utm_source=newsletter20171111/
A high school mild/moderate special education teacher demonstrates how she implements the gradual release of responsibility model through *I Do*, *We Do*, and *You Do* in creating a portrait. The teacher demonstrates the importance of direct instruction, modeling, and thinking aloud for all students, including sharing what a final product looks like as a reference. The teacher then uses prompting during the *We Do* and *You Do* phases, providing more and less support as needed as the students move towards completion of the assignment.

Scaffolds for Critical Thinking

www.teachingchannel.org/videos/scaffolding-critical-thinking
A high school teacher guest teaches in a fourth-grade classroom, providing scaffolded supports for students' understanding of the difference between things and ideas.

Interacting With Complex Texts: Scaffolding Meaning Making

www.teachingchannel.org/videos/middle-school-ela-unit-persuasion
A seventh-grade reading support teacher supports English Language learners in preparing to write persuasive essays.

eMedia Workshop

Teaching Matters: Scaffolding

www.youtube.com/watch?v=9gNjGD_W3dM
Presentation on instructional design principle of scaffolding from the Pennsylvania Department of Education.
explicitinstruction.org: Video-Elementary
This website contains videos of Dr. Anita Archer's modeling explicit teaching principles across common classroom activities. Dr. Archer's teaching is an elegant example of providing scaffolded instruction as she moves through an *I Do, We Do, You Do* approach to gradually ceding control to students.

Books

Archer, A. L., & Hughes, C. A. (2011). Explicit instruction: Effective and efficient teaching. In *What Works for Special-Needs Learners*, (Harris, K., & Graham, S., Series Editors). New York, NY: Guilford Press.

Fisher, D., & Frey, N. (2010). *Visible learning for literacy, Grades K–12: Implementing the practices that work best to accelerate student learning.* Thousand Oaks, CA: Corwin Press.

Fisher, D., Frey, N., & Hattie, J., (2016). *Guided instruction: How to develop confident and successful learners.* Alexandria, VA: ASCD.

Klingner, J., & Vaughn, S., Boardman, A., & Swanson, E. (2012). Now *we get it: Boosting comprehension with Collaborative Strategic Reading.*, San Francisco, CA: Josey Boss.

Lapp, D., Moss, B., Grant, M. C., & Johnson, K., (2016). *Turning the page on complex texts: Differentiated scaffolds for close reading instruction (Grade Specific Classroom Scenarios for Common Core State Standards).* Bloomington, IN: Solution Tree Press.

Oczkus, L.D. (2010). Reciprocal Teaching: *Powerful strategies and lessons for improving reading comprehension* (2nd ed.), Newark, DE: International Reading Association.

Web-Based Resources

IRIS Module: This module provides explanations and examples of three approaches to scaffolding (content, task, material). *Providing Instructional Supports: Facilitating mastery of new skills* https://iris.peabody.vanderbilt.edu/module/sca/#content

Intervention Central: Academic and behavior interventions. Videos and featured tools to support instruction, behavior, and executive skills. interventioncentral.com

edHelper: Graphic organizers and other tools to support learning. https://edHelper.com

Teacher Vision: Graphic organizers and other tools to support learning. https://teachervision.com

16
Use Explicit Instruction
Charles A. Hughes, Paul J. Riccomini, and Jared R. Morris

Chapter Introduction

This chapter begins by describing and defining explicit instruction followed by a list of key instructional behaviors or *elements* that make instruction "explicit." Next, a brief summary of selected research supporting the effectiveness of explicit instruction is presented, after which we provide a detailed description of how the key instructional elements are used during a typical explicit lesson. The chapter ends with a discussion of the explicit instruction element, "Provide Purposeful Practice," along with descriptions of how to implement three effective practice strategies (i.e., distributed, interleaved, and retrieval practice).

Introduction to Explicit Instruction

Explicit instruction is comprised of a group of research-supported instructional elements used in concert to design and deliver instruction in ways that provide sufficient support needed by students to successfully engage during an explicit lesson. Archer and Hughes (2011) state:

> It is called explicit because it is an unambiguous and direct approach to teaching that . . . is characterized by a series of supports or scaffolds, whereby students are guided through the learning process with clear statements about the purpose and rationale for learning the new skill, clear explanations and demonstrations of the instructional target, and supported practice with feedback until independent mastery has been achieved.[1]

Hughes, Morris, Therrien, and Benson (2017) define explicit instruction as:

> a group of research-supported instructional behaviors used to design and deliver instruction that provides needed supports for successful learning through clarity of language and purpose, and reduction of cognitive load. It promotes active student engagement by requiring frequent and varied responses followed by appropriate affirmative and corrective feedback, and assists long-term retention through use of purposeful practice strategies.[2]

Thus, at its core, explicit instruction is a group of effective teaching behaviors that provide appropriate amounts of clarity, guidance, and support to students who would not be able to learn in their absence.

Common elements included in explicit instruction are listed in Table 16.1 and are organized into four categories, *content*, *design*, *delivery*, and *practice*.[3] *Content* involves selecting academic skills that are important, that is, that are used frequently, now and in the future. It also includes arranging content in ways that are logical (e.g., in sequence, separating similar skills and concepts initially to avoid confusion), as well as segmenting or "chunking" complex or multi-step skills and strategies for instruction in order to reduce cognitive load by teaching smaller amounts at a time. The next category of elements, *design of instruction*, includes making clear what will be learned in the lesson, discussing its importance, and, if appropriate, linking it to past learning. Other design elements in this category include presenting new content using clear models as well as providing guided practice with gradual lessening of supports.

Elements in the third category, *Delivery of instruction*, are used as a lesson progresses. For example, in order to keep students engaged and focused on critical content, teachers provide multiple opportunities to respond to questions and prompts about the content being taught (see HLP 18 for an expanded treatment of promoting active student engagement). Student responses provide information about how well students are understanding what is being taught, thus helping teachers make

Table 16.1 16 Key Elements of Explicit Instruction

Instructional area	Element
Content	1. Focus instruction on critical content.
	2. Sequence skills logically.
	3. Break down complex skills and strategies into smaller instructional units.
Design of instruction	4. Design organized and focused lessons.
	5. Begin lessons with a clear statement of the lesson goals and your expectations.
	6. Review prior skills and knowledge before beginning instruction.
	7. Provide step-by-step demonstrations.
	8. Use clear and concise language.
	9. Provide an adequate range of examples and non-examples.
	10. Provide guided and supported practice.
Delivery of instruction	11. Require frequent responses.
	12. Monitor student performance closely
	13. Provide immediate affirmative and corrective feedback.
	14. Deliver the lesson at a brisk pace.
	15. Help students organize knowledge.
Purposeful practice	16. Provide distributed and cumulative practice.

Note. Adapted from *Explicit Instruction: Effective and Efficient Teaching*, by A. L. Archer and C. A. Hughes, 2011, pp. 2–3. Copyright by 2011 by The Guilford Press.

appropriate instructional adjustments (e.g., slow down or speed up, reduce or increase support, etc.). Requiring frequent responding also allows teachers to give corrective and affirmative feedback in a timely fashion (see HLPs 8 and 22 for expanded treatments of feedback). Finally, in order to help students retain, recall, and apply what they have learned, teachers design *purposeful practice* activities.

Research on Explicit Instruction: A Summary of Summaries

Over the past several decades, a substantial amount of research has been published providing support for a direct and explicit approach to teaching. This research has been conducted with students with and without disabilities as well as students described as "at-risk," "struggling," or "low-achieving" and in a number of academic areas (e.g., reading, math, written expression, cognitive learning strategies, vocabulary). Due to space constraints, a detailed, systematic review of this research is not provided. Instead, two lists of selected research summaries conducted over the last 25 years in which explicit instruction was found to be effective are provided in Table 16.2.

The first list contains Institute of Science (IES) Practice Guides published through What Works Clearinghouse. These Practice Guides are based on analyses of researched instructional interventions used to teach a variety of academic subjects (e.g., reading comprehension, writing) and published in peer-reviewed journals. The second group of citations listed in Table 16.2 are published literature reviews and meta-analyses in which effective instructional interventions that included elements of explicit instruction were found to be effective for teaching academic skills to students with learning disabilities.

To this point we have described what explicit instruction is, provided a closer look at the instructional elements commonly included in explicit instruction, and presented a brief summary of a large body of convergent research supporting it as effective, especially for learners who can be characterized as struggling. Next, we describe the "anatomy" of a typical explicit lesson.

A Typical Explicit Lesson Format

As presented above, the key elements of explicit instruction are designed for several purposes, such as making instructional expectations and goals clear; keeping students focused, engaged and responding; and providing guidance and support that allows them to be successful. The following section is intended to provide examples of how those elements are used when delivering an explicit lesson.[4] The structure and elements of a typical explicit lesson are illustrated in Figure 16.1.

Opening

A lesson's opening includes ensuring students are ready to learn the new content, a brief preview of what is to be learned, and why the content is important to learn. If necessary, some illustration (e.g., a graphic organizer) of how the new content is linked to or "fits" with previous, related content is provided and discussed with students.

Gain Student Attention

If a train leaves the station without some of the passengers on board, the engineer can keep going or return to pick up the passengers. In the first option, the late passengers won't reach their destination, and in the second, time will be wasted. Similarly, if some students are not "ready to learn" when the lesson begins, they will not be "on the train," and teachers will face the same decisions as the engineer. Thus, the first task of the teacher when starting a lesson is to obtain the attention of all the students.

Table 16.2 A Sample of Special Education Research Syntheses and IES Practice Guides Identifying Explicit Instruction as Highly Recommended or Having Strong Effects on Academic Achievement

	Authors, Year	Title
IES Practice Guides	Baker et al., 2014	Teaching academic content and literacy to English learners in elementary and middle school
	Frye et al., 2013	Teaching math to young children: A practice guide
	Gersten et al., 2009	Assisting students struggling with mathematics: Response to Intervention (RtI) for elementary and middle schools
	Graham et al., 2012	Teaching elementary school students to be effective writers: A practice guide
	Herrera, et al., 2016	Summary of 20 years of research on the effectiveness of adolescent literacy programs and practices
	Kamil et al., 2008	Improving adolescent literacy: Effective classroom and intervention practices: A practice guide
	Siegler et al., 2010	Developing effective fractions instruction for kindergarten through 8th grade: A practice guide
	Star et al., 2015	Teaching strategies for improving algebra knowledge in middle and high school students
Literature Review/Meta Analyses	Christenson, et al., 1989	Critical instructional factors for students with mild handicaps: An integrative review
	Gersten, 1998	Recent advances in instructional research for students with learning disabilities: An overview
	Graham, et al., 2012	A meta-analysis of writing instruction for students in the elementary grades
	Kroesbergen & Van Luit, 2003	Mathematics interventions for children with special educational needs: A meta-analysis
	Solis et al., 2012	Reading comprehension interventions for middle school students with learning disabilities: A synthesis of 30 years of research
	Swanson, 2001	Searching for the best model for instructing students with learning disabilities
	Therrien, et al., 2011	Science instruction for students with learning disabilities: A meta-analysis

Note. Adapted from "Explicit instruction: Historical and contemporary contexts," by C. A. Hughes, J. R. Morris, W. J. Therrien, and S. K. Benson, 2017, *Learning Disabilities Research and Practice, 32*(3), pp. 140–148.

For example, a teacher may say something like, *"One, two, three, eyes on me!"* or *"Clear your desks, get out (name materials), and when you are ready, eyes up here."* There are many ways to do this, and there is no "right" way: The important thing is that all students are "on board" (e.g., have the correct materials, looking at the teacher).

Opening

Gain Student Attention
Preview
- Provide students with a clear statement of goals and expectations.

  "Opening it up"

- Discuss the relevance of the target skill (or larger goal).
Review
- Review critical prerequisite skills.
- Verify students have the prerequisite skills and background knowledge.

Body

Model (I do it)
- Draw student attention to important features of the content through modeling/think-alouds.
- Present a wide range of examples and non-examples.
- Show and Tell (Demonstrating and Describing).
- 3 c's = Clear, Consistent, Concise
- Involve students.
- Provide several models.

  "Teaching it"

Prompted or Guided Practice (We do it)
- Provide successful engagement by using systematically faded supports/prompts (e.g., tell them what to do, ask them what to do, then remind them what to do.)
Check or Unprompted Practice (You do it)
- Insure all students are able to demonstrate understanding with high rates of accuracy.

Closing

Review critical content.
Preview the content of the next lesson.
Assign independent work (Practice).

  "Closing it up"

Practice

Independent Practice (e.g., distributed practice, cumulative practice, interleaved practice, testing/retrieval practice).

  "Purposeful practice"

Other Important Features: (a) Select critical content, (b) Provide opportunities for students to respond and receive feedback, (c) Segment complex skills, and (d) Maintain a brisk pace.

Figure 16.1 Structure of a Prototypical Explicit Lesson

Source: Illustrates the structure (e.g., major sections and subsections) of a prototypical explicit instruction lesson. Adapted from *Explicit Instruction: Effective and Efficient Teaching*, by A. L. Archer and C. A. Hughes, 2011, pp. 2–3.

State the Goal of the Lesson

Usually a straightforward statement is all that is needed. For example, "*Today we are going to continue our unit on writing. Last time you learned how to write introductory paragraphs when writing a short, expository essay, and today we are going to learn how to write a detail paragraph that follows the introductory paragraph.*"

Discuss Relevance of the Target Skill

To attempt to answer the age-old student question, "*Why do we have to learn this?*", teachers often discuss the relevance of the skill or strategy being taught. In addition to "why," this conversation often includes "where" and "when" the new skill can be used. For example, the teacher might start the discussion by asking students why it is important to provide details when writing about a topic as well as when and where they are required to write short essays and what the positive outcomes are if they are able to write clearly.

Review

Often, in order to learn new content, students need to have mastered previously taught content. A lesson can quickly fall apart if students don't remember (or haven't been taught) prerequisite skills or information required to learn the new content. Thus, teachers go beyond assuming students know the prerequisites and spend some time *verifying* they do. For example, a teacher might say, "*Before you learn how to write a detail paragraph, I want to see if you remember what makes a good introductory paragraph. I am giving you some paragraphs to look at. You are to decide which ones are good introductory paragraphs as well as explain why they are good. I will also ask you why the others are not good examples.*" The teacher then provides the paragraphs, walks around and monitors students as they work, and, when they indicate readiness to respond, asks questions such as, "*Everybody, is the first paragraph a good example of an introductory paragraph, yes or no?*" When the teacher signals, students respond simultaneously with a verbal "yes" or "no" thumbs up or down, or by displaying a yes or no card. She then might say, "*You all agreed it is a good example.*" "*Why do you think it is a good example?*" "*Give me a thumbs-up when you are ready to answer.*" "*I see all the thumbs are up.*" "*What do you think, John?*" Following John's response, the class adds and discusses any additional criteria for what makes a "good" introductory paragraph. When the teacher is satisfied students are ready to learn the next type of paragraph, the lesson moves to the body.

Body

The body of the lesson is where instruction on the new content occurs. It has three major parts, the model, prompt, and check. These parts are sometimes referred to as "I do," "We do," and "You do."[5]

Model

The model ("I do") is the first phase of teaching new content and accordingly is a critical part of the learning process, especially for students with learning difficulties. Modeling is used when students are learning how, and sometimes when, to "do" something. It is used for simple (e.g., how to write the letter 'b') to complex skills (e.g., how to use a heuristic to critically analyze original historical documents, how to apply an editing strategy).[6] A model includes two teacher behaviors: demonstrating and describing.[7] "Describing" during a model is often referred to as a think-aloud whereby teachers, as they "demonstrate," vocalize the important aspects of performing the skill (e.g., the sequence of the steps used to solve a problem, how the steps are performed). Accordingly, teachers "verbally highlight" what they are thinking and doing for the purpose of explicitly providing students visual and auditory access to expert thinking and performance. The primary role of students during this process is to watch and listen, that is, to observe.

Three factors impacting the effectiveness of modeling are clarity, conciseness, and consistency of language. Clarity of the teacher's language (e.g., using vocabulary students understand, minimizing grammatical complexity) impacts how well students understand what they are observing.[8] Conciseness involves using only words needed to enhance comprehension. Because students must understand and remember the key parts of the model when they begin to practice the skill in the prompt step, excessive and extraneous wording will hamper their retention. Finally, using key vocabulary during the model in a consistent manner can reduce possible confusion. For example, when modeling how to write the lower-case manuscript letter 'h', teachers avoid using different words to describe their actions when they model (e.g., use both "curved" and "arched" lines and "middle" and "dashed" lines). Instead, teachers select vocabulary words appropriate for their students and use them consistently to reduce confusion during initial learning.

To summarize, wording should be brief, focus on key actions, and consistently used. Developing an effective model involves planning, editing, and rehearsal. "Winging it" often leads to a confusing model, and that leads to confused learners!

Typically, several models are provided, and the number of models is dependent on how complex and/or novel the content is. One method for deciding when sufficient models have been provided is to involve students in the model. This is done by asking the students to "*help me with the next item/problem.*" Involving students keeps them engaged as well as provides the teacher an assessment of whether they are beginning to internalize the wording and processes used to complete the new skill. For example, "*I want you to help me write the letter 'h'. Where do I start, everybody?*" (teacher provides think-time and then signals for a group response—students say, in unison, "the top line"). "*That's right!*" (teacher puts her writing implement on the top line). "*Then I go down to the where, everybody?*" (again, think time is provided and followed by a signal to respond and students say "bottom line" followed by teacher drawing a line from the top to the bottom line). "*Then I go to the where, everybody?*" "*Yes, to the middle line. Now I . . .?*" "*Excellent remembering! I curve to the bottom line.*" Note that if the teacher had not used consistent and concise wording when she was modeling, students would not have answered her questions in unison. When students respond correctly to these questions, they are ready to move to the prompt step.

Prompt

The prompt step ("We do") occurs when students begin to practice the new content with teacher support. Support through prompting allows students to practice the new skill at a high level of success, which in turn builds their confidence. As students demonstrate success, the level of prompting and support is systematically faded until they perform the skill without prompts.

Prompting can take three forms: physical, verbal, and visual. Verbal and visual prompts are most commonly used when teaching academic skills and strategies to students with high-incidence disabilities. Verbal prompts take the form of teacher directions, questions, or reminders presented as students perform the new skill. For example, a highly supportive verbal prompt for learning how to add two-digit addition problems might be: "*Let's do some together. I will tell you what to do as we work through the problem. First, we add the ones' column. What is 4 + 2? Yes, it is 6. Write 6 under the ones' column. Next, we add the tens' column. What is 3 + 6? Correct again! Write the 9 under the tens' column. So, 34 + 62 is 96.*" This level of prompt is referred to as a "tell" prompt because students are told exactly what to do in terms of the new process being learned. Note that the teacher did "ask" students what the sums of the columns were, but that was because the students already knew their addition facts and the teacher wanted to keep them engaged by making responses. Keep in mind that prompts don't always start at such a high level of support (i.e., tell). The starting point for prompting is based on the teacher's knowledge of her students and their prior knowledge related to the new skill. Thus, it may be more appropriate to start the prompt at a lower level (e.g., questions versus directives).

For example, verbal prompting may start at the "ask" level, whereby the teacher follows the same format and language as the "tell" prompt described above, but turns the directives into questions. For example: *"Now let's do some together. I will ask you what to do as we work through the problem. First, which column do we add first? Yes, the tens' column. What two numbers will you add? Right again! What is the sum of 4 + 2? Yes, it is 6. Where will you write the 6? Excellent, under the tens' column. Which column do you add next?"* And so on.

When students have demonstrated success during the "ask" prompt, the teacher fades the prompt further by using a "remind" prompt. For example, *"Let's do another. Don't forget which column you start with."* If students are successful with just a reminder or hint, they begin to practice solving problems without prompting.

Check

After students perform the new skill or strategy accurately with no direct prompting—but before they are asked to do so independently at their desks or home—they go through a "checking" process. Here they perform the skill or strategy under the watchful eye of the teacher, allowing her to catch mistakes or misunderstandings and provide timely feedback. This process in turn reduces the chance of practicing errors.

Present Examples and Non-Examples When Appropriate

Often, explicit instruction is used when teaching not only *how*, but also *when*, to use a new skill or procedure. For example, when teaching academic rules, multi-step strategies, or vocabulary, students learn not only *how* to use these skills, they also learn when they should be applied—or not. Learning to discriminate *when* or *when not* to use a strategy or rule requires the use of examples *and* non-examples. Without this discrimination students often tend to over-generalize the use of the skill (they use it when they should not).

A non-example is similar to an example but is missing a critical aspect or attribute of the rule or concept. An *example* for teaching the math rule *"when the sum of a column is greater than 9, then regroup,"* would be an addition problem where at least one of the sums of a column in the problem is greater than 9, thus allowing students to practice using the rule (e.g. 42 + 38). A *non-example* for this rule would be an addition problem where *none* of the sums of a column are greater than 9 (e.g., 42 + 37)—it is missing the attribute of "greater than 9." To illustrate, if a teacher was teaching this rule and using a *non*-example during the "ask" prompt, it would sound something like: *"Please touch the next problem on your paper/screen* (teacher observes if all students are attending to the correct problem on their sheets). *Great, you are all looking at the correct problem. Everybody, let's read the problem* (teacher signals and students respond). *Excellent, it is 42 + 37. Everybody, which column will you add first?* (signal—response) *Yes, the ones' column. Add the ones' column, and when you have the answer, look at me. What is the sum, everybody? Yes, it's 9. Our rule says, 'when the sum of a column is greater than' what everybody? Correct, greater than 9. Is it greater than 9 everybody? Agreed, it is not greater than 9. So, will you regroup? Why not?* (Give think time and when all students indicate they are ready to answer the teacher calls on a student.) *Cicely? Right again! You remembered the rule is only used when the sum of a column is greater than 9."*

Close

When students demonstrate a high level of accuracy (e.g., 90 to 95%) during the check step or when the time allotted for the lesson is at an end, the close provides a quick way to "wrap things up." A typical close has three parts: review, preview, and assign independent practice.

Review

A quick review of content covered during the lesson is provided, usually by asking students questions. For example, asking *"What are the factors that make up a good detail paragraph?"* and/or *"How do you know if you need to regroup when adding multiple digit addition problems?"* This is often a good time to provide group affirmative feedback about what they did as learners during the lesson. For instance, *"You all did an excellent job of listening and paying attention and are starting to write some great detail paragraphs!" "Your writing is so much more interesting and informative when you provide more details and examples!"*

Preview

Following the review, the teacher tells students what will be covered in the next lesson. For example, *"Tomorrow we will continue working on detail paragraphs"* or *"Tomorrow, I will check your homework to see if you wrote a good detail paragraph, and if you did, we will move on to learning how to finish an essay using a summary paragraph."*

Assign Independent Practice

If, at lesson's end, students can perform the skill at a high level of accuracy with no prompting (i.e., have shown they are ready to practice the skill independently), it can be assigned as seat work, group work, or homework. If they cannot accurately practice the skill independently, practice should be delayed until they can. In its place, the teacher can decide to assign previously taught, related skills.

Tips for Designing and Delivering an Explicit Lesson

The "typical" lesson format presented above includes all major components. However, not all are used all the time in all lessons. For example, going over the rationale for learning a new skill can be unnecessary (and a less efficient use of instructional time) when it has been discussed several times previously (e.g. students know *why* and *when* it is important to write clearly). Or, if a new unit is starting and there are no prerequisite skills pertinent to the new content, prerequisite skills are not required. Sometimes (though not often) the prompt step is not used (e.g. when teaching a vocabulary word that is easy for a group of students to understand such as a basic, concrete concept). However, eliminating some components of the lesson is not a good idea. For example, beginning a lesson without learner attention will likely result in having to reteach. Not providing a clear and concise model and/or skipping over the prompt and moving directly to the check can lead to student confusion and possible misunderstanding (and more reteaching). In short, including all components when needed is a far more efficient mode of instruction than a more haphazard approach.

Within an explicit instruction lesson, there is room to be "creative" and make adjustments—if those adjustments are based on teacher knowledge (versus assumptions) of what learners know and can do. This knowledge most often comes from requiring frequent student responses that function as on-the-spot assessments. These assessments allow teachers to make timely decisions such as whether the lesson should move to the next step (e.g., move from the model to the prompt, fade a prompt), stay at the step they are on (e.g., perform another model, involve them in another model), or move back a step (e.g., students are making too many errors as they begin the check step, so the teacher moves back to the prompt step). The big idea here is that in an explicit instruction lesson, *all* decisions are based on student performance.

As a final tip, we present an instructional routine that can be used during an explicit lesson: Instructional Transition Statements (ITSs). These are teacher statements that prompt or cue students about what is happening next and what they are expected to do as they transition through the parts of an explicit lesson. Consistent use of ITSs helps maintain instructional pace and student attention. Examples of where ITSs could be used during an explicit lesson and example teacher statements are presented in Table 16.3.

Narrowing the Focus

Given that several of the elements of explicit instruction (e.g., providing feedback and increasing student engagement by providing many opportunities to respond) are topics of other chapters in this book (i.e., HLPs 8, 12, 15, 18, 20, and 22), we decided to end the chapter by focusing on the element

Table 16.3 Making the Structure of an Explicit Lesson More Explicit: Using Instructional Transition Statements (ITSs)[*]

	When to Use ITSs	Example ITSs
OPENING		
	Gain Attention/Starting Lesson	"One, two, three, eyes on me!"
		"Let's get ready to learn!"
	Review Prerequisite Skills/Knowledge	"Let me see if you remember how to. . ."
		"Show me you can still do. . ."
	Discuss Relevance	"Let's talk about why, where, and when learning . . . will help you."
	Link New Content to Previous Content	"Let's discuss how what we are learning today fits with what we have been learning."
BODY		
	Model	"Watch and listen while I show and tell you how to. . ."
	Involve the Students in Model	"Now I want you to help me as I do another one."
	Prompt	"Let's do some together."
		"Your turn to do some with my help."
	Check	"I think you are ready to try some on your own."
CLOSE		"Great work! Let's close the lesson down."

[*] Using ITSs is an instructional routine. ITSs are statements that prompt students about what to do and expect as they progress through an explicit lesson. Consistent use of ITSs helps maintain instructional pace and student attention. (C.A. Hughes, 2017).

of purposeful practice. We chose to discuss this topic because it typically does not get much coverage despite its importance in the learning process. Specifically, people cannot become competent users of newly learned skills if they don't practice them using effective practice strategies in purposeful and deliberate ways.[9] Put another way, if they (the students) don't remember it (the content of instruction), you (the teacher) did not really teach it!

While practice is an important part of learning for all students, it is especially essential for students with learning disabilities given documented problems in various aspects of memory as well as attention and processing speed.[10] Additionally, explicit, well-designed, and purposeful practice strategies, along with feedback, have been identified as one of the most import instructional components for these learners.[11] Below, we present, three research-based practice strategies: distributed practice, interleaved practice, and retrieval practice.

Mrs. Johnson, a first-year special education teacher, has been focusing her instructional planning on developing explicit instruction lessons (see Table 16.3: Opening and Body). Specifically, she devoted substantial time to gaining students' attention, reviewing necessary prerequisite skills, and modeling, guiding, and checking for understanding; however, due to time constraints, she was using the practice sheets that accompanied the core mathematics program. She was very pleased with the progress of her students, especially during the initial stages of learning, but her progress monitoring data was indicating students were not retaining the high levels of accuracy with minimal support demonstrated during the closing of the lessons. Recognizing that her current practice structures may be the issue preventing her students from retaining the content, she decides to learn how to better structure practice opportunities to make them more purposeful. In this case, the purpose is to promote long-term retention.

Distributed Practice

Description of the Strategy

Distributed practice, sometimes known as spaced practice, is performed by spacing out practice sessions over time (e.g., days, weeks, and months). Numerous studies, conducted over the course of almost 200 years, indicate the effectiveness of distributed practice for knowledge and skill acquisition and retention.

The amount of time scheduled for distributed practice sessions are often relatively short segments of time in comparison to massed practice. Massed practice and distributed practice are essentially opposites. Distributed practice is composed of shorter sessions or fewer problems spaced out over time, whereas massed practice consists of longer sessions within a short amount of time. Teachers and commercially produced curricula frequently implement massed practice, and although it can initially produce greater short-term retention than distributed practice, that retention diminishes quickly. Conversely, retention of material studied using distributed practice is slightly lower in the short term but quickly surpasses the retention gained through massed practice. Distributed practice has been shown to be effective for students with and without disabilities in variety of content areas.[12]

After initial learning, without continued practice retention decreases rapidly. Spaced practice helps to disrupt the forgetting of newly acquired knowledge and skills. As practice is repeated and spaced over time, retention (a) "resets" to high percentages after each session, (b) begins to decrease at a slower rate, and (c) levels out at sequentially higher levels, thus resulting in increased overall retention.[13]

How to Implement the Strategy

There are two methods used for implementing distributed practice, equal-interval spacing and expanding spaced schedule.[14] In equal-interval spacing, the intervals are the same distance apart, whereas in an expanding schedule, the interval distance increases with each successive interval. It was not until recently that studies identified a formula suggesting the optimal length of time between practice sessions, called "intersession intervals." The first step of the formula is to decide how long students need to retain information. This length of time is referred to as the "retention interval." While some content will hopefully be retained over a lifetime, there are situations, such as examinations, where the long-term retention goal is more finite. The next step is to multiply the retention interval by 0.1 to 0.2.[15] If the retention interval is a relatively short period of time, then multiplying by 0.1 might be optimal, while if the overall retention interval is longer in duration, using the multiplier 0.2 would likely produce superior results.[16] For example, if the desired retention interval is 90 days, multiplying that number by 0.2 provides the approximate intersession intervals, which is approximately 18 days.[17] Therefore, using 0.2 as the multiplier, practicing the material every 18 days would produce optimal retention in 90 days (see Figure 16.2).

The second variation of distributed practice is an expanding schedule of practice sessions. In an expanding schedule, each successive practice session is further apart than the previous one. For example, when a skill or concept is taught it would be practiced again three days later, nine days later, and 28 days later (see Figure 16.3).[18] While some studies have shown that an expanding schedule produces longer retention with increased efficiency (i.e., fewer practice sessions),[19] others found equal-interval and expanding schedules equally effective.[20]

In conclusion, distributed practice has a strong research base supporting its effectiveness for maintaining and retaining a variety of skills and knowledge with a variety of learners.[21] In addition to its *effectiveness*, distributed practice is also *efficient* in that it involves less time and effort and achieves better results than the typically used approach of massed practice.[22]

Following the guidelines for distributed practice, Mrs. Johnson decides to develop a schedule to provide distributed practice using an equal interval sequence. Because the progress monitoring

New Skill Learned

Practice Session 1 (18 days after initial learning)

Practice Session 2 (18 days after Practice 1)

Practice Session 3 (18 days after Practice 2)

Practice Session 4 (18 days after Practice 3)

Practice Session 5 (18 days after Practice 4)

Figure 16.2 Example of a Distributed Practice Equal Interval Schedule

Figure 16.3 Example of a Distributed Practice Expanding Schedule

data indicated student performance was beginning to drop about 21 days after initial instruction, she decides to allocate 15–20 minutes 18 days after the initial lesson for practice of that content. She will then provide additional practice every 18th day for 15–20 minutes. This spaced distributed practice should help her students maintain the concepts and skills. She will continue to collect data to determine if the equal-interval distributed practice is increasing her students' retention.

Interleaving Practice Format

Description of the Strategy

Interleaving practice format (IPF) is a design structure used to improve long term retention. It uses purposeful mixing-up of items within the same practice session.[23] Often, practice activities are structured in a format called blocking that involves grouping similar items together.[24] The blocking structure results in a student practicing the same skill consecutively multiple times before moving to a different skill. When students practice using the IPF structure they experience greater learning gains across time, increased retention, and improved generalization when compared to practice sessions formatted in a blocking design.[25]

The improved learning outcomes associated with IPF are due in part to the mixed sequence of the problem types which require students to think more deeply about the strategy and/or approach necessary to apply to the skill or solution. The learner must carefully consider each problem and select the most appropriate strategy as it comes up.[26] Additionally, the varying sequence of problem types requires the learner to continuously *retrieve* the appropriate strategy from long-term memory compared to a blocking structure in which the appropriate strategy stays in short-term memory.[27] Repeated retrieval from long-term memory reinforces neural connections, resulting in more robust learning. Thus, by simply adjusting how problems are organized on a practice sheet, teachers have the ability to improve their students' learning outcomes, retention rates, and ability to discriminate and transfer information.

In addition, research on IPF also demonstrates that interleaving the sequence of problems during practice sessions is more important than the number of items practiced. In other words, mixing up items is more effective than how many items are practiced.

Practice sheet sequenced in a **BLOCKING** structure

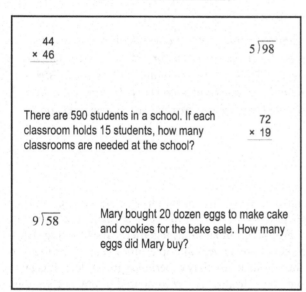

- Problems are grouped according to type: 2x2 multiplication, 1x2 division, and word problems (aaa bbb ccc).

- Requires minimum thought because students recognize the process in advance and are simply applying it to consecutive problems.

- Initial learning benefits, but decreased long term retention.

Practice sheet designed in **INTERLEAVING** practice format

- Problems involve multiplication and division computation and word problems.

- Problem types are alternating in an abc abc sequence.

- Requires students to think more deeply about the process by alternating problem types.

- Initial learning may feel delayed, but produces better long-term learning.

Figure 16.4 Blocking vs. Interleaving Practice Format

How to Implement the Strategy

There are four important considerations when developing IPF structured practice sheets. The first is identifying problems that correspond to the targeted concepts and skills of the lesson(s). The second consideration requires reviewing the different problem types identified and sequencing the problems in an alternating pattern so that students are not practicing the same problem types consecutively. Problems from previous lessons are used to mix up the sequence. This *mixed sequence* is the essential element of the IPF structure and where teachers should place the most emphasis when developing their IPF materials; however, researchers are still in the process of determining the most effective sequence. Therefore, teachers should experiment with varying sequences and types of problems to determine the most effective sequence for a specific class. Technology applications may also assist in the implementation of IPF structured practice. If you have access to software programs with the capability for controlling practice items, setting up the computer practice following IPF guidelines is an excellent option (refer to Figure 16.6). Keep in mind the IPF design is particularly useful for practicing similar problems that are easily confused by students. For example, problems involving finding the perimeter, area, and volume of objects are similar in process but often cause confusion for students (e.g., students use the procedure for finding a *perimeter* when calculating *area*). Sequencing practice problems following an "a-b-c, a-b-c, a-b-c" design (e.g. *area, perimeter, volume . . . area, perimeter, volume . . . area, perimeter, volume*) forces students to focus on each problem more deeply, resulting in deeper learning.[28]

Third, we strongly recommend that students and parents are informed that with the new IPF design, students may progress a little slower at first but that this format will result in better long-term retention and recall. Explaining the IPF structure to parents and students before implementation and describing this initial, but temporary, feeling of slower learning can reduce anxiety about its use. The fourth and last consideration is that it is beneficial to novice learners if they are given a blocked practice format during initial practice before switching to the IPF format.[29]

In summary, the IPF does not require changing or adjusting instruction, only slight adjustments to the sequence of practice problems that will likely produce larger and longer lasting performance outcomes.

> *Mrs. Johnson realizes the majority (if not all) of the practice sheets accompanying the math curriculum are structured in a blocking format. She believes while this structure might help at the initial stages of learning it also might have a negative impact on long-term retention. Mrs. Johnson decides to embed interleaving practice opportunities across the course of each unit. Following the IPF guidelines, she will use the scope and sequence to determine which problem types can be grouped together in one practice sheet. She will identify three problem types and develop a practice sheet that mixes the problem types so that students do not practice the same problem multiple types consecutively. For example, she will develop a practice sheet where students practice calculating the area of a figure, then calculate the perimeter of a figure, and then calculate the surface area of a 3D figure. She will include nine total problems so that the students have three opportunities to practice each problem type in a mixed structure. Since blocked practice appears to be important early, she will add regular IPF practice opportunities once students have demonstrated high levels of accuracy with minimal support. Mrs. Johnson will pay special attention to the progress monitoring data to determine if this IFP practice is increasing student retention across the course of the school year and adjust as necessary.*

Retrieval Practice Technique

Description of the Strategy

Retrieval practice (RP) is a technique teachers can use to significantly improve student retention of content over long periods of time; it is one of the most effective practice techniques available to educators.[30] RP, or practice testing, was researched beginning a century ago (see *testing effect*).[31] Interest in this practice strategy has been renewed as educational researchers seek high leverage practices.

An RP activity requires learners to recall information purely from memory with no assistance from textbooks or notes. When teachers use RP activities with their students on a regular basis as they learn new content, the result is longer retention of the material.[32] In short, test-like activities that require students to recall information with no aids is much more effective than traditional study procedures (e.g., taking notes from text, highlighting, re-reading) when it comes to retaining the information accurately and over time.[33]

How to Implement the RP Technique

Although the RP technique is relatively simple to understand and implement, there are four critical design aspects to consider in order to maximize learning benefits for students. Teachers have many options for the type of activity that requires students to practice recalling information with no assistance. A list of RP activities is included in Table 16.4.

First, RP activities are effective in both formal assessment situations as well as informal low-stakes activities.[34] The testing effect and its positive outcomes for retention is well documented, however, given the controversy about the amount of testing currently in schools,[35] we recommend using a "low or no" stakes type of ungraded activity designed for the purpose of improving learning. This can be done using a variety of activities that have one thing in common: students are required to actively recall information with no assistance. For example, you may develop a *self-check* routine for students to engage in every fourth or fifth day of school. Students are given several questions based on essential learning objectives and are required to answer them from free recall. A grade is not assigned and only feedback that allows student to self-assess their learning is provided.

Second, the format of the question embedded in the RP activity is an important consideration. The question format in the RP activity does not have to match the actual assessment format; open response questions have a positive impact on multiple choice tests. The key ingredient does not appear to be the question format, but rather the emphasis on *unassisted active recall* of the information. We recommend using a variety of short answer and/or fill-in-the blank question formats in the above described *self-check routine* as well as the activities listed in Table 16.4.

Third, feedback is also an integral part of RP activities, especially when students answer incorrectly or are not able to recall any of the targeted information. Given the requirement of active and unsupported recall, students will make mistakes, and this is when providing feedback is essential, or the misconceptions will remain.[36] Continuing with the *self-check routine*, providing feedback in the form of right or wrong immediately following the activities is an option, but providing more

Table 16.4 Retrieval Practice Activities

Activity	Description	Frequency
Flash Card Q&A	Short answer questions or vocabulary terms are placed on flash cards. Students are paired and ask each other the questions and then discuss the answer. Answer is provided on the back, so feedback is embedded in the activity.	First 10 minutes of class every fourth day
Throw-Back-Thursday Ticket Out the Door	Students are given a question related to the topics in the previous week's lesson and write down everything that they can remember about the question. Feedback is provided the next day in the first five minutes of class.	Every Thursday or when appropriate based on sequence of content
Jeopardy Type Games	Any type of game that encourages unassisted recall and equal opportunities for students to answer questions. Questions could be drawn from recent chapters.	Every second Friday of the month
Self-Check Quizzes	A self-check activity is not graded and includes short answer questions that students have to answer. The answers are immediately corrected through a class discussion where students share answers and discuss both incorrect and/or correct answers.	Every sixth day or as much as appropriate

Note. This list is not a comprehensive list of activities.

elaborate feedback may improve retention. Teachers could have students exchange their self-check papers while displaying the correct answers on the board, and the teacher could elaborate upon commonly missed questions in the form of a group discussion. Regardless of the question format and the formal/informal type of RP activity, corrective feedback must become a common feature of all RP activities.

The fourth and perhaps most complex aspect to consider is the dosage and timing of the RP activities. In general, a common theme and/or statement emerges in this collection of research related to the dosage issue, *more testing is better*,[37] but an important consideration within the *dosage* is the timing of the RP activities. Providing students opportunities to retrieve the same information multiple times is much more effective than only providing one or two opportunities for RP; however, research demonstrates greater gains when the opportunities are purposefully spaced (versus consecutive RP activities). It appears that more RP activities that are purposefully spaced result in even stronger retention for students; in other words, more RP condensed into a short period is *not* as effective as spacing those RP activities across a longer period of time. Unfortunately, researchers have not clearly identified the exact timing; thus, our recommendation is that teachers experiment with different spacing of RP activities to better determine the "sweet spot" to realize the optimum benefits on retention.

In summary, the RP activities do not require changing initial instruction or adjusting sequence of content, but rather planning to provide activities that require *unassisted active recall* of targeted information *spaced* at regular intervals. The addition of *low-stakes* RP activities paired with *feedback* and the already existing assessments has the potential to produce significantly greater retention of important content taught across the course of the school year.

Mrs. Johnson has learned very quickly that a characteristic of her struggling students is that they do not test well. For some reason, students who are demonstrating mastery on practice and informal types of activities, score poorly on the exam or test. She decides that implementing the retrieval practice technique might benefit her students when they take the exams, especially the high-stakes exams. She develops a series of what she calls "check yourself practice tests" that resemble the more important formal tests and exams. She develops a regular check yourself practice test routine for every ninth day of school. She explains to the students that this will be a way for us to check our learning before the exams. The information we get from these "check yourself" practice tests will help determine what you might need extra help on and what you already know. Each check yourself practice test will include three or four problems from the previous sections and require students to produce an answer (no multiple choice). This will most often take the form of pencil and paper, but she also plans to use a Jeopardy-like game structure and computer software that is available.

Wrap Up

As teachers, it is our primary responsibility to teach our students the skills and knowledge they need to be successful in school and beyond. To do so, we need to use the most effective techniques available to us at the time, and their effectiveness needs to be established through well-designed, peer-reviewed research. This is not to say everything we do—or don't do—in classrooms must have a research base, only that when possible it is best to base our decisions on research rather than opinion. Explicit instruction and the instructional elements that compose it have a strong research support that is based on how students learn. It is not the only way to teach; however, it is the most effective approach for teaching academic skills to students who need additional support and guidance, clarity, feedback, and yes, practice.

Notes

1 Archer, A. L., & Hughes, C. A. (2011). *Explicit instruction: Effective and efficient teaching.* New York, NY: Guilford Press, p. 1.

2 Hughes, C. A., Morris, J. R., Therrien, W. J., & Benson, S. K. (2017). Explicit instruction: Historical and contemporary contexts. *Learning Disabilities Research and Practice, 32*(3), 143. doi:10.1111/ldrp.12142

3 Archer, A. L., & Hughes, C. A. (2011). *Explicit instruction: Effective and efficient teaching.* New York, NY: Guilford Press.

   Hughes, C. A., Morris, J. R., Therrien, W. J., & Benson, S. K. (2017). Explicit instruction: Historical and contemporary contexts. *Learning Disabilities Research and Practice, 32*(3), 140–148. doi:10.1111/ldrp.12142

4 Archer, A. L., & Hughes, C. A. (2011). *Explicit instruction: Effective and efficient teaching.* New York, NY: Guilford Press.

5 Archer, A. L., & Hughes, C. A. (2011). *Explicit instruction: Effective and efficient teaching.* New York, NY: Guilford Press.

6 De La Paz, S., & Felton, M. K. (2010). Reading and writing from multiple source documents in history: Effects of strategy instruction with low to average high school writers. *Contemporary Educational Psychology, 35*(3), 174–192. doi:10.1016/j.cedpsych.2010.03.001

   Hughes, C. A. (2011). Effective design and delivery of task-specific learning strategy instruction for students with learning disabilities. *Focus on Exceptional Children, 44*(2), 1–16.

7 Archer, A. L., & Hughes, C. A. (2011). *Explicit instruction: Effective and efficient teaching.* New York, NY: Guilford Press.

8 Titsworth, S., Mazer, J. P., Goodboy, A. K., Bolkan, S., & Myers, S. A. (2015). Two meta-analyses exploring the relationship between teacher clarity and student learning. *Communication Education, 64*(4), 385–418. doi:10.1080/03634523.2015.1041998.

   Hollo, A., & Wehby, J. H. (2017). Teacher talk in general and special education elementary classrooms. *The Elementary School Journal, 117*, 616–641. doi:10.1086/691605

9 Dunlosky, J., Rawson, K. A., Marsh, E. J., Nathan, M. J., & Willingham, D. T. (2013). Improving students' learning with effective learning techniques promising directions from cognitive and educational psychology. *Psychological Science in the Public Interest, 14*(1), 4–58. doi:10.1177/1529100612453266

   Schwartz, D. L., & Goldstone, R. (2016). Learning as coordination: Cognitive psychology and education. In L. Corno & E. M. Anderman (Eds.), *Handbook of educational psychology* (3rd ed., pp. 59–74). New York, NY: Routledge.

10 Swanson, H., & Ashbaker, M. (2000). Working memory, short-term memory, speech rate, word recognition and reading comprehension in learning disabled readers: Does the executive system have a role? *Intelligence, 28*(1), 1–30. doi:10.1016/S0160-2896(99)00025-2

11 Vaughn, S., Gersten, R., & Chard, D. J. (2000). The underlying message in LD intervention research: Findings from research syntheses. *Exceptional Children, 67*(1), 99–114.

   Swanson, H. L., & Deshler, D. (2003). Instructing adolescents with learning disabilities: Converting a meta-analysis to practice. *Journal of Learning Disabilities, 36*(2), 124–135. doi:10.1177/002221940303600205

12 Grassi, J. R. (1971). Effects of massed and spaced practice on learning in brain-damaged, behavior-disordered, and normal children. *Journal of Learning Disabilities, 4*(5), 237–242. doi:10.1177/002221947100400501

   Dunlosky, J., Rawson, K. A., Marsh, E. J., Nathan, M. J., & Willingham, D. T. (2013). Improving students' learning with effective learning techniques promising directions from cognitive and educational psychology. *Psychological Science in the Public Interest, 14*(1), 4–58. doi:10.1177/1529100612453266

Gettinger, M., Bryant, N. D., & Fayne, H. R. (1982). Designing spelling instruction for learning-disabled children: An emphasis on unit size, distributed practice, and training for transfer. *The Journal of Special Education, 16*(4), 439–448. doi:10.1177/002246698201600407

Cepeda, N. J., Vul, E., Rohrer, D., Wixted, J. T., & Pashler, H. (2008). Spacing effects in learning: A temporal ridgeline of optimal retention. *Psychological Science, 19*(11), 1095–1102. doi:10.1111/j.1467-9280.2008.02209.x

Gerbier, E., & Toppino, T. C. (2015). The effect of distributed practice: Neuroscience, cognition, and education. *Trends in Neuroscience & Education, 4*(3), 49–59. doi:10.1016/j.tine.2015.01.001

13 Kang, S. H. K., Lindsey, R. V., Mozer, M. C., & Pashler, H. (2014). Retrieval practice over the long term: Should spacing be expanding or equal-interval? *Psychonomic Bulletin & Review, 21*(6), 1544–1550. doi:10.3758/s13423-014-0636-z

14 Cepeda, N. J., Vul, E., Rohrer, D., Wixted, J. T., & Pashler, H. (2008). Spacing effects in learning: A temporal ridgeline of optimal retention. *Psychological Science, 19*(11), 1095–1102. doi:10.1111/j.1467-9280.2008.02209.x

Gerbier, E., & Toppino, T. C. (2015). The effect of distributed practice: Neuroscience, cognition, and education. *Trends in Neuroscience & Education, 4*(3), 49–59. doi:10.1016/j.tine.2015.01.001

15 Carpenter, S. K., Cepeda, N. J., Rohrer, D., Kang, S. H. K., & Pashler, H. (2012). Using spacing to enhance diverse forms of learning: Review of recent research and implications for instruction. *Educational Psychology Review, 24*(3), 369–378. doi:10.1007/s10648-012-9205-z

16 Carpenter, S. K., Cepeda, N. J., Rohrer, D., Kang, S. H. K., & Pashler, H. (2012). Using spacing to enhance diverse forms of learning: Review of recent research and implications for instruction. *Educational Psychology Review, 24*(3), 369–378. doi:10.1007/s10648-012-9205-z

17 Cepeda, N., Coburn, N., Rohrer, D., Wixted, J., Mozer, M., & Pashler, H. (2009). Optimizing distributed practice theoretical analysis and practical implications. *Experimental Psychology, 56*(4), 236–246. doi:10.1027/1618-3169.56.4.236

Cepeda, N. J., Pashler, H., Vul, E., Wixted, J. T., & Rohrer, D. (2006). Distributed practice in verbal recall tasks: A review and quantitative synthesis. *Psychological Bulletin, 132*(3), 354–380. doi:10.1037/0033-2909.132.3.354

18 Kang, S. H. K., Lindsey, R. V., Mozer, M. C., & Pashler, H. (2014). Retrieval practice over the long term: Should spacing be expanding or equal-interval? *Psychonomic Bulletin & Review, 21*(6), 1544–1550. doi:10.3758/s13423-014-0636-z

19 Nakata, T. (2015). Effects of expanding and equal spacing on second language vocabulary learning: Does gradually increasing spacing increase vocabulary learning? *Studies in Second Language Acquisition, 37*(4), 677–711. doi:10.1017/S0272263114000825

20 Karpicke, J. D., & Roediger, H. L. (2010). Is expanding retrieval a superior method for learning text materials? *Memory & Cognition, 38*(1), 116–124. doi:10.3758/MC.38.1.116

21 Benjamin, A. S., & Tullis, J. (2010). What makes distributed practice effective? *Cognitive Psychology, 61*(3), 228–247. doi:10.1016/j.cogpsych.2010.05.004

Cepeda, N. J., Pashler, H., Vul, E., Wixted, J. T., & Rohrer, D. (2006). Distributed practice in verbal recall tasks: A review and quantitative synthesis. *Psychological Bulletin, 132*(3), 354–380. doi:10.1037/0033-2909.132.3.354

Rohrer, D., & Taylor, K. (2006). The effects of overlearning and distributed practice on the retention of mathematics knowledge. *Applied Cognitive Psychology, 20*(9), 1209–1224. doi:10.1002/acp.1266

22 Rohrer, D., & Pashler, H. (2007). Increasing retention without increasing study time. *Current Directions in Psychological Science, 16*(4), 183–186. doi:10.1111/j.1467-8721.2007.00500.x

23 Rohrer, D. (2012). Interleaving helps students distinguish among similar concepts. *Educational Psychology Review, 24*, 355–367. doi:10.1007/s10648-012-9201-3

Rohrer, D., Dedrick, R. F., & Stershic, S. (2015). Interleaved practice improves mathematical learning. *Journal of Educational Psychology, 107,* 900–908. doi:10.1037/edu0000001

Taylor, K., & Rohrer, D. (2009). The effects of interleaved practice. *Applied Cognitive Psychology, 24,* 838–848. doi:10.1002/acp.1598

24 Abushanab, B., & Bishara, A. J. (2013). Memory and metacognition for piano melodies: Illusory advantages of fixed-over random practice order. *Memory & Cognition, 41,* 928–937. doi:10.3758/s13421-013-0311-z

Kang, S. H. K. (2017). The benefits of interleaved practice for learning. In J. C. Horvath, J. M. Lodge, & J. Hattie (Eds.), *From the laboratory to the classroom: Translating science of learning for teachers* (pp. 79–93). New York, NY: Routledge.

Kornell, N., & Bjork, R. A. (2008). Learning concepts and categories: is spacing the "enemy of induction"? *Psychological Science, 19,* 585–592. doi:10.1111/j.1467-9280.2008.02127.x

Zulkiply, N., Mclean, J., Butt, J. S., & Bath, D. (2012). Spacing and induction: Application to exemplars presented as auditory and visual text. *Learning and Instruction, 22,* 215–221.

25 Rohrer, D., Dedrick, R. F., & Burgess, K. (2014). The benefit of interleaved mathematics practice is not limited to superficially similar kinds of problems. *Psychonomic Bulletin and Review, 21,* 1323–1330. doi:10.3758/s13423-014-0588-3

Rohrer, D., Dedrick, R. F., & Stershic, S. (2015). Interleaved practice improves mathematical learning. *Journal of Educational Psychology, 107,* 900–908. doi:10.1037/edu0000001

26 VanderStoep, S. W., & Siefert, C. M. (1994). Learning "how" versus learning "when": Improving transfer of problem-solving principles. *Journal of the Learning Science, 3,* 93–111.

27 Pan, S. C. (2015, August 4). *The interleaving effect: Mixing it up boosts learning.* Retrieved 25/4/2017, from www.scientificamerican.com/article/the-interleaving-effect-mixing-it-up-boosts-learning/

28 Kang, S. H. K. (2017). The benefits of interleaved practice for learning. In J. C. Horvath, J. M. Lodge, & J. Hattie (Eds.), *From the laboratory to the classroom: Translating science of learning for teachers* (pp. 79–93). New York, NY: Routledge.

Rohrer, D., Dedrick, R. F., & Burgess, K. (2014). The benefit of interleaved mathematics practice is not limited to superficially similar kinds of problems. *Psychonomic Bulletin and Review, 21,* 1323–1330. doi:10.3758/s13423-014-0588-3

Rohrer, D., Dedrick, R. F., & Stershic, S. (2015). Interleaved practice improves mathematical learning. *Journal of Educational Psychology, 107,* 900–908. doi:10.1037/edu0000001

29 Kang, S. H. K. (2017). The benefits of interleaved practice for learning. In J. C. Horvath, J. M. Lodge, & J. Hattie (Eds.), *From the laboratory to the classroom: Translating science of learning for teachers* (pp. 79–93). New York, NY: Routledge.

Rohrer, D., Dedrick, R. F., & Burgess, K. (2014). The benefit of interleaved mathematics practice is not limited to superficially similar kinds of problems. *Psychonomic Bulletin and Review, 21,* 1323–1330. doi:10.3758/s13423-014-0588-3

Rohrer, D., Dedrick, R. F., & Stershic, S. (2015). Interleaved practice improves mathematical learning. *Journal of Educational Psychology, 107,* 900–908. doi:10.1037/edu0000001

30 Adesope, O. O., Trevisan, D. A., & Sundararajan, N. (2017). Rethinking the use of tests: A meta-analysis of practice testing. *Review of Educational Research, 87*(3), 659–701.

Putman, A. L., Nestojko, J. F., & Roediger III, H. L. (2017). Two strategies to make it stick. In J. C. Horvath, J. M. Lodge, & J. Hattie (Eds.), *From the laboratory to the classroom: Translating science of learning for teachers* (pp. 95–121). New York, NY: Routledge.

31 Abbott, E. E. (1909). On the analysis of the factors of recall in the learning process. *Psychological Monographs, 11,* 159–177.

Dunlosky, J., Rawson, K. A., Marsh, E. J., Nathan, M. J., & Willingham, D. T. (2013). Improving students' learning with effective learning techniques promising directions from cognitive and educational psychology. *Psychological Science in the Public Interest, 14*(1), 4–58. doi:10.1177/1529100612453266

32 Pashler, H., Bain, P., Bottge, B., Graesser, A., Koedinger, K., McDaniel, M., & Metcalfe, J. (2007). *Organizing instruction and study to improve student learning* (NCER 2007–2004). Washington, DC: National Center for Education Research, Institute of Education Sciences, U.S. Department of Education.

33 Adesope, O. O., Trevisan, D. A., & Sundararajan, N. (2017). Rethinking the use of tests: A meta-analysis of practice testing. *Review of Educational Research, 87*(3), 659–701.

Dunlosky, J., Rawson, K. A., Marsh, E. J., Nathan, M. J., & Willingham, D. T. (2013). Improving students' learning with effective learning techniques promising directions from cognitive and educational psychology. *Psychological Science in the Public Interest, 14*(1), 4–58. doi:10.1177/1529100612453266

34 Adesope, O. O., Trevisan, D. A., & Sundararajan, N. (2017). Rethinking the use of tests: A meta-analysis of practice testing. *Review of Educational Research, 87*(3), 659–701.

35 Layton, L. (2015, October 24). Study says standardized testing is overwhelming nation's public schools. *The Washington Post*. Retrieved from www.washingtonpost.com

36 Adesope, O. O., Trevisan, D. A., & Sundararajan, N. (2017). Rethinking the use of tests: A meta-analysis of practice testing. *Review of Educational Research, 87*(3), 659–701.

Dunlosky, J., Rawson, K. A., Marsh, E. J., Nathan, M. J., & Willingham, D. T. (2013). Improving students' learning with effective learning techniques promising directions from cognitive and educational psychology. *Psychological Science in the Public Interest, 14*(1), 4–58. doi:10.1177/1529100612453266

Putman, A. L., Nestojko, J. F., & Roediger III, H. L. (2017). Two strategies to make it stick. In J. C. Horvath, J. M. Lodge, & J. Hattie (Eds.), *From the laboratory to the classroom: Translating science of learning for teachers* (pp. 95–121). New York, NY: Routledge.

37 Dunlosky, J., Rawson, K. A., Marsh, E. J., Nathan, M. J., & Willingham, D. T. (2013). Improving students' learning with effective learning techniques promising directions from cognitive and educational psychology. *Psychological Science in the Public Interest, 14*(1), 4–58. doi:10.1177/1529100612453266

Putman, A. L., Nestojko, J. F., & Roediger III, H. L. (2017). Two strategies to make it stick. In J. C. Horvath, J. M. Lodge, & J. Hattie (Eds.), *From the laboratory to the classroom: Translating science of learning for teachers* (pp. 95–121). New York, NY: Routledge.

Key Resources

1. *explicitinstruction.org.* This companion site to the Archer and Hughes (2011) book (cited in the endnotes) includes free access to a number of videos of the first author using explicit instruction with elementary and secondary students across various subject areas.

2. Hughes, C. A. (2011). Effective design and delivery of task-specific learning strategy instruction for students with learning disabilities. *Focus on Exceptional Children, 44*(2), 1–16. This article (cited in the endnotes) provides an extended example of how the elements of explicit instruction are used to teach cognitive learning strategies in the area of reading comprehension and short essay writing.

3. *Make it Stick.* Brown Roediger, & McDaniel (2014). This book (cited in the endnotes) presents multiple examples of developing and using effective practice strategies. Writing style is engaging and easy to read.

4. Dunlosky, J., Rawson, K. A., Marsh, E. J., Nathan, M. J., & Willingham, D. T. (2013). Improving students' learning with effective learning techniques promising directions from cognitive and educational psychology. *Psychological Science in the Public Interest*, *14*(1), 4–58. doi:10.1177/1529100612453266. This article is written in a more "scholarly" style and can be somewhat technical in places. However, the information contained is very detailed and includes suggestions for implementing them in the class room.

5. Video: Kennedy, M. J., Peeples, K. N., Romig, J. E., Mathews, H. M., Rodgers, W. J. (2017). High Leverage Practice #16: Use Explicit Instruction. https://vimeo.com/239774145. This video contains explanations of the elements of Explicit Instruction as well as clips several teachers using them in their classrooms. https://vimeo.com/266046762

Note. This list is not a comprehensive list of resources.

17
Using Flexible Grouping
Lawrence Maheady, Tim Zgliczynski, and Gliset Colón

Introduction

Special education teachers use flexible grouping to differentiate instruction and meet individual student needs. Grouping patterns change often depending on lesson goals and objectives and may include (a) small groups of same or mixed ability, (b) pairs, (c) whole-class, and (d) individual instruction.[1] Grouping arrangements are used flexibly to accommodate learning differences, promote in-depth academic discussions, and facilitate collaborative student interactions. Teachers use a variety of grouping formats at different times as determined by student skills, prior knowledge, and/or interest.

Within flexible grouping arrangements, students can work collaboratively or independently, and groups may be teacher or student led. The general goal is to give students opportunities to interact with peers in meaningful ways while meeting important learning goals.[2] Research has also found that small, *mixed-ability* groupings promote improved academic and social outcomes (e.g., higher achievement, improved interpersonal relationships, and more positive self-concepts).[3] Flexible grouping promotes on-task behaviors, teaches personal and social responsibility, and improves student social skills.[4] Smaller groups may also be particularly valuable for students with disabilities and culturally and linguistically diverse learners who require explicit, intensive instruction in reading *and* opportunities for collaborative group work with more proficient classmates.

Narrowing the Focus

Given the multiple formats that flexible groupings embody and the frequency with which regrouping occurs, it is difficult to describe it as a distinct and replicable high leverage practice (HLP). Rather, it consists of multiple instructional arrangements that are used for varied purposes and differing amounts of time during typical school days. Discussion of all possible configurations and respective evidence bases is beyond the scope of this chapter. Instead, the focus is on one facet of flexible grouping—the effective and efficient use of small, mixed-ability groups to improve educational outcomes for students with and without disabilities.

Chapter Overview

1. Describe the rationale and purposes served by small instructional groups, particularly mixed-ability groups using cooperative learning structures.

2. Outline major steps for teachers to implement mixed-ability groups with fidelity.
3. Provide a sample lesson that serves as a model for the use of mixed-ability grouping and that integrates cooperative learning structures and instructional technology.

Small Group Instruction

This section describes the essential functions and major components of small group instructional practices and provides a rationale for their use. Particular emphasis is placed on the use of small, mixed-ability groups and how they can be used with Spencer Kagan's cooperative learning structures.[5] Special education teachers can use same-ability (*homogeneous*) and mixed-ability (*heterogeneous*) small groups to meet students' learning goals. Homogeneous groups are used to provide focused, intensive instruction for students with *similar* instructional strengths, needs, and/or interests. They are configured often to meet short-term instructional goals and objectives.[6] To maximize instructional intensity, teachers reduce group sizes (i.e., one to three students has been demonstrated as most effective for improving achievement),[7] provide additional time to ensure student mastery, and/or use interventions that produce high rates of student responding.[8] Chapter 20 (Use Intensive Instruction) describes same-ability small groups in more detail; this chapter focuses solely on the use of mixed-ability groupings.

Mixed-ability groups are designed to include students who *differ* academically (e.g., achievement or ability levels), demographically (e.g., gender, ethnicity, and language dominance), and/or interpersonally (e.g., social and behavioral competence). Academically, groups include students with a range of subject matter knowledge and skills (e.g., high-, high-medium, low-medium, and low-performers); demographically, they reflect the gender, ethnic, and linguistic/cultural composition of the classroom; and interpersonally, groups may include socially skillful students and those with behavioral challenges. Teachers use mixed-ability groups to (a) increase active student engagement in academic discussions, (b) engage students at differing ability levels in sharing knowledge and skills, and (c) improve interpersonal relationships among students with and without disabilities and across racial and ethnic backgrounds.[9]

Research has also shown positive outcomes for students with disabilities. It is estimated, for example, that there is a five- to six-year range in student reading and math achievement levels in typical fourth-grade, inclusive classrooms across the country. These differences are often compounded by diverse cultural and linguistic backgrounds, varied SES-levels, multiple student interests and motivation levels, and disparate learning histories. Given this wide range of needs and abilities, small group instruction can provide students with more opportunities to respond and receive positive and corrective feedback from peers and teachers within individual lessons. Both variables contribute significantly to improved academic achievement.[10]

If structured appropriately, small mixed-ability groups also make more efficient use of teacher and student time. As noted, students get more response opportunities and feedback within lessons, more knowledgeable team members increase groups' likelihood of success (i.e., less need for teacher correction), and teachers gain valuable performance-based feedback to help differentiate instructional time and support.[11] Mixed-ability groups may also reduce discipline problems by distributing students with behavioral issues across different groups and including good social models within each team. Finally, mixed-ability groups create unique teaching arrangements that engage lower and higher performing students in common tasks. Low performers get to see and work with more knowledgeable and skillful peers (i.e., good academic models), and higher achievers benefit from teaching and helping teammates improve their academic competence.

Simply placing students into mixed-ability groups, however, does not guarantee high engagement or academic success. As many teachers can attest and applied researchers have confirmed, *unstruc-*

tured small groups, mixed-ability or not, do not function well.[12] In these groups, students tend to be off-task more often, become disruptive, and seldom reach instructional goals. Mixed-ability groups are also prone to "hog" and "log" effects. Hogs are individuals within teams who dominate interactions, whereas logs typically remain silent and unresponsive; the latter often reflects the small group performance of students with disabilities and those who are culturally and linguistically diverse. The key, therefore, is to ensure that mixed-ability groups are well-formed and *structured* to maximize academic productivity and enhance interpersonal relationships.

Cooperative Learning Groups

Cooperative learning is probably the most well-known and extensively researched instructional approach that uses small, mixed-ability groups. A long and robust research base indicates cooperative learning (a) increases academic achievement, (b) enhances interpersonal relationships, (c) reduces inequitable achievement outcomes, and (d) improves student social skills.[13] Although there are many different cooperative learning models (e.g., Learning Together, Jigsaw, and Student Team Learning), this chapter highlights the use of Kagan's cooperative learning structures.[14]

There are over 150 Kagan cooperative learning structures (e.g., Numbered Heads Together, Sage-N-Scribe, and Quiz-Quiz-Trade) that can be used to meet a wide range of instructional objectives (i.e., academic, behavioral, and interpersonal) across most age and grade levels and throughout all lesson parts (i.e., opening, body, and closing). These structures have a relatively strong research base[15] and are easy to implement, flexible, and widely disseminated commercially. Structures organize student interactions within groups around four basic principles: (a) positive interdependence, (b) individual accountability, (c) equal participation, and (d) simultaneous interaction. In well-structured Kagan groups, all students are engaged actively, equally, and simultaneously.

Using Kagan Structures With Mixed-Ability Groups

There are six basic steps for using Kagan's structural approach with mixed-ability groups. Although individual structures differ in specific implementation requirements, most if not all incorporate the following steps. Table 17.1 shows two short fidelity checklists (i.e., Numbered Heads Together and Rally Robin) that can be used to ensure that structures are implemented as intended.

1. Create mixed-ability groups. The first step is to break the whole class into small groups of two to six students (preferably four) who differ in demographic characteristics and academic competence (e.g., high- to low-achieving). Base group size on existing contextual factors like number of students and their academic and interpersonal competence, instructional goals and objectives, available physical space, and staff training and support.[16] Groups can be formed randomly or systematically, used for short (within lessons) or long (e.g., six weeks) durations, and reconstituted as needed (e.g., under-performing or not working well together). Random assignment is used to reduce bias and maximize heterogeneity within teams, and it is usually done by flipping coins, rolling dice, picking numbers or names from jars, and/or using random number generators or charts.

Mixed-ability groups can also be formed systematically based on student achievement levels in relevant subject areas (e.g., math, literacy, or science). One method ranks students *privately* from highest to lowest (1 = highest to 24 = lowest performing) and assigns them to different groups based on rank (e.g., student #1 to group A, student #2 to group B, #3 to group C, and so on). This results in small groups that are heterogeneous within and homogeneous across (i.e., all groups have high (H), high-average (HA), low-average (LA), and low (L) achievers). Mixed-ability groups can also be formed using *split-half pairings*. Students are ranked again from highest to lowest, but the list is divided in half and placed side-by-side (e.g., students ranked 1 to 12 and 13 to 24). The two highest

Table 17.1 Two Fidelity Checklists for Two Kagan Cooperative Learning Structures: Numbered Heads Together and Rally Robin

---

General Directions:

After observing the class session for a minimum of 20 minutes, check **Yes** next to each item that was *present* during your observation. Check **No** if a particular activity was *not present* during your observation.

Numbered Heads Together

Instructional Activities	*Yes*	*No*
1. Students are seated in small, mixed ability groups.	____	____
2. Students within teams are numbered 1–4.	____	____
3. Teacher-led, whole-group instruction occurs.	____	____
4. Teacher asks knowledge-based question to whole class.	____	____
5. Teacher tells pupils to "put your heads together, come up with the best answer you can, and make sure everyone on the team knows the answer."	____	____
6. Students write individual answers on white boards and share when given signal.	____	____
7. Teacher says, "Boards up," and scans responses.	____	____
8. Students raise boards, teacher randomly picks one numbered student to respond.	____	____
9. Teacher asks, "How many agree, disagree, and/or can add to the answer?"	____	____

*Sub-Total*____ / 9 = _____ %

Comments: _____
_____
_____
_____

Rally Robin

Instructional Activities	*Yes*	*No*
1. Students are seated in small, mixed–ability groups.	____	____
2. Teacher asks academic-related question.	____	____
3. Teacher tells student to pair with shoulder or face partner.	____	____
4. Teacher indicates which partner will start ("A goes first").	____	____
5. Partners go back and forth until answers run out or teacher signals that time is up.	____	____

*Sub-Total*____ / 5 = _____ %

Comments: _____
_____
_____
_____

students in each column (#1 and #13) are paired and assigned to one group, then the next two highest (# 2 and #14) are paired and designated for another group, and so on moving down the columns. The result is that the top "high" students work with top "low" students, and the lowest "high" students work with the lowest "low" students.[17]

2. Create positive interdependence within groups. Once students are in mixed-ability groups, teachers create positive interdependence within each team by establishing conditions that make it more likely those students will work well together. Positive interdependence has been described as an arrangement in which the success of one individual increases the probability of others' success. In these relationships, students are more likely to work together because it maximizes the likelihood of their own success. Special education teachers can create positive interdependence in at least four different ways (i.e., learning goal, task, role, and reward). Positive interdependence in *learning goals* can be established by (a) setting class- or team-wide goals and criteria (e.g., the class/team earns recognition if they answer 85% of math problems correctly), (b) getting group members to agree on preferred team responses, and/or (c) randomly picking individuals to share group knowledge and skills. *Task* interdependence is created by providing one set of materials for group members to share and/or giving each member different parts (i.e., content or materials) that must be combined to complete assignments. *Role* interdependence is developed by assigning separate and rotating roles and responsibilities to group members (e.g., captain, encourager, recorder, and timekeeper), preparing them to play these roles, and then recognizing them for doing so. In one structure (e.g., Showdown Captain), for example, one team member (captain) is responsible for dictating questions/problems, another praises correct or well-formed responses (encourager), a third writes student responses (recorder), and another manages instructional time (timekeeper). Finally, *reward* interdependence is established by providing positive consequences based on individual and/or collective group performance. Groups earn rewards, for example, if their average performance meets criteria (e.g., group average of 80% or higher) and/or if one randomly selected team member meets or exceeds the criteria. Initially, teachers may want to use one or two ways to foster positive interdependence (e.g., shared goals and tasks) and then gradually increase methods as students become more procedurally competent.

3. Use materials and directives to promote effective, efficient, and equal student interactions. Kagan's cooperative learning approach provides extensive instructional resources to promote frequent, productive, and positive interactions among students in mixed-ability groups. The Kagan mat, for example, provides visual cues and a common nomenclature to encourage effective and efficient interactions among group members (see Figure 17.1). As shown, Kagan mats have numbers (1 to 4), letters (A and B), and role designations (i.e., shoulder versus face partners) that are used for multiple purposes. Teachers can use the numbers, for example, to determine who (a) responds to teacher-led, academic questions (i.e., "all number 3s show/tell your answers"), (b) goes first in a discussion or activity (e.g., "Bs go first"), and (c) interacts with whom in the group (e.g., "face" or "shoulder" partners). Face partners are typically seated across from one another while shoulder partners sit side-by-side. Teachers use short directives (e.g., "discuss with face partners" and "Bs go first") to promote effective, consistent, and efficient group interactions. The common language saves instructional time and gives teachers multiple ways to have students interact with different peers throughout lessons.

1. Embed structures to maximize and equalize participation. Table 17.2 provides a list of some Kagan structures, their primary purposes, and a brief summary of how to implement them. Most structures are designed to engage all students simultaneously and ensure everyone has equal response opportunities. Numbered Heads Together, for example, is an alternative question-answering structure that requires all group members to write answers to each teacher-led question on dry erase

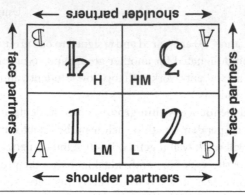

Figure 17.1 Kagan Cooperative Learning Mat

Table 17.2 Some Common Kagan Structures and Response Techniques to Use With Mixed-Ability Groups

Activity	Purpose	Number of Students	Summary
Jot Thoughts (Kagan & Kagan, 2009)	Peer Collaboration	2–4	Teacher poses a question or prompt with a time limit. Students are given slips of paper or sticky notes. Students take turns writing ideas/answers on notes and place them in the center of the table without overlapping.
Sage-N-Scribe (Kagan & Kagan, 2009)	Peer Tutoring	2	Teacher poses numerous questions to students. Partner A (the Sage) begins to instruct partner B on how to solve the question as partner B writes. Partners may coach each other. Partners switch roles for the next question.
Showdown (Kagan & Kagan, 2009)	Peer Tutoring	2–4	Students are given a set of questions. Teacher selects one student to begin as Showdown Captain. Captain selects first question and reads to the group. Teammates solve question and signal when ready. Showdown Captain says, "Showdown!" Team shares and discusses answers. Next student in line becomes Captain for the next question.
Round Robin (Kagan & Kagan, 2009)	Peer Collaboration	4	Teacher poses a problem/question with multiple answers. Students go in order and provide the group with answers, one at a time, until the group runs out of ideas or the teacher calls time.
Mirrors On (Biffle, 2013)	Choral Response	Whole Group	Teacher says, "Mirrors on!" Students repeat the phrase. Teach speaks and gestures and the students must echo each phrase and movement. Teacher says, "Mirrors off!" Students end the echo.
Broken Mirrors On	Choral Response	Whole Group	Similar to Mirrors On. Teacher begins with regular Mirrors On but omits parts of his/her statements. Students must echo the phrase and insert the missing information.
Fist to Five	Self-Evaluation	Whole Group	Teacher prompts students to rate their understanding on a 1 (I don't know this) to 5 (I'm an expert) scale using their fingers. Students close their eyes and share level of understanding with the teacher by raising the appropriate number of fingers.
Gallery Walk	Self-Evaluation	Whole Group	After the completion of an assignment, students are allowed to get up and quietly walk around a room to see peers' work. Teacher may allow students to record positive comments or provide feedback on peers' work.

boards. When finished, students are directed to "put your heads together" (i.e., turn over boards, share and discuss information, agree on best team responses, and make sure all team members know the answer(s)). Teachers *randomly* call a number from one to four (e.g., spins a spinner) and all those "numbered" students stand and share answers. Other students are asked if they agree or disagree and/or if they can "add to" responses (e.g., "how many number 4s can provide more detail?"). Unlike voluntary hand-raising, all students are expected to write, share, and discuss their responses to each teacher question when using Numbered Heads Together.

Sage-N-Scribe requires students to alternate roles with face- or shoulder-partners to answer questions and/or solve academic-related problems. One student (A) serves as Sage and verbally instructs the Scribe (student B) on how to solve a problem. The Scribe must write the solution as the Sage dictates but may also provide corrective feedback if s/he believes the solution is incorrect. In the sample lesson, for example, students work to solve inequality problems by writing appropriate symbols in answer boxes. If student B agrees with the solution, no changes are made, and the Sage praises the Scribe for good work. Students then reverse roles and follow the same procedures on each subsequent item. If disagreements occur, other group members are consulted and, if necessary, the teacher intervenes. Again, all students are actively engaged simultaneously, and response opportunities are equalized.

5. **Monitor student learning and group interaction.** While students are actively engaged in small group work, teachers watch and listen to gauge student understanding, progress, and interpersonal competence. Teachers should observe group interactions formally by moving through the class and asking a few simple questions. Is everyone actively engaged and using the structures as intended? Are all students getting a similar number of response opportunities, and how well are they performing? Are there common problems that require re-teaching, and how productive are individuals and groups? It is equally important to provide positive and/or corrective feedback on students' academic, behavioral, and/or interpersonal performance. Feedback should not be intrusive or disrupt student attention and interactions. Rather, use brief descriptive statements that acknowledge student understanding and progress (e.g.., "great job Cynthia and Greg, that's three consecutive correct responses"), inform them of how accurately they used structures (e.g., "you followed Greg's directions correctly, nicely done"), and/or highlight how well they worked together (e.g., "you took turns and gave one another positive feedback, great work").

6. **Hold students accountable individually and collectively**. Although mixed-ability groups in general, and Kagan structures in particular, *can* improve students' academic and interpersonal performance, there is no guarantee that they will always do so. Therefore, teachers must assess individual and group outcomes before, during, and after their use. Individual assessment strengthens personal accountability (e.g., "I really do need to know this"), and group assessments create the positive interdependence upon which structures were developed. Assessment of individual and collective student outcomes can be facilitated through the use of instructional technologies. For example, Table 17.3 provides a list of electronic systems that allow students to respond simultaneously, receive feedback, and collaborate on an interdependent level and facilitate teacher data collection responsibilities.

These systems are used to collect formative data on student engagement and understanding more efficiently. Plickers, for example, is a set of downloadable response cards with different geometric figures and embedded small letters (a, b, c, or d) on one side (see Figure 17.2). Students use the cards to respond to teacher questions. They hold them with their answers facing up; since all cards are different and letters are written so small, students do not know how one another responded. Teachers scan student responses with cell phones or tablets, record the data, and provide feedback to individuals

Table 17.3 Electronic Response Resources for Assessing Student Engagement and Understanding

Website	Response Type	Description
Nearpod www.nearpod.com	• Multiple choice • Poll • Drawing • Short response	Teacher can upload or create PowerPoint slides and insert activities for students between slides. Students engage in slide activities, and teacher can share student work on all student devices in real time.
Plickers www.plickers.com	• Multiple choice • True/false	Teacher poses questions on a display, and students hold up response cards with ambiguous symbols. Teacher scans cards with a cell phone or tablet.
Kahoot! https://getkahoot.com	• Multiple choice • Quiz • Discussion • Survey	Teacher poses questions on a display, and students respond via individual devices. Student receive immediate corrective feedback and can remain anonymous.
Socrative www.socrative.com	• Multiple choice • Short response • True/false	Teacher creates virtual classrooms where students can answer questions in varying formats. Student answers can be shared with peers as exemplars.
Verso http://versoapp.com	• Short response	Teacher can post questions where student respond with blog-like posts. Teacher can then group students and provide feedback based on responses.
Quiz Socket www.quizsocket.com	• Multiple choice	Teacher can write a question on the board, and students respond via personal devices. No planning or preparation is required.
Poll Everywhere www.polleverywhere.com	• Poll	Teacher posts a poll question, and students answer, anonymously or not, on individual devices using a web code.
Mentimeter www.mentimeter.com	• Multiple choice • Poll • Short answer • Word cloud	Teacher creates an online slideshow. Students are able to answer on individual devices using a web code. Students may post anonymously or not.

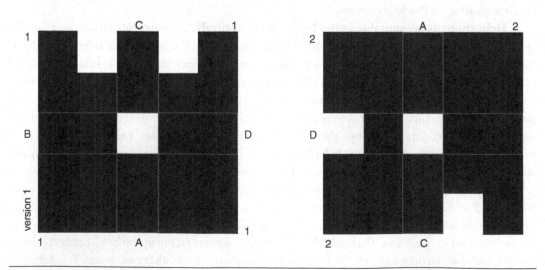

Figure 17.2 Plicker Response Cards That Students Use to Respond to Teacher Questions

and/or the entire class. Teachers can also use Kahoot! To pose and display questions to which students respond via individual devices and receive immediate, corrective, and anonymous feedback.

Using Flexible Groups: A Sample Lesson

Background Information

> **Group being taught:** Third-grade inclusive classroom consisting of 24 students, ages 8–9. Eight students receive special education services. Three students have a learning disability, two have Attention Deficit Hyperactivity Disorder, and three have autism spectrum disorder.

> **Skill to be taught:** Students are continuing a unit on developing number sense and are using less than and greater than symbols to make comparisons between numbers in an inequality.

> **Lesson objective:** Given several pairs of two-digit numbers, students will select and write the correct symbol (< or >) to show an inequality with 90% accuracy.

> **Prerequisite skill(s):** Reading/writing two-digit numbers, knowledge of Kagan Structures (Jot Notes, Sage-N-Scribe, and Showdown)

> **Notes:** Students are seated in groups of four and assigned based on classroom-level assessments. Each group had high-, high-medium, low-medium, and low-performing students.

Anticipatory Set/Lesson Opening

Teacher begins by activating prior knowledge using a Jot Note Activity. Students are asked to take out a set of Post-it notes and write numbers that are more than 20 but less than 40. The teacher rolls a die to determine which student will begin. Each student has a number (e.g., 1, 2, 3 or 4) as determined by the Kagan mat located at the center of their table. The first student writes a single number between 20 and 40 on a Post-it note and places it in the center of the table. Students then take turns adding a single number to the center of the table. This process continues until the students are out of numbers or the teacher calls time.

When time is called, students at each table review their contributions and check for any errors. The teacher then rolls the die again to see which number student at each table can share one of the groups' numbers. The numbers are then placed on the board for the whole class to see.

Example: **20**, 21, 22, 23, . . ., 39, **40**.

The teacher will point out that all numbers to the right of 20 are greater than 20 and all numbers left of 40 are less than 40. The teacher also notes that this method of number comparison is long and difficult; however, there is a much easier way to compare such numbers. The teacher reviews the importance of the target skill using a fist-to-five response technique. First, s/he asks students how confident they feel with writing numbers greater than or less than a given set of numbers. Students close their eyes and respond using the fist-to five-technique, which allows them to show the number of fingers corresponding to their level of understanding (5-very confident, 4-somewhat confident, 3-not sure, 2-not too confident, 1-not confident at all). If the teacher sees most students are confident, s/he proceeds with the body of the lesson. If students still require more practice, s/he provides another example using the numbers 10 and 20. The teacher may also informally assess prior knowledge through response-card prompting where students are asked questions related to numbers between 20 and 40, and they write responses on white boards and then hold them up in unison.

Body of the Lesson

Teacher introduces the less than (<) and greater than (>) symbols.

(I Do)

The teacher models several inequality number pairs (e.g., 15 < 20, 38 > 32) and conducts several *mirrors on* sequences where students repeat the teacher's words and gestures for several more inequality examples. To conduct a *mirrors on* sequence, the teacher speaks the words "mirrors on," and students stand at attention to mimic teacher actions and words until the teacher says, "mirrors off". The teacher writes two numbers on the board (e.g., 27 and 30) and then uses his/her body to make the < or > symbol with their arms as they stand between the two numbers. As the teacher moves, s/he also thinks aloud. The teacher says, "I know 30 is larger than 27, and I always want my greater than symbol to eat the larger number since it looks like an alligator mouth. So I must want to hold my hands this way and eat the 30!" Students follow the example and hold their arms in the same direction as the teacher. The teacher leads students in using this response to several more examples. After more examples, the teacher announces the class is now doing *broken mirrors on*. During this process, the teacher simply writes two numbers on the board and stands between them. When prompted, students must show the proper < or > sign as they stand and face the teacher, but the teacher makes no gestures and simply verbalizes the numbers on the board. The teacher monitors student responses during the *mirrors on* and *broken mirrors on* demonstration to assess student understanding and determine if moving to cooperative learning structures is appropriate.

(We Do)

Teacher selects one student to help model Sage-N-Scribe, a paired peer-tutoring structure, in front of the class. Students pair up with their shoulder partner, and each pair is given a set of 12 inequalities on individual index cards. Working with shoulder partners allows students to work with like-model students (high with high-medium/low with low-medium) to build confidence for larger group work later in the lesson. The teacher instructs all pairs to take out the first inequality and read it and then instructs them to solve it. Student A takes the role of Sage first and instructs student B, the Scribe, on which symbol (< or >) to write in the box. If student B agrees with the chosen symbol, the pair flips their card over and prepares to present their answer to the teacher. When all pairs are ready, the teacher prompts the class to show their answers.

The teacher then instructs students to switch roles, and student B becomes the Sage while student A acts as the Scribe. Another inequality is selected by the teacher, and the process is repeated. The pairs switch off and complete four examples with their shoulder partner. The teacher provides answers to the whole class once the four cards are completed. Next, the teacher tells students to switch partners and work with their face partner at their respective tables. Student A begins as the Sage and student B scribes for the first example. This continues as students switch off for four more examples. The teacher then provides answers to the whole class once the four cards are completed.

After reviewing pairs' answers, the teacher directs students to complete the final four inequalities using Showdown. Each table works together as a heterogeneous group of four, with each student taking the role of captain for one of the four remaining inequalities. Students are now working in mixed-ability groups at the same table but have had substantial practice to allow for positive interdependence in the group. Each student in the group has a copy of each inequality for response purposes. Student 1 takes the role of Showdown Captain first and directs all group members to solve his/her inequality and to give a thumbs up when ready. When all students are ready, the Showdown Captain yells "showdown" and all group members hold up their index card to show their answers to the captain, who checks for accuracy. If any corrections are required, the Showdown Captain works with other group members to provide guidance and feedback. Likewise, group members are responsible for checking the accuracy of the Showdown Captain. Next, student 2 becomes the Showdown Captain, and the same procedure is followed. Each group member serves as Showdown Captain. At the end of the lesson, all students will have answered the remaining four inequalities and received corrective feedback.

(You Do)

At the conclusion of the We Do section, students are given a worksheet of 10 inequalities and are directed to complete the problems by placing < or > in each blank. As students work, the teacher passes out Plicker (www.plickers.com) response cards. Plickers is a response card system where students hold up individual quick response (QR) code symbols to answer multiple choice questions. The teacher, having uploaded the worksheet questions to the Plickers website, is prepared to collect student responses using his/her cellphone and a free Plickers application. This response card system is an improvement over white boards or paper response cards because each card is unique, therefore preventing students from glancing at others' answers, and the teacher is provided with formal assessment data on how students answered.

Once students have completed the worksheet, the teacher displays the first question on the Plickers website, and students hold their QR cards showing A for less than and B for greater than. The teacher unveils the answer after all students have responded, and students are allowed to adjust the next question on their worksheet before answering subsequent questions, making use of immediate, corrective feedback. This process continues until all 10 questions have been reviewed.

Closing of the Lesson

The teacher praises students for properly applying less than and greater than symbols to inequalities. The teacher restates the learning objective and asks students to respond once more using the "fist to five" to collect information on student comfort level regarding inequalities. The teacher informs students they will add the symbol of equal (=) to the comparison of two numbers, and the class continues to learn about new ways to compare numbers. Worksheets and Plicker data are collected and analyzed to determine the need for remediation in upcoming lessons.

Wrap Up

This chapter described small, mixed-ability groups with embedded cooperative learning structures to represent one type of instructional arrangement within the flexible grouping HLP. Here, mixed-ability groups were structured to promote positive interdependence, individual accountability, equal participation, and simultaneous responding;[18] principles that can be embedded into almost any lessons, at any age/grade levels, and/or across multiple subject areas. Small, mixed-ability groups, however, represent only a small proportion of practices used in flexible grouping and an even smaller part of what is known as evidence-based practice(s) (EBP) in special education (e.g., formative assessment, feedback, and meta-cognitive strategies).[19]

Tips

1. **Seek other Kagan structures to meet your students' needs.** We would encourage you to seek out other teachers who are using these strategies for advice, as well as professional development opportunities to expand your skill in using these practices. This can help you become fluent with a core set of cooperative learning structures that can be used to meet a range of student needs.
2. **Expand your instructional repertoire to include other effective grouping practices.** Other chapters in this book can be used to improve your ability to work effectively with both large

and small same-ability groups. The chapter on explicit instruction, for example, describes how teachers design and deliver instruction in ways that result in meaningful and successful engagement for all students while providing them with frequent opportunities to respond and receive performance-based feedback. The chapter on active student engagement offers a variety of "low tech" strategies for getting all students involved during both large and small group instruction, and the chapter on intensive instruction provides useful information for working effectively with same-ability groups to address foundational skills to access grade-level content.

3. **Continue to learn from your students and you will not go wrong.** As B. F. Skinner noted, the learner is never wrong.[20] The only way you will know if learners are making progress, however, is by closely monitoring their ongoing performance. If we knew *in advance* which teaching practices would work with our students, then teaching would be much easier. Unfortunately, we don't know. While high leverage and evidence-based practices increase our likelihood of success, they cannot guarantee it. No matter what practice you use, be sure to closely monitor students' ongoing performance to determine what is and is not working and use this information to make subsequent decisions about which practices to use and with which students. See Chapters 6 (Use Assessment Data) and 10 (Functional Behavioral Assessment) for more information about practices to closely monitor student performance.

Notes

1 Hoffman, J. (2002). Flexible grouping strategies in the multiage classroom. *Theory into Practice*, *41*(1), 47–52.
   Vaughn, S., & Bos, C. S. (2012). *Strategies for teaching students with learning and behavior problems* (8th ed.). Upper Saddle River, NJ: Pearson.
2 Vaughn, S., Schumm, J. S., Klingner, J., & Saumell, L. (1995). Students' views of instructional practices: Implications for inclusion. *Learning Disability Quarterly*, *18*(3), 236–248.
3 Kagan, S., & Kagan, M. (2009). *Kagan cooperative learning*. San Clemente: Kagan Publishing.
4 Velantino, C. (2000). *Flexible grouping*. Houghton Mifflin Company. Retrieved from www.eduplace.com/science/profdev/articles/valentino.html
   Bellanca, J., & Fogerty, R. (2001). *Blueprints for achievement in cooperative classroom* (3rd ed.). Thousand Oaks, CA: Corwin Press.
5 Castle, S., Deniz, C. B., & Tortora, M. (2005). Flexible grouping and student learning in a high-needs school. *Education and Urban Society*, *37*(2), 139–150.
6 Cohen, E. G., & Lotan, R. A. (2014). *Designing group work: Strategies for the heterogeneous Classroom* (3rd ed.). New York, NY: Teachers College.
7 Iverson, S., Tunmer, W., & Chapman, J. (2005). The effects of varying group size on the reading recovery approach to preventive early intervention. *Journal of Learning Disabilities*, *38*, 456–472.
8 McLeskey, J., & Waldron, N. L. (2011). Educational programs for elementary students with learning disabilities: Can they be both effective and inclusive? *Learning Disabilities Research and Practice*, *26*(1), 48–57.
9 Hattie, J. (2009). *Visible learning: A synthesis of over 800 meta-analyses relating to achievement*. London: Routledge.
   Kagan, S., & Kagan, M. (2009). *Kagan cooperative learning*. San Clemente: Kagan Publishing.
10 Heward, W. L., & Wood, C. R. (2015, April). *Improving educational outcomes in America: Can a low-tech, generic teaching practice make a difference?* Oakland, CA: The Wing Institute. Retrieved from www.winginstitute.org/uploads/docs/2013WingSummitWH.pdf
11 Gillies, R. M. (2003). Structuring cooperative group work in classrooms. *International Journal of Educational Research*, *39*(1–2), 35–49.
12 Kagan, S., & Kagan, M. (2009). *Kagan cooperative learning*. San Clemente: Kagan Publishing.

13 Hattie, J. (2009). *Visible learning: A synthesis of over 800 meta-analyses relating to achievement.* London: Routledge.

Johnson, D. W., & Johnson, R. T. (2002). Learning together and alone: Overview and meta-analysis. *Asia Pacific Journal of Education, 53*(1), 95–105.

Johnson, D. W., & Johnson, R. T. (1987). Research shows the benefits of adult cooperation. *Educational Leadership, 45*(3), 27–30.

Johnson, D. W., Johnson, R. T., & Maruyama, G. (1983). Interdependence and interpersonal attraction among heterogeneous and homogeneous individuals: A theoretical formulation and a meta-analysis of the research. *Review of Educational Research, 53*(1), 5–54.

Johnson, D. W., Maruyama, G., Johnson, R. T., Nelson, D., & Skon, L. (1981). Effects of cooperative, competitive, and individualistic goal structures on achievement: A meta-analysis. *Psychological Bulletin, 89*(1), 47–62.

Slavin, R. E. (1987). Ability grouping and student achievement in elementary schools: A best evidence synthesis. *Review of Educational Research, 57*(3), 293–336.

Slavin, R. E. (1990). Achievement effects of ability grouping in secondary schools: A best evidence synthesis. *Review of Educational Research, 60*(3), 471–499.

Stevens, R. J., & Slavin, R. E. (1990). When cooperative learning improves the achievement of students with mild disabilities: A response to Tateyama-Sniezek. *Exceptional Children, 57*(3), 276–280.

14 Kagan, S., & Kagan, M. (2009). *Kagan cooperative learning.* San Clemente: Kagan Publishing.

15 Hunter, W. C., Maheady, L., Jasper, A. D., Williamson, R. L., & Stratton, E. (2015). Numbered heads together as a Tier I instructional strategy in a multi-tiered systems of support. *Education and Treatment of Children, 38*(3), 345–362.

McMillen, C., Mallette, B., Smith, C., Rey, J., Jabot, M., & Maheady, L. (2016). The effects of numbered heads together on the science quiz performance of a 9th grade class. *Journal of Evidence-Based Practices for Schools, 15*(1), 65–89.

16 Slavin, R. E. (1987). Ability grouping and student achievement in elementary schools: A best evidence synthesis. *Review of Educational Research, 57*(3), 293–336.

17 Fuchs, L. S., Fuchs, D., Kazdan, S., & Allan, S. (1999). Effects of peer-assisted learning strategies in reading with and without training in elaborative help giving. *The Elementary School Journal, 99*(3), 201–219.

18 Kagan, S., & Kagan, M. (2009). *Kagan cooperative learning.* San Clemente: Kagan Publishing.

19 Hattie, J. (2009). *Visible learning: A synthesis of over 800 meta-analyses relating to achievement.* London: Routledge.

Horner, R. H., Carr, E. G., Halle, J., McGee, G., Odom, S., & Wolery, M. (2005). The use of single-subject research to identify evidence-based practice in special education. *Exceptional Children, 71*(2), 163–179.

20 Skinner, B. F. (1984). The shame of American education. *American Psychologist, 39*(9), 947–954.

Key Resources

Kagan Publishing, P.O. Box 72008, San Clemente, CA 92673–2008; 1-800-933-2667 or (949) 545–6300; Fax (949) 545–6301; www.KaganOnline.com; Orders@KaganOnline.com

Pinterest

This site is an online pinboard, a visual representation on a social book marketing site. You can share images you find online and/or you can directly upload images onto Pinterest. You can also share your pins on Twitter and Facebook. One particularly relevant location includes 100+ ways to use group students for instruction
www.pinterest.com/explore/grouping-students/

Center for Teaching at Vanderbilt University

This site focuses primarily on how to use cooperative learning groups effectively. It provides numerous learning guides for teachers, explicit examples across numerous age and grade levels, and empirical evidence to support its effectiveness.
https://cft.vanderbilt.edu/guides-sub-pages/setting-up-and-facilitating-group-work-using-cooperative-learning-groups-effectively/

The Lookstein Center for Jewish Education

This is a mini-site for using small, heterogeneous groups. It contains sample units and lessons; the primary focus is on Jewish education. The site also includes professional articles and material and important educational links.
www.lookstein.org/heterogeneous/hetero_instruct.htm

Dare to Differentiate

Dare to Differentiate provide tips for using flexible grouping; information on grouping students by ability; information on collaborative learning; and a special small group learning page.
https://daretodifferentiate.wikispaces.com/Flexible+Grouping

Project IRIS

IRIS is a national center designed to improve educational outcomes for students, particularly those with disabilities from birth to age 21, through the use of evidence-based practices and interventions. Two particularly relevant modules include (a) video on the use of flexible grouping and (b) a case study on effective room arrangements.
https://iris.peabody.vanderbilt.edu

18
Use Strategies to Promote Active Student Engagement
William L. Heward

When students respond frequently to a well-designed lesson, three benefits ensue: more learning, less off-task and inappropriate behavior, and their teacher gets immediate feedback on the lesson's effectiveness. The positive correlation between active student engagement and academic achievement is one of the most well established and robust findings in all of educational research.[1] Many peer-reviewed studies have demonstrated a functional relation between increased student engagement and enhanced learning. These experiments have been conducted in preschool, elementary, and secondary classrooms and with various curriculum content taught to general and special education students, with instructional arrangements including one-to-one tutoring, peer-mediated instruction, and small group and whole-class lessons.[2] Significantly, active student engagement is a defining feature of teaching practices, with the largest effect sizes on achievement: cumulative review (0.88), quantity of instruction (0.84), student verbalization (0.64), and mastery learning (0.58).[3]

When teachers increase active student engagement, off-task and disruptive behavior decreases. Researchers have replicated this finding with general and special education students in pre-K through secondary classrooms in urban, rural, and suburban schools.[4] For example, in a study conducted in two urban fourth-grade classrooms, the nine most disruptive boys, who were also the lowest performers, were observed during daily math lessons. When their teachers shifted from calling upon one student at a time to answer questions to having every student answer in unison by holding up a response card, immediate and substantial reductions in disruptive behavior occurred for all nine students.[5]

Tactics that promote active student engagement are valuable not only because of the practice they afford students but also because of the feedback they provide to teachers. In an effort to assess student learning, teachers often ask, "Do you understand?" (an unreliable practice at best because many students will answer "Yes" when they may not understand at all). When lessons entail high rates of active student engagement, teachers need never wonder if their students are "getting it." The accuracy and firmness of their students' responses let teachers judge lesson effectiveness in real time. Teachers can adjust a lesson on the fly by providing additional instructional trials on a particular concept or skill or skipping ahead as students' performance dictates.

An additional benefit of teaching practices that promote active student engagement: students prefer lessons in which they respond at high rates to lessons in which they are expected to passively attend or wait for the teacher to call on one student at a time to respond.[6] In one study, 95% of kindergarten children indicated they liked answering teacher questions by holding up response cards better than raising their hands to be called upon.[7]

Narrowing the Focus

Educators measure student engagement during instruction in various ways, the most common being time on task; academic learning time (ALT: the time a student spends engaged with academically relevant materials of moderate difficulty);[8] opportunities to respond (OTR: the number or rate of lesson-related questions or prompts a teacher provides to the group or individual students);[9] and active student response (ASR).[10]

Figure 18.1 relates these measures to one another in the context of potential, planned, and delivered instruction. ASR, the most direct and sensitive measure of student engagement, is represented by the bull's eye. Active student response occurs each time a student makes a detectable, lesson-specific response. Responses qualifying as ASR are as varied as teachers' objectives for their lessons: words read, sentences written, ratios computed, distances measured, musical scales played, artistic genres identified, and molecules analyzed may all count as ASR.

As a metric of student engagement, ASR offers important advantages:

- As a direct measure of student responses to instruction, ASR reveals what Benjamin Bloom[11] called an alterable variable: a factor that influences student learning and that teachers can control.
- ASR yields more information about student performance than time-based measures. For example, on-task or ALT data showing that two students each spent 15 minutes working on algebra problems would not reveal that one student solved 30 problems while the other student calculated just 5.

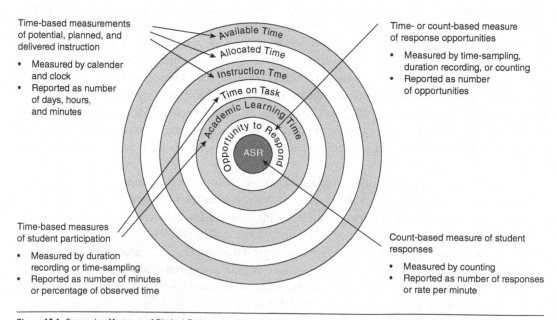

Figure 18.1 Comparing Measures of Student Engagement in the Context of Potential, Planned, and Delivered Instruction

Source: Adapted from "Three 'Low-Tech' Strategies for Increasing the Frequency of Active Student Response During Group Instruction" by W. L. Heward, 1994. In R. Gardner III, D. M. Sainato, J. O. Cooper, T. E. Heron, W. L. Heward, J. Eshleman, & T. A. Grossi (Eds.), Behavior Analysis in Education: Focus on Measurably Superior Instruction (pp. 287). Monterey, CA: Brooks/Cole.

- ASR data are collected and reported as rate of response (typically the number of responses per minute). Rate measures are sensitive to changes in instructional practices and unlimited by ceilings, as are engagement measures reported as duration of time or percentage of observed intervals.
- ASR can be measured in lessons taught in any instructional format (e.g., teacher-led whole class or small group, peer mediated, self-directed), setting (e.g., classroom, science lab, music room, gym, community-based instruction), or curriculum area.
- ASR data are easy to obtain: teachers—or students themselves—tally the number of responses.

Chapter Overview

1. Describe challenges of group instruction and a possible solution.
2. Describe how to implement choral responding to increase active student engagement and learning.
3. Describe how to use response cards to increase active student engagement and learning.

Group Instruction: Difficult Challenge and a Possible Solution

Students spend most of their school days in groups. Teacher-led group instruction is the most common instructional format in the regular classroom, regardless of grade or student performance level.[12] A study entailing 1,277 observations over 327 hours in elementary and secondary classrooms found that 63% of available class time was devoted to group instruction (49% whole class, 14% small group).[13]

Teaching more than one student at a time, be it a small group of 4 or a classroom of 24, is demanding. Group instruction presents teachers with five major tasks: maintain students' attention, give each student sufficient opportunities to respond, provide feedback for students' responses, monitor students' learning, and prevent and address disruptive behavior. The challenges posed by group instruction hold particular significance for students with disabilities and the teachers, both general and special educators, responsible for their learning. Most students with disabilities spend the majority of the school day participating in Tier I instruction in inclusive general education classrooms. Most Tier II interventions are delivered to small groups.

Meeting the challenges posed by group instruction is so difficult that when students just pay attention and do not misbehave, a lesson may be considered a success. While on-task behavior is desirable—an on-task student is more likely to learn than an off-task one—accepting a high level of on-task behavior as evidence of an effective lesson is a mistake. Students can pay attention but make no lesson-related responses. And the research is clear: lessons in which students make many responses produce more learning than lessons in which students passively attend.[14]

Teachers know active student engagement is important. The most prevalent practice for obtaining student participation during group instruction is asking questions to the class and calling on students who volunteer to answer by raising their hands. While this practice provides ASR for the student called upon to answer, his or her classmates are usually passive observers at best. Calling upon individual students is problematic for another reason: high achievers answer most questions while students with disabilities and low achievers, for whom active participation is needed most, make few or no responses.[15]

The challenge: keeping *every student* actively engaged throughout group lessons. A solution: practices that encourage all students in the group to respond simultaneously to teacher-posed questions. Researchers have demonstrated the effectiveness of several such "high-ASR" techniques, chief among them choral responding (CR) and response cards (RC). In addition to strong research evidence supporting their use, CR and RC are "low-tech" practices in that they are inexpensive, require few if any materials, require no equipment to maintain or software to keep current, are not susceptible to internet/connection glitches, are easy for teachers to learn to implement, and can be applied immediately in any classroom.

Choral Responding

Choral responding—students responding orally in unison to a series of teacher-posed questions—is the simplest, quickest way to increase student engagement. CR can be used effectively with any curriculum content meeting three criteria: (a) each question has only one correct answer; (b) each question can be answered with a brief oral response or verbal chain (e.g., counting by fives); and (c) the questions can be presented at a lively pace. Teachers have designed CR-based lessons for basic academic skills such as math and reading, subject matter content such as history and science, and sequences of steps for solving higher-level problems. CR can also be used with existing curriculum materials.[16] For example, in one study general education teachers enhanced the effectiveness of a published, core-reading program with CR.[17]

Peer-reviewed studies reporting positive effects of CR on student engagement, learning, and behavior have been published since the 1980s.[18] CR has been used successfully with students from preschool through high school, with general education students,[19] and with students with various disabilities.[20] When used in a well-designed program, CR can produce measurable learning outcomes in a single lesson.[21]

Choral Responding Procedures

CR is a relatively simple instructional practice that teachers report as easy to learn.[22] Figure 18.2 describes the basic procedure and suggested guidelines for conducting choral responding. Brief, two-to-three-minute bouts of CR can be used to review key points from previous lessons, to prime students' background knowledge when introducing new content, at various points during a lesson, and as an end-of-the-lesson review.

Example of a CR-Based Lesson

Simply increasing student engagement is no guarantee of improved learning. Students should respond to a well-designed sequence of examples and non-examples and receive positive and corrective feedback as illustrated in the script for a lesson teaching the greater than and less than arithmetic symbols shown in Figure 18.3.

Response Cards

Response cards (RC)—items students hold up simultaneously to display their answers to teacher-posed questions—are another low-tech alternative to one-student-at-a-time participation. With *pre-printed RCs*, students select the card with the answer of their choice. Examples include yes/true and no/false cards, colors, historical figures or events, traffic signs, chemical symbols from the periodic table, parts of speech, and artistic genres. A single RC with multiple answers printed on different sections can also be used (e.g., setting, characters, theme, point of view, and plot for a lesson on parts of a narrative story). Students hold up their cards with closed fingers or a plastic clothespin indicat-

- *Give Clear Directions and Model the Activity*—Tell students the types of questions to be asked and demonstrate one or two trials by acting out the roles of teacher and students. For example: "How many hydrogen atoms in a molecule of methane?" [pause briefly, give signal for students to respond] "Four."
- *Provide a Brief Thinking Pause Before Signaling Students to Respond*—Let the complexity of the question/problem and students' relative level of mastery determine the duration of the pause. If a thinking pause greater than four or five seconds is required for students to answer, break the content into smaller chunks.
- *Signal Students to Respond*—Use a clear, consistent auditory and/or visual signal for students to respond. For example, "Class," "How many?," a finger snap, or a hand or arm movement. Saying "Get ready" immediately before signaling the students' response promotes unison responding.
- *Provide Positive and Constructive Feedback*—When you hear only correct answers confirm and/or praise and immediately present the next question. When one or two incorrect responses are heard, (1) confirm the majority response and restate the correct answer in context with the question (e.g., "Yes. A molecule of methane contains hydrogen atoms."), and (2) repeat the question a few trials later. When you hear more than a few incorrect responses, (1) state the correct answer with a *brief* explanation, (2) immediately repeat the question for CR, and (3) present the same question again several trials later.
- *Intersperse Individual Turns*—Now and then, instead of signaling a CR, call on an individual student. Present the question before calling a randomly selected student's name so students cannot predict when they will be called on. Individual turns are a great way to give students with special needs opportunities to shine in front of their classmates. After a target student chorally voices a correct response, repeat the question several trials later and call on that student to answer individually.
- *Maintain a Lively Pace*—When teachers conduct CR at a fast pace, students make more responses, respond with higher accuracy, and engage in less off-task behavior. Prepare questions and examples prior to the lesson so you can focus on students' responses and move from one learning trial to the next without hesitation.

Figure 18.2 Guidelines for Choral Responding

Source: Adapted from W. L. Heward and C. L. Wood, 2015, Improving Educational Outcomes in America: Can a Low-Tech, Generic Teaching Practice Make a Difference? Oakland, CA: Wing Institute.

ing their answers. Figures 18.4 and 18.5 show examples of teacher-prepared preprinted RC for various lessons.

With *write-on RCs* students mark their answers on blank cards that they erase between learning trials. Write-on RCs can be custom-made for specific subject matter. Music students might mark notes named or played by the teacher on a response card with permanent treble and bass clef scales. Students in a driver's education class could look at projected photos of traffic patterns and draw where their car should go on response cards with various street and highway configurations as permanent backgrounds.

Teachers can obtain a set of 40 durable write-on RCs from a 4-by-8-foot sheet of white laminated bathroom board (available from home improvement stores). The cost is about $25, including the charge for cutting the sheet into 9-by-12-inch RCs. Other materials that can be used as write-on RCs include small chalkboards, laminated file folders, and plastic plates. Dry-erase markers are available at office supply stores; paper towels, old socks, or wash clothes make excellent RC erasers.

Effectiveness of RC

More than two dozen peer-reviewed studies on RCs have compared RCs to the practice of calling upon individual students who have raised their hands to answer. These studies have produced a

Teacher and Student Script	Number Sets on the Chalkboard			

Step 1: Identify the bigger number	Before		After	
Teacher: "I'm going to point to some numbers. When I touch under the numbers, you say which number is bigger." *Point under the first set.* "Get ready." **Students:** "Eight" **Teacher:** "Yes, eight is correct!" *Teacher circles the number eight and touches under the next set.* "Get ready." **Students:** "Seven." **Teacher:** "Way to go! Seven is bigger than two! *Teacher circles the number seven. Repeat for last three sets.* *Erase numbers and write new number sets.*	8 2 9 7 4	3 7 10 6 3	⑧ 2 9 ⑦ ④	3 ⑦ ⑩ 6 3

Step 2a: State rule about bigger numbers	Before		After	
Teacher: "Listen to this rule. The big number gets two dots. Say that." **Students:** "The big number gets two dots." **Teacher:** "Yes, the big number gets two dots." *Point under the first set of numbers.* "When I touch under the numbers, you say which number is bigger." *Point under the first set.* "Get ready." **Students:** "Six." **Teacher:** "You got it! Six is bigger! So, which number gets two dots?" **Students:** "Six." **Teacher:** *Makes two dots next to the six* (shown in the after box). *Repeat for next two number sets.*	3 5 4	6 8 1	3 5 4:	:6 :8 1

Step 2b: State rules about bigger and smaller numbers	Before		After	
Teacher: "Listen. The big number gets two dots. Say that." **Students:** "The big number gets two dots." **Teacher:** "Listen. The small number gets only one dot. Say that." **Students:** "The small number gets only one dot." *Repeat until students can firmly say both rules.* **Teacher:** *Point under the third set of numbers.* "Which number is bigger? Get ready." **Students:** "Ten." **Teacher:** Yes, ten. So, which number gets two dots?" **Students:** "Ten." **Teacher:** *Makes two dots next to the ten.* "Which number gets only one dot?" **Students:** "Five." **Teacher:** "Super work. Five only gets one dot." *Makes one dot next to the five. Repeat next two sets. Erase and write new number sets.*	10 0 6	5 3 4	10: 0. 6:	.5 :3 .4

Figure 18.3 Script for a Choral-Response-Based Lesson on the > and < Math Symbols

similar pattern of findings in favor or RCs: much higher rates of ASR, higher scores by students on quizzes and tests of lesson content, and student preference for RCs.[23] In addition to increased student engagement and learning outcomes, several studies have found improved on-task behavior and/or decreases in disruptive behavior when students used RCs.[24]

Step 3: Draw > and < symbols	Before		After
Repeat Step 2b with new number sets. After the first set, show students how to connect the dots. **Teacher:** "Now I'm going to show you how to connect the dots. Watch me." *Draw a line from the higher dot of the bigger number to the single dot of the smaller number, and back to the lower dot of the bigger number (see after box).* *Present the remaining number sets.* *Show examples of correctly drawing lines and examples of incorrectly drawing the lines. Have students CR if you are "right" or "wrong."* *Erase and write new number sets.*	4 9 8 0 4	1 3 7 10 5	4 > 1 9 > 3 8 > 7 0 < 10 4 < 5
Step 4: Read number sentences with > and < symbols	**Before**		**After**
Repeat steps 1–3. After the first number set, show students how to read the number sentence: **Teacher:** "Listen. Another word for bigger is greater. What is another word for bigger?" **Students:** "Greater." **Teacher:** "Yes, another word for bigger is greater. Way to go! Listen. Another word for smaller is lesser. What is another word for smaller?" **Students:** "Lesser." **Teacher:** "You got it! I will read the first number sentence. Watch and listen." **Teacher:** "Eight is greater than two. Your turn to read the number sentence." **Students:** "Eight is greater than two." *Repeat for remaining number sets.* *Write more number sets. Have students CR through all the steps. Call on an individual student at times to assess his or her performance.*	8 8 4 3 6	2 10 7 1 8	8 > 2 8 > 10 4 < 7 3 > 1 6 < 8

Figure 18.3 (Continued)

Figure 18.4 Teacher-Prepared Preprinted Response Cards

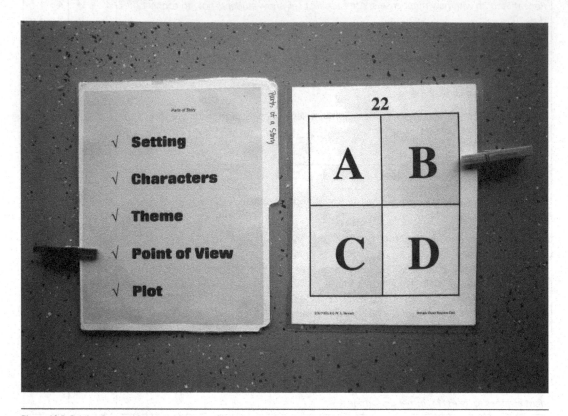

Figure 18.5 Teacher-Prepared Preprinted Response Cards

How to Use RC

Figure 18.5 contains suggestions for using RC.

Wrap Up

Participants at the 2013 annual summit meeting hosted by Wing Institute for Evidence-Based Practice identified 46 practice elements related to effective instruction (e.g., cumulative review, classroom rules and procedures, data collection, formative assessment, guided practice, teacher-student relations). Recognizing that teachers cannot be expected to master and implement every practice, participants were asked to "prioritize those practices you consider most important." The group of 20 experts in general and special education ranked *high rates of student responding* as the most important teaching practice. Not surprisingly, active student engagement is inherently intertwined and supportive of other HLPs featured in this volume. ASR is a defining feature of explicit instruction (HLP 16) and a requisite element of intensive instruction (HLP 20). ASR also provides teachers with frequent opportunities to provide positive, constructive feedback to students (HLP 22).

Unison response techniques such as choral responding and response cards boost student engagement markedly. When a fourth-grade teacher implemented response cards in daily social studies lessons, each of the six students targeted for observation answered 30 more questions per 20-minute lesson than when their teacher called upon one student at a time to answer.[25] Extending this gain in ASR of using response cards for just 20 minutes per day over the course of a 180-day school year would enable each student to make more than 5,000 additional academic responses. If teachers

All Types of Response Cards

- Model several trials and have students practice using their RCs.
- Give clear cues when students are to hold up and put down their cards.
- Maintain a lively pace throughout the activity; keep intervals between trials short.
- Remember that students can learn from watching others; do not let them think looking at classmates' RCs is cheating.

Preprinted Response Cards

- Design the cards to be easy for you and students to see (e.g., consider size, print type, color codes).
- Make the cards easy for students to manipulate and display (e.g., put answers on both sides, attach a group of related cards to a ring; see Figure 18.4).
- Begin instruction on new content with a small set of fact/concept cards (perhaps only two); gradually add cards as students' skills improve.

Write-On Response Cards

- Limit language-based responses to one to three words.
- Keep a few extra markers on hand.
- Be sure students do not hesitate to respond because they are concerned about spelling mistakes: (a) provide several practice trials with new terms before the lesson begins; (b) write new terms on the board, and tell students to refer to them during the lesson; and/or (c) use the "don't worry" technique: tell students to try their best and that misspellings will not count against them.
- Many students enjoy doodling on their RCs. Now and then after a good lesson, let students draw on them for a short time.

Adapted from W. L. Heward, R. Gardner III, R. A. Cavanaugh, F. H. Courson, T. A. Grossi, & P. M. Barbetta, 1996, Everyone Participates in This Class: Using Response Cards to Increase Active Student Response. *Teaching Exceptional Children, 28*(2), 4–10.

Figure 18.5 Recommendations for Using Response Cards

incorporated CR and RC in multiple lessons across the school day, students would make tens of thousands more responses per school year, perhaps a million more responses to the curriculum by graduation day.

Imagine students leaving high school after making a million more responses during their K–12 careers. Wouldn't that help close the achievement gap? Hopefully, teachers will give researchers the opportunity to answer that question someday.

Tips

1. **Individualize to meet student needs.** A student who does not speak might use an augmentative communication device to chorally respond with classmates. A student with visual impairment might use a RC embossed with braille. Some students may use preprinted RCs while classmates use write-on RCs during the same lesson. A peer might assist a student with a motor impairment to display her RCs.
2. **Remember: The instructional items students respond to and the feedback received for those responses determine what is learned.** Some educators mistakenly believe high-ASR lessons featuring CR and RC can only produce low-level, rote learning because students make simple

responses. The form or topography of students' responses does not determine what they learn. A single-word response, such as "next" or "oxygen," might demonstrate that a student has recognized a new vocabulary item, acquired a bit of factual knowledge, deduced a logical outcome, or identified a step in a complex problem-solving sequence.

3. **Remember: More ASR is not always better.** Although too much practice is rare in most classrooms,[26] common sense and some research suggest ceilings above which additional practice is a waste of time.[27] The number of practice trials needed for mastery is an unknown and variable target, but frequent ASR helps teachers identify and hone in on it.

4. **Expand your repertoire of student engagement practices.** Other high-ASR practices with solid research support include fluency-building activities,[28] guided notes,[29] class-wide peer tutoring,[30] and collaborative learning arrangements (see HLP 17). Digital tools for increasing engagement are also available[31] (see Twyman & Heward, in Key Resources).

5. **Encourage "good noise."** Students prefer moving over sitting passively, talking over enforced silence. Keep CR and RC activities upbeat and fast moving. Recognize and praise participation. Incorporate games and group contingencies for responding on signal. Let students earn the privilege of presenting questions to their classmates for unison response. Have fun!

Notes

1 Greenwood, C. R., Delquadri, J., & Hall, R. V. (1984). Opportunity to respond and student academic achievement. In W. L. Heward, T. E. Heron, D. S. Hill, & J. Trap-Porter (Eds.), *Focus on behavior analysis in education* (pp. 58–88). Columbus, OH: Merrill.

  Ellis, E. S., Worthington, L. A., & Larkin, M. J. (1994). *Executive summary of research synthesis of effective teaching principles and the design of quality tools for educators.* (Technical Report No. 6). Eugene, OR: University of Oregon, National Center to Improve the Tools of Educators. Retrieved 6/7/2017, from http://eric.ed.gov/?id=ED386854

2 MacSuga-Gage, A. S., & Simonsen, B. (2015). Examining the impact of opportunities to respond on student outcomes: A systematic review of the literature. *Education and Treatment of Children, 38*(2), 211–240.

3 *Effect size* is a statistical measure of the strength or magnitude of one variable's influence on another. Hattie concluded that instructional practices with effect sizes of +0.4 and above on learning contribute to valuable student achievement outcomes. Hattie, J. (2009). *Visible learning: A synthesis of over 800 meta-analyses relating to achievement.* New York, NY: Routledge. [Note: with an effect size of 0.71, high rates of responding ranked third among all teaching practices analyzed by Hattie.].

4 Armendariz, F., & Umbreit, J. (1999). Using active responding to reduce disruptive behavior in a general education classroom. *Journal of Positive Behavior Interventions, 1*(3), 152–158.

  Haydon, T., Marsicano, R., & Scott, T. M. (2013). A comparison of choral and individual responding: A review of the literature. *Preventing School Failure, 57*, 181–188.

  Wood, C. L., Mabry, L. E., Kretlow, A. G., Lo, Y., & Galloway, T. W. (2009). Effects of preprinted response cards on students' participation and off-task behavior in a rural kindergarten classroom. *Rural Special Education Quarterly, 28*(2), 39–47.

5 Lambert, M. C., Cartledge, G., Lo, Y., & Heward, W. L. (2006). Effects of response cards on disruptive behavior and participation by fourth-grade students during math lessons in an urban school. *Journal of Positive Behavioral Interventions, 8*, 88–99.

6 Randolph, J. J. (2007). Meta-analysis of the research on response cards: Effects on test achievement quiz achievement, participation, and off-task behavior. *Journal of Positive Behavioral Interventions, 9*, 113–128.

7 Wood, C. L., Mabry, L. E., Kretlow, A. G., Lo, Y., & Galloway, T. W. (2009). Effects of preprinted response cards on students' participation and off-task behavior in a rural kindergarten classroom. *Rural Special Education Quarterly, 28*(2), 39–47.

8 Fisher, C. S., Berliner, C. D., Filby, N. N., Marliave, R., Cahen, L. S., & Dishaw, M. M. (1980). Teaching behaviors, academic learning time, and student achievement. In C. Denham & A. Lieberman (Eds.), *Time to learn* (pp. 7–22). Washington, DC: National Institute of Education.

9 MacSuga-Gage, A. S., & Simonsen, B. (2015). Examining the impact of opportunities to respond on student outcomes: A systematic review of the literature. *Education and Treatment of Children, 38*(2), 211–240.

Stichter, J. P., Lewis, T. J., Whittaker, T. A., Richter, M., Johnson, N. W., & Trussell, R. P. (2009). Assessing teacher use of opportunities to respond and effective classroom management strategies: Comparisons among high- and low-risk elementary schools. *Journal of Positive Behavior Interventions, 11,* 68–81.

10 Greenwood, C. R., Delquadri, J., & Hall, R. V. (1984). Opportunity to respond and student academic achievement. In W. L. Heward, T. E. Heron, D. S. Hill, & J. Trap-Porter (Eds.), *Focus on behavior analysis in education* (pp. 58–88). Columbus, OH: Merrill.

Stanley, S. O., & Greenwood, C. R. (1983). How much "opportunity to respond" does the minority disadvantage student receive in school? *Exceptional Children, 49,* 370–373.

11 Bloom, B. S. (1980). The new direction in educational research: Alterable variables. *Phi Delta Kappan, 61,* 382–385.

12 Hollo, A., & Hirn, R. G. (2015). Teacher and student behaviors in the contexts of grade-level and instructional grouping. *Preventing School Failure, 59*(1), 30–39.

13 Scott, T. M., Alter, P. J., & Hirn, R. (2011). An examination of typical classroom context and instruction for students with and without behavioral disorders. *Education and Treatment of Children, 34*(4), 619–642.

14 MacSuga-Gage, A. S., & Simonsen, B. (2015). Examining the impact of opportunities to respond on student outcomes: A systematic review of the literature. *Education and Treatment of Children, 38*(2), 211–240.

Haydon, T., Marsicano, R., & Scott, T. M. (2013). A comparison of choral and individual responding: A review of the literature. *Preventing School Failure, 57,* 181–188.

Heward, W. L. (1994). Three "low-tech" strategies for increasing the frequency of active student response during group instruction. In R. Gardner III, D. M. Sainato, J. O. Cooper, T. E. Heron, W. L. Heward, J. Eshleman, & T. A. Grossi (Eds.), *Behavior analysis in education: Focus on measurably superior instruction* (pp. 283–320). Monterey, CA: Brooks/Cole.

15 Hunter, W. C., Maheady, L., Jasper, A. D., Williamson, R. L., Murley, R. C., & Stratton, E. (2015). Numbered heads together as a Tier 1 instructional strategy in multitiered systems of support. *Education and Treatment of Children, 38*(3), 345–362. [See discussion of research on hand raising on p. 349.].

16 Sindelar, P. T., Bursuck, W. D., & Halle, J. W. (1986). The effects of two variations of teacher questioning on student performance. *Education and Treatment of Children, 9,* 56–66.

Sainato, D. M., Strain, P. S., & Lyon, S. L. (1987). Increasing academic responding of handicapped preschool children during group instruction. *Journal of the Division of Early Childhood Special Education, 12,* 23–30.

17 Bursuck, W. D., Smith, T., Munk, D., Damer, M., Mehlig, L., & Perry, J. (2004). Evaluating the impact of a prevention-based model of reading on children who are at risk. *Remedial and Special Education, 25,* 303–313.

18 Sindelar, P. T., Bursuck, W. D., & Halle, J. W. (1986). The effects of two variations of teacher questioning on student performance. *Education and Treatment of Children, 9,* 56–66.

Sainato, D. M., Strain, P. S., & Lyon, S. L. (1987). Increasing academic responding of handicapped preschool children during group instruction. *Journal of the Division of Early Childhood Special Education, 12,* 23–30.

19 Kretlow, A. G., Cooke, N. L., & Wood, C. L. (2012). Using in-service and coaching to increase teachers' accurate use of research-based strategies. *Remedial and Special Education, 33*(6), 348–361.

Maheady, L., Michielli-Pendl, J., Mallette, B., & Harper, G. F. (2002). A collaborative research project to improve the performance of a diverse sixth grade science class. *Teacher Education and Special Education, 25*(1), 55–70.

20 Kamps, D. M., Dugan, E. P., Leonard, B. R., & Doust, P. M. (1994). Enhanced small group instruction using choral responding and student interaction for children with autism and developmental disabilities. *American Journal on Mental Retardation, 99,* 60–73.

Sterling, R., Barbetta, P. M., Heward, W. L., & Heron, T. E. (1997). A comparison of active student response and on-task instruction on the acquisition and maintenance of health facts by fourth grade special education students. *Journal of Behavioral Education, 7,* 151–165.

21 Kretlow, A. G., Wood, C. L., & Cooke, N. L. (2011). Using in-service and coaching to increase kindergarten teachers' accurate delivery of group instructional units. *The Journal of Special Education, 44*(4), 234–246.

22 Kretlow, A. G., Cooke, N. L., & Wood, C. L. (2012). Using in-service and coaching to increase teachers' accurate use of research-based strategies. *Remedial and Special Education, 33*(6), 348–361.

23 Schnoor, C. I., Freeman-Green, S., & Test, D. W. (2016). Response cards as a strategy for increasing opportunities to respond: An examination of the evidence. *Remedial and Special Education, 37*(1), 41–51.

Horn, C. (2010). Response cards: An effective intervention for students with disabilities. *Education and Training in Autism and Developmental Disabilities, 45,* 116–123.

24 Wood, C. L., Mabry, L. E., Kretlow, A. G., Lo, Y., & Galloway, T. W. (2009). Effects of preprinted response cards on students' participation and off-task behavior in a rural kindergarten classroom. *Rural Special Education Quarterly, 28*(2), 39–47.

Lambert, M. C., Cartledge, G., Lo, Y., & Heward, W. L. (2006). Effects of response cards on disruptive behavior and academic responding by fourth-grade urban students. *Journal of Positive Behavioral Interventions, 8,* 88–99.

25 Narayan, J. S., Heward, W. L., Gardner III, R., Courson, F. H., & Omness, C. (1990). Using response cards to increase student participation in an elementary classroom. *Journal of Applied Behavior Analysis, 23,* 483–490.

26 Chard, D. J., & Kame'enui, E. J. (2000). Struggling first-grade readers: The frequency and progress of their reading. *The Journal of Special Education, 34,* 28–38.

Stichter, J. P., Lewis, T. J., Whittaker, T. A., Richter, M., Johnson, N. W., & Trussell, R. P. (2009). Assessing teacher use of opportunities to respond and effective classroom management strategies: Comparisons among high- and low-risk elementary schools. *Journal of Positive Behavior Interventions, 11,* 68–81.

27 Cuvo, A. J., Ashley, K. M., Marso, K. J., Bingju, L. Z., & Fry, T. A. (1995). Effect of response practice variables on learning spelling and sight vocabulary. *Journal of Applied Behavior Analysis, 28,* 155–173.

28 Tam, K. Y. B., Heward, W. L., & Heng, M. A. (2006). A reading intervention program for English-language learners who are struggling readers. *The Journal of Special Education, 40,* 79–93.

29 Konrad, M., Joseph, L. M., & Itoi, M. (2011). Using guided notes to enhance instruction for all students. *Intervention in School and Clinic, 46,* 131–140.

30 Maheady, L., Mallette, B., & Harper, G. F. (2006). Four classwide peer tutoring models: Similarities, differences, and implications for research and practice. *Reading and Writing Quarterly, 22,* 65–89.

31 Twyman, J. S., & Heward, W. L. (2016). How to improve student learning in every classroom now. *International Journal of Educational Research* doi:10.1016/j.ijer.2016.05.007.

Key Resources

Heward, W. L., & Wood, C. (2015, April). *Improving educational outcomes in America: Can a low-tech, generic teaching practice make a difference?* Oakland, CA: The Wing Institute. Retrieved from www.winginstitute.org/uploads/docs/2013WingSummitWH.pdf

Twyman, J. S., & Heward, W. L. (2016). How to improve student learning in every classroom now. *International Journal of Educational Research* doi:10.1016/j.ijer.2016.05.007.

Twyman, J. S., & Tincani, M. (2016). *Enhancing engagement through active student response.* Philadelphia: Center on Innovations in Learning. Retrieved from www.centeril.org/publications/Active%20Student%20Response%20(Final).pdf

19

Use Assistive and Instructional Technologies

Maya Israel

Introduction

Educational technology can be broadly defined as technology for teaching and learning.[1] These types of technologies can shape the educational outcomes of students with disabilities by increasing access to instructional content as well as offering flexible and engaging ways of interacting with that content. Special education teachers (SET) support the use of three distinct types of educational technologies when working with students with disabilities: (a) assistive technologies (AT), (b) general instructional technologies, and (c) content-specific instructional technologies.[2] Although these are distinct types of technologies, in reality, teachers who become proficient in supporting students' learning with technology will find that there is often overlap between the categories.

AT is defined in the 2004 reauthorization of the Individuals with Disabilities Education Act (IDEA) as, "Any item, piece of equipment, or product system, whether commercially acquired off the shelf, modified, or customized, that is used to increase, maintain, or improve the functional capabilities of a child with a disability."[3] These technologies support the individual needs of students and include a range of technologies, from no- and low-tech solutions such as raised-line paper and highlighter pens to higher-tech solutions such as augmentative and assistive communication devices (AAC), tablet devices with apps, digital textbooks, and text-to-speech. There are two components of AT: the devices and technologies themselves and the services necessary to all students to make use of those devices in an effective and efficient manner.

As compared with AT, instructional technologies are broader and typically benefit a wider range of learners.[4] These can include both general technologies that are used across content areas (e.g., multi-media presentations) or content-specific technologies (e.g., calculators and scientific probeware). Table 19.1 provides examples of both general and content-specific technologies commonly found in schools.

School districts often have access to numerous assistive and instructional technologies available to teachers. However, teachers may find themselves uncomfortable with using unfamiliar technology, may not know the extent of technologies available in their school districts, and do not have a framework for how to choose, use, or evaluate the effectiveness of assistive and instructional technologies to support students with disabilities. Special education teachers should remember that they do not have to be experts in all assistive and instructional technologies; they can leverage the expertise of professionals in their school districts such as assistive technology

Table 19.1 Examples of General and Content-Specific Technologies Found in K–12 Schools

General Instructional Technologies	Content-Specific Instructional Technologies
Word processing software	Calculators in mathematics
Digital cameras	Thermometers and scientific probes in science
Video conferencing software	Scratch programming in computer science
Concept mapping software	Library of Congress website in social studies

coordinators, special education administrators, content-area teachers, and district-wide curriculum coordinators.

Narrowing the Focus

This chapter provides specific recommendations about how special education teachers can begin to incorporate both assistive and instructional technologies into their instruction. Because technologies rapidly change, rather than focusing on specific technologies, this chapter provides general recommendations that can be applied to a broad range of technologies. The chapter begins with general guidelines for choosing assistive technologies. These guidelines are designed to ensure that teachers have a roadmap for evaluating students' needs and how technologies can be used to address those needs. The next part of the chapter focuses on suggestions for using instructional technologies within the context of content-area instruction to support access, engagement, and learning for students with disabilities. The chapter then transitions to Universal Design for Learning, as this planning and instructional framework can help teachers consider how to bring both assistive and instructional technologies into their instruction in ways that can increase access and engagement for all learners, including those with disabilities. The chapter ends with tips and resources for further exploration into assistive and instructional technologies.

Chapter Overview

1. Describe the rationale for incorporating assistive and instructional technologies into teaching and learning for students with disabilities.
2. Outline the steps for making instructional decisions for adopting assistive and instructional technologies.
3. Provide a model for using the Universal Design for Learning (UDL) framework for integrating both instructional and assistive technologies into instruction.

Supporting Learning Through Assistive Technologies

This section provides suggestions for selecting and using assistive technologies (AT) to provide access to the general curriculum for students with disabilities (SWD). Although AT vary widely and can address a broad range of needs, the primary focus of this section will be on *access to curriculum* rather than on technologies that support communication, mobility, or social development. There is a great deal of research on the effectiveness of providing students with AT to support their instructional needs. However, many schools are unprepared to address the AT needs of students with disabilities[5] or may only consider AT for students with more significant disabilities rather than the full range of SWD who qualify to receive special education services.[6]

Evaluating Students' Needs for Assistive Technologies

When conducting an Individual Education Program (IEP) meeting for a student with disabilities, special education teachers along with the rest of the team must evaluate the student's needs of AT, regardless of the type of disability. Typically, there is a section on the IEP with a checkbox that indicates that the team has considered the AT needs of the student. However, AT consideration should be an ongoing process rather than just a "one time" consideration.

1. Evaluate Whether the IEP Team Has the Collective Expertise Necessary to Evaluate AT for the Student

Often, in the IEP meeting, the special education teacher has the most extensive expertise in AT as well as in how the student's needs match with AT options. However, there are times when the special education teacher does not have extensive knowledge in AT, or the support needs of the student are so complex that additional expertise is necessary.[7] In cases where the IEP team does not have necessary expertise to thoroughly evaluate the student's AT needs, an AT coordinator or designated AT administrator should be included in the IEP meeting.

2. Consider the AT Needs of Students as Related to Goals, Access to the General Education Curriculum, and Extracurricular Activities

There are several models for considering the AT needs of students with disabilities. One well-established model focuses on an acronym called the Student, Environment, Tasks, and Tools (SETT) process.[8] This is a collaborative decision-making process wherein the team focuses on (a) the student's strengths and needs, (b) the environments in which the student learns and socializes as well as the supports within those environments, (c) the tasks that the student is expected to do, and finally (d) the tools including AT devices and services that might support the student in successfully achieving the desired tasks. Beyond AT consideration processes such as the SETT process, the Quality Indicators for Assistive Technology (QIAT) consortium provides a list of specific guidelines in eight areas that are important for developing and delivering AT. These guidelines also describe common errors that are often made in AT service delivery. These resources guide the IEP team in considering the student's needs and IEP goals, barriers to achieving those goals, and how AT might be used to help the student be more independent and successful in achieving those goals.

IEP teams should strategically chose an AT consideration procedure (such as the SETT process) and then implement that process consistently across IEP meetings for both AT device and accompanying services. Below is a checklist based on the IDEA (2004) on providing AT services alongside the AT devices.

Checklist of Guidelines for AT Services

- Evaluate for AT needs
- Purchase or rent the AT device
- Customize, repair, or replace the AT device
- Coordinate with specialists or therapists about the use of the AT device (e.g., speech therapists)
- Provide training to the student and their family on using the AT device
- Provide professional development and assistance to teachers and other professionals working with the student on the use of the AT device

3. Directly Integrate AT Into IEP Goals

When developing IEPs for students with disabilities, one way to ensure that AT will be used to support learning is to write IEP goals that reflect the use of AT.[9] For example, a student's Present Level of Academic Achievement and Functional Performance might read, "River is an eighth-grade student with a specific learning disability in reading. Her listening comprehension is at the seventh-grade level. When reading print materials independently, River's reading comprehension is at the fourth-grade level. When using text-to-speech software with digital text on her computer, River reads independently at the sixth-grade level." From this information, the IEP team can then create IEP goals that integrate River's AT. For example, an IEP goal for River might start with, "By May of 2018, when using text-to-speech with digital text at the seventh-grade level, River will. . . "

4. Collect and Analyze Data About the Student's Use of the AT Across Instructional Settings

For AT to be effective, it must be matched to the student's needs, the tasks that the student is expected to perform, the student's buy-in for using the AT, and the student's proficiency in using the AT.[10] Therefore, even with the best decision-making process at the IEP meeting, there is a need for continued data collection and analysis to evaluate the appropriateness and effectiveness of the technology. For example, River might know how to effectively use text-to-speech software when working one-on-one with the special education teacher but does not use this AT when completing homework or when in the general education classroom. On the other hand, the evaluation might reveal that River struggles with navigating the updated text-to-speech software that was recently installed on the computer. One way to collect data is through student self-assessment. Figure 19.1 provides an example of a self-assessment data form.

5. Revisit AT Determinations

Based on the data collection and analysis, the student's AT usage would then be reevaluated to see whether changes to the AT devices or services are required. In the case wherein River does use the AT in settings outside of one-on-one support, the team might decide that there is a need for generalization strategies rather than strategies to increase proficiency in the use of the text-to-speech software. In the case wherein River lacks proficiency with the software, the team might plan for continued modeling and supports or even consider a change in software. Thus, AT determinations should be considered continually in a similar manner that IEP goals are continually assessed and evaluated.

Integrating Instructional Technologies Into Core Academic Content

Unlike AT, which is designed to meet the individual needs of students with disabilities, instructional technologies (IT) are intended to be used broadly by a wide range of learners with and without disabilities. IT falls into two primary categories: (a) those technologies that are general and used across content areas and (b) technologies that are content specific.[11] As a special education teacher, it may not be realistic to be an expert in all of these technologies, but it is important to have enough proficiency to understand accessibility features and challenges within these technologies, the affordances of the technologies in supporting learning and engagement of students with disabilities, and how these technologies might be used within purposeful planning using the UDL framework. The following list describes technology tasks that special education teachers should consider. Given the broad range of technologies that students use in schools, SET should utilize content teachers, technology coaches, and other support staff in their school districts to help address these technology tasks.

Assistive Tech Self Assessment: Dictation Software

How's this software working for me?

What do I think about this tool?

	1	2	3	4	5	
I hate it.	○	○	○	◉	○	I love it.

Where do I use this tool?

	Math	English/Language Arts	Science	Social Studies	Health	Other
At school	○	○	○	◉	○	○
For homework	○	○	○	◉	○	○

I have difficulty with:

☐ Opening the app on my iPad.

☐ Logging into my account.

☐ Finding and turning on the mic.

☑ Dictating clearly enough so the software recognizes my voice.

☐ Making corrections.

☑ Saving my work.

☐ Communicating to teachers that I need to use this as an accommodation.

☐ Other:

Figure 19.1 Assistive Technology Student Self-Assessment Questionnaire

1. **Evaluate the affordances of the technologies to increase learning and engagement.** Schools are investing a great deal of money and resources in general technologies[12] with the addition of initiatives such as one-to-one computers[13] and the purchase of tablet devices.[14] Many general technologies available to all students have numerous features that can support students with disabilities regardless of whether these supports are built into their IEPs. For example, computers,

interactive white boards, and mobile devices all have features that could support students with disabilities if aligned to students' instructional demands. When considering the pros and cons of these technologies, evaluate how these technologies can minimize reading challenges, increase engagement, reduce cognitive load, or provide additional methods of presenting information. A few examples include: (a) Students can access opportunities to reinforce math understanding through watching videos and engaging in math problem solving through websites such as Khan Academy; (b) Content Acquisition Podcasts (CAPs) can be used to increase vocabulary proficiency in science instruction;[15] and (c) calculators may reduce the cognitive load for conceptual understanding, limit tedious calculations, and decrease math anxiety.[16] For example, teachers can display the procedures for graphing inequalities using Desmos (www.desmos.com), which is a free web-based graphing calculator, to the entire class on an interactive white board. Once students have seen worked examples, they can then use the same software on their mobile devices or computers to attempt the same problems. Given the wide range of instructional technologies, teachers must evaluate the effectiveness for their instructional purposes. There are numerous rubrics available to help teachers evaluate technologies such as mobile apps so that they do not have to create their own evaluation system.[17] These rubrics evaluate not only accessibility but also match between instructional objectives and the technology, intended age/grade level, opportunities for practice, and level of visual and auditory distraction.[18]

2. **Evaluate accessibility barriers in the instructional technologies.** Although instructional technologies are designed to engage learners in academic content, these technologies are typically not designed with accessibility in mind. Thus, even though they seem engaging and fun, some technologies might present accessibility barriers for students with disabilities. For example, a science teacher might decide to provide students with a virtual frog dissection experience prior to the actual lab activity in order to provide background knowledge, dispel misconceptions, and introduce procedures. However, if that virtual dissection software or app requires reading for participation or if the app does not provide explicit step-by-step directions to guide students' participation, students with print-based disabilities or those who struggle with complex multi-step problem solving would find the technology inaccessible. If, however, the virtual dissection software is compatible with a text-to-speech application and had scaffolding to support a guided experimental approach, those particular barriers to engagement would diminish. In another example, the Desmos graphing calculator has proactively addressed accessibility in several ways. First, it integrates a screen reader. Second, it is compliant with common web accessibility standards. Third, it includes audio as well as visual supports. For example, it includes an audio trace that allows students to use the right and left arrows to navigate along the curve of a graph while the screen reader calls out the coordinates. In this way, the software calls out intersections as well as changes tone as the audio trace moves vertically and horizontally along the graph. If the app was not proactively designed to allow for flexibility in use or integration with text-to-speech software, it would remain inaccessible. However, because Desmos was proactively designed to integrate with screen readers, multiple options are available to students. Thus, examining technologies from the perspective of accessibility is critical to understanding whether those technologies are useful and appropriate for all learners.

3. **Explicitly teach students how to use the technologies for learning.** We cannot assume that because students are surrounded by technologies, they will know how to use new technologies strategically to support their own learning and engagement. Therefore, it is important to (a) explicitly tell students the purpose of the technologies for supporting learning, (b) model how to use those technologies, (c) guide students from teacher-directed to independent uses of the

technologies, and finally (d) support their generalization so that they can use those technologies independently and in appropriate contexts. For example, if students are expected to animate mathematics story problems within the Scratch programming environment (https://scratch.mit. edu/), they must be taught to log into Scratch, the purposes of each of the programming blocks, how the programming blocks fit together, and the problem-solving steps necessary to go from

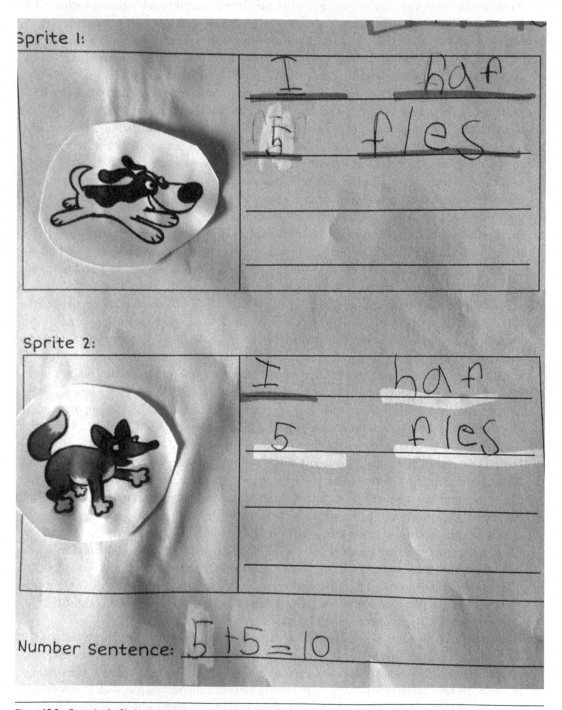

Figure 19.2a Example of a Student's Animated Story Problem in Scratch

Figure 19.2b Example of a Student's Animated Story Problem in Scratch

a written story problem on paper to an animated story problem in Scratch. The teacher might adopt an "I do, we do, you do" approach wherein they would explain how Scratch can offer a creative avenue in which students can animate their math story problems, model the steps to use chosen blocks to animate the story problem, guide students through examples with visual supports and checklists, and then provide feedback to them as they complete their own animated story problems. Figure 19.2 provides an example wherein a teacher guided a student through animating a simple addition story problem. The student chose to develop his story problem about the number of fleas on two dogs. In this example, to provide some explicit guidelines, the teacher provided the student with a checklist of both the mathematics requirements and the Scratch blocks that she expected to see in the animated story problems.

4. **Evaluate the effectiveness of the technologies to support learning.** Just like all pedagogical approaches, it important to reflect upon whether the technologies integrated into instruction have the intended instructional outcomes. For example, when providing access to videos that provide background knowledge about instructional content, are these videos effectively providing that background knowledge? Are the students accessing the videos? Is the vocabulary appropriate within the videos?

Throughout this process, it is helpful to consistently consider students' evolving needs, technology solutions, and outcomes of using those technologies. Table 19.2 provides some guiding questions that can support instructional decision making for integrating technology into teaching and learning.

Using Universal Design for Learning (UDL) to Embed Technology Within Instruction

Planning and teaching through the UDL framework provides diverse learners with increased opportunities to engage in learning.[19] This process starts with teachers' belief that their instruction should be engaging and accessible to all their students. This inclusive mindset can then lead to proactively planning instruction in a way that accounts for the diversity present in most classrooms. Although UDL and technology should not be considered synonymous, technology frequently plays an import-

Table 19.2 Reflective Questions for Integrating Technology Into Instruction for Students With Disabilities

Technology and UDL Self-Reflection	Example
What are the students expected to learn and do?	The seventh-grade student is expected to conduct a scientific inquiry investigation and develop and refine a scientific model about charge polarization as part of their Next Generation Science Standards (NGSS) science curriculum.
Why might this be relevant or important to my students?	Students have probably experienced a situation where they walked across the carpet in socks and then "zapped" someone or have taken off a sweatshirt quickly and their hair "stood up." These situations might be good ways of engaging them in the scientific phenomenon associated with charge polarization.
What barriers exist to fully engaging in the instruction?	Students are expected to (a) read about charge polarization in their textbooks, (b) conduct two inquiry investigations, (c) draw a model explaining their hypothesis about what occurred in their inquiry investigations, and (d) develop a conceptual understanding of complex concepts such as positively and negatively charged electrons, transfer of electrons from one object to another, insulators, and attraction and repulsion.
What technologies can address these barriers?	Text-to-speech software alongside electronic texts could address reading challenges. Audio recorders can be used alongside the students' drawings to reduce writing load. Pictures and videos can be used to provide background knowledge about the scientific phenomena.
How can students gain proficiency in these technologies?	If the students are using these technologies in other content areas, the teacher can encourage them to use the technologies within this science unit. If the technologies are new, the teacher can model and guide the students to independent use of the technologies. For technologies that can be used collaboratively among peers (e.g., audio record explanations of the scientific models), the teacher can pair students to work together.
How will we know if the technology is effective?	The student knows how to access, navigate through, and proficiently use the technologies independently. The student independently chooses to use the technologies to support learning. For example, the student decides to watch a video explaining charge polarization wherein someone rubs a balloon on their head and then "sticks" the balloon to the wall.

ant role within UDL-based instruction.[20] Because UDL begins with planning instruction that meets the needs of all learners, considering how technology supports learning should be an essential component of planning and teaching.

Teaching through the UDL framework can seem daunting to teachers because they must consider not only how to teach their curriculum but also how to infuse flexibility into that curriculum so that students can learn in a manner that supports their needs and capitalizes on their strengths. Additionally, teachers must have enough background knowledge to evaluate both the general and content-specific technologies available for that instruction to understand how to integrate these technologies within UDL-based instruction. Therefore, teaching through the UDL framework should be considered a process wherein teachers gain expertise over time and become more comfortable with experience.

Teaching through the UDL framework informs teachers in considering every aspect of instruction, including instructional goals, instructional delivery methods, materials, and assessments.[21] Because this planning process can seem daunting, it is helpful to consider planning through the three principles outlined by Meyer and Rose (2002). The following section provides details about each of the three UDL principles and methods of considering technology integration within them.

1. **Use technology to increase engagement.** To motivate and challenge students appropriately, it is important to first consider how students might engage with the instructional content. Teachers can begin by asking questions such as, "Why is this important to my students?" and "How might I find ways to increase my students' engagement in this content?" By reflecting on these questions, teachers can begin considering ways of increase engagement and then consider what technologies may be available to support that engagement. For example, in a lesson about bacteria and viruses, the teacher might design a lesson wherein students begin by conducting online research about an area of interest such as the discovery of antibiotics or about the differences between pathogens that cause food poisoning versus the common cold. General technologies that could be embedded into this introductory lesson could include online resources that students could access on the class website (e.g., videos and pictures of different pathogens). Content-specific technologies could include microscopes wherein students can engage in initial exploration of various pathogens and make comparisons. This introductory activity could have similar guidelines with checklists to guide the students' exploration and offer structure and purpose. By allowing some choice in how to engage students in learning, students with different interests can all become engaged in the instruction.

2. **Use technology to increase access to content.** Because students have different background knowledge, strengths, and challenges, they will not necessarily benefit equally from the same content-delivery methods. For example, some students will have difficulty with reading about bacteria and viruses in their textbooks, while others will prefer this method of content delivery. Therefore, it is important to present content in different ways so that all students have access to the instructional content. Within the bacteria and viruses unit, along with class discussions and inquiry activities, the teacher might consider integrating videos about bacteria and viruses and digital reading materials that are accessible through text-to-speech. They might also include Content Acquisition Podcasts (CAPs)[22] to support general understanding as well as explicit ties to vocabulary by providing narration of student-friendly definitions of vocabulary along with associated visuals. By considering how technology can support content learning, SET can begin to integrate multiple access points to learning for their students that will allow them to have access to the content regardless of challenges such as with reading, background knowledge, or memory.

3. **Use technology to provide options for students to demonstrate their understanding.** Students may find themselves in positions where content assessments do not measure actual learning but rather unintended measures such as writing ability or test-taking strategies. Teachers should, therefore, consider how to assess learning in a manner that does not impose unnecessary barriers to the learners. For example, assessments do not necessarily have to all be paper and pencil tests. Assessments can leverage technologies such as multimedia presentations, videos, illustrations, and written products that make use of accessibility features such as speech recognition software. By allowing students to demonstrate their learning in technology-mediated and alternative formats, students can leverage their strengths rather than only areas in which they struggle. In the bacteria and viruses unit, for example, students can create PowerPoint presentations about the differences between pathogens. They may also play video games aligned to the Next Genera-

tion Science Standards (NGSS) such as the Filament Games product called *You Make Me Sick!* (www.filamentlearning.com/products/bacteria-and-viruses-unit-you-make-me-sick) in which students engineer a pathogen or pick one from within the game and attempt to infect a person with that pathogen in a manner consistent with the characteristics of that pathogen.[23]

As seen in the examples above, the three UDL principles can be used to reduce barriers to learning as well as increase engagement. It can take time for teachers to gain experience in how to use UDL within their instruction. Therefore, teachers should not consider UDL as an "all or nothing" framework, nor should they expect that they will quickly gain knowledge of all different technologies that can increase engagement and learning. Rather, they should reflect upon how to gradually gain experience in UDL and the technology skills that can support UDL-aligned instruction.

Putting It All Together

When considering both AT and IT to support learning for students with disabilities, it becomes apparent that there can be significant overlap between AT and IT. For example, most computers have text-to-speech features built into their operating systems. Many students, those with and without disabilities, may find these accessibility features useful. They may use text-to-speech to play back their own written essays to check for accuracy or to listen along to their history textbooks. These features, therefore, can be considered both AT and IT. For the purpose of instructional decision making, however, it is important to remember that the IEP team decides which technologies are necessary to reduce barriers to learning for students with disabilities, and those technologies must be written into the IEP and always be made accessible to students. These same features, however, can be available to all learners even if they do not have IEPs requiring their use. Figure 19.3 provides a cyclical decision-making process that teachers can use in thinking about technologies from both a UDL perspective and AT perspective.

Wrap Up

Special education teachers have an important role in supporting students' learning with both assistive and instructional technologies. This chapter described strategies for implementing both types of technologies to support students with disabilities as well as how the Universal Design for Learning (UDL) framework could be used to consider technology integration.

Tips

1. **Collaborate with content teachers, technology coordinators, and other special education teachers to learn about new technologies or "tricks" to using familiar technologies.** As a special education teacher, you cannot be expected to have deep expertise in how all technologies can support learning across all subject areas. Consequently, it is essential to collaborate with content teachers and other experts in the school district that may provide insight into how technology can support students with disabilities in the content areas. For example, many schools are now including computer science classes for all students. Because most SET do not have a significant background in K–12 computer science instruction, it would be helpful to speak with the computer science teacher to learn about which curricula, software, and programming environments

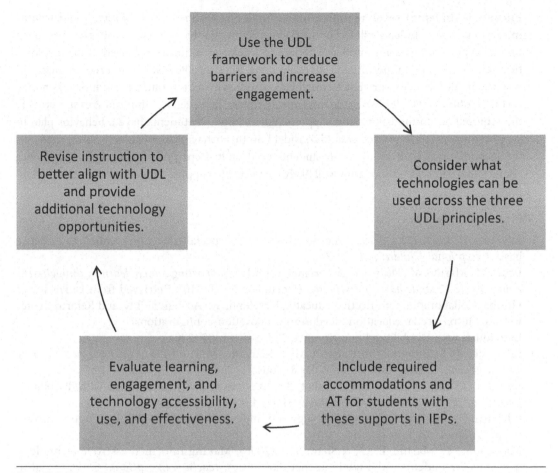

Figure 19.3 UDL and AT Instructional Considerations Cycle

are being used and to ask questions about accessibility, accommodations, and support needs within these technology-rich environments.[24]

2. **Spend time tinkering with unfamiliar technologies.** Do not feel intimidated by new technologies. Rather, give yourself time (e.g., 20 minutes once a week) to explore new accessibility features in familiar technologies or general features in new technologies. When, invariably, you find yourself stuck, acknowledge that the process of encountering barriers and addressing those barriers in technologies is a natural part of learning new technologies. Additionally, there is a good chance that your students will also confront similar barriers, so it is helpful to document these challenges so that you can proactively address them with your students. In the computer science example, it might seem exceptionally intimidating to learn the programming language that your students are learning in class. However, having some fluency in those programming languages will help you advocate for the necessary accommodations and supports for your students. If your fifth-grade students are learning to use the Scratch programming language (like in the example associated with Figure 19.2), spend some time tinkering in that environment. You should also ask to see the general education teacher's lesson plan in order to understand the big ideas being taught. This way, your exploration of the software is purposeful.

3. **Encourage students to explore unfamiliar technologies with necessary supports and accommodations.** Some students will feel hesitant to use unfamiliar technologies. Just as teachers need time to explore and become familiar with new technologies, students will need similar exploration time. Giving them "permission" to explore, get stuck, problem solve, and request help will help them take chances with new technologies as well as avoid too much frustration when they do hit roadblocks. While giving students time to explore, however, it is important to still provide the required accommodations and supports. For example, if students have a behavior plan to support on-task behaviors, you should consider how that behavior support can be integrated into the technology-rich environment. If students need multi-steps problems broken into smaller chunks, that same accommodation will likely be needed to support technology-rich instruction.

Notes

1 Edyburn, D. L. (2013). Critical issues in advancing the special education technology evidence base. *Exceptional Children, 80*(1), 7–24.
2 Israel, M., Marino, M., Delisio, L., & Serianni, B. (2014). *Supporting content learning through technology for K-12 students with disabilities* (Document No. IC-10). Retrieved from University of Florida, Collaboration for Effective Educator, Development, Accountability, and Reform Center website http://ceedar.education.ufl.edu/tools/innovation-configurations/
3 Individuals with Disabilities Education Act, 20 U.S.C. § 1400 (2004).
4 Billingsley, B. S., Brownell, M. T., Israel, M., & Kamman, M. L. (2013). *A survival guide for new special educators*. New York: John Wiley & Sons.
5 Bouck, E. C. (2016). A national snapshot of assistive technology for students with disabilities. *Journal of Special Education Technology, 31*(1), 4–13.
6 Edyburn, D. L. (2006). Assistive technology and students with mild disabilities. *Focus on Exceptional Children, 32,* 1–24.
7 Marino, M. T., Marino, E. C., & Shaw, S. F. (2006). Making informed assistive technology decisions for students with high incidence disabilities. *Teaching Exceptional Children, 38*(6), 18–25.
8 Zabala, J. (1995, October). *The SETT framework: Critical areas to consider when making informed assistive technology decisions*. Paper presented at the Closing the Gap Conference on the Use of Assistive Technology in Special Education and Rehabilitation, Minneapolis, MN. Retrieved from http://files.eric.ed.gov/fulltext/ED381962.pdf
9 Carl, D., Zabala, J., & Karger, J. (2015). *Accessible educational materials and the IEP*. Wakefield, MA: National Center on Accessible Educational Materials. Retrieved [insert date] from http://aem.cast.org/about/publications/2015/aem-iep.html
10 Israel, M., Marino, M., Delisio, L., & Serianni, B. (2014). *Supporting content learning through technology for K-12 students with disabilities* (Document No. IC-10). Retrieved from University of Florida, Collaboration for Effective Educator, Development, Accountability, and Reform Center website http://ceedar.education.ufl.edu/tools/innovation-configurations/
11 Israel, M., Marino, M., Delisio, L., & Serianni, B. (2014). *Supporting content learning through technology for K-12 students with disabilities* (Document No. IC-10). Retrieved from University of Florida, Collaboration for Effective Educator, Development, Accountability, and Reform Center website http://ceedar.education.ufl.edu/tools/innovation-configurations/
12 McKnight, K., O'Malley, K., Ruzic, R., Horsley, M. K., Franey, J. J., & Bassett, K. (2016). Teaching in a digital age: How educators use technology to improve student learning. *Journal of Research on Technology in Education, 48*(3), 194–211.
13 Zheng, B., Warschauer, M., Lin, C. H., & Chang, C. (2016). Learning in one-to-one laptop environments: A meta-analysis and research synthesis. *Review of Educational Research, 86*(4), 1052–1084.

14 Chandler, M., & Tsukayama, H. (2014). Tablets proliferate in nation's classrooms, taking a swipe at the status quo. *Washington Post, 17*.

15 Kennedy, M. J., Rodgers, W. J., Romig, J. E., Lloyd, J. W., & Brownell, M. T. (2017). Effects of a multimedia professional development package on inclusive science teachers' vocabulary instruction. *Journal of Teacher Education, 68*(2), 213–230.

16 Hasselbring, T. S., Lott, A. C., & Zydney, J. M. (2005). *Technology-supported math instruction for students with disabilities: Two decades of research and development.* Retrieved December, 12, 2005.

   Maccini, P., & Gagnon, J. C. (2000). Best practices for teaching mathematics to secondary students with special needs. *Focus on Exceptional Children, 32*(5), 1.

   Bouck, E. C., Satsangi, R., & Flanagan, S. (2016). Focus on inclusive education: Evaluating apps for students with disabilities: Supporting academic access and success. Bradley Witzel (Eds.). *Childhood Education, 92*(4), 324–328.

17 Maccini, P., & Gagnon, J. C. (2000). Best practices for teaching mathematics to secondary students with special needs. *Focus on Exceptional Children, 32*(5), 1.

18 Bouck, E. C., Satsangi, R., & Flanagan, S. (2016). Focus on inclusive education: Evaluating apps for students with disabilities: Supporting academic access and success. Bradley Witzel (Eds.). *Childhood Education, 92*(4), 324–328.

   Ok, M. W., Kim, M. K., Kang, E. Y., & Bryant, B. R. (2016). How to find good apps: An evaluation rubric for instructional apps for teaching students with learning disabilities. *Intervention in School and Clinic, 51*(4), 244–252.

19 Edyburn, D. L. (2013). Critical issues in advancing the special education technology evidence base. *Exceptional Children, 80*(1), 7–24.

20 Israel, M., Marino, M., Delisio, L., & Serianni, B. (2014). *Supporting content learning through technology for K-12 students with disabilities* (Document No. IC-10). Retrieved from University of Florida, Collaboration for Effective Educator, Development, Accountability, and Reform Center website http://ceedar.education.ufl.edu/tools/innovation-configurations/

   Marino, M. T. (2009). Understanding how adolescents with reading difficulties utilize technology-based tools. *Exceptionality, 17*(2), 88–102.

   Rappolt-Schlichtmann, G., Daley, S. G., Lim, S., Lapinski, S., Robinson, K. H., & Johnson, M. (2013). Universal design for learning and elementary school science: Exploring the efficacy, use, and perceptions of a web-based science notebook. *Journal of Educational Psychology, 105*(4), 1210.

21 Rose, D. H., & Meyer, A. (2002). *Teaching every student in the digital age: Universal design for learning.* Association for Supervision and Curriculum Development, Alexandria, VA.

22 Kennedy, M. J., Rodgers, W. J., Romig, J. E., Lloyd, J. W., & Brownell, M. T. (2017). Effects of a multimedia professional development package on inclusive science teachers' vocabulary instruction. *Journal of Teacher Education, 68*(2), 213–230.

23 Israel, M., Wang, S., & Marino, M. T. (2015). A multilevel analysis of diverse learners playing life science video games: Interactions between gaming content, learning disability status, reading proficiency, and gender. *Journal of Research in Science Teaching, 53*(2), 324–345.

24 Israel, M., & Ray, M. (2017). Practical strategies for including students with learning and cognitive disabilities in K-8 computer science, *CSTA Voice, 13*(3), 6–7.

Key Resources

- CAST: www.cast.org/
- Universal Design for Learning Research and Implementation Network: http://udl-irn.org/
- Maryland Department of Education Learning Links Assistive Technology and UDL Resources: https://marylandlearninglinks.org/?s=Assistive+technology+and+Universal+Design+for+learning
- Universal Design for Learning: Recommendations for Teacher Preparation and Professional Development Innovation Configuration: http://ceedar.education.ufl.edu/wp-content/uploads/2014/08/IC-7_FINAL_08-27-14.pdf

- Supporting content learning through technology for K–12 students with disabilities: http://cee-dar.education.ufl.edu/wp-content/uploads/2014/09/IC-10_FINAL_09-10-14.pdf
- Quality Indicators for Assistive Technology Consortium: www.qiat.org/index.html
- Understood Assistive Technology Resources: www.understood.org/en/school-learning/assistive-technology/assistive-technologies-basics

20
Provide Intensive Instruction
Devin Kearns, Marney S. Pollack, and Victoria M. Whaley

Introduction

Intensive instruction is an approach to identifying academic and social behavior challenges and designing a system of support to address those needs systematically. Intensive instruction systems must (1) be driven by data, (2) increase in intensity in response to student need, and (3) be individualized for each student. Intensive instruction is designed for students with the most severe and persistent learning difficulties—in this chapter, specifically learning academic skills.

Narrowing the Focus

There is little question that many students require intensive instruction. Students with significant cognitive and developmental disabilities, severe behavioral and emotional disorders, and/or substantive physical and health-related impairments often need data-driven and individualized instruction. Here, we focus our attention on two groups: (1) students with learning disabilities (LD), that is, high-incidence language-based disabilities that affect students' ability to respond, and (2) students with severe and persistent academic difficulties at risk for LD but not yet identified.[1] Put differently, we emphasize the use of intensive instruction for students who have not responded to *secondary prevention* in a *multi-tier support* (MTS) or a *responsiveness-to-intervention* (RTI) *system*, whether or not they are receiving special education services. Intensive intervention is part of an MTS/RTI system. As described later, it is the third tier of instruction for students who require more intensity than lower tiers permit.

Many students with LD and those at risk of academic failure require intensive instruction to succeed in school and life. Statistics indicate, for example, that students with LD frequently fail to catch up to their peers—a trend that begins even in elementary school.[2] Students who struggle with reading in first grade have an 88% chance of having difficulty in fourth grade.[3] This problem persists throughout school such that about one-third of the variability in 11th grade reading comprehension can be predicted from first-grade reading skills.[4] By high school, the average student with LD reads 3.4 grade levels below peers without learning disabilities.[5] So, an 11th grade student would be reading at a 7.6 grade level. The problem is not unique to reading. In mathematics, 95% of children who exhibit difficulty in fifth grade continue to show performance below the 25th percentile in high school.[6] In the United States, the Common Core State Standards[7] have placed strong emphasis on the use of language to explain solutions to mathematics problems, and the introduction of these standards appears to be intended to address a gap between students with LD and students with high achievement on fractions understanding in fourth grade.[8]

The long-term consequences of low academic achievement are pernicious. Students with LD frequently drop out of school—more than 25% (vs. 10% among all students). Challenges may persist beyond school; only 46% of individuals with LD report being employed, with 8% unemployed and all others not in the labor force.[9] Moreover, 67% of individuals identified as LD in the labor force earn less than $25,000 per year compared with 45% among all Americans.[10] Students identified with LD may have health problems including obesity, increased smoking rates, and decreased exercise rates. Moreover, 41% of incarcerated people were students who dropped out of school.[11] In short, persistent academic problems increase risk for post-secondary financial, health, and legal difficulties. Academic intensive instruction has the potential to change these possible, very sad, outcomes.

The statistics showing the need for intensive instruction make the goal of closing the gap seem flatly unattainable. This is not the case. Changing students' trajectories is very hard, but several researchers indicate that well-structured intensive intervention systems can reverse these trends.[12] A synthesis of 18 reading intervention studies found that participating students with LD experienced positive academic outcomes, particularly when they received small group instruction,[13] while another reported that students with mathematics difficulties provided with intensive instruction showed far greater growth than peers who did not.[14]

Chapter Overview

1. Describe data-based individualization (DBI) as a validated and preferred way to deliver intensive instruction.
2. Provide a case study to illustrate how the DBI process is applied with Maria, a student making insufficient academic progress in primary and secondary prevention.
3. Discuss important questions and issues that school-based teams must address to successfully implement the DBI model.

An Approach to Intensive Intervention

Data-based individualization (DBI) is a validated way of providing intensive instruction[15] and we therefore focus on this approach here. Data-based individualization is designed to support individual students who have exhibited insufficient progress in *primary prevention* and *secondary prevention* (*Tiers 1* and *2*, respectively) in a three-tier MTS system. In other words, DBI is not part of *primary prevention* (*Tier 1*) or *secondary prevention* (*Tier 2*). Rather, school teams begin the DBI process with children who have already demonstrated insufficient progress in primary and secondary prevention. Figure 20.1 shows how DBI fits into an MTS/RTI system. The details of the DBI system for students who require *tertiary intervention* (i.e., *Tier 3*) comprise the remainder of this chapter. The steps in the process are these: (1) implementing a level-appropriate secondary prevention program, (2) monitoring progress, (3) examining diagnostic assessment data, (4) planning adaptations, and (5) continuously cycling through core DBI activities. Table 20.1 provides short summaries of these five steps that align with the next five sections.

To provide some context, we provide a case study that describes the entire process. The case study of Maria is given in Figure 20.2. We suggest reading the case study before reading the remainder of the chapter.

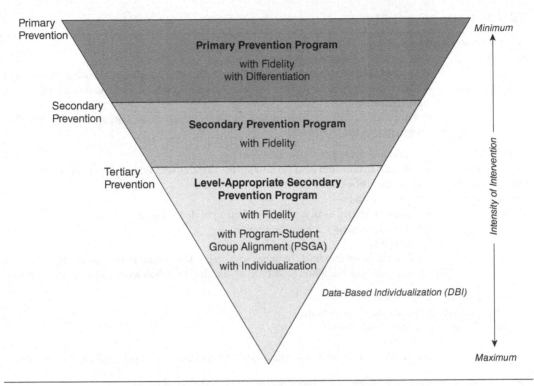

Figure 20.1 DBI in the Context of an MTS or RTI System

DBI Step 1: Implementing a Secondary Prevention Program

DBI begins with the implementation of a program, but it should not usually be the same program that the student did during Tier 2. In general, Tier 2 participation works best for students whose instructional level is no more than one grade level below their grade in school. Students who require DBI are almost always more than a grade level below, so participation in Tier 2 is no longer appropriate.

In our case study, Tier 2 is represented as Step Zero. Maria participated in Tier 2 programs throughout third grade with some progress, but she was falling very far below expected grade-level benchmarks. Now in fourth grade, the problem appears even more serious, and instruction in the Tier 2 program is not benefitting her. So, it makes little sense to continue using the same program.

In short, no student should continue participation in a previously ineffective secondary prevention, so educators should not use the same program that did not help the student in Tier 2. Students should participate in programs at their instructional level. We still call these secondary prevention programs, as there are rarely meaningful differences between the components of Tier 2 and Tier 3 programs. For example, a program like Reading Mastery[16] is designed as a primary prevention program but is frequently used for Tier 2, Tier 3, or both—and school teams puzzle over placing it in the tier system. There is no need to puzzle: Teams should not try to put a program in a tier. Rather, they should select programs that have good evidence of success with students with intensive academic needs and use those. We refer to these as secondary prevention programs.

Using a Program

Successful implementation of DBI depends on using a secondary prevention program. However, the phrase "use a program" evokes an immediate negative visceral reaction from some educators. The

Table 20.1 Steps in the DBI Process

Step 1: Use of a research-based secondary prevention program	Program should be • validated by rigorous experimental studies • implemented with groups of students who have not responded to secondary prevention • used for secondary prevention, but—in DBI—at the student's instructional level Interventionists • first provide small group instruction with only those adjustments agreed upon in collaboration with the school team
Step 2: Use of progress monitoring to track student improvement	Progress monitoring assessments should be • general outcome measures (usually) with reliability and validity for target skills • done weekly or more frequently Progress should be • evaluated relative to an aimline based on a pre-defined goal • adequate based on tracking the aimline If progress is • adequate: Interventionist continues with Step 1 and continues monitoring progress • inadequate: Interventionist collaborates with the DBI *school team* and moves to Step 3.
Step 3: Examination of diagnostic assessment data	Data include • standardized assessments • teacher-made tests • observations Discussion focuses on how the data might reveal issues in the dimensions of the taxonomy
Step 4: Creation of a student-specific intensive intervention plan	During the school team meeting, the team agrees on a plan that • is based on the examination of the diagnostic assessment data • focuses on one or more areas of the taxonomy • includes the ideas most likely to increase achievement
Step 5: Implementing plan, tracking response, and cycling back to Step 3 as needed	The interventionist • implements the plan • tracks the student's progress closely • every four weeks, meets with the school team to evaluate the student's performance data relative to the student's aimline If progress is • adequate: Continue as is • inadequate: Return to Step 3

first author once gave a DBI presentation to a school administrator who told him, "Don't say program." We understand this reaction, but we are insistent on this point. The question is then obvious: If you understand that some educators dislike programs, why insist that everyone uses them?

Our recommendation to use a program reflects the importance of data and practicality. In terms of data, high-quality research studies have shown that some programs are particularly effective for improving student achievement. If an available program has evidence of success for students with learning difficulties, why would we not use it? In terms of practicality, programs can make the interventionist's work simpler and more strategic. Most programs provide all learning materials, examples for demonstration and practice, and clear language for instruction, so interventionists do not need to plan these things. Rather, their planning time can be used to consider how to implement lessons, to clarify their own understanding, and to anticipate what might be difficult for students. However,

Step		

0 — Tier 2 With a Secondary Prevention Program

Maria is a fourth-grade student who has been receiving interventions through the RTI process since spring of second grade. By adding a secondary prevention program throughout third grade, she approached the minimum benchmarks until spring. Since the start of fourth grade, she has not made adequate progress despite her participation in the secondary prevention program.

1 — Data-Based Individualization: Implement a Secondary Prevention Program With Fidelity

The school team decides to use DBI to intensify her instruction. First, the team makes instructional groups for all DBI students and puts Maria with similar-level peers.
The team selects an instructional-level (first grade) word-reading secondary prevention program. The team decides to measure progress with first-grade oral reading fluency (ORF) because it is good for tracking decoding and fluency improvement, in line with the intervention focus. The team also selects a rate-of-improvement goal for Maria.
The interventionist begins to deliver the program, 40 minutes, four days per week.

2 — Data-Based Individualization: Monitor Progress

Over the next six weeks, ORF is administered 1-2 times per week as the interventionist provides instruction in the word-reading program. Some of the students in the group are following their aimlines, but Maria starts to fall below her aimline. After four data points (about four weeks) below the aimline, the interventionist decides to ask the school team to discuss Maria's DBI plan at the next meeting.

3 — Data-Based Individualization: Examining Diagnostic Assessment Data

The team meets to review data and create a plan to intensify intervention. Here are the data:

1. The interventionist shows Maria's sight word data. She has about 80% correct. The incorrect ones all have more than one syllable.
2. The general education teacher reports that Maria does not mind reading in a small group, except when the words are "too long." She asks for help on these words all the time.
3. Her parents have found that she tends to substitute different words if she doesn't know them. Examples include "floater" for "flower" and "different" for "division."

The interventionist reports that Maria is frequently off task during small group intervention time. The team adds a self-monitoring system to improve attention and participation.

4 — Data-Based Individualization: Planning Adaptation

The team has hypothesized that there is an alignment problem. The program includes some strategies for reading long words, but they have not reached those lessons. The team decides to continue with the program but supplement it with practice breaking words up using prefixes and suffixes.

The interventionist reports that Maria is frequently off task during small group intervention time. The team adds a self-monitoring system to improve attention and participation.

5 — Data-Based Individualization: Continuous Cycling

The interventionist implements the plan and monitors her progress. The team reconvenes in four weeks time. Maria's progress monitoring data shows no (or negative) progress on ORF, and she is still well below the aimline. She has not responded to this intervention.

Reconvening in four weeks time, the team sees that Maria's progress is on track.

This was not the right adaptation

Figure 20.2 A Case Study of Data-Based Individualization

not all programs are created equal; the program should be good. What defines a "good" program? Put simply, it is research-based, systematic and explicit, and focused on foundational skills.

A Good Program Is Research-Based

Research-based (or sometimes research-validated and perhaps evidence-based) means that the program has been tested by researchers and found to be effective. It is often hard to tell if a program is research based, but excellent websites are now available to evaluate programs. We provide a list of some in Table 20.2.

A Good Program Is Explicit and Systematic

A standardized program is explicit and systematic. Explicit means that it includes models of expected performance and scaffolded practice and involves effective supporting practices. Systematic means that each lesson is similar in design and that the program includes a complete sequence of lessons that gradually increase in difficulty and lead toward mastery of critical academic skills.

A Good Program Focuses on Foundational Skills

This means the program addresses critical skills that support grade-level expectations. After Grades 2 and 3, standards involve the assumption that students have the requisite supporting skills. For example, in adolescent literacy instruction students learn discipline-specific literacy.[17] However, many students lack foundational skills in word recognition (e.g., phonics) and building mental models of texts (e.g., understanding the main idea). In mathematics, students often lack basic calculation skills[18] and problem solving using schemas.[19] Difficulties with these foundational skills are one important reason students with intensive academic needs fail to meet grade-level standards. Secondary prevention programs should fill these holes.

What to Do When You Do Not Have a Program

We recommend programs, but know from experience that educators report having difficulty getting a program for a variety of reasons:

- School and/or school district/board administrators have already committed to a curriculum or instructional approach, and they will not purchase one that does not align with its implementation.
- Administrators are willing to purchase a program but do not have the funds to do this.
- A program at the students' instructional level does not exist (especially in secondary).

These issues defy easy resolution, but we make these points for educators to consider. Before purchasing a new program, make sure one is not already available. Often, schools put aside research-based programs in favor of newer programs (research-based or not), but the old ones are often still in storage and can be used. If one cannot be found, consider using the recommended websites to find one of the few very inexpensive programs that are available.

For interventionists in secondary schools and who are teaching areas that have few programs (e.g., specific mathematics skills), you can still design instruction in ways that are research-based, systematic and explicit, and focused on foundational skills. The idea is to find research-based resources for teaching foundational skills and use them systematically and explicitly. Table 20.3 provides some examples of teacher-friendly, research-based resources.

Table 20.2 Websites That Help Evaluate Secondary Prevention Programs

Website	Website Address	Content	Screen Shot
What Works Clearinghouse	https://ies.ed.gov/ncee/wwc/FWW/Index	Evaluates research in interventions EC-12 in academic and social/emotional behavioral interventions	
National Center for Intensive Intervention Tools	www.intensiveintervention.org/chart/instructional-intervention-tools	Presents individual studies into specific intervention programs in reading, writing, and math in elementary and middle school	
Best Evidence Encyclopedia	www.bestevidence.org/index.cfm	Summarizes scientific evidence for particular programs in reading and math	
Evidence For ESSA	www.evidenceforessa.org	Reports evidence on a variety of intervention programs using the standards provided by the Every Student Succeeds Act	
Evidence-Based Information Network	http://ebi.missouri.edu	Includes a series of useful briefs regarding specific intervention approaches and programs in math and reading	

Table 20.3 Resources for Finding Research-Based Practices

Domain	Description	Source
Secondary reading comprehension	A book containing research-based strategies including collaborative strategic reading	Klingner, Vaughn, and Boardman (2015). *Teaching Reading Comprehension to Students With Learning Difficulties*
Secondary reading comprehension	A resource for implementing collaborative strategic reading	Collaborative Strategic Reading website: https://outreach.colorado.edu/programs/details/id/652
Foundational and higher-level skills in reading and mathematics	A website with information about a wide range of research-based practices in reading and mathematics	IRIS Center at Vanderbilt University: *https://iris.peabody.vanderbilt.edu*
Elementary and middle-school foundational reading skills and reading comprehension	A set of programs to prevent reading disabilities	Peer-Assisted Learning Strategies website: http://vkc.mc.vanderbilt.edu/pals
Elementary foundational reading skills	A book containing research-based strategies for teaching early reading skills, fluency, and comprehension	Honig, Diamond, and Gutlohn (2008). *Teaching Reading Source Book*
Foundational and higher-level skills in reading and mathematics	A resource containing information about a wide range of evidence-based instructional strategies	Evidence-Based Intervention Network website: http://ebi.missouri.edu/
Elementary math skills	A book containing information regarding evidence based intervention approaches in math	Riccomini and Witzel (2010) *Response to Intervention in Math*
Elementary math skills	A book containing information regarding evidence-based intervention approaches in math	Witzel and Little (2017). *Teaching Elementary Math to Struggling Learners*

Although books and websites can provide research-based instructional materials focused on foundational skills, these materials must still be used systematically and explicitly. This means designing explicit lessons based on the resources, perhaps using an *Explicit Instruction* book for ideas, and creating a sequence of lessons to help students build their skills.[20] Programming strategies is no small matter, so we strongly recommend an initial search for existing programs. Creating a program using strategies is much harder—but sometimes necessary.

Implementing a Secondary Prevention Program with Fidelity

When a program is located—or a set of strategies is programmed—the interventionist begins implementation. The interventionist works hard to implement the program as designed, that is, with *fidelity*. When we work in schools, we often find that interventionists use only some parts of programs, or use the materials but in their own way, not according to program design. For example, interventionist Mr. K is using *Building Reading*, a research-based, standardized beginning-reading curriculum.

However—without discussing with the school team—he uses about half the materials, creates his own activities, and explains things his own way. In a sense, instead of implementing *Building Reading*, he has created a new program called *Reading Words with Mr. K*. However, his program is not research-based or standardized. The school team can no longer evaluate how the group responded to *Building Reading* or systematically change its implementation because the program was never actually attempted. Program implementation often occurs in a small group setting, and the team and interventionist might decide that the program would be implemented best with some adjustments to the program for the entire group. This would be a team decision, and fidelity would mean implementation with these agreed-upon changes.

DBI Step 2: Monitoring Student Progress With a Progress Monitoring System

Monitoring students' progress as they participate in intervention is critical for DBI. Progress monitoring is a reliable way to decide if students are responding to intervention within the secondary prevention program. It allows school teams to decide whether students are making adequate progress or whether they require DBI Steps 3 and 4. In our case study, progress monitoring data made it clear to the interventionist and the school team that Maria's intervention was not working.

What Progress Monitoring Is

Progress monitoring (sometimes called *curriculum-based measurement*; CBM) refers to the administration of short assessments at regular intervals (usually weekly and sometimes more frequently) that allow school teams to track whether students are making progress in the secondary prevention program. DBI is critically dependent on effective progress monitoring because the key decisions of the process—to continue instruction as is or to go to Step 3 and Step 4 of DBI—are made using these data. Without a good progress monitoring system, school teams cannot know if their activities are making a difference.

There are two categories of progress monitoring measures, *general outcome* and *mastery measures*. The former refers to assessments that index student achievement overall—across all skills in a grade level (e.g., first-grade reading skills). The latter refers to assessments that track progress toward a specific standard (e.g., reading sight words). In general, DBI is implemented using general outcome measures.

Good progress monitoring systems must have several critical features. First, they must have (1) known (and high) reliability and validity and (2) enough forms to allow frequent administration. In terms of the number of forms, DBI requires administration weekly—or even more often.[21] So, it is critical that teachers have enough different versions at the same level, so students do not take the same test repeatedly, as increased exposure to the same items could potentially affect their scores.

Even if progress monitoring systems meet these criteria, teachers sometimes think the measures seem strange or unhelpful. A strange test is the Maze (it has other names like Daze in some cases), and teachers wonder how it is helpful. The answer is that it is a valid measure of reading comprehension because it measures reading comprehension well even though it takes less than three minutes to administer.[22] The critical thing about progress monitoring measures is that they tell you whether instruction is working. They answer the question "How is DBI going?" If they do this well, we should use them, but this means that they are not necessarily diagnostic—they do not provide information about *how* to improve instruction. This can feel frustrating, but progress monitoring is very helpful because when data are graphed, student performance can be seen, and good instructional decisions can be made.

What Progress Monitoring Is Not

Many commonly used assessments in schools are not suitable for progress monitoring. This can be confusing because publishers sometimes refer to these tests as progress monitoring assessments, or school teams have a history of using them that way. Even when an assessment is designed to be administered several times over the course of a year, there are two primary aspects of these assessments that disqualify them from use as progress monitoring instruments. One is if the level of difficulty keeps changing. Some published programs come with tests of recently taught skills, but they are not progress monitoring assessments as we are defining them because the level of difficulty keeps changing. The other is that the measure is not validated. Many popular systems for evaluating student progress are not supported by empirical data that they are good indices of student performance. We urge readers to examine assessments carefully to see if they are general outcome measures that are appropriate for progress monitoring. In many schools, they are not.

Choosing a Progress Monitoring System and Measure

School teams getting started with DBI must first select a progress monitoring system to use, that is, a published assessment package that comes with a set of validated progress monitoring tests for teachers. Then, they must decide what assessments within the system to administer for students in DBI.

Choosing a System

No doubt, schools should choose systems with adequate reliability and validity. It can be hard to determine if a measurement system has these features, so we recommend using the National Center for Intensive Intervention's Academic Progress Monitoring Tools Chart (www.intensiveintervention. org/chart/progress-monitoring). This includes information about the quality of measures and costs associated with their use. For example, some systems require annual subscriptions. Some offer ways to administer assessments using technology (e.g., a tablet). They can also offer graphing tools to track progress. In our experience, DBI data are best tracked using graphs designed for DBI, so we urge teams to choose measures that have good reliability and cost a reasonable amount. School teams can evaluate the advantages and disadvantages of each system using the NCII chart and choose one that makes sense for their context.

Choosing a Measure

Within a published progress monitoring system, there are different types of assessments for different grades and skills. For example, kindergarten-level progress monitoring might include an assessment of how quickly students say the sounds made by different letters, but second-grade progress monitoring often involves timed reading of short passages (a task called oral reading fluency; ORF). In reading and mathematics, the chosen assessment should focus on instructional needs in foundational lower-order or higher-order skills (see Figure 20.3). In reading, these are word recognition and reading comprehension. In mathematics, these are computation and problem-solving. Figure 20.3 shows different assessments for these domains. For a given group of students, the school team must select the measure that is best aligned with the focus of the secondary prevention program. For example, if the team chooses a secondary prevention program focused on problem-solving schemas, it would not make sense to measure only students' computation because problem solving is a higher-order foundational skill for which concepts and applications is a better assessment. The point is that the measure must focus on lower-order or higher-order skills based on the nature of the intervention.

Higher-order skills incorporate lower-order skills and additional language-based knowledge and skills like understanding of syntactic structures or background and vocabulary knowledge. Lower-order

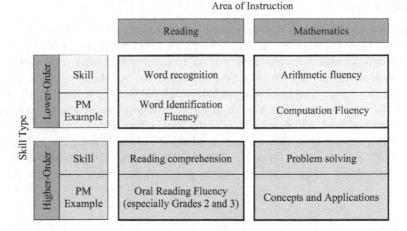

Figure 20.3 Types of Progress Monitoring Assessments by Area of Instruction and Skill Type

skills are essential supports for higher-order skills. These are only examples of progress monitoring measures. Others are available at each grade.

Choosing a measure also requires selecting the correct level for the student. Remember that we are usually not using a grade-level secondary prevention program, so it would not make sense to use a grade-level progress monitoring measure. If an interventionist monitors student progress with a grade-level measure, the student scores may be so low that it does not appear they are improving at all. Therefore, the school team should select a measure that would be sensitive enough to detect changes in student performance.

Choosing the correct level is tricky and unscientific. At the beginning of DBI, the interventionist tests students using a measure that is appropriate for their needs, using the level of measurement that seems appropriate based on prior performance and the level of the secondary prevention program. If a fourth grader receives instruction in a secondary prevention program for second-grade students, start with a second-grade progress monitoring measure. Then, the interventionist—perhaps in collaboration with the school team—would decide whether the student's performance is in the right zone, meaning that the score is not too low (we would not notice progress) or too high (the scores may be very inconsistent and hard to interpret). The Goldilocks rule (i.e., it should be "just right") applies, but deciding what is just right must be left to interventionist and school team judgment.

When it is difficult to decide on a measure, one possible solution is to use two levels of the measure (e.g., third- and fourth-grade passage reading fluency). The interventionist might (1) track performance on both all year or (2) administer both for the first four-week period and then choose the one that seems most sensitive to improvement. In other words, if a student seems to show progress on one measure (probably one at a lower grade) and not the other, track the one that shows the progress. This is perfectly acceptable: If we can see progress easily, we will also be able to tell when it stalls.

It is important to choose wisely because it is not possible to change the measure once DBI has started. It is not even possible to use different grade levels for the same type of measure. For example, passage reading fluency for Grade 3 cannot be compared to fluency for Grade 4, even though the skill is the same: Grade 4 texts have more challenging words, so reading 90 correct words per minute on Grade 4 passages requires more skill than reading 90 correct words per minute on Grade 3 passages.

Setting a Goal

DBI requires school teams to establish ambitious but reasonable goals for students to reach by the end of the year. The first step in establishing a goal is to collect baseline data by administering the same progress monitoring assessment three times over two weeks and taking the median of students' three scores (i.e., neither the best nor worst and not the average) as the best reflection of student performance. Once the student has completed three assessments, the school team can set two kinds of goals, benchmark goals and rate-of-improvement goals. Another type of goal, an intra-individual goal, will require more data. The authors have developed a form to track and graph student progress that allows users to select one of the three goals below (www.dropbox.com/s/xa2kdr75pv48voo/One-Document%20DBI%20Student%20Meeting%20Record-Blank%202017_10_31.xlsx?dl=0). Figure 20.4 shows the graph produced from the data for the case study student.

Benchmark Goals

After the first three data points are collected, a benchmark goal can be set based on the median. Here, the school team examines the technical manual for their chosen progress monitoring measure and finds the end-of-year expectation—that is, the 50th percentile—for the measure. The technical manual gives the benchmarks based on the grade of the measure. So, if the interventionist measures a sixth grader's progress with a fourth-grade measure, the benchmarks for fourth grade are used.

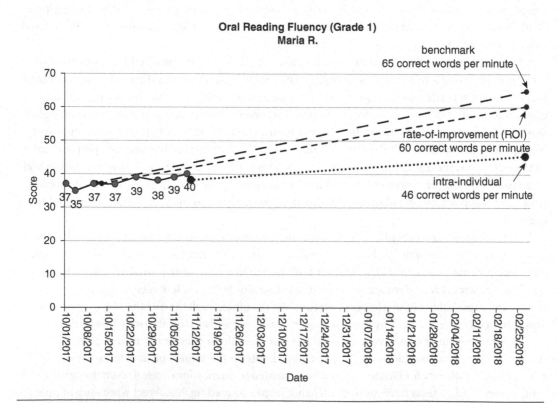

Figure 20.4 Potential Aimlines and Goals for Maria Based on Benchmark, Rate of Improvement (ROI), and Intra-Individual Progress

Rate of Improvement Goals

The median of the first three points can also be used for a rate-of-improvement (ROI) goal: This is based on the expected rate of improvement for students as given by the technical manual for the progress monitoring system—measured on a weekly basis. For example, the technical manual might specify that average second graders read one more word per minute each week they are in school. A student who started at 70 words per minute would be at 90 words per minute after 20 weeks. As with benchmark goals, the expected ROI is based on the expected improvement for a student in that grade level. In this example, that would be for a second grader. The only challenge is that some progress monitoring systems do not report rates of improvement, and it is hard to calculate them by hand. The authors have calculated them for some systems and can provide them if they are available or explain how to calculate them if not (see contact information at the end).

Intra-Individual Goals

The third way to set a goal is to do it with an intra-individual approach, but it is not possible with only three data points—it requires eight. Intra-individual goals are based on performance within (intra-) student (individual) at the point they participate in DBI. To use this goal, the interventionist uses a formula to calculate the student's current rate of improvement (i.e., the slope), increase that by 50%, multiply that slope by the number of weeks remaining in the school year, and add this amount to the starting point (the median of the first three weeks). This description of how to calculate the intra-individual goal is probably too brief for readers to do the calculation easily, but the NCII website has an Excel document school teams can use,[23] and the authors can provide assistance if needed. In this chapter, it should be clear that teams can set goals based on individual students' progress, not just an external standard.

Selecting the Goal and Drawing the Aimline

The three different goal-setting approaches will produce different goals, and the school team should select the one that seems reasonable, that is, the student has a good chance of meeting the goal. This is not a scientific decision—it is based on the collective knowledge of the school team about the student. It is not essential that the team is exactly right about the goal—the goal can be changed if it is too ambitious or insufficiently ambitious. The purpose of the goal is to create an expectation for student growth that will guide the team when evaluating progress at their meetings.

Regardless of how goals are set, based on the benchmark, rate-of-improvement, or intra-individual approach, the school team uses the goal to create an aimline—a link between the student's current performance and the desired end of year outcome. The school team's hope is that the student's performance will track the aimline, that is, follow it across the year or exceed it. The aimline shows the team when a student's performance is inadequate (i.e., consistently below the line). Figure 20.4 shows three possible goals and their dotted aimlines.

These goals are set based on the end date for intensive intervention. In this example, DBI begins in October and ends in March. Typically, the end of intervention is the same as the end of the school year. The benchmark goal (65 correct words per minute [CWPM]) is the 50th percentile for the grade level of the measure (first grade), copied from the manual for the progress monitoring system. The rate-of-improvement goal (60 CWPM) is calculated based on the amount of growth (more words read in a minute) an average first grader makes each week. This is also taken from the manual. These goals can be chosen after the interventionist has collected three data points. The intra-individual goal (46 CWPM) is calculated by estimating the student's current rate of progress (how much Maria improves each week) and accelerating that rate by 50% over the remainder of the year. Maria has made slow progress at the beginning of the year, so the intra-individual goal is low. The school team needs to decide which of these goals is best for Maria.

In Maria's case, the school team did not wait to calculate the intra-individual goal (after seven weeks) but chose a rate-of-improvement goal in Week 3. Figure 20.5 shows the graph with only Maria's data after Week 3 and the ROI aimline and goal. They chose the ROI goal because they thought Maria can make progress at that rate despite her initially slow improvement. (Figure 20.4 showed the different options. This figure shows the actual decision.) The vertical line indicates the point at which the goal was chosen and the DBI process started.

Evaluating Progress

Once the school team has (1) selected a measure focused on the right skills at the right student level and (2) set a goal based on initial data, the interventionist tracks progress weekly—or more frequently and plots it. The key question is whether student performance is tracking the aimline. If progress falls below the line for four weeks, the student is not responding. If progress falls around the aimline—sometimes below, sometimes above—that shows good progress. If the student's scores are always above the aimline, the instructional program is clearly working, so the team might conclude that their selected goal was not ambitious enough and redraw the aimline based on a different goal.

What interventionists and school teams are generally considering is whether the data indicate that the student requires further individualization. They want to address cases where students are not responding as soon as possible. When they find a student's performance is consistently below the aimline, the team goes to the next DBI step. In Maria's case, she appears to reach the aimline for just

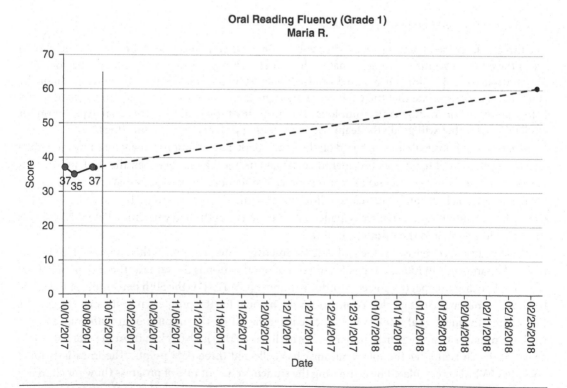

Figure 20.5 Maria's Data, Aimline, and Rate-of-Improvement Goal Set After Week 3

one week. Then, she has four data points below the line, and the interventionist decides to discuss Maria's performance with the school team.

DBI Step 3: Examining Diagnostic Assessment Data

Some students do not respond to the secondary prevention program as measured by progress monitoring scores relative to the aimline. In these cases, the student's data have consistently fallen below the aimline. A school team examines the data for the individual student who has failed to respond to secondary prevention. They consider multiple sources of data including progress monitoring charts, teacher observations, classroom assessments, and reports from others who work with the student. An important part of this step is for the team to make sure educators bring useful data to a student meeting. Useful data are not confined to progress monitoring. They can include student work samples, informal observations, information gleaned from progress monitoring assessments, and reports from different educators and specialists. Data should help the team understand all possible reasons for the student's lack of response. With the right data in hand, the team can make good hypotheses about the causes of non-response. Once all relevant data are shared, the team hypothesizes the causes of the student's difficulty.

The process of formulating hypotheses is strategic. Team members discuss them as they relate to the dimensions of the taxonomy of intervention adaptations. The taxonomy includes five dimensions of adaptation and broad categories of ways to make changes and is used to organize a school team's thinking. Instead of identifying problems at random, they can link each piece of data to a particular taxonomy dimension. For example, if a student is consistently late to the group and complains of headaches, the team would consider related dimensions. The team might hypothesize that the student has a long history of academic failure and just needs a motivation system (behavior support). Alternatively, it might be that the program is not connected well enough with the student's needs: It might be too easy or too hard or focus on the wrong skill. Table 20.4 describes each taxonomy dimension, and Table 20.5 gives examples of diagnostic assessment data and how they might lead to hypotheses about the cause of non-response in each dimension.

Some specialists who attend meetings might have expertise to help the team make good hypotheses—even if they have limited knowledge of the student. For example, a behavior specialist might notice that a student's disruptive behaviors immediately precede a particular activity; others may not have noticed this pattern. The team should coordinate to have educators with potentially relevant expertise available when discussing particular students. For example, consider a student who has struggled to articulate how a mathematics problem was solved—even when it was solved correctly. The interventionist might think that the challenge relates to language, so the speech-language pathologist might be invited to examine the student's written responses and help form hypotheses whether the student's current instructional program has sufficient alignment with the need to use language more precisely. The speech-language pathologist might even identify a particular language-related cause from all of the data. For Step 3, the team goal is to decide on a set of ideas about what might be critical impediments to student success in DBI. Figure 20.2 Step 3 shows the data the team has to decide the best adaptations for Maria.

DBI Step 4: Planning Adaptations

Step 4 immediately follows Step 3—occurring within the same meeting. It involves using the hypotheses to decide what might be effective adaptations to the student's current intervention program. The team will consider adaptations related to each hypothesis they create. Then, they consider which of these has the maximum chance of improving student outcomes. They also consider which of these is

Table 20.4 Taxonomy of Intervention Adaptations

Taxonomy Dimension	What It Is	Potential Adaptations
Dosage	The amount of time the student spends practicing.	• Repeat, strategically reorder, or create lessons. • Increase the amount of intervention time per day or number of lessons per week. • Decrease group size. • Increase opportunities to respond/practice in each lesson (see Comprehensiveness).
Alignment	How well the program addresses a student's academic skill deficits in foundational skills (higher-order or lower-order).	• Add or change the skills taught to address the full set of student deficits in a curricular area. • Adjust to minimize or eliminate instruction on already-mastered skills. • Change the strategy for teaching a skill when the current strategy may not be effective.
Attention to Transfer	Whether the program includes opportunities to practice skills outside of the original context (e.g., applying word decoding to sentences; applying rational number concepts to problem solving).	• Increase and/or improve opportunities to transfer the skills to other formats and contexts. • Increase and/or improve instruction on making connections to related skills.
Use of Explicit Instruction Principles	How much the program provides explanations in simple, direct language; modeling; repeated opportunities for practice with gradual release of responsibility; clear questions at the appropriate cognitive level; many opportunities to respond; immediate feedback; and brisk pacing.	• Clarify explanations and add additional examples for modeling. • Increase or better structure guided or independent practice opportunities (i.e. practice with fading support). • Improve phrasing of questions at the student's appropriate performance level requiring a variety of response formats. • Increase number of opportunities for students to respond actively to teacher questions in a variety of response formats. • Provide feedback that is more immediate, specific, positive, corrective, and/or frequent.
Behavior Support	The extent to which self-regulation, motivation, executive function, or strategies to minimize non-academic behaviors.	• Increase and/or improve strategies to improve self-regulation or executive function. • Increase and/or improve strategies to minimize nonproductive behavior.

most feasible, that is, easiest for the interventionist to implement. For example, some interventionists might easily be able to increase dosage by lengthening lessons, particularly if they have control over their schedules and can adjust students' schedules as well. Other interventionists may have no schedule control, making it difficult to add time. So, feasibility of increasing dosage will be dependent on context.

In sum, the team's task is to weigh the benefits of a given adaptation against its feasibility and select the highest-benefit most-feasible adaptations from among those proposed. School teams will often include more than one adaptation in their plan, but it is important that the plan is sustainable.

Table 20.5 Examples of Diagnostic Data and Hypotheses for Non-Response to Problem-Solving Program

Taxonomy Dimension	Example Data	Example Hypothesis
Dosage	• Progress monitoring data: There is a positive trend (slope) for the concepts and applications measure. • The trend is not sufficient for the student to reach the aimline.	The student needs more exposure to the content.
Behavior Support	• School psychologist observation: The student is very energized at the beginning of the lesson—when the activity involves computation practice. • Special education teacher report: The student complains of headaches and gives other excuses toward the end of the lessons—when the activity involves problem solving.	The student dislikes problem-solving and uses headaches and other excuses to get out of the lesson.
Alignment	• Special education teacher report: In the 45 minute period, 15 minutes are devoted to practice with computation of whole numbers using standard algorithms. • Standardized test: Student's performance on grade-level computation is at about the 35th percentile.	The student does not need that much time on computation. Daily fluency practice is important, but it can probably be reduced to five minutes.
Use of Explicit Instruction Principles	• General education teacher report: The student tends not to participate in group activities that require students to describe their thinking processes and multiple ways to solve problems. • Special education teacher report: In the resource room class, the student did well in the previous unit on total problems. The manual for the secondary prevention program provided a very clear introduction to the concepts. In the present unit, another teacher borrowed the manual and the special education teacher taught the strategy from memory. • Parent report: Student enjoys homework assignments and applying information.	The general education context is difficult because the student is not getting enough clear explanations of key problem-solving concepts, and the need to solve problems in many different ways is making that harder. The student's success with total problems—taught explicitly—provides further evidence, as does the challenge in the current unit where the teacher does not have the support of the manual to give good examples and model clearly.
Attention to Transfer	• Work samples: Student generally has 70 to 80% of answers correct on daily independent practice. The problems that involve application of the same problem-solving strategy to unique contexts are usually incorrect.	The student is learning to do the skill but only in the ways it is taught explicitly. The student cannot extend this to less obvious situations.

Part of the interventionist's job will be to track fidelity of implementation of the plan through to the next meeting. In this case, the interventionist will really just note whether the plan has been implemented as the team discussed. The plan, then, must be something the interventionist believes is manageable. Often implementation is the responsibility of multiple people beyond the interventionist. Implementing a motivation system based on accumulating points, for example, might involve the student sharing the number of points earned each day with the general educator, particularly if the student and general educators have a strong relationship. So, the general educator will be responsible for asking the student about the points during the lesson with the interventionist. In this way, the general educator has a role beyond that of the interventionist. Figure 20.2 Step 4 (left side) shows initial adaptations made for Maria.

Step 5: Continuous Cycling Through the Core DBI Activities

Step 5 is easy to describe and critically important. The interventionist implements the intervention plan with fidelity—that is, using the secondary prevention program with adaptations agreed on by the school team. As the intervention plan is implemented, student progress is measured weekly or more often. After four to six weeks, the school team convenes to review student progress, comparing their progress to the established aimline. If student scores are falling around the aimline—sometimes above and sometimes below—then the plan is appropriate, and the intervention should continue. If all scores are above the aimline, the team will discuss why the plan might be working well, and the interventionist would continue the intervention with fidelity to the school team's plan. The school team's most important work occurs when student's progress always falls below the aimline. The student is not achieving relative to the team's expectations (i.e., Maria starts to track the aimline two weeks after setting the goal; the next four data points fall below the line, indicating inadequate response to instruction). The group repeats Step 3 and Step 4 to change the plan. Figure 20.6 shows how this might occur in Maria's case.

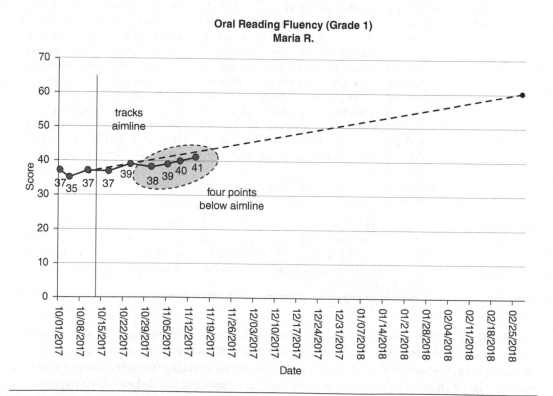

Figure 20.6 Maria's Progress After Selecting the ROI Goal

When the interventionist presents student progress monitoring data to the team, it can be emotionally taxing. The interventionist may feel sensitive, feeling somehow responsible for the student's lack of success. We have been interventionists and experienced this sadness—and even shame—when students do not achieve, so interventionists may feel the same way when presenting data showing a lack of progress.

When schools implement DBI, no one should feel any kind of shame when students do not achieve. If the intervention plan is implemented with fidelity, then student failure to respond is not the interventionist's fault. Rather, the problem was either the plan itself or uncontrollable external factors. When we say the problem was the plan, we mean that the team's plan was not effective. The team simply needs to change the plan by completing Steps 3 and 4 again. In terms of uncontrollable external factors, inadequate attendance is most often the issue. We have worked with school teams that realize the problem only at the meeting. In one instance, the student was supposed to receive 25 days of intervention between meetings, but student and teacher absence meant that the student received just 13 days of intervention, half the time. If a student is chronically absent, the team might write a new plan that addresses this specifically.

However, the problem is frequently that the DBI plan has not been implemented with fidelity. Sometimes interventionists do not implement all parts of the plan, or they change the plan without discussing this with the team. These changes are problematic for two reasons. First, the interventionist and the school team worked together to come up with a plan, so everyone should expect it to be implemented as designed. Second, it is hard to know if the plan worked or not. Data-based individualization is a systematic process but only if the adaptations are implemented as intended. The interventionist is rarely the only person involved in the plan. In many cases, other team members have responsibilities within the plan, and they also need to complete their tasks. Otherwise, the plan has not been implemented with fidelity. Figure 20.7 shows a fidelity of implementation checklist used to track whether the student has received the intended interventions.

Plan Elements		Implementer
Activity 1	Add 5 minutes of affix reading	Interventionist
Activity 2	Teach special long-word reading strategies	Interventionist
Activity 3	Complete 5 minutes reading long words using strategies	Interventionist
Activity 4	Teach Maria self-monitoring system	Behavior Support Specialist
Activity 5	Implement self-monitoring in class	Interventionist
Activity 6	Check in with Maria to provide positive feedback on monitoring	Assistant Principal

Write Y or N under each number to say whether you did that activity on this date.

Date	1	2	3	4	5	6	Notes
12/19/2017	Y	Y	-	-	-	-	
12/20/2017	Y	Y	-	-	-	-	
12/21/2017	Y	-	Y	-	-	-	Completed Activity 2
12/22/2017	N	-	N	-	-	-	Half day with assembly; no intervention
1/3/2018	Y	-	Y	-	-	-	First day back
1/4/2018	Y	-	Y	-	-	-	
1/5/2018	Y	-	Y	Y	-	-	Started self-monitoring teaching
1/8/2018	Y	-	Y	Y	-	Y	
1/9/2018	Y	-	N	N	-	N	Lesson cut short
1/10/2018	N	-	N	N	-	N	Maria absent
1/11/2018	Y	-	Y	N	Y	Y	First day of self-monitoring

Figure 20.7 Fidelity Checklist for Implementation of DBI plan

The top section, "Plan Elements," lists the activities that have been added to the secondary prevention program. This checklist is based on the second round of adaptations that included the addition of self-monitoring. Note that the interventionist is not the only implementer. The behavior specialist and the assistant principal also have responsibilities. The section below shows whether each activity was completed. In this case, some activities are not relevant at certain points, indicated by the dash (-). For example, the self-monitoring strategy is not taught until early January, and Maria does not start using it without immediate support from the behavior specialist until January 11. At the next meeting, the team will use this simple fidelity checklist to decide whether they implemented the intended plan. In this case, the plan has been implemented for about three weeks, and the school team appears to be following their plan. However, the data also show that the self-monitoring strategy has been implemented fully for only one day because of a shortened lesson and Maria's absence. If she does not show a pattern of good response after another week, the team might decide that she simply needs more time to see the effects of self-monitoring.

When plans are not successful, we have observed school teams look at external factors (beyond attendance) to explain the student's lack of response, (e.g., factors related to students' parents and home communities). We understand this impulse because the team may feel frustrated the plan did not work, but external factors should *not* become the focus. This belief comes from one simple fact: We cannot control what happens outside of school. As a result, adaptations must focus on what can be done at school. For example, homework may be important, but its completion is outside the school's control, and our obligation is to meet students' intensive needs through DBI in school.

In fact, the entire purpose of DBI is to meet student needs with the most severe and persistent academic problems. We certainly agree that factors outside of school can affect student achievement, and these factors can inform adaptations the team makes. However, we have observed schools that focus on these external factors rather than creating a new plan in their meetings. As we have already said, when the plan was implemented with fidelity, the problem was that the plan was not effective. School teams should focus on selecting new adaptations that will make the time the student spends in school more beneficial.

The meeting outcome should be a new plan and implementation of the secondary prevention program with adaptations the team thinks will increase achievement. After that, the interventionist implements the plan, and the team convenes regularly to examine student progress and create new adaptations as needed. Figure 20.8 shows how the school team decided to make changes for Maria and the results of those changes. Her data do not yet track the aimline, but the school team decides she is responsive for two reasons. (1) Winter break (the period within the gray box) appears to have stopped progress, but this has nothing to do with Maria or the plan itself. (2) Her data appear to be moving closer to the aimline. They are not making changes to the plan because it seems to have some effect, but they will monitor her data closely because she is not yet at the aimline.

Wrap Up

We hope that readers finish this chapter believing that DBI (1) has a simple structure in its five steps, (2) can work when implemented as designed, and (3) cannot be implemented without considerable planning and collaboration. We have worked in many schools where implementing DBI seems daunting, with the need for progress monitoring systems, programs, school teams, and a focus on fidelity. However, many schools have seen change in two ways: (1) Educators begin to focus on internal, controllable factors (i.e., not external ones). (2) Educators across the school—that is, outside of special education—begin to adopt elements of DBI like systematic use of progress monitoring.

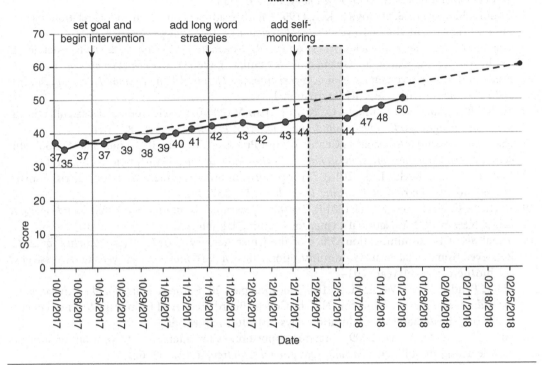

Figure 20.8 Maria's Data Following the Second Round of Adaptations

Put simply, we have seen DBI work, and our observations align with empirical data showing this. We encourage readers to explore the NCII website to think about how they might begin implementing DBI. Then, after learning and planning, we hope readers will begin their own work to implement this system. In the words of one experienced DBI teacher mentor, "It's not easy, but it works."

Contact Us

There are at least two ways to get support for DBI implementation. One is to visit the NCII website and explore their resources. There is also contact information for Center staff. They can provide support if you contact them directly. The other is to contact the authors. You can contact Devin Kearns by email at devin.kearns@uconn.edu. He can provide direction related to specific concerns—including very practical considerations—based on seven years of work with schools implementing DBI. Additional resources and exemplars are listed below and can also be found in the figures and tables.

Notes

1 Fuchs, D., Fuchs, L. S., & Stecker, P. M. (2010). The "blurring" of special education in a new continuum of general education placements and services. *Exceptional Children, 76*, 301–323.

2 Francis, D. J., Shaywitz, S. E., Stuebing, K. K., Shaywitz, B. A., & Fletcher, J. M. (1996). Developmental lag versus deficit models of reading disability: A longitudinal, individual growth curves analysis. *Journal of Educational Psychology, 88*, 3–17.

3   Juel, C. (1988). Learning to read and write: A longitudinal study of 54 from first through fourth grades. *Journal of Educational Psychology*, *80*, 243–255.

4   Cunningham, A. E., & Stanovich, K. E. (1997). Early reading acquisition and its relation to reading experience and ability 10 years later. *Developmental Psychology*, *33*, 934–945.

5   Wagner, M., Marder, C., Blackorby, J., Cameto, R., Newman, L., Levine, P., & Davies-Mercier, E. (with Chorost, M., Garza, N., Guzman, A., & Sumi, C.). (2003). *The achievements of youth with disabilities during secondary school. A report from the National Longitudinal Transition Study-2 (NLTS2)*. Menlo Park, CA: SRI International.

6   Shalev, R. S., Auerbach, J., Manor, O., & Gross-Tsur, V. (2000). Developmental dyscalculia: Prevalence and prognosis. *European Child and Adolescent Psychiatry*, *9*, II/58–II/64.

7   National Governors Association Center for Best Practices, & Council of Chief State School Officers. (2010). *Common core state standards English language arts*. Washington, DC: Authors.

8   Malone, A. S., & Fuchs, L. S. (2016). Error patterns in ordering fractions among at-risk fourth-grade students. *Journal of Learning Disabilities*, *50*, 337–352.

9   Cortiella, C., & Horowitz, S. H. (2014). *The state of learning disabilities: Facts, trends and emerging issues*. New York, NY: National Center for Learning Disabilities.

10 Social Security Administration Office of the Chief Actuary. (2017). *Wage statistics for 2014*. Retrieved from Social Security Administration Office of the Chief Actuary website www.ssa.gov/cgi-bin/netcomp.cgi?year=2014

11 Ma, J., Pender, M., & Welch, M. (2016). Education pays 2016: *The benefits of higher education for individuals and society*. Princeton, NJ: The College Board. Retrieved from https://trends.collegeboard.org/sites/default/files/education-pays-2016-full-report.pdf

12 Fuchs, L. S., & Fuchs, D. (2009). Creating opportunities for intensive intervention for students with learning disabilities. *Teaching Exceptional Children*, *42*(2), 60–62.

     Fuchs, L. S., & Fuchs, D. (2001), Principles for the prevention and intervention of mathematics difficulties. *Learning Disabilities Research & Practice*, *16*(2), 85–95.

     Vaughn, S., Klingner, J. K., & Bryant, D. P. (2001). Collaborative strategic reading as a means to enhance peer-mediated instruction for reading comprehension and content-area learning. *Remedial and Special Education*, *22*, 66–74.

     Fuchs, L. S., Fuchs, D., & Compton, D. L. (2010). Rethinking response to intervention at middle and high school. *School Psychology Review*, *39*, 22–28.

13 Wanzek, J., & Vaughn, S. (2007). Research-based implications from extensive early reading interventions. *School Psychology Review*, *36*, 541–561.

14 Fuchs, D., Fuchs, L. S., & Fernstrom, P. (1993). A conservative approach to special education reform: Mainstreaming through transenvironmental programming and curriculum-based measurement. *American Educational Research Journal*, *30*, 149–177.

15 Stecker, P. M., Fuchs, L. S., & Fuchs, D. (2005). Using curriculum-based measurement to improve student achievement: Review of research. *Psychology in the Schools*, *42*, 795–819.

     Capizzi, A. M., & Fuchs, L. S. (2005). Effects of curriculum-based measurement with and without diagnostic feedback on teacher planning. *Remedial and Special Education*, *26*, 159–174.

     Deno, S. L., & Mirkin, P. K. (1977). *Data-based program modification: A manual*. Reston, VA: Council for Exceptional Children.

     Fuchs, L. S., Deno, S. L., & Mirkin, P. K. (1984). The effects of frequent curriculum-based measurement and evaluation on pedagogy, student achievement, and student awareness of learning. *American Educational Research Journal*, *21*, 449–460.

     Fuchs, L. S., Fuchs, D., & Hamlett, C. L. (1989). Effects of instrumental use of curriculum-based measurement to enhance instructional programs. *Remedial and Special Education*, *10*(2), 43–52.

16 Engelmann, S., Bruner, E., Hanner, S., Osborn, J., Osborn, S., & Zoref, L. (1995). *Reading mastery*. Columbus, OH: SRA/McGraw-Hill.

17 Lee, C. D., & Spratly, A. (2010). *Reading in the disciplines: The challenges of adolescent literacy.* New York, NY: Carnegie Corporation of New York.

18 Fuchs, D., Fuchs, L. S., & Compton, D. L. (2012). Smart RTI: A next-generation approach to multilevel prevention. *Exceptional Children, 78,* 263–279.

19 Jitendra, A. K., & Star, J. R. (2011). Meeting the needs of students with learning disabilities in inclusive mathematics classrooms: The role of schema-based instruction on mathematical problem-solving. *Theory into Practice, 50,* 12–19.

20 Archer, A. L., & Hughes, C. A. (2011). *Explicit instruction: Effective and efficient teaching.* New York, NY: Guilford Press.

21 Christ, T. J., Zopluoglu, C., Monaghen, B. D., & Van Norman, E. R. (2013). Curriculum-based measurement of oral reading: Multi-study evaluation of schedule, duration, and dataset quality on progress monitoring outcomes. *Journal of School Psychology, 51,* 19–57.

22 Dewey, E. N., Powell-Smith, K. A., Good, R. H., & Kaminski, R. A. (2015) *DIBELS next technical adequacy brief.* Eugene, OR: Dynamic Measurement Group, Inc.

23 Kearns, D. M. (2016). *Student progress monitoring tool for data collection and graphing* [computer software]. Washington, DC: U.S. Department of Education, Office of Special Education Programs, National Center on Intensive Intervention. Retrieved from www.intensiveintervention. org/resource/student-progress-monitoring-tool-data-collection-and-graphing

Key Resources

Honig, B., Diamond, L., Gutlohn, L., & Cole, C. L. (2008). *Teaching reading sourcebook: Consortium on Reading Excellence.* Novato, CA: Arena Press.

Kearns, D. M. (2016). *Student progress monitoring tool for data collection and graphing* [computer software]. Washington, DC: U.S. Department of Education, Office of Special Education Programs, National Center on Intensive Intervention. Retrieved from www.intensiveintervention.org/ resource/student-progress-monitoring-tool-data-collection-and-graphing

Kearns, D. M., Lemons, C. J., Fuchs, D., & Fuchs, L. S. (2014). Essentials of a tiered intervention system to support unique learners: Recommendations from research and practice. In J. Mascolo, D. Flanagan, & V. Alfonso (Eds.), *Essentials of planning, selecting, and tailoring interventions for the unique learner* (pp. 56–91). Hoboken, NJ: Wiley.

Klingner, J. K., Vaughn, S., & Boardman, A. (2015). *Teaching reading comprehension to students with learning difficulties* (2nd ed.). New York, NY: Guilford Press.

Riccomini, P. J., & Witzel, B. S. (2010). *Response to intervention in math.* Thousand Oaks, CA: Corwin Press.

Witzel, B. S., & Little, M. E. (2016). *Teaching elementary mathematics to struggling learners.* New York, NY: Guilford Press.

21
Teach Students to Maintain and Generalize New Learning Across Time and Settings

Mary Catherine Scheeler, David L. Lee, and Andrew M. Markelz

Introduction

Generalization involves performing a behavior in settings other than the original teaching environment.[1] Maintenance is also important in the learning process and occurs when behavior persists after instruction has occurred. Effective teachers must have knowledge of strategies in order to build generalization and maintenance components into lessons when designing and implementing instruction. In doing so, students can use their new learning (hereafter referred to as behavior) in a variety of places and with a variety of people. Many teachers provide instruction using evidence-based practices during the acquisition phase of learning, but unless generalization and maintenance are also considered, students may not be able to access their new behavior in applied settings, such as at home or the playground. It is our contention that both generalization and maintenance should be programmed systematically.

Students with disabilities are educated in general education classrooms now more than ever before. They are in settings where they must use skills they may have initially learned in more structured settings and with more supports. Expecting learners to automatically transfer newly learned skills when supports have been withdrawn is asking a lot of students and, in fact, may be setting them up for failure. It is meaningless to change any learner's behavior unless the change is made to last (maintenance) and the new behavior occurs in settings other than the original training site and in the absence of the original trainer (generalization).[2] Most teachers can think of an example when a student was able to demonstrate new skills (academic, behavioral, or social) in one setting, but not in another. Likewise, most teachers can think of an example when a student's behavior did not persist over time, with a student forgetting a skill from one day to the next! Fortunately, there are practices that teachers can use to improve the likelihood that behavior will persist and actually transfer to other settings including but not limited to the general education classroom.

Narrowing the Focus

Specific techniques for teaching students to generalize behavior may include (a) teaching behaviors that can be used in many different situations, (b) teaching the behavior in several different settings with several different instructors, (c) varying instructions and reinforcers, and (d) programming for common stimuli between the natural and teaching settings. Instructing students so that behaviors maintain may include (a) attending to reinforcement schedules, (b) overlearning new behaviors, and (c) instructing self-management strategies. Effective teachers thoughtfully and carefully choose strategies for maintenance and generalization at the onset of teaching new academic and/or social skills and build them into the instructional program.

This chapter provides an overview of specific techniques teachers can use to promote generalization along with recommendations for identifying the most appropriate techniques to use in their unique instructional settings. We also focus on ways teachers can promote maintenance of behavior so newly acquired skills persist over time. Finally, we describe ways to collect and use data to promote and ensure that behavior is indeed maintained and generalized to other settings. We will provide specific strategies that teachers can use to analyze data and make sound instructional decisions as a result.

Chapter Overview

1. Identify techniques for promoting generalization of behavior.
2. Identify techniques to promote maintenance of behavior.
3. Describe ways to measure and collect data and use it to promote generalization and maintenance of behavior.

Promoting Generalization of Behavior

Skill development progresses in an orderly sequence: initial accuracy (acquisition), fluency, maintenance, and generalization.[3] In order to plan for generalization, teachers should first determine if the new skill can be performed accurately and fluently in the instructional setting, where the maximum level of support is available.[4] At the same time, however, teachers should begin to think about how generalization may impact the usefulness of the targeted skill. Generalization involves demonstrating or performing a behavior in settings that are different from the original teaching environment.[5] Behaviors may also show generalization over time and across behaviors. Generalization across behaviors and settings is known as stimulus generalization, whereas generalization over time is known as response maintenance, or maintenance (tendency for behavior to occur after programmed contingencies are removed). In this chapter, we will talk about both types of generalization.

Programming for Generalization

This section focuses on generalization of behavior across settings. We describe the essential features and major components of generalizing behavior to different settings with different people. Particular emphasis is placed on explaining the techniques and describing ways to apply them with students with special needs in general education settings. The techniques we describe can be used with any age and grade level, although they may have to be adapted by using age and grade-level appropriate materials. Stokes and Baer categorized the following techniques for programming generalization.[6] Each technique can be used individually or in combination to enhance generalization.

1. **Sequential Modification.** The teacher applies the same techniques that successfully changed behavior in one setting to all settings where the target behavior is desirable. For example, a ninth-grade student who struggles with taking tests may be taught a test-taking strategy in social studies. Once she has learned to use the strategy with social studies tests, she is taught to apply the strategy in her science class when she takes a test. She then moves on to the next class, then the next (sequentially) until she has generalized using the strategy in all settings. The skill of applying

a test-taking strategy is modified (i.e., generalized) from where she first learned the behavior to all other settings where she needs to use it.

2. **Natural Maintaining Contingencies.** Sometimes learning a skill can, in fact, provide its own reinforcement. Teachers can help their students with this by teaching them to recognize reinforcement that is available in the natural environment and to recruit reinforcers or recognize subtle forms of "social reinforcement." We cannot assume that learners will always have the skill set to acquire or recognize reinforcers across settings without instruction. For example, researchers taught fourth graders to ask, "How am I doing?" in a special education class to recruit reinforcers. The students generalized the skill to their general education class, and praise from their teachers increased, as well as academic performance.[7] In addition, some students may not recognize the subtleties of nonverbal communication such as a head nod in approval. Instructing students to recognize subtle reinforcers may increase the potential for naturally occurring reinforcers.

3. **Train Sufficient Exemplars.** A behavior should be taught in a number of different settings with a number of different persons. Too often insufficient examples, both in number and variety, are provided to assist the generalization process. For example, a first-grade student may need to improve social skills. He is learning a greeting response using the prompt, "How are you feeling today?" He is successful in his responses when his first-grade teacher asks him this question and usually will respond with an appropriate answer about how he is feeling and follow up by saying, "How are you?" to his teacher. His teacher asks others in the school (principal, therapist, paraprofessional) to interact with the student and provide the same or similar prompts so that he practices his new greeting/response with others; thus, a generalized response is practiced.

4. **Train Loosely.** Lessons taught under looser, more variable conditions lead to increased generalization.[8] Unless one skill is a prerequisite for another, it is not necessary to train students to master one skill before beginning instruction on another. Therefore, randomly varying non-critical aspects of instruction may lead to greater generalization.[9] Varying non-critical aspects of instruction means building a reasonable degree of "looseness" into teaching[10] and may include such things as using more than one teacher to teach the new skill or strategy, varying where it is taught (placement in the classroom, teaching from a sitting or standing position), varying tone of voice and choice of words, and so on. The important thing to remember is that the teacher introduces unpredictability as often as he can.

5. **Use Indiscriminable Contingencies.** Reinforcement is used to increase and/or maintain behaviors. Indiscriminable contingencies are when students do not know when reinforcement will happen, thus promoting the likelihood that desirable behaviors are continued. For example, Mr. Rene wants his students to work quietly in small groups. Knowing his students enjoy positive attention, he walks around the room and provides verbal praise to groups that are working quietly, making this behavior more likely to occur in the future. Another example of using indiscriminable contingencies is using the "Three Jars" technique. The first jar contains slips of paper with behaviors and criteria printed on them (e.g., raise hand 100% of time to answer a question). The second jar is labeled "who" and contains slips of paper with individual names or names of the entire class written on them. The third jar is "rewards" and contains slips of paper with rewards the students desire printed on them. The teacher picks one slip from each jar at the beginning of the lesson but does not tell the students who or what she has chosen. At the end of the lesson, the teacher determines if the behavior was met according to the criteria, and if so, the students earn the reward. During instruction, the students do not know what the behavior is (that the teacher is looking for), nor do they know what students are being observed for the behavior. From continu-

ous to intermittent, and fixed to variable, schedules of reinforcement are thinned to more closely resemble delivery of reinforcement in more natural settings. When a teacher uses indiscriminable contingencies, the students are never quite sure when reinforcement will occur and what behaviors will be reinforced, making it more likely that they behave appropriately so they will get the reinforcement when it becomes available. We will describe schedules of reinforcement later in the chapter in the section on maintenance of behavior change.

6. **Program Common Stimuli.** This occurs when the teacher deliberately programs similar stimuli in the training setting and in the setting where generalization is desired. The teacher can do this by bringing elements of the training setting into the natural setting (e.g., the general education classroom) or by bringing elements of the natural setting (general education classroom) into the training setting. For example, the same rules are posted in both the special education and general education classrooms. Classroom expectations are consistent across settings and teachers, and therefore, appropriate student behaviors are more likely to generalize between the two. When a special education teacher uses the same materials to teach math that the student will need to use in the general education math classroom (same book, calculator, ruler, number line, etc.), she is programming common stimuli. A teacher who is preparing her students with intellectual disabilities to work in a grocery store will use this technique when she brings in actual groceries and paper bags from the local grocery store to teach the student how to bag groceries. The student may also bring something from the original training setting, such as a schedule with a breakdown of the steps he learned for a task (such as bagging groceries and collecting grocery carts), into the natural setting. Teachers using this generalization technique should be on the lookout for common elements between the classroom setting and the setting where they want the student to use the new skill, including in the home. Teachers could work with parents, where appropriate, to promote generalization of techniques, e.g., assignment completion such as homework or managing specific behaviors such as using words to express emotions when angry or upset. Programming common stimuli may, on the surface, seem to be the opposite of training loosely. Remember, use train loosely by varying non-critical aspects of the lesson (e.g., teach from a sitting position some days, stand other days). The goal is to introduce some degree of "looseness" and unpredictability to encourage generalization. When using program common stimuli, the teacher systematically uses critical aspects of the lesson to increase generalization, (e.g., use the same calculator in the special education classroom when teaching math that the student will use in the general education math class).

7. **Mediate Generalization.** With this technique, the learner is taught to monitor and report on his own generalization of appropriate behavior. It involves training in self-management. For example, a seventh-grade student with behavioral difficulties has made substantial progress in curbing disruptive behaviors with a daily behavior report card when working with his special education teacher. A daily behavior report card is a tool that can be used to deliver feedback and provide reinforcement to students on targeted behaviors during specific periods or throughout the day. The student enjoys receiving positive feedback on his report card from his mother and always remembers to remind his special education teacher to fill out his daily report card. The student should be taught to use his daily behavior report card with his general education teachers to mediate the generalization of appropriate behaviors to his other classes.

8. **Train to Generalize.** Verbal instructions can be used to help promote generalization. For example, if a learner has sufficient receptive verbal ability, a teacher can tell her that if she engages in a particular behavior in a new setting she will receive a preferred item. A behavior reward system could also be implemented with this same student, who often fails to complete her homework on

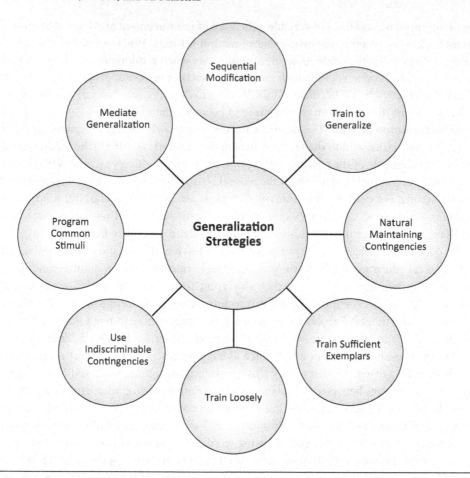

Figure 21.1 Generalization Strategies

time. Following several successful days of using the reward system in one setting, the program could be expanded to other teachers/classes in order to generalize the behavior of completing and returning homework to other classes. The student (as well as her other teachers) should be explicitly told that her new behavior of completing homework must generalize to her other classes and that she will receive reinforcement for doing so.

Helping learners achieve generalized change in desirable behaviors is one of the most challenging tasks that teachers face, but it is also one of the most important.[11] After all, no one learns a generalized lesson unless a generalized lesson is taught.[12] Fortunately, generalization techniques are available, and with careful planning are fairly easy to implement. The important thing is to systematically include generalization in lesson planning and implementation instead of what often is referred to as train and hope, where we teach the learner and hope the learning continues!

Promoting Maintenance of Behavior

Why include maintenance of behavior when we talk about generalizing newly acquired skills to new settings, people, and/or other behaviors? The learner cannot generalize a behavior if she cannot maintain the behavior in the first place, so maintenance is integral to the learning process. Think about a time that you learned a new behavior. Over time, your skill level likely diminished if you did not adequately practice the behavior. Perhaps the behavior diminished because it was not reinforced appropriately. Assuming a reinforcer is individualized and effective for a student in increasing behavior, the teacher also must use a schedule to deliver the reinforcement. All behavior is maintained by some schedule of reinforcement. Schedules of reinforcement can be thought of as the terms under which a reinforcer will be delivered. Unless they are systematically included in teaching, they risk being under-utilized tools in affecting behavior change in academic settings, thus resulting in the behavior not continuing in the learner's repertoire of skills.[13]

This next section describes the essential features and major components of maintaining behavior in the absence of instruction. Particular emphasis is placed on describing how teachers can use reinforcement schedules to ensure that behavior persists for students with special needs in general education settings.

Types of Reinforcement Schedules

Continuous Schedules of Reinforcement

There are two types of reinforcement schedules, continuous and intermittent. With continuous schedules, a reinforcer (e.g., praise or a tangible item such as a sticker or token) is provided each time the desired behavior occurs. For example, when learning a new skill, a teacher may provide a reinforcer each time a child zips his jacket or ties his shoes independently. Obviously, a person does not go through life obtaining a reinforcer each time he performs a given skill. The delivery of reinforcers may be delayed, such as getting a paycheck every month, or the frequency of reinforcers may be reduced, such as when a student receives verbal praise for a job that is particularly well done. In some cases, however, going from getting a high five or "Good job" for each and every occurrence to no reinforcement at all results in severe reduction of the behavior. This process is called extinction and is one of the problems associated with continuous schedules of reinforcement (i.e., when the delivery of reinforcers stops abruptly, responding also decreases or stops altogether). A second issue with using continuous schedules of reinforcement is that the student may become satiated for that reinforcer. (It becomes too much of a good thing, and no longer desired.) Varying the types of reinforcers could prevent this from happening.

Intermittent Schedules of Reinforcement

Although continuous schedules of reinforcement are good to use with acquisition of new behavior, we need to be careful to not just abruptly stop the reinforcement once the behavior is acquired. This is where intermittent schedules are advantageous. Intermittent schedules are used to deliver reinforcement after some of the responses rather than after each one.

Intermittent schedules can be used to give reinforcement after a certain number of responses (ratio schedule), or after a specific period of time (interval schedule). If the number of responses or passage of time is set (e.g., after every three correct responses or after every three minutes), we refer to the schedules as fixed ratio (number) or fixed interval (time). However, it is best to move from fixed schedules to variable schedules where reinforcement is delivered on an average number of responses or interval of time.

Thinning Schedules of Reinforcement

The process of moving from a rich (i.e., continuous schedule) to an intermittent schedule is called thinning the schedule of reinforcement. Thinning can result in slightly lower rates of a behavior but

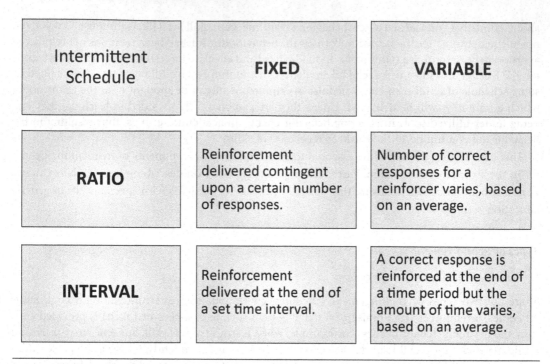

Figure 21.2 Intermittent Schedules of Reinforcement

will make that behavior more persistent over time. For example, sometimes Matt gets praised for completing eight math problems, sometimes for completing three, and sometimes for completing four. He never knows when he is going to get praise, so he continues to complete his math work. (His teacher praises him on an average of every five completed problems, a variable ratio schedule of reinforcement.) The reinforcement is indiscriminate, i.e., Matt does not know when he will get praised; he just knows that he will. Another example is that Matt gets praised for staying on task. (Matt likes verbal praise.) Sometimes Mr. Wright praises him for staying on task after eight minutes, sometimes after three minutes, and sometimes after four minutes. He never knows when he is going to get praise, so he continues to stay on task. (His teacher praises him on an average of every five minutes, a variable interval schedule of reinforcement.) The reinforcement is indiscriminate. Matt does not know when he will get praised for staying on task; he just knows that he will.

Teachers need to be aware of thinning schedules too quickly before the learner can adapt. Reducing the amount of reinforcement may decrease the behavior to undesired levels. For example, Ms. Avery was delivering praise to Laytisha for being on task every two minutes, and Laytisha's on-task behavior improved. The teacher thinned the schedule of reinforcement to every five minutes, but Laytisha's on-task behavior did not maintain. She became disruptive again. Ms. Avery should return to the most recent schedule that was successful in maintaining the behavior and proceed more gradually (e.g., every three minutes).

Other Ways to Promote Maintenance

Another way to promote maintenance, in addition to working with schedules of reinforcement, is to build in the opportunity for overlearning trials and distributed practice.[14] Overlearning is defined as repeated practice after an objective has been reached. Optimally, this translates to 50% of the number of trials necessary to acquire the skill.[15] For example, it takes Kai eight lessons to learn the steps to multiply fractions with unlike denominators. In order to provide for overlearning and promote maintenance, his teacher adds four more sessions to ensure the behavior persists and that Kai uses his new skills with a variety of different examples.

One final strategy for promoting maintenance is to teach learners to manage their own behavior. After all, who better to be responsible for monitoring, reinforcing, and maintaining less dependence on the teacher than the student? Self-management is defined as the capacity to regulate one's own behavior and includes techniques the teacher is already doing, such as goal setting, self-evaluation and reflection, self-reinforcement, and self-instruction (e.g., prompting oneself through a task, "Do this first, then this. . .").[16] Ultimately, if teachers have independence for their students as a goal, then they must teach students to be independent.[17] Teaching students self-management skills is a huge step forward in accomplishing this goal. The following is an example of what this could look like:

1. **Set a goal.** Teacher asks, "You wrote three sentences for your story yesterday, Ben. How many do you think you can write today?"
2. **Self-evaluation.** Teacher asks Ben to check to make sure he has used the correct parts of a sentence by checking with a rubric.
3. **Self-reinforcement.** Teacher asks Ben to award himself the predetermined number of points or tokens he earned for the task. (The teacher may also want to keep a record for reliability purposes.)
4. **Self-instruction.** Teacher tells Ben to prompt himself (under his breath) while writing with such statements such as, "I need a capital letter to start, need a noun and verb, put punctuation at the end. . .". This works particularly well when the teacher models how to do this by doing a task while talking to herself, quietly.

Making sure that behavior will be maintained is an important part of overall teaching. We teach our students to do academic tasks, such as reading, writing, or using appropriate learning strategies, and of course, we want our students to continue to perform these tasks after the teaching ends. The same thing applies to learning social and behavioral skills. It is frustrating for the teacher and a waste of time for both teachers and students if behavior does not persist. Continuous schedules of reinforcement work well for teaching a new behavior, but for the behavior to persist over time, teachers should use intermittent schedules (preferably variable ratio or variable interval) and also use reinforcers that occur in the student's natural environment.[18]

As with all of the techniques we have covered so far, it is important to collect data on the behavior so that the teacher can determine if the generalization technique, schedule of reinforcement, or self-management technique is effective and producing the desired behavior. This leads us to the final section of the chapter, describing ways to measure and collect data and use it to promote generalization and maintenance of behavior.

Using Data to Monitor Generalization and Maintenance

No instructional plan works every time as designed. Data collection is a key step that can help teachers readily identify components of programs that may be in need of revision. Lee and colleagues list five steps that can be used to monitor the effectiveness of programs.[19] These steps can be used for both generalization and maintenance programs.

1. **Schedule a time and location for data collection.** Data collection, like many other important activities in our lives, must be scheduled in order for it to occur consistently. Prior to design-

ing the actual data collection system, teachers must consider when and where to collect data. When collecting data to evaluate programs designed to enhance generalization, teachers must first identify the focus of generalization, which may include a separate location, other people, or different instructional stimuli, and then note the time when the generalized behavior should occur. Similarly, to collect maintenance data, teachers must decide when to collect data after the instruction has ended. For example, a teacher may decide to monitor the maintenance of a particular learning strategy two, four, and six weeks after instruction has been completed.

2. **Define the behavior of interest.** Ultimately, assessment data allow for the evaluation of programs. When the data show meaningful change in behavior, programs are often continued. When the data show little behavior change, teachers can work to modify instruction until positive results are observed. A key to this process is collecting data on the behavior of interest reliably over time. To achieve adequate levels of reliability, the behavior targeted for generalization and/or maintenance must be defined in a very clear manner. Strong definitions refer to observable behavior, are clear to all professionals involved in the program, and differentiate instances of the behavior, as well as non-instances.[20]

3. **Collect data.** The first step in collecting data on target behaviors is to determine which system of data collection will give the clearest picture of student performance. Selection of a data collection system should be guided by a question. Table 21.1 shows assessment questions and corresponding data collection systems.

4. **Summarize the data.** Data on data sheets are very difficult to interpret. In order to best determine behavior change over time, data should be graphed using a line graph. Oftentimes, instructional data and generalization/maintenance data are collected and shown on the same graph. These types of displays can give teachers data regarding both the effectiveness of instruction and generalization/maintenance programming. In Figure 21.3, the graph depicts both instructional and generalization data across baseline and instruction conditions. In Figure 21.4, the graph depicts baseline and instruction data, as well as maintenance data collected for three weeks after the completion of instruction.

5. **Interpret data.** Steps 1–4 are very important. However, it is only in implementing Step 5 that program improvement can actually occur. In this step, teachers should examine their graphed data between baseline (i.e., prior to instruction) and instruction phases to compare differences in student performance. Three scenarios are common for generalization. First, both instructional and generalization data show improvement relative to baseline. In this case, the program is progressing as desired and changes are likely not necessary. Second, the student's performance in the instructional environment (i.e., non-generalization setting) is progressing as planned, but

Table 21.1 Assessment Questions and Collection Systems

Assessment Question	Data Collection System
How many times does the behavior occur?	Use a simple count of the number of times the targeted behavior occurs in the generalization setting or during maintenance trials.
How long does the behavior last?	Use a stopwatch to determine the duration of the target behavior.
How long does it take the behavior to begin?	Use a stopwatch to determine the time between a prompt and the target behavior.

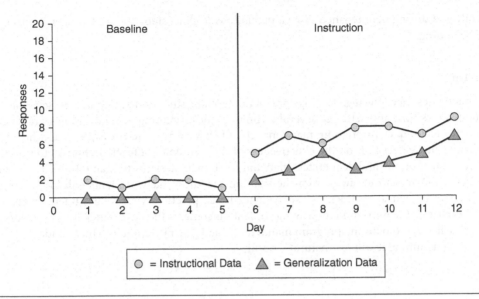

Figure 21.3 Baseline, instructional, and generalization data

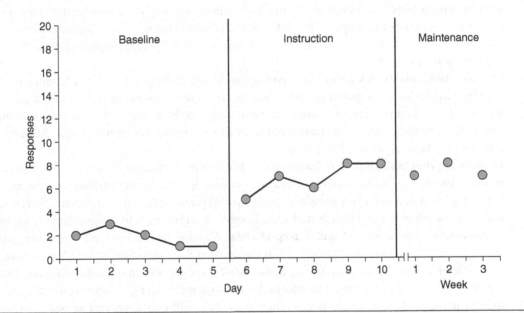

Figure 21.4 Baseline, Instruction, and Maintenance Data

generalization of the targeted behavior does not occur. Given these data, it is likely that the generalization program is ineffective. In this case, the teacher should review methods to increase generalization and modify the program accordingly. Finally, the student's performance in both the instructional and generalization settings is below criterion. These data show that both the instructional and generalization programs are ineffective and should be revised. Maintenance data are often a little more clear-cut. Maintenance is demonstrated when, at a later date, the behavior is at a level similar to that of the last few instruction phase data points. However, if data collected during maintenance show a precipitous decline, steps should be taken to strengthen responding.

Wrap Up

This chapter described the high leverage practice of teaching students to maintain and generalize new learning across time and settings. Several techniques for promoting generalization were described along with techniques to promote maintenance of behavior, ways to measure it, and how to collect data to make decisions on the effectiveness of the techniques a teacher chooses to use. Unless teachers systematically and deliberately plan and teach their students to maintain behavior and use their new skills in settings away from the training site, most likely, students will lose these skills. Effective special education teachers use evidence-based practices with their students with special needs because of the impact on improving student outcomes.[21] Effective, efficient special education teachers will also promote and program maintenance and generalization into their students' learning rather than assuming it will just naturally occur.

Tips

1. **Identify appropriate generalization strategy(ies) based on the skill and instructional setting prior to instruction.** One size does not fit all when programming for generalization. Different strategies may be more appropriate for different skills. Identifying generalization as an objective prior to instruction will encourage teachers to reflect on the skill being taught and plan accordingly for generalization.

2. **Maintain behaviors with schedules of reinforcement.** Continuous schedules of reinforcement may be used for newly acquired behaviors but must be faded as soon as possible to intermittent schedules of reinforcement to promote maintenance of the behavior. To continue thinning schedules of reinforcement, fade from fixed schedules of reinforcement to variable. Just make sure you reinforce generalized responses.

3. **Identify appropriate reinforcers individually.** What may act as a reinforcer for one student, another student may find aversive. For example, one student may enjoy verbal praise, whereas another student does not enjoy the attention that verbal praise brings. It is important, therefore, to ensure the reinforcer that is delivered actually serves as a reinforcer to that particular student.

4. **Purposefully plan to collect and interpret data.** Classrooms are busy environments, and teachers have full workloads. Collecting and interpreting data, therefore, should be intentionally implemented so that student data demonstrate whether generalization and maintenance are occurring. Data can then be used to inform decisions on maintaining or altering the program.

5. **Involve parents.** Parents are the first teachers their child will ever have, and among the most important. When parents are taught to apply behavioral techniques with their son/daughter, not only does the behavior continue in the natural environment, but programming common stimuli occurs in both settings (school and home), promoting generalization and maintenance.

6. **Teach students to regulate their own behaviors.** Look for ways to help students monitor their behaviors through technology such as iPads, smartphones, even buzzers set to go off at intervals. This could systematically increase the opportunities to receive feedback and reinforcement for the student while making him or her more independent and responsible for maintaining the desirable behavior.

7. **Stop wishing it will happen and make it happen.** Remember to make programming for maintenance and generalization part of your teaching repertoire. Assume generalization will not happen unless you deliberately make it happen.

Notes

1 Lee, D. L., & Axelrod, S. A. (2005). *Behavior modification: Basic principles* (3rd ed.). Austin, TX: PRO-ED.

2 Alberto, P., & Troutman, A. (2013). *Applied behavior analysis for teachers* (9th ed.). Upper Saddle River, NJ: Pearson.

3 Haring, N. G., & Eaton, M. D. (1978). Systematic instructional procedures: An instructional hierarchy. In N. G. Haring, T. C. Lovitt, M. D. Eaton, & C. L. Hansen (Eds.), *The fourth R: Research in the Classroom* (pp. 23–40). Columbus, OH: Merrill.

4 Haring, N. G., & Liberty, K. A. (1990). Matching strategies with performance in facilitating generalization. *Focus on Exceptional Children, 22*(8), 1–16.

5 Cooper, J. O., Heron, T. E., & Heward, W. L. (2007). *Applied behavior analysis* (2nd ed.). NJ: Pearson.

6 Stokes, T. F., & Baer, D. M. (1977). An implicit technology of generalization. *Journal of Applied Behavior Analysis, 10,* 349–367.

7 Craft, M. A., Alber, S. R., & Heward, W. L. (1998). Teaching elementary students with developmental disabilities to recruit teacher attention in a general education classroom: Effects on teacher praise and academic productivity. *Journal of Applied Behavior Analysis, 31,* 399–415.

8 Stokes, T. F., & Baer, D. M. (1977). An implicit technology of generalization. *Journal of Applied Behavior Analysis, 10,* 349–367.

9 Alberto, P., & Troutman, A. (2013). *Applied behavior analysis for teachers* (9th ed.). Upper Saddle River, NJ: Pearson.

10 Baer, D. M. (1999). *How to plan for generalization* (2nd ed.). Austin, TX: PRO-ED.

11 Cooper, J. O., Heron, T. E., & Heward, W. L. (2007). *Applied behavior analysis* (2nd ed.). NJ: Pearson.

12 Baer, D. M. (1999). *How to plan for generalization* (2nd ed.). Austin, TX: PRO-ED.

13 Lee, D. L., & Belfiore, P. J. (1997). Enhancing classroom performance: A review of reinforcement schedules. *Journal of Behavioral Education, 7,* 205–217.

14 Alberto, P., & Troutman, A. (2013). *Applied behavior analysis for teachers* (9th ed.). Upper Saddle River, NJ: Pearson.

15 Alberto, P., & Troutman, A. (2013). *Applied behavior analysis for teachers* (9th ed.). Upper Saddle River, NJ: Pearson.

16 Alberto, P., & Troutman, A. (2013). *Applied behavior analysis for teachers* (9th ed.). Upper Saddle River, NJ: Pearson.

17 Alberto, P., & Troutman, A. (2013). *Applied behavior analysis for teachers* (9th ed.). Upper Saddle River, NJ: Pearson.

18 Lee, D. L., & Axelrod, S. A. (2005). *Behavior modification: Basic principles* (3rd ed.). Austin, TX: PRO-ED.

19 Lee, D. L., Vostal, B. R., Lylo, B., & Hua, Y. (2011). Collecting behavioral data in general education settings: A primer for behavioral data collection. *Beyond Behavior, 20,* 22–30.

20 Hawkins, R. P., & Dobes, R. W. (1977). Behavioral definitions in applied behavior analysis: Explicit or implicit? In B. C. Etzel, J. M. LeBlanc, & D. M. Baer (Eds.), *New developments in behavioral research: Theory, method, and application* (pp. 167–188). Hillsdale, NJ: Erlbaum.

21 Cook, B. G., Landrum, T., Tankersley, M., & Kauffman, J. M. (2003). Bringing research to bear on practice: Effecting evidence-based instruction with students with emotional or behavioral disorders. *Education and Treatment of Children, 26,* 345–361.

Key Resources

Alberto, P., & Troutman, A. (2013). *Applied behavior analysis for teachers* (9th ed.). Upper Saddle River, NJ: Pearson.

Stokes, T. F., & Baer, D. M. (1977). An implicit technology of generalization. *Journal of Applied Behavior Analysis, 10*, 349–367.

22
Providing Positive and Corrective Feedback

Kristen Merrill O'Brien, Michelle M. Cumming,
and Elizabeth Bettini

Introduction

Ms. Donavan: *"Alejandra, nice job using a figure to think about this word problem—that is a great strategy. I wonder how you might use the strategy list to think about what to do next?"*

Mr. Nguyen: *"Javier, I notice that you are working hard on this essay. I wonder if you might be spending too much time on this section, though; I am worried you won't have time to complete it. Sometimes, I use a timer to help me track how much time I have. Would that be helpful for you now?"*

Ms. Bejarano: *"I really appreciate how you took a deep breath and said, 'I can do it,' and tried again when you hit that rough spot. Great persistence, Demaree."*

Ms. Kovaleski: *"This part is correct, but I think you might have made an error over here. Do you see this word here? It is another word for 'add,' or 'plus.' Do you know what to do differently now?"*

In all of these statements, teachers are providing students with feedback on their performance, letting them know what they did well and/or what they need to improve. Instructional feedback is essential for learning, providing students with key information about their progress towards a learning goal, including what they know, what they still need to know, and how they can learn it.[1] Research consistently indicates that providing students with effective instructional feedback has a powerful effect on their learning and is an essential core teaching practice.[2]

However, not all feedback is equal; some kinds of feedback are more effective at promoting students' ability and motivation to learn new content and to independently apply metacognitive (i.e., thinking about their thinking) learning strategies. Furthermore, some students may need different kinds of feedback than others, depending on their prior knowledge, skill, and motivation. Certain forms of feedback are more helpful when students have extensive knowledge and skill, while others are more appropriate for students who have more limited understanding or ability. Some feedback statements promote learning processes and independence, while others provide less information to guide students' learning. Researchers have identified the most effective ways for teachers to use instructional feedback and maximize student success.

Narrowing the Focus

Given the extensive body of research on the use of feedback, the many types and features of feedback, and the various scenarios in which feedback may be used and/or adapted, a complete review of feedback research is beyond the scope of this chapter. Additionally, the unique characteristics of feedback used to guide students' behavior is discussed as a separate high-leverage practice (HLP) in Chapter 8. We, therefore, focus this chapter on the essential features of feedback provided by educators to improve student learning. Specifically, we discuss how feedback can be aimed at various levels (i.e., task, process, and self-regulation) to influence its effectiveness. We also provide best practice recommendations on how to use corrective, goal-oriented feedback to guide student learning. Throughout the chapter, we highlight important aspects of feedback as an HLP by using instructional examples.

Chapter Overview

1. Describe the rationale and purposes for providing positive and corrective feedback.
2. Describe how to effectively use feedback at various levels to improve student learning and promote self-regulation.
3. Provide examples of how to use feedback to increase student learning in class.

Providing Instructional Feedback

As a teacher, feedback can be one of the most powerful tools available to increase student achievement. To improve their learning, students need to know how they are progressing toward academic goals; feedback is the information provided by teachers, peers, or oneself about an individual's instructional performance or understanding.[3] Instructional feedback is important for helping students to understand content and to develop effective strategies for learning. It is, therefore, critical that educators gain the knowledge and skills to provide effective instructional feedback.

Guiding Feedback Questions

According to Hattie and Timperley's feedback model, to improve students' academic achievement, it is necessary to bridge the gap between students' current levels of understanding and their learning goals, which can be accomplished by answering three overarching feedback questions.[4] Although the three questions can be used by students for self-directed feedback, we focus our examples and this chapter on teacher-directed feedback that is student centered. The teacher, therefore, asks the following feedback questions about the student's learning ("I" refers to the student), and then uses this information to guide his or her feedback to the student.

1. ***Where am I going?*** Feedback that answers the first feedback question directs students' attention towards learning goals and the criteria for achieving these goals. Providing feedback makes the expected outcome clear for students and communicates to them what reaching the learning objective looks like. For example, Mr. Alvarez tells Christian, "Your goal today is to write one paragraph that summarizes the findings of your science experiment, and it should include the results and whether your hypothesis was correct or not."
2. ***How am I going?*** Feedback that addresses this question provides students with information about how they are progressing toward a learning goal (e.g., how close they are to achieving the learning goal, whether they accurately understand something). When providing information related to progress and how to proceed towards a learning goal, teachers give information in terms of

task criteria, previous performance, or specific task successes or failures. For example, Mrs. Cole says to Bree, "You've done a great job of adding details about the planet Mars on your poster, but remember to also list at least three similarities and differences between Mars and Earth."

3. *Where to next?* Feedback that answers the last question helps students to plan next steps for how to advance their learning. By examining where to go next, students can better self-regulate their learning, gain instructional strategies, better identify what they do and do not yet understand, deepen their understanding, and choose the next challenging goal appropriate for their learning outcomes. For example, Miss Han tells Jon, "You've learned important features of the US Constitution in today's lesson, so next we're going to read this passage about the Bill of Rights, and you'll need to use what you learned about the Constitution to answer discussion questions with a partner. As you work, think about how your thoughts about the Constitution's role in our country may have changed and what you want to learn more about next."

These three feedback questions are interrelated and lead students on a path towards reaching their learning goals, from clarifying the criteria to reach a goal (Where am I going?), to how they are progressing (How am I going?), to what needs to be done next to make further progress (Where to next?). Specifically, answering these questions through feedback provides students with a clear roadmap that directs them in how best to reach their academic goals and deepen their learning.

Using Feedback to Scaffold Students' Learning

How effectively the answers to the three feedback questions maximize students' academic success is dependent upon students' current learning needs and the level at which they would benefit from feedback. Specifically, feedback can be provided at three levels:[5]

(1) task level (i.e., understanding and doing the task),
(2) process level (e.g., understanding the strategies needed to do the task), and
(3) self-regulation level (e.g., self-monitoring actions).

When teachers are aware of students' learning needs, they can better target feedback at the appropriate level to enhance the effectiveness of provided feedback. Task-level feedback is related to surface-level learning; the student learns content, remembers it, and applies acquired knowledge to a task. While the task level is foundational, too much focus on only providing specific task-level feedback can limit students in understanding how to accomplish learning goals beyond the immediate task. A deeper level of learning requires more complex constructions of understanding, cognitive processes, and generalizability of knowledge to other tasks, which would take place at the process or self-regulation levels. To help students progress from surface learning of new material to deeper understanding of that material, feedback must start at the task level, move to the process level, and then, finally, the self-regulation level. Therefore, to ensure that feedback is effective in enhancing students' learning and performance, it is important for teachers to understand students' current learning needs and provide targeted feedback at the correct level. Next, we describe more in depth the three feedback levels that progress from task, to process, to self-regulation, and Table 22.1 illustrates examples of feedback at each level.

Task Level

Feedback about the task, which is also known as corrective feedback, is one of the most widely used and influential feedback methods to improve student performance, with a wealth of research sup-

Table 22.1 Feedback Levels: Progressing From Task to Self-Regulation

Feedback Level	Optimal Use	Examples	Feedback Starters
Task: Feedback on whether the task was performed correctly or incorrectly	With new material or when student is struggling	"Jill, you provided a thorough description of the protagonist, but did not write about the antagonist." "Juan, you wrote correct answers to each question on your science paper, but did not provide evidence from the experiment to support your answers."	"Is your answer correct/incorrect?" "Your goal is to . . . so you'll need to. . ." "You have done the first part correctly . . . to fully meet the criteria, you need to. . ." "How can you elaborate on your answers?" "This is not accurate. Follow my example to correct it."
Process: Feedback on current and alternative strategies needed to do the task	When student has some understanding and is becoming proficient with the material	"Wow, Jemar, the first part of your essay is really organized, but the rest of the essay is disorganized. Let's think about how we can improve your work. What strategies did you use during writing?" "You've done well on the first half of your math assignment, Shasta, but you're stuck on this one question. Does it look similar to other problems you've solved so far? How did you solve those?"	"What did you get wrong and why?" "What strategies did you use to. . .?" "What questions can you ask about (the task)?" "What other helpful information is in the handout?"
Self-Regulation: Feedback that guides learner in self-evaluation, self-monitoring, and help-seeking	When student is highly proficient or experienced with the task	"Jeff, since you've completed your history assignment, go back through and check your responses. As you read, think about how confident you are in your answers and why." "Aria, I like how you looked in a resource book to discover whether your answers were correct. For the answers that are incorrect, do you know why you got them wrong? What else could you try?" Specific Strategies: • Self-instruction • Self-evaluation • Help-seeking • Goal-setting/planning • Self-monitoring	"How can you check/evaluate your own work?" "What did you do to answer. . .?" "How does your answer compare to. . . ?" "What goals do you have and what have you accomplished?" "How has your understanding changed?"

porting its effectiveness.[6] It is focused on how well a task is being performed and whether content was correct or incorrect. For instance, if students performed a task correctly, then the teacher could offer feedback on what was done well to encourage students to continue doing the task accurately. Conversely, if a task was done incorrectly, then the teacher could provide feedback to students on how they could improve their performance. For example, the teacher could point out where students went amiss, provide the correct answer, and/or highlight additional information that was needed to accurately complete the task. Researchers have found that for task-level feedback to be effective, it must be specific to the task, simple rather than complex, and specific to the student's performance.

Process Level

Feedback that is provided at this level is focused on the processes that an individual uses to perform a task. This type of feedback is especially important when teachers want to enhance student understanding and deepen learning.[7] At the process level, teachers can help students understand what strategies they used to perform the task accurately. If students performed the task incorrectly, teachers can provide feedback on strategies or information searching cues to help them correct and improve their performance. For example, a teacher could help students develop *task-specific* strategies to complete an assignment and skills to identify errors. Additionally, they could provide feedback on *information search* strategies by helping students to develop skills to identify additional information needed to correctly perform the task. Process-level feedback is influential in improving students' confidence in performing tasks, as well as self-efficacy.[8]

Self-Regulation Level

Feedback at the self-regulation level involves providing students with feedback that helps them to regulate their thoughts, feelings, and actions towards an academic goal. The intent is for teachers to provide feedback that helps students use internal feedback and cognitive processes to self-manage their learning through such strategies as self-monitoring (i.e., observing and recording performance), self-evaluation (i.e., evaluating performance), and self-help seeking (i.e., searching for help to improve performance).[9] Specifically, teacher-directed feedback at the self-regulation level encourages students to use metacognitive skills (i.e., thinking about their thinking) to determine the level at which they understand a task, the strategies they used, and their progression towards academic goals. For instance, teachers can provide feedback at the self-regulation level by helping students to appraise and monitor their own work (e.g., "How can you track your work during the science experiment? How confident are you in your answers?"), evaluate the information provided (e.g., "What does the information have in common, and how does it compare to the previous experiment?"), and reflect on their own learning (e.g., "How have your ideas changed after doing this activity?"). When teachers provide feedback at the self-regulation level, they encourage students to increase their engagement in a task, seek out further feedback, and use feedback information to improve task performance and deepen learning. Importantly, researchers have found that more successful students tend to use self-regulation strategies to direct their own learning and rely less on the teacher for feedback.[10]

Ineffective Feedback: The Self Level

We have described how teachers can help students answer three important feedback questions that are aimed at the task, process, or self-regulation levels. Feedback, however, at the self level is commonly used in classrooms and is less effective at helping students reach their learning goals. Feedback at the self level refers to giving evaluative feedback about the student as a person and not the student's performance of a task (e.g., "Good girl," "You're so smart"). Although self-level feedback is used frequently in classrooms, these statements have been found to have little impact on improving student learning and can, in fact, lower student engagement.[11] Even when used in combination with task-level feedback, self-level feedback can have a negative effect on student performance.[12] One of the main reasons self-level feedback is so ineffective is that it does not provide students with useful information to answer the three feedback questions (Where am I going? How am I going? Where to next?). Thus, we encourage teachers to avoid self-level feedback and instead incorporate instructional feedback that is aimed at the task, process, and self-regulation levels.

Effective Feedback Features

Researchers have identified key features of feedback, provided at any level, that can either promote or impede student learning.[13] In this section and in Table 22.2, we discuss ways to increase the use of effective feedback and ways to avoid less effective practices.

Table 22.2 Examples of Effective Feedback Features

Feedback Feature	Examples	Non-Examples
Provide clear, specific feedback that verifies and elaborates.	"Zakia, these details about research on genetically modified crops really help me understanding why you've come to this conclusion. I wondered about how you will help your classmates understand those details when you present this in our class debate."	"Great job on your persuasive essay Zakia! Keep working on the language some more."
Provide feedback that is focused on the task or process, not the learner.	"Brandon, nice work creating a visual representation of this word problem. That is a great strategy! If you can't figure out what to do after that, it is sometimes a good idea to re-read the word problem and make sure that you've put all of the numbers and shapes in the right places."	"Brandon, you are such a good artist! But, you need to be more precise when creating your graphics."
Provide immediate feedback, especially for struggling learners.	"Dashawn, I can see that you've started solving this equation correctly, writing down the PEMDAS strategy steps, and solving the parentheses and exponents. Can you remind me, do we do all of the multiplying before all of the dividing, or do we do multiplying and dividing in the order they show up in the equation?"	"Dashawn, even though you used the PEMDAS strategy, you got all of these questions wrong. We don't do all of the multiplying first, we do multiplying and dividing in the order they show up in the equation. We have ten minutes left if you'd like to redo these."
Use goal-directed feedback.	"Melanie, I can see that you've read this passage and made careful notes about who the characters are. But, let's take a look at the comprehension questions at the end. Are they asking about the characters? [pause for answer] No, they are asking about the mood. So our goal, when reading, is to pay really close attention to the story's mood. Can you re-read it with that in mind?"	"Melanie, I think you might need to re-read the story again. I am not sure you picked up on the right details when you read it the first time."
Focus feedback on misunderstandings rather than a lack of information.	"Jon, I notice that you have incorrectly conjugated -ir verbs. Let's go back and learn how to conjugate -ir so that you know how to do this before you work more on this worksheet."	"Jon, I've marked the ones that are incorrect, please go ahead and fix it."
Consider students' developmental level and abilities when giving feedback.	"Beatriz, I can see that you have worked hard on this assignment, but that it was a pretty challenging assignment. Let's go through each part together, and we can talk about what you've done well and what you should change."	"Beatriz, your answers are the shortest in the class. You didn't write enough."

Effective Feedback: What to Do

1. **Provide clear, specific corrective feedback that verifies and elaborates.** Effective feedback not only verifies the answer, but it also elaborates on the accuracy of the student's response. When giving feedback, tell the student whether his or her answer is correct or incorrect, and elaborate by discussing the correct answer or explaining why the student's response is incorrect. For example, if a student incorrectly identifies a shape in math, instead of simply responding, "Wrong answer," the teacher can provide clear, specific feedback by saying, "No, that isn't a circle because this shape has three sides and three vertices, so this is a triangle." Telling students specific ways to improve their responses is much more effective than only telling them if they are right or wrong. Additionally, giving students feedback that is clear and specific provides them with explicit ways to revise their responses, will be less frustrating, and provides scaffolding to learners. Correcting student errors through clear, specific feedback is particularly beneficial when they are struggling with the content.

2. **Provide corrective feedback that is focused on the task or process, not the learner.** Feedback should draw attention to the learner's performance (e.g., "You did a nice job checking your resources!") rather than the individual's self as a person (e.g., "You're so smart!").

3. **Provide immediate feedback, especially for struggling learners.** Feedback should be provided immediately to promote accurate, efficient learning. Immediate feedback allows students to use the provided information while working toward the learning goal and is, therefore, particularly important to use with struggling learners and when teaching new skills. For example, if students are reading sight words in a small group, the teacher should immediately correct any misread words rather than waiting until all the sight words have been read.

4. **Use goal-directed feedback.** To be most effective, feedback should help students close the gap between their current performance and an instructional goal. To do so, teachers must provide specific, appropriate goals that clarify for students the criteria for successful goal attainment. When students know their objectives for learning tasks, they can adjust their actions and track their performance. Thus, teachers' feedback to students should focus on the instructional goal and student performance toward achieving that goal.

5. **Focus feedback on misunderstandings rather than a lack of information.** Feedback occurs after instruction, so if a student lacks information, then more instruction is needed before feedback should be provided. Provide feedback on students' misunderstandings of content rather than their lack of knowledge. For instance, if a student does not know how to do long division, rather than providing feedback on the errors on the student's division worksheet, the teacher should provide more instruction. Conversely, if a student knows how to do long division but subtracted incorrectly in a problem, the teacher should provide feedback about this error.

6. **Consider students' developmental level and abilities when giving feedback.** To be effective, feedback should be aligned with students' prior knowledge and ability levels. Feedback should be provided in amounts that support meaningful learning (i.e., enough to support improvement, but not so much the student feels overwhelmed) and in a way that the feedback is clear and understandable to the learner (i.e., using language the student understands).

Effective Feedback: What to Avoid

1. **Avoid providing person-focused praise with feedback.** For example, do not use statements like "Good boy," "Nice job," or "You're a really good student." These types of statements do not provide information related to the task and distract the student from the performance goal.

2. **Avoid the use of hints that end with the correct answer.** Although hints can be used to scaffold student learning, they can be overused when they result increasingly in the correct answer.[14] For example, when asking the answer to an addition problem, the teacher would not want to provide hints such as "It's greater than 10. It's less than 13. You're getting warmer!" A more effective practice is to prompt students to use strategies or cues to use previously learned skills. In this scenario, the teacher could instead prompt students, "Think about the addition strategy we practiced yesterday. If one of the numbers is 10, what can you do to add the numbers?"

3. **Use caution with providing overall grades.** Giving students summative grades at the end without providing information about their learning progress (e.g., specific information about what they did well or poorly) does not improve student achievement.

4. **Do not use feedback that compares a student to peers.** Doing so draws attention to the student's self rather than the learning tasks and goals, can be discouraging, and fails to promote student learning. In addition, it can create a competitive culture in the classroom, which is not conducive to learning for most students. Instead of comparing students to others, focus feedback on the student's individual progress.

Additional Factors to Consider When Providing Feedback

The kind of feedback that is effective depends on other factors, such as student characteristics and ability levels. Researchers have found that students from different cultures experience and respond differently to various forms of feedback. For example, people from collectivist cultures (e.g., China, Japan) tend to prefer indirect, group-level feedback, while people from individualistic cultures (e.g., United States, Canada) tend to prefer direct, individual-level feedback.[15]

Student ability level also plays a role; for instance, low-achieving students benefit from immediate feedback, which provides information on the spot so students can adjust performance quickly and enhance accurate learning. Conversely, high-achieving students benefit more from delayed feedback, which allows them to self-monitor and self-correct their responses before verifying the answer through teacher-provided feedback.[16] Furthermore, the effect of feedback depends on whether and how students receive and use feedback; some students know how to think about and use feedback to improve their work, while others might need to be taught this skill. Finally, feedback provided by peers can greatly influence student learning in positive or negative ways.[17] Peer feedback that is incorrect, for example, can hinder student learning, while accurate peer information can foster student achievement.

We, therefore, recommend that teachers take their students' cultural backgrounds and ability levels into consideration when delivering feedback and explicitly teach students how to receive and use instructional feedback. Further, teachers should monitor their use of feedback and its effect on student learning to determine whether they should make adjustments to better support individual students.

Using Effective Feedback to Scaffold Students Toward Self-Regulation: An Example

Feedback can have a significant effect on student learning when it follows what researchers have shown to be critical features (e.g., clear, specific, immediate) and gives students information about their learning goals and their progress towards reaching them. Furthermore, feedback can be most powerful when it answers the three feedback questions and is aimed at the appropriate level, which can help scaffold students' learning from the beginning task level, to the process level, and ultimately the self-regulation level. In this section, we provide an in-depth example of how a beginning special educator, Ms. Landry, learns about and uses positive and corrective feedback to effectively target her students' individual needs and support them in meeting learning goals.

Ms. Landry, a first-year special education teacher in a fifth-grade inclusive classroom, has been teaching her students how to write essays on historical figures. The students have been drafting, revising, and editing their essays, so in today's lesson, Ms. Landry is holding individual meetings with her students to provide feedback on their work. Due to the diverse population of her students, including those with disabilities, she knows that they have varying writing abilities. She first meets with Dominique and notices that there are many grammar and spelling errors in her essay. Ms. Landry tells Dominique, "Wow, there are a lot of errors in your paper. I'm not going to look at this until you have fixed them, so get to work." The student stares at the teacher for a moment, goes back to her desk, and mumbles to herself, "I don't know what I'm supposed to do. . . " Instead of working, she gives up and lays her head on the desk and pretends to sleep.

Ms. Landry calls her next student over for his writing conference. Aaron has a good essay overall, but Ms. Landry notices that his paper is lacking depth and detail. She tells him, "Aaron, you're so smart, but you could do better in this essay. Let me give you a hint . . . more information is needed." Aaron smiles and nods his head confidently. He returns to his desk, puts his pencil to the paper, pauses, and then mutters, "She wants more information, but I have no idea how I'm going to do that, which section I should put the information in, what information would be most important, or where I should look. What does she mean?"

Ms. Landry is feeling excited about her writing conferences with her students and the chance to give them feedback on their work. She calls up her next student, Heta, who is a strong writer and independent worker. Ms. Landry smiles brightly at Heta and says, "This is a great paper, but I noticed that this paragraph could be improved. You are one of my best writers and are such a good girl. I know you can figure it out!" Heta agrees that she can, but when she attempts to write, she stares blankly at her page and says, "I have no idea why this paragraph is weak, and what I can do to make it better. I guess I'll check my spelling." She proofreads the paragraph, uncertain of what to do next.

After the student meetings, Ms. Landry is surprised when she discovers that her students have made limited improvements on their essays. She is perplexed and talks to the school's learning strategist, Ms. Bentley, to figure out what she should do. After Ms. Bentley learns the types of feedback Ms. Landry provided her students on their writing, she teaches Ms. Landry how to use more effective feedback to scaffold students' learning at the appropriate feedback level (i.e., task, process, and self-regulation levels) and provides helpful tips.

After learning more about the importance of feedback and how to use it effectively, Ms. Landry sets up new writing meetings with her students. She realizes that Dominique is struggling with the task of writing the essay, which is evident in her grammar and spelling errors; it is clear she needs corrective feedback at the task level. Ms. Landry starts Dominique's writing conference by saying, "Today I'm going to help you see and understand what you did well and what needs to be improved. Let's look through your essay together to find what you did right and what needs to be fixed." She then proceeds to point out what Dominique did correctly and incorrectly grammatically. During the process, Ms. Landry realizes that many of Dominique's errors are on comma use, which signals a lack of knowledge on commas. Thus, before providing additional feedback, Ms. Landry gives her additional instruction on the mechanics of comma use.

During the next writing conference, Ms. Landry realizes that Aaron has knowledge about writing details, but he is ready for a deeper understanding of strategies and processes used to include details in his essay; thus, Aaron would benefit from feedback at the process level. As she is preparing to meet with Aaron, Ms. Landry remembers that she was instructed to avoid providing feedback at the self level because it distracts students from their learning goals and provides no insight about next steps they need to take. When meeting with Aaron, Ms. Landry states, "Your paper is written well grammatically, but needs more details. Remember that your learning goal is to include details in your essay about the historical figure. Read back through your paper and make sure you use the strategy of asking who, what, where, when, and why. Also, pay close attention to when your paragraphs are really short, since that's probably a good sign that you need more detail."

Finally, Ms. Landry thinks about Heta's writing and the type of feedback she will need during her writing conference. Heta is the strongest writer in the fifth-grade class, with foundational knowledge of how to write an essay and strategies to use during writing, and Ms. Landry knows that she could improve her writing even more by gaining greater self-regulation. Therefore, Ms. Landry provides Heta feedback at the self-regulation level to help her self-monitor and direct her own writing. Her intent is to encourage Heta to deepen her engagement and learning. Ms. Landry tells Heta, "I want you to learn how to rely on yourself a bit more when writing. Let's take a look at the paragraph that needs more work. Any idea what is wrong with this paragraph? How do you think this paragraph is different from the other ones in your essay? Can you think of a strategy you can use to strengthen it? How will you know when it is a well-written paragraph?"

After using effective feedback with her entire class, Ms. Landry notices a marked improvement in her students' abilities to meet their writing goals. She realizes how important it was to avoid providing feedback at the self level because it would not give students guidance about how to meet their learning goals. She also recognizes how important it was to target feedback at the appropriate level. For instance, providing Dominique feedback at the process level or self-regulation level would have been inappropriate since she first needed to understand how to perform the writing task; since process or self-regulation-related feedback would have been unhelpful, Ms. Landry provided task-level feedback. In all, Ms. Landry saw firsthand how feedback can be used effectively to help close the gap between students' current performance and their learning goals, and she is going to start applying her new knowledge of instructional feedback across subjects.

Wrap Up

As an educator, using corrective instructional feedback can greatly improve your students' academic success. In this chapter, we explained the features of effective feedback and important considerations when providing feedback. We also outlined key components of Hattie and Timperley's feedback model, including guiding feedback questions for teachers and students to consider and the levels at which feedback can be aimed.[18] To illustrate the levels of feedback, we showed how to scaffold students' learning from the task level, to the process level, and finally to the self-regulation level. Providing positive and corrective feedback is a critical evidence-based practice for all educators, and one that can have a powerful influence on student success.

Tips

1. **Create a positive learning environment for feedback to be well received by students.** For feedback to be effective, teachers must create a safe learning environment that is built on mutual respect and trust.[19] Students should trust that the teacher's feedback is intended to help them toward their learning goals. To do so, establish positive teacher-student relationships by getting to know your students, valuing their input, and using culturally responsive practices (see HLP 7 for more information). We also encourage teachers to use effective classroom management techniques (e.g., establishing classroom rules and procedures) to create a safe, structured environment for students. Keep in mind that teachers may need to directly teach students with disabilities how to receive and use feedback to progress towards their learning goals (see HLP 16 for how to use explicit instruction).

2. **Plan for and monitor your use of instructional feedback.** We encourage you to plan how you will use instructional feedback that is targeted to each student's individual needs. There are many

modes (e.g., orally, in writing, visually) and levels (e.g., task, self-regulation) of feedback, and it is critical that you prepare for how to provide instructional feedback. We recommend that you monitor your use of instructional feedback by collecting data informally (e.g., observation) and formally (e.g., assessments) on students' learning progress and documenting and reflecting on the feedback you provide. Using the information you gather, examine how you are using feedback and whether your feedback is effectively meeting students' needs.

3. **Combine feedback with other HLPs.** As noted in this chapter, feedback is a complicated technique that can promote or hinder students' learning. Being able to effectively provide corrective feedback requires the use of other essential teaching techniques. When you acquire and successfully use other HLPs, you are better able to provide feedback to your students. For example, if you can identify learning goals for your students (HLP 12) and can adapt tasks and materials toward those learning goals (HLP 14), you have key skills necessary to provide corrective, goal-oriented feedback that will improve your student's academic outcomes.

Notes

1 Brookhart, S. M. (2008). *How to give effective feedback to your students.* Alexandria, VA: Association for Supervision and Curriculum Development.

2 Hattie, J., & Timperley, H. (2007). The power of feedback. *Review of Educational Research, 77,* 81–112. doi:10.3102/003465430298487

   Thurlings, M., Vermeulen, M., Bastiaens, T., & Stijnen, S. (2013). Understanding feedback: A learning theory perspective. *Educational Research Review, 9,* 1–15. Retrieved from https://doi.org/10.1016/j.edurev.2012.11.004

3 Hattie, J., & Timperley, H. (2007). The power of feedback. *Review of Educational Research, 77,* 81–112. doi:10.3102/003465430298487

4 Hattie, J., & Timperley, H. (2007). The power of feedback. *Review of Educational Research, 77,* 81–112. doi:10.3102/003465430298487

   Hattie, J., Gan, M., & Brooks, C. (2017). Instruction based on feedback. In R. E. Mayer & P. A. Alexander (Eds.), *Handbook of research on learning and instruction* (2nd ed., pp. 376–417). New York, NY: Routledge.

5 Hattie, J., & Timperley, H. (2007). The power of feedback. *Review of Educational Research, 77,* 81–112. doi:10.3102/003465430298487

   Hattie, J., Gan, M., & Brooks, C. (2017). Instruction based on feedback. In R. E. Mayer & P. A. Alexander (Eds.), *Handbook of research on learning and instruction* (2nd ed., pp. 376–417). New York, NY: Routledge.

6 Sheen, Y. (2004). Corrective feedback and learner uptake in communicative classrooms across instructional settings. *Language Teaching Research, 8*(3), 263–300. Retrieved from https://doi.org/10.1191/1362168804lr146oa

   Hattie, J., & Timperley, H. (2007). The power of feedback. *Review of Educational Research, 77,* 81–112. doi:10.3102/003465430298487

7 Hattie, J., Gan, M., & Brooks, C. (2017). Instruction based on feedback. In R. E. Mayer & P. A. Alexander (Eds.), *Handbook of research on learning and instruction* (2nd ed., pp. 376–417). New York, NY: Routledge.

8 Hattie, J. (2012). *Visible learning for teachers: Maximizing impact on learning.* New York, NY: Routledge.

9 Hattie, J., Gan, M., & Brooks, C. (2017). Instruction based on feedback. In R. E. Mayer & P. A. Alexander (Eds.), *Handbook of research on learning and instruction* (2nd ed., pp. 376–417). New York, NY: Routledge.

10 Hattie, J., & Timperley, H. (2007). The power of feedback. *Review of Educational Research, 77,* 81–112. doi:10.3102/003465430298487

Hattie, J., Gan, M., & Brooks, C. (2017). Instruction based on feedback. In R. E. Mayer & P. A. Alexander (Eds.), Handbook of research on learning and instruction (2nd ed., pp. 376–417). New York, NY: Routledge.

11 Hattie, J., Gan, M., & Brooks, C. (2017). Instruction based on feedback. In R. E. Mayer & P. A. Alexander (Eds.), *Handbook of research on learning and instruction* (2nd ed., pp. 376–417). New York, NY: Routledge.

12 Hattie, J., & Timperley, H. (2007). The power of feedback. *Review of Educational Research, 77,* 81–112.   doi:10.3102/003465430298487

13 Hattie, J., & Timperley, H. (2007). The power of feedback. *Review of Educational Research, 77,* 81–112.   doi:10.3102/003465430298487

Shute, V. J. (2008). Focus on formative feedback. *Review of Educational Research, 78,* 153–189. Retrieved from https://doi.org/10.3102/0034654307313795

Chan, P. E., Konrad, M., Gonzalez, V., Peter, M. T., & Ressa, V. A. (2014). The critical role of feedback in formative instructional practices. *Intervention in School and Clinic, 50,* 96–104. Retrieved from https://doi.org/10.1177/1053451214536044

14 Shute, V. J. (2008). Focus on formative feedback. *Review of Educational Research, 78,* 153–189. Retrieved from https://doi.org/10.3102/0034654307313795

15 Hattie, J., Gan, M., & Brooks, C. (2017). Instruction based on feedback. In R. E. Mayer & P. A. Alexander (Eds.), *Handbook of research on learning and instruction* (2nd ed., pp. 376–417). New York, NY: Routledge.

16 Mason, B. J., & Bruning, R. H. (2001). *Providing feedback in computer-based instruction: What the research tells us.* CLASS Research Report No. 9 Center for Instructional Innovation, University of Nebraska-Lincoln.

Shute, V. J. (2008). Focus on formative feedback. *Review of Educational Research, 78,* 153–189. Retrieved from https://doi.org/10.3102/0034654307313795

17 Hattie, J. (2012). *Visible learning for teachers: Maximizing impact on learning.* New York, NY: Routledge.

18 Hattie, J., & Timperley, H. (2007). The power of feedback. *Review of Educational Research, 77,* 81–112.   doi:10.3102/003465430298487

19 Chan, P. E., Konrad, M., Gonzalez, V., Peter, M. T., & Ressa, V. A. (2014). The critical role of feedback in formative instructional practices. *Intervention in School and Clinic, 50,* 96–104. Retrieved from https://doi.org/10.1177/1053451214536044

Key Resources

Brookhart, S. M. (2008). *How to give effective feedback to your students.* Alexandria, VA: Association for Supervision and Curriculum Development.

Hattie, J., & Timperley, H. (2007). The power of feedback. *Review of Educational Research, 77,* 81–112. doi:10.3102/003465430298487

Making Feedback Meaningful. www.teachingchannel.org/videos/personalize-feedback-for-students

Missouri Educational Systems and Instruction for Learning (MOEduSAIL) Feedback Course. www.moedu-sail.org/courses/feedback/

Wiggins, G. (2012). Seven keys to effective feedback. *Educational Leadership, 70,* 10–16. Retrieved from www.ascd.org/publications/educational-leadership/sept12/vol70/num01/Seven-Keys-to-Effective-Feedback.aspx

23
Some Final Thoughts Regarding High Leverage Practices

*James McLeskey, Lawrence Maheady, Bonnie Billingsley,
Mary T. Brownell, and Timothy J. Lewis*

Much of the work related to high leverage practices and practice-based teacher preparation is supported by research and the wisdom of practice from other professions. For example, an examination of how expertise is developed across professions reveals that a critical first step is defining the core practices that all professionals must learn to use before beginning their work.[1] These core practices have been identified in professions ranging from airline pilots to plumbers, from cosmetologists to physicians. Identifying core practices in many of these professions has been simplified by the fact that immediate and highly consequential feedback is provided when a practice is not performed well. For example, all plumbers are required to learn to appropriately install a faucet (i.e., ensuring that it does not leak, among other things) before entering the profession. This is such an obvious and important core practice that a master plumber would never suggest that an initially licensed plumber should begin practice before learning to perform this task. Furthermore, ignoring this core practice could undermine licensing and ultimately the credibility and utility of the profession. Similarly, all airline pilots must learn to land a plane in a cross-wind before beginning to fly a plane, as not performing this skill with proficiency could well lead to disastrous consequences. Such core practices in these and other professions are often very obvious, and all agree that they are necessary for beginning practice and the credibility of the profession.

Identifying core practices in education has not proven to be as straightforward as in many other professions, primarily because skilled instructional practice is so complex, coupled with the fact that the consequences of not using these core practices take time to be identified (e.g., it takes time to know that a student is not making sufficient progress in learning to read). However, over the last several decades, research and the wisdom of practice have been used to identify a range of practices that are effective in improving student achievement or behavior.[2] This information from practice and research provided the foundation for developing high leverage practices for special education teachers.[3]

Obviously, developing a set of core practices is only a necessary first step. The critical next step is designing effective approaches that provide support to future and current teachers as they develop expertise in employing these practices in classrooms. Extensive research has been conducted regarding how this occurs across professions.[4] Similar to the experiences of many teachers, complex practices in other professions are not learned by simply reading about them in a book or listening to someone talk about the practice. Rather, expertise in professions is gained through well-structured opportunities to practice particular skills in authentic settings with support and feedback.[5] When used in teacher education, these practice-based opportunities "provide candidates time to apply content pedagogy, to gain real experience, to understand school relationships—and, most importantly—to work with students within a supervised context."[6]

As we are sure every teacher and teacher educator recognizes, this is not a simple task. However, we are confident that work on HLPs and practice-based teacher education has the potential to substantially improve teacher preparation and, ultimately, outcomes for students with disabilities and others who struggle to succeed in school. Much of this optimism comes from the fact that this new direction in teacher preparation reflects the core values that have provided the foundation of instruction in special education for many years. That is, if someone needs to learn something, we should identify what the person needs to learn and provide well-supported, systematic instruction until the learning is demonstrated. We should do no less for future teachers as they gain expertise in using instructional practices that have high potential for improving student academic and behavioral outcomes. While all of us have much to learn as we undertake this complex task, we have some final thoughts for teachers and teacher educators in the sections that follow that may help make this change somewhat more manageable.

Some Final Thoughts for Teachers

As we are sure you recognize, the high leverage practices we have described in this book are not all that is needed to be an effective special education teacher. For example, knowledge regarding a range of topics including culturally responsive practice, child development, and so forth is needed to guide decision making regarding the use of these practices. Furthermore, teaching is complex and unpredictable, often requiring teachers to use professional judgment to make quick decisions regarding how to adapt a practice or resolve a unique problem for a specific student. Professional judgment develops over a number of years. For the most part, the HLPs address more routine, predictable aspects of practice for special education teachers. What we anticipate is that as you learn to use the HLPs with proficiency, this will provide a foundation of effective practices that you can employ frequently to improve student outcomes and build your confidence as you develop as a professional. As this occurs, you will continually have opportunities to improve your expertise related to the use of teacher judgment as you collect data regarding student performance and carefully observe how your practice influences student outcomes.

Given the number and complexity of the high leverage practices, gaining expertise related to their use should continue well into your teaching career. This includes both learning to use new practices that would be especially useful for your students, as well as enriching what you have already learned about other HLPs. Of course, learning to use complex practices in the classroom is not a simple task. For many years, professional development that was provided by most school districts was not particularly helpful. This professional development typically consisted of an expert or "sage on the stage" who described an effective practice, showed videos of the practice in action, discussed the practice with teachers, and so forth, and then departed, leaving the teachers on their own to learn to use the practice in their classrooms. This type of information can be useful to a point, but it just does not go far enough.

How professional development is provided in many schools is changing based on research regarding how teachers gain expertise in using complex practices.[7] Teachers now often work in collaborative groups to support one another in learning about effective practices and how to use them in their classrooms. In addition, many schools have coaches available to provide modeling and feedback in teachers' classrooms as they learn to use a practice. If these types of collaborative learning opportunities are available in your school, we would encourage you to take advantage of them.

Another resource for learning to use HLPs in your classroom that is available to all teachers is to seek out other teachers who have expertise in using these practices. These teachers will often be willing to have you observe them use the practice in their classroom and will respond to any questions you have about the practice. Your principal also may be willing to arrange a time when this teacher can come to your classroom to provide coaching regarding the use of the practice. To expand the group of teachers who might provide this support, we would encourage you to seek out general education teachers as well as special educators. As we noted in the introductory chapter of this book, we have had general educators tell us that many of the HLPs for special education teachers are important practices that should be used in inclusive classrooms by general educators. We agree with this perspective and have found that general educators can provide excellent models for how to use some of the HLPs in their classrooms. For example, it is likely that fellow teachers can assist you in identifying general education colleagues who have expertise related to practices such as collaborating with other professionals (HLP 1); the use of formative assessment (HLP 6); establishing a consistent, organized, and respectful classroom (HLP 7); and a number of the instruction HLPs such as scaffolding instruction (HLP 15), using flexible grouping (HLP 17), and providing feedback (HLP 22).

Finally, research has clearly demonstrated that there is nothing more important to improving outcomes for students with disabilities and others who struggle in school than improving the practice of their teachers. We know that improving instruction is a challenging endeavor and very much appreciate the many teachers we know and have worked with who have taken on this demanding task. We hope you find that the information we have provided regarding high leverage practices in the preceding chapters will make this task somewhat more manageable as you learn to employ HLPs in your classroom. All the best in this endeavor!

Some Final Thoughts for Teacher Educators

To state the patently obvious, using HLPs as part of teacher preparation is complex and requires many changes in the content and structure of programs. Fortunately, scholars are beginning to conduct research and write position papers and program descriptions that provide insight into how these changes occur that should prove useful to teacher educators who are beginning this work. We initially provide some thoughts from a faculty member who has been actively engaged in this work for several years, Paula Lancaster, a professor and Director of Teacher Education at Grand Valley State University in Grand Rapids, Michigan (see Figure 23.1). This is followed by brief descriptions of resources that we have found useful related to the use of high leverage practices as the core curriculum of practice-based teacher preparation (see Table 23.1).

Conclusion

Collective action among those who prepare teachers and provide continuing professional development is needed to enact this new vision of teacher preparation and professional development. There are obvious risks involved, primary among them the possibility that, as has occurred in the past with major initiatives to improve teacher preparation, there will be a "proliferation of approaches driven more by the trend than by a deep understanding of how people learn to enact ambitious professional practice."[14] Given this history, let us proceed with caution, but let us begin to enact this new vision of teacher preparation that promises to build bridges between schools and teacher preparation programs, and improve the preparation of teachers in ways that will substantially benefit students with disabilities and others who struggle in schools.

Work focused on HLPs and practice-based teacher preparation has occurred in Michigan over the past few years thanks to significant partnerships supported by TeachingWorks (teachingworks.org) and the CEEDAR Center (http://ceedar.education.ufl.edu/) at the Universities of Michigan and Florida, respectively. I mention these partnerships because, while I am proud of what we have accomplished at Grand Valley State University, we have benefited tremendously from the wisdom and support of colleagues across the state and country. Further, whether you are undertaking this endeavor at an individual institution or across a state, a core team of committed colleagues is helpful and makes the work much more meaningful, fruitful, and manageable.

As was mentioned earlier in this chapter, identifying and adopting a set of HLPs is a necessary first step. When we considered embedding HLPs into our program, we anticipated fielding questions from our peers. A shift as substantial as this one is worthy of scrutiny and discussion, so we committed extensive time to addressing questions, facilitating discussions, and distributing shared readings related to high leverage practices and practice-based teacher education. Knowing and sharing that background information is critically important in helping colleagues contextualize and understand all that is involved in the shift toward a focus on HLPs. I can say definitively that every moment we invested in these conversations was time well spent. Affording faculty opportunities to raise questions and study available literature and material on HLPs demonstrates the significance of this shift and makes the work that follows much more logical and palatable.

As we looked at the HLPs, we acknowledged that we teach about most of them in our program. Ensuring that beginning teachers can actually enact these practices requires changing the manner in which they are prepared. We had been offering substantial field experiences, but we learned that we needed to be more deliberate about earlier and targeted opportunities for approximation and enactment of practices. Taking the first steps was challenging. We decided on a two-pronged approach that allowed us to leverage small successes and progress with a few committed faculty who focused deeply on a couple of HLPs, coupled with slower, big-picture efforts from the broader faculty.

For example, we chose a course required of all teacher candidates that is taught by faculty members who were invested in HLP work and targeted HLPs 16: Use explicit instruction, and 22: Provide positive and constructive feedback to guide students' learning and behavior (those happen to be present in both general and special education HLP lists from CEC and TeachingWorks). In doing so, we developed a model implementation process that others might replicate. With the larger group of faculty, we began mapping the HLPs onto our curriculum. Based on professional literature,[8] we developed and distributed a table to all faculty who teach courses required in our preparation programs asking them to identify in which courses they already do, or could, represent a particular practice, deconstruct or decompose a practice, approximate enactment of a practice either via role-play or a focus on isolated components, and finally enact the practice with children and youth. This exercise provided us with baseline information regarding the practices that faculty felt were being addressed to some degree and served as a conversation starter for how we needed to adjust our preparation pedagogy. Our current work is focused on these pedagogical and curriculum changes as well as developing materials and assessments to support faculty. I highly recommend consulting the resources noted in this chapter as a starting point for similar efforts.

The last component of our HLP focus I mention has been a game-changer for us. We are part of two critical learning communities with select K–12 partners. In both of these communities we convene regularly with teachers, principals, instructional coaches, and our candidates to focus on developing common language and understanding of the HLPs and transitioning beginning-level teachers from their training programs to the classroom. Put simply, we spend a couple of hours a month watching video or role-play of teaching, taking it apart, and sharing our understandings of what we saw, what feedback should be given, and how to strengthen our own skills as well as our profession. Many of us have agreed that our time together is some of the most meaningful continuous improvement work we have done, in part because these activities look and feel like how our entire enterprise should be working, and this emphasis on HLPs has enabled it to happen. Focusing on practice and the work educators do on a day-to-day basis is immensely satisfying and, in many ways, has served as a reminder of how powerful a force teaching is.

Figure 23.1 Thoughts From a Teacher Educator: Paula Lancaster, Director of Teacher Education, Grand Valley State University

Table 23.1 Recommended Resources for Teacher Educators Related to HLPs

1. Benedict et al. (2016). *Learning to Teach: Practice-Based Teacher Education.*[9]	• This brief document describes essential features for providing high-quality, structured, and sequenced opportunities to practice within teacher preparation programs. • Describes teacher preparation programs that have enacted innovative strategies to embed practice-based opportunities into existing coursework and field experiences. • Describes several practice-based approaches that have been found to increase beginning teacher candidates' capacity for teaching. • Identifies potential action steps that EPPs and districts can take to improve candidates' opportunities to practice.
2. Grossman et al. (2009). *Redefining teaching, re-imagining teacher education.*[10]	• This article provides an argument for re-conceptualizing teaching and teacher preparation to improve teacher practice. • Describes new directions in teacher education including organizing around core practices, reimagining the curriculum, and addressing pedagogical issues for teacher education programs. • Addresses the organizational challenges that teacher education programs must address as they support candidate learning of core practices in practice-based settings.
3. McDonald et al. (2013). *Core practices and pedagogies of teacher education: A call for a common language and collective activity.*[11]	• This article provides a review of changes in teacher education that have led to an emphasis on better supporting teachers in learning to use knowledge in action. • Provides a review of why core practices are a critical foundation for practice-based teacher preparation. • Describes a learning cycle that may be used to engage candidates in authentic and ambitious instructional activities as they learn to enact core practices based on a situated perspective on learning. The cycle includes introducing and learning about the activity; preparing for and rehearsing the activity; enacting the activity with students; and analyzing enactment and moving forward.
4. McLeskey et al. (2017). *HLPs for Special Education Teachers.*[12]	• This short book was written by CEC's High Leverage Practices Writing Team that developed HLPs for K–12 special education teachers. • Includes an introduction to the HLPs and a description of how they were developed. • Provides background information, description, and a brief research synthesis for each of the HLPs.
5. Windschitl et al. (2012). *Proposing a core set of instructional practices and tools for teachers of science.*[13]	• An article that discusses why the identification of core practices is critical to improving the practice of teachers. • Reviews research informing the development of core practices. • Describes the development of core practices in science education. • Describes supporting tools and how they were used to support candidates in learning to use core practices in science education teacher preparation programs. • Reflects on unexpected insights that arose from beginning to engage in this work.

Notes

1 Ericsson, A., & Pool, R. (2016). *Peak: Secrets from the new science of expertise.* New York, NY: Houghton Mifflin.

2 American Psychological Association (APA). (2015). *Top 20 principles from psychology for preK—12 teaching and learning.* Retrieved from www.apa.org/ed/schools/cpse/top-twenty-principles.pdf

   Cook, B., & Tankersley, M. (Eds.). (2013). *Research-based practices in special education.* Boston, MA: Pearson.

   Hattie, J. (2008). *Visible learning: A synthesis of over 800 meta-analyses relating to achievement.* New York, NY: Routledge.

3 McLeskey, J., Barringer, M., Billingsley, B., Brownell, M., Jackson, D., Kennedy, M., . . . Ziegler, D. (2017). *High leverage practices in special education: The final report of the HLP Writing Team.* Arlington, VA: CEC & CEEDAR Center.

4 Ericsson, A., & Pool, R. (2016). *Peak: Secrets from the new science of expertise.* New York, NY: Houghton Mifflin.

5 Benedict, A., Holdheide, L., Brownell, M., & Foley, A. (2016). *Learning to teach: Practice-based preparation in teacher education.* Special Issues Brief, Center on Great Teachers & Leaders at American Institutes for Research, CEEDAR Center, University of Florida (pp. 1–44). Retrieved from http://ceedar.education.ufl.edu/wp-content/uploads/2016/07/Learning_To_Teach.pdf

6 Benedict, A., Holdheide, L., Brownell, M., & Foley, A. (2016). *Learning to teach: Practice-based preparation in teacher education.* Special Issues Brief, Center on Great Teachers & Leaders at American Institutes for Research, CEEDAR Center, University of Florida (pp. 1–44, 2). Retrieved from http://ceedar.education.ufl.edu/wp-content/uploads/2016/07/Learning_To_Teach.pdf

7 Desimone, L. (2011). A primer on effective professional development. *Phi Delta Kappan, 92*(6), 68–71.

   McLeskey, J. (2011). Supporting improved practice for special education teachers: The importance of learner centered professional development. *Journal of Special Education Leadership, 24*(1), 26–35.

   Webster-Wright, A. (2009). Reframing professional development through understanding authentic professional learning. *Review of Educational Research, 79*(2), 702–739.

8 Goodwin, A. L. & Kosnik, C. (2013). Quality teacher educators = quality teachers? Conceptualizng essential domains of knowledge for those who teach teachers. *Teacher Development, 17*(3), 334–346.

   Kazemi, E., Ghousseini, H., Cunard, A., & Turrou, A. C. (2016). Getting inside rehearsals: Insights from teacher educators to support work on complex practice. *Journal of Teacher Education, 67*(1), 18–31.

   McDonald, M., Kazemi, E., & Kavanaugh, S. (2013). Core practices of teacher education: A call for a common language and collective activity. *Journal of Teacher Education, 64*(5), 378–386.

9 Benedict, A., Holdheide, L., Brownell, M., & Foley, A. (2016). *Learning to teach: Practice-based preparation in teacher education.* Special Issues Brief, Center on Great Teachers & Leaders at American Institutes for Research, CEEDAR Center, University of Florida (pp. 1–44). Retrieved from http://ceedar.education.ufl.edu/wp-content/uploads/2016/07/Learning_To_Teach.pdf

10 Grossman, P., Hammerness, K., & McDonald, M. (2009). Redefining teaching: Re-imagining teacher education. *Teachers and Teaching: Theory and Practice, 15*(2), 273–290.

11 McDonald, M., Kazemi, E., & Kavanaugh, S. (2013). Core practices of teacher education: A call for a common language and collective activity. *Journal of Teacher Education, 64*(5), 378–386.

12 McLeskey, Barringer, M., Billingsley, B., Brownell, M., Jackson, D., Kennedy, M., . . . Ziegler, D. (2017). *High leverage practices in special education: The final report of the HLP Writing Team.* Arlington, VA: CEC & CEEDAR Center.

13 Windschitl, M., Thompson, J., Braaten, M., & Stroupe, D. (2012). Proposing a core set of instructional practices and tools for teachers of science. *Science Education, 96*(5), 878–903.

Goodwin, A. L., & Kosnik, C. (2013). Quality teacher educators = quality teachers? Conceptualizing essential domains of knowledge for those who teach teachers. *Teacher Development, 17*(3), 334–346.

Kazemi, E., Ghousseini, H., Cunard, A., & Turrou, A. C. (2016). Getting inside rehearsals: Insights from teacher educators to support work on complex practice. *Journal of Teacher Education, 67*(1), 18–31.

14 McDonald, M., Kazemi, E., & Kavanaugh, S. (2013). Core practices of teacher education: A call for a common language and collective activity. *Journal of Teacher Education, 64*(5), 378–386, 379.

Contributors

Alana Oif Telesman, The Ohio State University
Allison Bruhn, University of Iowa
Amber Benedict, University of Florida
Andrew Hashey, SUNY College at Old Westbury
Andrew M. Markelz, The Pennsylvania State University
Angela L. Patti, SUNY Buffalo State
Anna Osipova, California State University, Los Angeles
Annmarie Urso, SUNY Geneseo
Arfang Dabo, Michigan State University

B. Keith Ben, University of Central Arkansas
Barbara Mitchell, University of Missouri
Benjamin Riden, The Pennsylvania State University
Blair Lloyd, Vanderbilt University
Bryan Cook, University of Hawaii

Carl Liaupson, University of Arizona
Carrie A. Davenport, The Ohio State University
Cathy Newman Thomas, Texas State University
Charles Hughes, The Pennsylvania State University
Chris Riley-Tillman, University of Missouri
Christian Shabey, Brigham Young University
Corrine Gist, The Ohio State University
Cynthia Baughan, University of North Carolina at Charlotte

Dane DiCesare, Brock University
Daniel Pyle, Weber State University
David L. Lee, The Pennsylvania State University
Dawn Hamlin, SUNY Oneonta
Dee Berlinghoff, Mount Saint Mary College
Devin Kearns, University of Connecticut
Dia Jackson, American Institutes for Research

Elizabeth Bettini, Boston University
Erica Lembke, University of Missouri
Erica Mason, University of Missouri
Erica McCray, University of Florida

Gliset Colon, SUNY Buffalo State
Grace Francis, George Mason University

Heather Hatton, University of Missouri
Howard Wills, University of Kansas Center for Research, Inc.

Imad Zaheer, Montclair State University

Jarod R. Morris, The Pennsylvania State University
Jen Freeman, University of Connecticut
Jennifer Urbach, University of Northern Colorado
Jessica Gugino, SUNY Fredonia
Jocelyn Washburn, Virginia Tech
Joseph Wehby, Vanderbilt University
Judith Winn, University of Wisconsin-Milwaukee

Karrie Shogren, University of Kansas
Kathleen Pfannenstiel, American Institute of Research
Kelly Acosta, University of Florida
Kimberly Vannest, Texas A&M University
Kristen L. McMaster, University of Minnesota
Kristen Merrill O'Brien, George Mason University
Kristie Asaro-Saddler, University of Albany
Kristin L. Sayeski, University of Georgia
Kyena Cornelius, Minnesota State University, Mankato

Lee Kern, Lehigh University
Lisa A. Rafferty, SUNY Buffalo State
Lisa Monda-Amaya, University of Illinois

Maria R. Helton, The Ohio State University
Marilyn Friend, Marilyn Friend, Inc.
Marney S. Pollack, University of Connecticut
Mary Catherine Scheeler, The Pennsylvania State University
Maya Israel, University of Illinois
Mayumi Hagiwara, University of Kansas
Meg Kamman, University of Florida
Michelle Hosp, University of Massachusetts at Amherst
Michelle M. Cumming, Florida International University
Moira Konrad, The Ohio State University

Natalie Williams, Weber State University
Nicole Pyle, Utah State University

Pamela Stecker, Clemson University
Pamela Williamson, University North Carolina at Greensboro
Paul Riccomini, The Pennsylvania State University
Paula Lancaster, Grand Valley State University
Peggy Weiss, George Mason University

R. Alex Smith, University of Missouri
Regina Hirn, University of Louisville
Rob O'Neill, University of Utah

Sara McDaniel, The University of Alabama
Scott Dueker, The Ohio State University
Shannon Budin, SUNY Buffalo State
Sheila R. Alber-Morgan, The Ohio State University
Steve Goodman, Michigan's Integrated Behavior and Learning Support Initiative, Ottawa Area
   Intermediate School District

Talida State, Mountclair State University
Tammy Barron, Western Carolina University
Terrance Scott, University of Louisville
Terri Hessler, Ohio State University at Newark
Timothy Zgliczynski, SUNY Buffalo State
Tracy Gershwin Mueller, University of Northern Colorado
Troy Mariage, Michigan State University

Victoria M. Whaley, University of Connecticut
Vivian Correa, University of North Carolina at Charlotte

William L. Heward, The Ohio State University

Index

Note: **Boldface** page references indicate tables. *Italic* references indicate figures.